CW01238234

SISTERHOOD AND AFTER

SISTERHOOD AND AFTER

An Oral History of the UK Women's
Liberation Movement, 1968–Present

Margaretta Jolly

OXFORD
UNIVERSITY PRESS

OXFORD
UNIVERSITY PRESS

Oxford University Press is a department of the University of Oxford. It furthers
the University's objective of excellence in research, scholarship, and education
by publishing worldwide. Oxford is a registered trade mark of Oxford University
Press in the UK and certain other countries.

Published in the United States of America by Oxford University Press
198 Madison Avenue, New York, NY 10016, United States of America.

© Oxford University Press 2019

All rights reserved. No part of this publication may be reproduced, stored in
a retrieval system, or transmitted, in any form or by any means, without the
prior permission in writing of Oxford University Press, or as expressly permitted
by law, by license, or under terms agreed with the appropriate reproduction
rights organization. Inquiries concerning reproduction outside the scope of the
above should be sent to the Rights Department, Oxford University Press, at the
address above.

You must not circulate this work in any other form
and you must impose this same condition on any acquirer.

Library of Congress Cataloging-in-Publication Data
Names: Jolly, Margaretta, author.
Title: Sisterhood and after : an oral history of the UK women's liberation
movement, 1968–present / Margaretta Jolly.
Description: New York, NY : Oxford University Press, [2019] |
Series: Oxford oral history series | Includes bibliographical references and index.
Identifiers: LCCN 2019000513 (print) | LCCN 2019004017 (ebook) |
ISBN 9780190658854 (Updf) | ISBN 9780190658861 (Epub) | ISBN 9780190658847 (hardcover)
Subjects: LCSH: Feminism—Great Britain—History. | Feminists--Great Britain—History.
Classification: LCC HQ1597 (ebook) | LCC HQ1597 .J65 2019 (print) | DDC 305.420941—dc23
LC record available at https://lccn.loc.gov/2019000513

9 8 7 6 5 4 3 2 1

Printed by Sheridan Books, Inc., United States of America

For Nick

CONTENTS

Foreword by Sally Alexander   ix
Acknowledgments   xiii

Introduction: The Sound of Feminist Memory   1
1. Telling Feminist Histories   8
2. Oral History and Feminist Method   40
3. Forming Feminists: Growing Up in the 1940s, 1950s, and 1960s   62
4. Campaigning and Coming of Age in the 1970s   89
5. Guilty Pleasures? Feminism and Everyday Life in the 1980s   121
6. Friend or Foe? Men and Feminism Through the 1990s   159
7. Happiness: Late Feminist Lives and Beyond in the 2000s   204
Conclusion: Archiving Hope: The Future of Feminist Memory   242

Notes   251
Selected Bibliography   299
Index   311

FOREWORD

Sally Alexander

Sisterhood and After offers us a new history of the women's liberation movement through the twentieth century and beyond. Margaretta Jolly's deep listening to the oral archive focuses on feeling as well as the changing times of women's lives. Reading the book is an unnerving experience, since as one of the group behind the making of this archive, I'm also one of the interviewed.

Women's liberation was a spontaneous, iconoclastic movement whose impulse and demands reached far beyond its estimated twenty thousand activists in the mid-1970s. Women's refuges, law centres, nurseries, rape crisis centres, publishing houses, magazines, journals, peace camps, and more were made in the name of all women, as were the four—by 1978 seven—demands. Inspired by civil rights, black power, national liberation movements, the utopianism of 1968, Britain's movement followed close in the wake of industrial militancy among Ford seamstresses and Hull fishermen's wives and families. The movement's political touchstones were both revolution and democracy, the small group was its signature practice, and sexual difference was its foundational myth. Most women in the movement wanted a grassroots movement grounded in everyday life, as Sue O'Sullivan, a worker in women's health, puts it. Women's daily lives in Britain—then as now—were significantly unequal and different.

Margaretta Jolly ventures deep into the hearts and minds of the sixty women interviewed in the Sisterhood and After Women's Liberation Oral History Project, whose oral life stories form the "archive of feeling"—shame, guilt, anger, hope, love—on which her book is especially based. She tracks not one movement but many. Socialists, Marxists, lesbians, radical and revolutionary feminists, "all of that was there," affirms Beatrix Campbell, journalist and author, recalling her own equivocal radical and socialist feminism. But Rosalind Delmar remembers the antagonism as women argued over the wording of the sixth demand—the right to define our own sexuality—in Edinburgh in 1974. Sexuality and violence—the most difficult issues to bear consciously in mind—evoked the strongest political memories among women interviewed.

Born around the Second World War, in the moment of reconstruction and Cold War, the women's liberation generation imbibed with their free milk, cod liver oil, secondary schools, and hospital clinics an audacity—the gift of previous generations' determination to build a better world after fascism and world war. Envy and fear as well as love went into their makeup. Fathers returned from war, replacing the infant in her mother's bed, bringing with them the birth of siblings. Some recall domestic violence, their mother's (as well as their own) abortions, or silent depression. You can hear the "intake of breath," Jolly notes, from almost all the interviewees when asked to speak about their mother. Fear of a third world war, palpable to a child who glimpsed or overheard, on radio or TV or in the Pathé News, stories of bloodshed in Palestine, India, Korea, or Suez, whose older brothers left for national service in postcolonial wars. Such memories resurfaced in the women's peace movements and camps of the 1970s and 1980s.

Women's liberation manifested these divisions—legacies of war, empire, and migrations. When Mukami McCrum, Scottish advocate for race and education rights, returned to visit family in Kenya, her mother noticed she had become sad and angry. Now Mukami always thinks about how she can avoid oppression "taking root" inside her, and she notices, too, the "silent woman," makes a space for her, invites her to speak. Gail Lewis, a founding member of the Brixton Black Women's group and a sociologist and psychotherapist, describes her disappointment that the predominantly white women's liberation movement did not at first acknowledge the intellectual work of black UK feminists. *Charting the Journey: Writings by Black and Third World Women* (1988), she remembers, received more recognition in the United States than in the United Kingdom. Black and Asian British feminists took their own distinctive paths and made careful alliances with white women: for instance, the Grunwick strike (1976), the Southall Black Sisters (1979), the Organisation of Women of African and Asian Descent (1979), refuges from domestic violence in Edinburgh and Liverpool. Jolly maps the local and regional black and Asian women's groups that changed the face and mental climate of Britain.

The democratic voice of women's liberation emerged through conversation and small-group action. Catherine Hall, historian—whose story of a marriage forms one of the editorial gems in this book—contrasts her isolation as a young mother with the fast friendships that emerged from consciousness raising. Stella Dadzie, writer and advocate of black women's rights, describes the spiritual and physical friendship another woman showed her in her time of deep mourning after the death of her mother. These and other instances established trust between women, the "thinking in common" (Virginia Woolf's phrase) that defended safe legal abortion and secured women's refuges, which today struggle to survive. After Margaret Thatcher's election in 1979, feminists moved into municipal and national politics. The United Nations Declaration on the Elimination of Violence against Women in 1993, affirmed by the international gathering of women in Beijing two years later, testifies to their success. Harriet Harman, Labour member of Parliament since 1982, claims that the legalization of adoption rights for lesbian and gay parents and in-vitro fertilization rights (2002 and 2008, respectively), childcare, lone mothers' right to work, and paternity leave fulfilled the early gender demands and body politics of the movement.

Women's liberation is an unfinished movement. Feminism is born anew with each generation. The past is always before us, to rephrase historian Sheila Rowbotham, while Mary Kelly's glittering glass "Multi-Story House" (2007) inscribes these women's dreams as well as the questions raised by their daughters and granddaughters. Margaretta Jolly captures the ebb and flow of a movement as lived by some activists and their effect on the mental and political landscape of their time. "Go listen to the archive" is her final wish—and then act.

ACKNOWLEDGMENTS

Oral history depends on the kindness, courage, and candor of people willing to give their stories to the public record. My first thanks go, therefore, to those whose oral history interviews form the heart of this book. Principally, I thank the sixty women who were recorded for Sisterhood and After: The Women's Liberation Oral History Project, not only for their time and trust, but also for their years of political dedication to the causes of justice and equality from which we all benefit. This book honours them and their achievements.

Oral history also requires hard, skillful, and often hidden work in creating, curating, and interpreting. I offer immense gratitude to the project's research fellow Rachel Cohen, doctoral student Freya Johnson-Ross, British Library Learning Programme writer Abi Barber, and transcribers and summarizers Susan Hutton, Susan Nicholls, Kerry Cable, Carolyn Mumford, Claire Sissons, and Bridget Lockyer. Filmmaker Lizzie Thynne provided ten beautiful films to accompany the oral histories, ably supported by Peter Harte. These are, with the oral histories, happily archived at the British Library. For these, and for her imaginative sound piece drawn from the recordings, *Voices in Movement*, I am extremely appreciative. I thank Ed Hughes from the University of Sussex, too, for the music that accompanied the piece. A project advisory board provided invaluable guidance and support. Members included Lynn Abrams, Lucy Bland, Esther Breitenbach, Janet Browne, Kathy Davis, Teresa Doherty, Kelly Foster, Mary Marshall Clark, Heidi Mirza, Ursula Owen, Luisa Passerini, Rob Perks, Avril Rolph, Anne-Marie Sandos, Barbara Taylor (who kindly chaired), Pat Thane, Anna Towlson, and Margaret Ward. I particularly thank Sally Alexander, also an advisory board member, in providing the foreword for this book, in editorially supporting the British Library Learning Programme, and in helping spark the Sisterhood and After collection in the first place. She is owed special gratitude for her time and wisdom.

I thank the librarians and archivists working in a variety of precious collections who were also essential to the making of Sisterhood and After as well as many other wonderful resources. Jude England and Rob Perks at the British Library were vital supports, along with Teresa Doherty at the Women's Library. Dr. Polly Russell, as British Library partner, interviewer, writer, and teacher, was the project's curatorial spark and engine. I cannot thank her enough for her visionary work throughout and her enduring friendship.

The experience of working with Nancy Toff, executive editor of Oxford University Press, and Rob Perks, Oral History Series editor, was enjoyable from the start; I also thank Sonia Tycko for her fine editorial support, Julia Turner, Wendy Walker, Elizabeth Vaziri, Lena Rubin, and Judith McConville for excellent help at production stage, and the anonymous readers of both grant application and manuscript for their suggestions.

My thanks also to colleagues and friends, especially Lucy Delap, Jay Prosser, Sasha Roseneil, Sue Thornham, Kate O'Riordan, and the International Auto/Biography Association, and to family, especially my father Richard Jolly, for ever-interesting political conversation. Most of all I thank Nick Fairclough for loving companionship from title page to index.

This research was funded by a Leverhulme Trust Research Project Grant and was supported by the University of Sussex, for which I am deeply grateful. The Humanities Research Centre and the Dictionary of National Biography team at the Australian National University enabled a Visiting Fellowship, for which I also owe thanks.

I have tried assiduously to contact every source and to obtain copyright permission. If, at the time of publication, it has not been possible to trace any authors cited, I would be pleased to hear from them. I very gratefully acknowledge permission to include brief extracts from the following people from *Sisterhood and After: The Women's Liberation Oral History Project*, 2010–2013, British Library Sound & Moving Image Catalogue: Stella Dadzie, reference C1420/20 © Dadzie; Rosalind Delmar, reference C1420/03 © Delmar; Mukami McCrum, reference C1420/39 © McCrum; Sue O'Sullivan, reference C1420/40 © O'Sullivan; Michelene Wandor, reference C1420/09 © Wandor. I also thank Lucy Delap and the British Library for permission to quote from *Unbecoming Men: Interviews on Masculinities and the Women's Movement, 1970–1991*, C1667 © British Library Board.

Thanks to the British Library for permission to quote from Stuart Hall interviewed by Paul Thompson; *Pioneers of Qualitative Research*, 2007, C1416/42 © British Library Board; the Black Cultural Archives for permission to quote from Gerlin Bean, in *Oral Histories of the Black Women's Movement: The Heart of the Race*, 2008–2010, Black Cultural Archives, London ORAL/1/BWM 3; The Trades Union Congress for permission to quote from Maureen Jackson, in Voices from the Workplace: *A TUC Oral History Project on Equal Pay* (London: Trades Union Congress, 2006); Hull Maritime Museum, for permission, under Creative Commons, to quote from "What Was the Headscarf Campaign? Interview with Mary Denness," in *Local Heroes: Hull's Trawlermen*, 2008; and the Kitzinger family, for permission to quote from Sheila Kitzinger's poetry.

I also thank the following for permission to reprint excerpts from my articles that have constituted earlier expressions of portions of this book:

Taylor & Francis for "Sisterhood and After: Individualism, Ethics and an Oral History of the Women's Liberation Movement" (co-authors Polly Russell and Rachel Cohen), *Social Movement Studies* 11, no. 2 (2012): 211–26.

Berghahn Books for "After the Protest: Biographical Consequences of Movement Activism in an Oral History of Women's Liberation in Britain" in *The Women's Liberation Movement: Impacts and Outcomes*, ed. Kristina Schulz (New York: Berghahn, 2017), 298–321.

INTRODUCTION: THE SOUND OF FEMINIST MEMORY

"The revolutionary who is serious must listen very carefully to the people who are not heard and do not speak. Unless attention is paid to the nature of their silence there can be no transmission of either memory or possibility and the idea and practice of transformation can accordingly not exist."[1] When Sheila Rowbotham issued that clarion call in 1969, it was hard to hear a feminist voice. Aged twenty-seven, she was living in London, a part-time teacher and full-time activist, a woman "in the process of casting off dependence," as she put it, yet surrounded by women who remained economically dependent on men and publicly silent.[2] How distant this seems now from the contemporary din of voices and images: post-feminism, new feminism, third wave, fourth wave, against waves, lean-in woman and lipstick lesbian, gender equality and gender queer, grrl-style, boygirls, and backlash. Feminist revolution today generates a clamorous soundscape.

Yet Rowbotham's belief that listening is essential to the transmission of memory and revolution remains true. Even as we debate what women's liberation means in the twenty-first century, we need to tune into past voices, sounds, and songs. Rowbotham's generation was special, as she knew, because it conjured a gender transformation, a "new man" alongside a "new woman," and social, economic, and racial equality through and in addition to a revolution of gender relations.[3] Moreover, the collective memory of those women who powered the women's liberation campaigns of the 1970s and 1980s is invaluable in its own right. After Blair, Bin Laden, Brexit, and Beyoncé, after equality mainstreaming and transgender rights, gay marriage and digital porn, with what late-life voices do they speak? How do their voices echo, and in what kitchens, bedrooms, boardrooms, classrooms, rented halls, and streets? What is the sound of feminist memory, and how will younger people hear, touch, taste, sing, and walk it?

This book is inspired by the humane form of oral history to explore the UK Women's Liberation Movement (WLM). The WLM revived the fight for women's rights, which had withered fifty years after the vote was won, bringing a new emphasis on personal, political, and social autonomy. "We're not beautiful, we're not ugly, we're angry," feminists cleverly protested at the Miss World beauty pageant in 1970, and at Greenham Common Women's Peace Camp in the 1980s they linked the cause of disarmament with mothering, land rights, and lesbian culture. These are two of the most spectacular protests of the "long" WLM. Between the late 1960s and the 1990s there were many more, just as artful and wide-ranging. My account includes strikes for equal pay for work of equal value, consciousness raising about domestic work, Reclaim the Night, lobbies to defend reproductive rights, feminist work in local government and schools, Women and Manual Trades' initiatives, and Women Against Fundamentalism's simultaneous protests against patriarchal religious revivals and Islamophobia.

My aim, however, is not to offer another chronological narrative of these achievements, nor a history of these headline actions. Rather, I expose the inside story of the movement as it formed, developed, and diversified, negotiating with parallel movements including antisexist men and the trade unions. I also point to the longer legacy of the WLM, through the "backlash" years of the 1990s and early 2000s toward today's feminist revitalization. By weaving individual stories through a thematic history of the WLM and collective life course structured by decade, I reenter the times within which the movement lived, from the so-called Swinging Sixties to the new century's so-called war on terror.

Exploring a history that spans four decades and four nations, as well as their porous borders, in a movement that mobilized at least twenty thousand activists in the United Kingdom necessarily requires selectivity. Happily, there is a rich range of feminist oral history available as source material: the "Heart of the Race" women's liberation collection at the Black Cultural Archives, the Feminist Archive North and Feminist Archive South, the Trade Union Congress Equal Pay Story, Lisa Power's oral history of the UK Gay Liberation Front, Brighton Trans*formed, and the Women's Liberation Music Archive were just a few that I used.[4] However, I drew mostly on the British Library's Sisterhood and After: The Women's Liberation Oral History Project (S&A), which I had the privilege of directing from 2010 to 2013. The project captures the histories of sixty feminist activists and intellectuals to give unparalleled insight into the campaigns, ideas, and lifestyles they pioneered from the late 1960s.

Despite the unfolding discourse about feminism, these women's own lives have received little sustained attention. In part, this reflects the inevitably politicized nature of the material and broad generalizations about positions, rather than more rounded portraits. In part, it is because feminists in Britain were often bashful, idealistic about their lack of leaders, and politically dispersed. Consequently they have been underestimated as social and philosophical pioneers. While in the United States, Steinem, Friedan, Walker, Morgan, Bunch, Nestle, Firestone, and Dworkin enjoy name recognition, as do Cixous, Irigaray, Kristeva, not to mention de Beauvoir, in France or Li Xiaojiang in China, too little is known about their UK counterparts, other than the charismatic but capricious Germaine Greer.

This book therefore brings to the wider record the stories of Amrit Wilson, author of the breakthrough book on Asian women in Britain's struggle in 1978, and Pragna Patel, director of Southall Black Sisters. Mary McIntosh left the Gay Liberation Front for socialist feminism and sparked the "YBA Wife" campaign, and Una Kroll was a militant campaigner for women's ordination. Sue Lopez, battling to get women's football ("soccer" in the United States) onto a professional pitch, emerges as a pioneer, as does Jenni Murray, BBC broadcaster who, though never sympathetic to radical feminism, remains an important mainstreamer for many WLM ideas. Zoë Fairbairns wrote the 1979 novel *Benefits*, the British equivalent to Marge Piercy's and Margaret Atwood's feminist sci-fi dystopias. The right to be free from male violence unites women around the world: this book illuminates the challenges of such campaigns amid militarized civil conflict through Karen McMinn's experiences as a lynchpin of Women's Aid Northern Ireland.

Such lives embody new ideas, from labour to psychology, violence, art, and education. These were crystallized in the United Kingdom by intellectuals including Juliet Mitchell, Catherine Hall, Lynne Segal, Gail Lewis, Ellen Malos, and Jalna Hanmer. For these women, notions of "equality" or even "equal rights" were insufficient. Women's liberation meant new ways of managing domestic work, new expressions of sexuality and family, new cultures. We see how this shaped people's lives, from Betty Cook leaving an abusive marriage to become a leader in Women Against Pit Closures, to Barbara Jones's success as one of England's few women builders. But we also see the varied, sometimes opposing philosophies that guided these efforts: Cook built on a history of working-class trade union activism championed by socialists Mitchell, Segal, and Lewis, for example; Jones was inspired by the radical feminism proposed by Hanmer. I also bring out strong differences in strategy—as Jane Hutt, Sheila Gilmore, and Valerie Wise speak of getting into representative politics, in contrast to the grassroots activism of Jo Robinson and Gail Chester.

Yet groups crossed over more often than is sometimes thought, ideologically, professionally, and personally, as we see when we pay attention to activists' later lives. Beatrix Campbell, a Communist-aligned firebrand in the early days, has become a leading campaigner for survivors of sexual abuse; Jan McKenley, a black women's rights activist, was coordinator of the largely white National Abortion Campaign in the late 1970s and later brought her political commitment to her job as a school inspector; Susie Orbach, therapist and author of *Fat Is a Feminist Issue*, worked with Dove Beauty's "real women" advertising campaign in the early 2000s. Catherine Hall rethought her early work on class and family as she confronted the cruelties of the British Empire—not merely academically but through life with her husband, Jamaican-born academic Stuart Hall. In turn, Hall's own oral history shows her influence on him—one of a small but significant group of pro-feminist men whose lives I also discuss as part of a more complex mapping of relationships, including transgendered activists as they now reflect on the movement.

This collective archive thus populates a landscape too often drawn in terms of ideological abstraction. Although there have been many personal accounts, the narratives of the WLM have overwhelmingly been structured as an argument about differences between feminist camps. Attention to individual voices refreshes and complicates the question of difference, between women and women's movements. These lives I describe were determined not only by structures of race, class, gender, sexuality, and physical ability, but by political education, age, and cultural taste. In contrast to the "prudent revolutionaries" of the early to mid-twentieth century, they were imprudent optimists about participatory democracy and revolution, critical of Barbara Castle's Equal Pay Act of 1970 for failing to address the deeper question of equal value, and hostile to the mainstream media.[5] Their explorations of new kinds of family, friendships, language, leisure, and loves were part of their quest for liberation that now focused as much on the soul and body as on representation in the public sphere. Here, oral history is an exceptional resource for documenting the personal moments of lives that reflected these more insistently intimate politics and also, less obviously, "structures of feeling" that societies produce, including within activism itself.[6]

It is not simply the first-person conversations in oral history that flesh out our understanding of feminism; the aura of the voice and inadvertently caught sounds are important in themselves. Consider these moments in the S&A oral histories: Una Kroll's silvery laugh as she recounts how the BBC told her that women's voices were too high for the radio; the click of Kirsten Hearn's knitting needles as she describes getting an audio version of *The Female Eunuch* more than a decade after it was published for sighted women; Jenni Murray's Chihuahuas yapping; Sheila Kitzinger mimicking the panting of sheep giving birth; Gail Chester's drawlingly comic account of her appalling sex education; Rebecca Johnson singing Greenham Common ballads; Juliet Mitchell's rocking chair; and the thunder outside Mukami McCrum's window when she recalls her Kenyan childhood. The intake of breath almost all took when an interviewer asked about their mothers—and indeed, my own, when I was asked. Sound is gendered beyond the question of speaking out, or up. It involves the pleasure of intimate spaces and the fear of a crowd; the painful relationship we have with the visual and the gaze; the domestic, the sensual and sexual; the bodily place in the world and its connection to others.[7]

Of course, this book can only *describe* the oral of oral history, imitating in print its special pleasure. And the voice can be deconstructed into learned elements of accent, social tone, or idiom, just as it can be politicized. So while I urge you to access the archives to hear the voices themselves (easily done via the British Library's website), here I invoke oral history's strength as a creative method. In doing so, I build on poststructuralist theorists such as Luisa Passerini and Alessandro Portelli, and feminist oral history as a branch of memory studies that attempts to put the politics of speaking and listening at its centre. Such memory studies include Sherna Gluck, Susan Armitage, and, in the United Kingdom, Mary Chamberlain—all formed in and by women's liberation movements. Chamberlain introduced her collection *Fenwomen*, for example, the first nonfiction publication of the feminist press Virago in 1975, with the telling words that:

> It seemed natural to use oral history to write a book about women's lives. Much of the political groundwork of the women's movement went on orally in consciousness-raising groups. Therefore a book which attempted to draw out past and present experiences of women should allow women to speak for themselves. . . . I wanted those histories to be testimonies which appeared intact and related to individuals.

I did not want those memories to be plundered, treated as inanimate documents, for evidence in support of a singular point.[8]

In making my case for a fuller social and emotional history of the stories of feminists of Chamberlain's generation, I also acknowledge that the WLM, as an identity formed in conversation with a many-sided discourse of liberation in the 1960s, was by no means the only women's movement of the period. Major and distinct initiatives were led by trade unionists in the women's labour movement and the Left; an autonomous black women's movement often defined itself precisely against the WLM, which was undoubtedly, though often unconsciously, centred in white majority culture and perspectives. The Gay Liberation Front included women who did not align themselves with the WLM, as did women in national independence groups, most obviously Northern Ireland. Taken together, these movements have sometimes been called the second wave of feminism, but this can overemphasize commonalities—just as can equating the first wave with Anglo-American suffrage activism. The term "feminist" itself reflects these debates: black women's movements often refuted the word for its white middle-class connotations, while more traditional lobby groups—also active during this period—focused on "women's rights."[9] While I do concentrate on those who identified explicitly with the WLM, I attempt to bring a realist ear to it, and to take account of its limits as well as its successes.

By using an oral historical approach, then, I want readers to hear memories that are still animated and interested, and to question common simplifications and stereotypes of feminists and women's activists. For this reason, the title of this book—and the oral history collection itself—proposes that we think of "sisterhood" as an important but imperfect idea. Women, in truth, are not sisters, and our discourse about feminism must attend as much to what happens "after" the forging of political solidarity, discovering ways to maintain, extend, relearn, or reinvent a movement. This is ever more important in today's complex and globalized patterns of gender struggle, where feminism has even at times become a mode of soft power for Western governments. Angela McRobbie's *The Aftermath of Feminism* reveals that feminism continues to be culturally vilified: surveys of younger women show them routinely condemning it as "repulsive" or "disgusting."[10] Alison Phipps's *Gender in a Neoliberal and Neoconservative Age* similarly shows the enduring construction of feminists as paranoid, grasping, antisex, and antimen.[11] Sara Ahmed pithily explains this through the public projection of the feminist bogeywoman as a "killjoy," lesbians in particular; black feminists are especially seen as "angry."¹² Feminists admittedly did not argue that women should be happy—an ambitious aim for anyone—but they should attain equal opportunities and agency. But this book will show that they are not killjoys, even as they also worry about the instrumental use of feminist ideas. Instead, I hope that learning about the real people who were involved, including their pleasures, faiths, depressions, fears, and arts, and by listening to their sounds as much as words, will open up a more generous understanding of what it has meant to live a feminist life in recent times. For those whose own futures are unfolding amid clamorous and contrary messages of opportunities and challenges, it is more important to hear and listen to the oral histories of revolutionaries than ever before.

1 TELLING FEMINIST HISTORIES

The story of women's activism in the United Kingdom since the late 1960s is compelling, romantic, and frustratingly elusive. Because it was a network of loosely related lobbying groups and communities rather than any singular organized campaign, the Women's Liberation Movement (WLM) eschewed leaders. Its bases were often modest community centres or living rooms. Dubbed a "second wave" of protest following the campaigns for women's rights in the late nineteenth and early twentieth centuries, the women's movement was a series of eddies and currents, carrying not only gender relationships but the conditions of postwar affluence and aspiration, anticolonialism, the Cold War, and more. While some women wanted to turn unrealized promises into realities, others were struggling for control over matters of life and death. There are many versions, then, of this history. In this context, feminists have chosen oral histories and autobiographical writings to document the story plurally, from Michelene Wandor's 1990 *Once a Feminist*, for which she gathered transcribed interviews with those at the first national WLM conference in 1970, to the plethora of feminist memory websites today.[1]

Oral history demonstrates the changeable meaning of the past. Some of the most interesting insights arrive through cross-checking and synthesizing interview statements with documentary sources. Accounts of the British women's movement after 1968, from the first overview written by Anna Coote and Beatrix Campbell in 1982 to doctoral theses today, show a change from a primarily celebratory approach to one that digs into the unevenness of alliances and different ideas of what political goals should be.[2] By comparing narratives of two origin stories, the working women's protests of 1968 in Hull's fishing industries and at the Ford Motor Company in east London, and another era-defining labour struggle, at Grunwick's photo-processing plant in west London in 1976–78, oral history particularly reveals complexities around the cross-class and cross-race alliances feminists sought. Meanwhile, accounts of the history of the first WLM conference at Ruskin College in 1970, when set alongside memories of the first conference of the Organisation for Women of Asian and African Descent (OWAAD) in 1979, show how mythic moments of togetherness for some can feel painfully exclusive or simply irrelevant for others. Yet political differences are only part of the story: just as interesting and valuable are the elements of humour and confession as activists on all sides review their pasts. Here, oral histories—when put together and in context—can check tendencies both to nostalgia and to bitterness, helping to structure a realistic as well as hopeful version of this complex collective past.

In 1982, Anna Coote and Beatrix Campbell summarized their view of the major concerns of their movement—work, family, legislation, unions, learning, culture, and sex—in the first book-length history of the UK WLM: *Sweet Freedom: The Struggle for Women's Liberation*.[3] "NO WOMAN SHOULD MISS THIS BOOK. NOR SHOULD ANY MAN," proclaimed the back cover.

Both aged thirty-five, Coote, deputy editor for the *New Statesman*, and Campbell, a jobbing journalist for *Time Out* and the *Morning Star*, were well aware of the challenge of writing history as it was happening. Their declared motive was to secure an accurate political record, since women rising up have "never yet secured the means of communicating their endeavours truthfully beyond the boundaries of their own movements. . . . Shall we late-twentieth-century feminists be reduced to fragments of political archaeology before we are even in our graves?" they asked. "This time we want to be sure that history doesn't repeat itself."[4]

They begin by looking back to the protest for suffrage by domestic servant Jessie Stephen, who in 1905 had helped set fire to Royal Mail letterboxes in Glasgow. Remarkably, Stephen lived until 1979 and was involved in the Bristol WLM in her late seventies.[5] Although letterboxes really did go up in flames, the bras that American activists flung into a "freedom trash bucket" to protest the Miss America pageant in 1968 did not. Rejecting media sensationalizing, Coote and Campbell described a movement of women reacting to "the fetishized femininity" of the 1950s, women who felt betrayed by the false promises of an era when they were apparently so much freer than the past. These tensions were ignited, they claimed, by other 1960s social causes: the civil rights and anti–Vietnam War movements in the United States and the Campaign for Nuclear Disarmament (CND) and the International Socialists, the newly radical Left, in the United Kingdom. In particular, they proposed that the WLM was propelled "out of socialism." Women in the WLM, in contrast to the reforming feminists of the midcentury, wanted revolution, not reform, in which women's liberation would accompany—indeed was premised on—the abolition of class and race exploitations.

These arguments have often been repeated in accounts of the movement since, and they remain important. However, even as *Sweet Freedom* appeared, there were disagreements about the narrative. Campbell remembers that although the book was stocked by Sisterwrite, "a lovely feminist bookshop in Upper Street," they "inserted a little slip saying, I think something to the effect of, 'This book is crap,' and challenging some of the section on sexual politics, I suppose."[6] The objection was driven by radical feminists who traced a genealogy not from socialism but principally from radical feminist groups such as the American Red Stockings, whose *Notes from the First Year* in 1970 circulated widely in the United Kingdom.

Amanda Sebestyen's 1979 *Feminist Practice: Notes from the Tenth Year* was another publication inspired by the wish to record a different lineage.[7] Her pamphlet included a "chart of feminist tendencies," whose anatomizing she clearly relished. Their names today read as esoteric, from Althusserians and Euro Communists to *Féministes révolutionnaires*, matriarchists, and female supremacists. Yet even Sebestyen had to apply a sticker to each, allowing that "it's one woman's view of the movement and not a definitive statement." Ironically, the objection came from Revolutionary Feminists, who refuted her description of them. Sheila Jeffreys's *Anticlimax* (1990) went on to offer a take on the history as a mortal combat by lesbian feminists against the male-dominated sexual revolution of the 1960s and against any feminist who believed that this revolution could be of any use to women.[8]

But a different history was simultaneously being conceived that was not on Sebestyen's chart at all: the protests by those concerned with civil rights, anticolonialism, and racialized poverty. Black and Asian women's activism, described prominently in Amrit Wilson's 1978 *Finding a Voice* and Beverley Bryan, Stella Dadzie, and Suzanne Scafe's 1985 *The Heart of the Race* claimed a distinct set of roots.[9] Dadzie explicitly refuted a genealogy from the white-majority WLM:

> I think we were influenced far more, at the time, by what was happening in the liberation movements on the African continent. There were more and more examples of Black women who were active in revolutionary struggles in places like Angola, Mozambique, Eritrea, Zimbabwe, and Guinea-Bissau. And those sisters weren't just picking

up a gun and fighting—they were making demands as women, letting it be known that they weren't about to make all those sacrifices just so that they could be left behind when it came to seizing power. So although we had begun to form women's caucuses and women's study groups, what Samora Machel had to say about women's emancipation made a lot more sense to us than what Germaine Greer and other middle-class white feminists were saying. It just didn't make sense for us to be talking about changing lifestyles and attitudes, when we were dealing with issues of survival, like housing, education, and police brutality.[10]

The difficulty of bringing together these strands—and indeed the question of whether we should—reflects a political problem as to how feminism is defined, and how it relates to other struggles. Coote and Campbell's case for how the new activism emerged and what it represented had its dissenters even as it appeared, but one point remains consistent across the narratives that have emerged since—the paradox that many of the first self-declared WLM activists were apparently "winners," members of a long baby boomer generation that enjoyed free school milk as toddlers, grammar school and

The coauthors of *The Heart of the Race: Black Women's Lives in Britain* (1984), Suzanne Scafe, Beverley Bryan, and Stella Dadzie (from left to right). Their groundbreaking work highlighting the activism of black and Asian women won the 1985 Martin Luther King Award for Literature. *Photo courtesy of Stella Dadzie*

university places as teenagers, and the Pill, if they wanted it, as young adults. Britain in the 1960s may not have been swinging for all, but the economy was strong, there was universal healthcare, and education was opening to women at all levels. Middle-class homes had televisions and washing machines, advertising became ubiquitous, and the consumer goods industries and service and public sectors were expanding.

The scale of change can be measured by the fact that in 1962, 42 percent of women worked outside the home, compared with 36 percent in 1951; by 1972 the figure had risen to 52 percent.[11] Labour's 1964 election victory after thirteen years of Conservative rule, like Kennedy's in the United States in 1960, seemed to herald new opportunities and change. Feminist theologian Sara Maitland remembers the 1960s as "Very Heaven," jettisoning the passive Marilyn Monroe ideal of the 1950s. Legendary writer Angela Carter sings that "truly, it felt like Year One, when all that was holy was in the process of being profaned, and we were attempting to grapple with the real relations between human beings."[12] Despite the deeply unequal starting points for women of different classes and races, new hopes flourished across the board.

The reason, then, that several hundred women launched what they called the Women's Liberation Movement around 1968, and which three years later attracted thousands to join marches, consciousness-raising groups, women's centres, and rape crisis networks across the four countries of the United Kingdom, was ironically *because* of the new opportunities. They revealed the social and economic fetters that still tied women in "silken threads."[13] The fiftieth anniversary of women winning the vote, celebrated in 1968, highlighted the reality of women's oppression through family, marriage, sex, culture, racism, and poverty. Girls dazzled by the gleaming images of movie stars Julie Christie and Rita Tushingham, singer Shirley Bassey, and fashion model Twiggy were quickly disillusioned by the reality of sexual double standards, backstreet abortion, unequal pay, limited opportunity, domestic violence, the loneliness of the nuclear family, the stigma of divorce, and the taboo of lesbian desire. Thus the WLM focused on language, ideas, and images as much as the law—as translator and therapist Rosalind Delmar put it, moving from representation in politics to the politics of representation.[14]

Newly educated women, especially those from families with social, political, or financial clout, were in a position to protest—they did not *want* or need to conform. Prime Minister Harold Wilson's Labour governments (1964–70) arguably did much to reduce social inequalities and promote social reform, including the 1967 Abortion Act, but growing economic difficulties led to austerity, forcing the abandonment of key policy goals in housing and education, and the reimposition of the requirement that patients pay for medication prescribed by their doctor. Such reversals, alongside the government's refusal to oppose the nuclear arms race and its postcolonial policies in Africa, disappointed those of more radical and impatient political aspirations. At the same time, there was pleasure and self-discovery all around. Alongside the rise of the WLM, the British black power movement, gay liberation, the early Green movement, even the struggles in Northern Ireland, was the frisson of living differently, flouting parental and peer expectations.[15] Writer Jenny Diski said that their generation rejected their parents' dream they be "materially successful and therefore, by definition, happy." Instead, "We looked at the apparent calm, at the possibility of an untroubled suburban life that trickled properly and uneventfully to the grave, and didn't like what we saw at all."[16]

This, paradoxically, is what Sheila Rowbotham analyzed in Britain's first "manifesto" for women's liberation: "Women and the New Politics." Published in the radical political and cultural newspaper *Black Dwarf* for its "Year of the Militant Woman" issue in January 1969, it gained wider circulation in Wandor's anthology of the first writings of the WLM.[17] Rowbotham epitomized this "winning" group of young women—daughter of a mining engineer (controlling, Conservative) and a housewife (Conservative but anarchical), she was infused with Methodist idealism at grammar school, influenced by American beats, Paris existentialists, and British CND activists, and mentored by radical historians Edward and Dorothy Thompson at Oxford, which crystallized her intellectual connections with the New Left. By the late 1960s she was in London, joyously exploring the counterculture, with a finger in most protest pies, and, thanks to a passion about education for working-class men, teaching at Tower Hamlets College, in East London.

Yet, as she explains in her memoir and oral history, too many patronizing or confusing sexual messages from supposed comrades illuminated an "inner bondage" not encompassed by the Marxist idea of exploitation.[18] Her heart sank when Tariq Ali, *Black Dwarf* editor, showed her the layout for her "Year of the Militant Woman" issue in 1969: the cover sported a "cartoon dolly bird" looking out from a "V" sign, holding a hammer and sickle. Below this image the designer had drawn a woman wearing overalls in comic-book style, her pocket buttons substituting for protruding nipples. The copy inside was laid out against a background of iconic but gratuitous naked images of John Lennon, Yoko Ono, and Marilyn Monroe.[19]

To his credit, Ali removed the offensive nudes, but Rowbotham failed to spot a few pages later a "nasty little personal ad the designer had inserted": "DWARF DESIGNER SEEKS GIRL: Head girl type to make tea, organise paper, me. Free food, smoke, space. Suit American negress."[20] Sexism and racism permeated everything, including the counterculture. This was what she, and the WLM, sought to confront. And Rowbotham's justly famous manifesto turned refusal into a visionary invitation:

> The so-called women's question is a whole people question. It is not simply that our situation can only be fundamentally changed by the total transformation of all existing social relations, but also because without us any such transformation can be only partial and consequently soon distorted. The creation of a new woman of necessity demands the creation of a new man.[21]

This call for total transformation measured the difference between the incomplete enfranchisement of women in the early twentieth century and meaningful economic and cultural equality. And it showed up the patriarchal limits of the New Left.

A tireless activist, brilliant visionary, and precipitant to the first national WLM conference, Rowbotham is rightly at the centre of movement histories. But she has herself, more than any other, influenced the account of the UK WLM as having come "out of socialism." "As a historian by trade I have lived a double life," she wrote of the early years, "participating in the women's movement while contributing to its chronicling and preserving archives."[22] In the first of these chronicles, written in 1970, she attributes the beginnings of activism to the initiatives of socialist women in Nottingham and London to support working-class women's protests, with only a hazy idea of political events in the United States and Germany. Though she acknowledges that a group of London-based Americans were setting up a consciousness-raising group in Tufnell Park, inspired more by transnational ideas of black power and anti–Vietnam War protests, her account puts working-class activism centre stage. Her belief that women's liberation directly depends on involving working-class women is reflected in the pieces she gathered for that groundbreaking issue of *Black Dwarf*: Audrey Wise on equal pay, Ann Scott on birth control, Lillian Bilocca's campaign for safe working conditions, and a personal piece by "an unsupported mother."[23] It is also evident in her influential histories of activism and *The Past Is Before Us* (1989), her first extended account of her own movement.[24]

Many women, however, joined the movement without having been part of any organized Left.[25] Lynne Harne, for example, who contacted a consciousness-raising group in 1971 after having seen the first national women's liberation march on television, said that "though there were many women who had been and still were politically on the left, there were also many others coming from the hippy counterculture, from being bored housewives, mothers going off their heads at home with their children, from being women with no reason for existence, except to service men."[26] Harne was a self-declared radical/revolutionary feminist.[27]

The "out of socialism" account has also now been balanced by historians concerned to include "liberal" or "equality feminist" activism—reformers rather than revolutionaries.[28] Others see that by the early 1960s that reformist tradition had become exhausted and embattled, timidly focused on the problems of married women, and that the WLM's demands were a dramatic advance. Yet Rowbotham, and indeed Juliet Mitchell, the other most influential intellectual of the early WLM, generally ignored the long influence of the equal rights struggle in the United Kingdom. Although Rowbotham later broadened her approach, her first accounts positioned even the suffrage campaigns as too reformist, Mary Wollstonecraft too bourgeois.[29] Similarly, Mitchell was far more inspired by de Beauvoir, Althusser, and Fanon—and the new Marxist black power and student movements—than by the abolitionists and liberals of Britain's feminist past. "For me, what matters about the women's movement is the Left; it's not that it is attached to the Left, *it is the Left*," she explained in 2011.[30]

However, the broader women's movement, even in the 1970s and 1980s, certainly did include women for whom women's liberation was more easily understood as women's "rights." These included the National Council of Civil Liberties woman's officer Harriet Harman, who later became a New Labour feminist stalwart; Liberal Party activist Lesley Abdela, who simply wanted 50/50 representation in Parliament; Jill Tweedie's "Letters from a Fainthearted Feminist" weekly column in the *Guardian*; or, though perhaps this is pushing it, lifestyle writer Shirley Conran, who proclaimed: "Life's too short to stuff a mushroom."[31]

The diversity that was the women's movement—or, more accurately, movements—involved awful factionalism: 1970s debates over sexual difference and radical-socialist conflicts, with a fatal split in 1978 at the final national WLM conference; bitter debates over racism, anti-Semitism, Northern Ireland, and lesbian feminism at the turn of the '80s. Poststructuralist ideas that stressed the malleability and uncertainty of identity helped deconstruct sisterhood as part of a necessary trajectory toward a more pluralistic movement in the 1980s.[32] Increasingly, the history of the WLM is being rewritten to show how a set of diverse initiatives came together in a coalitional movement that included strands of black activism, peace activism, and local government initiatives of both radical and socialist flavors, and also, importantly, the ongoing efforts of "equal rights" or "liberal" feminists, churchwomen, Women's Institute members, Soroptimists, and Fawcett Society supporters, who had become more ambitious in their demands for social and cultural transformation.[33] This approach also acknowledges the effects of the Conservative election victory in 1979 and the ascent of free-market capitalism under Thatcherism. The next big chapter in the history was of a new "opportunity structure": on the one hand, the New Right clamped down on the welfare state in which social movements had grown, but on the other, the Labour Party and the trade unions turned to women's votes and feminist ideas in their hour of need.

Tracking such opportunity structures, networks, and ideas, sociologists have also helped to tell the story of the fierce debates in the UK women's movements over strategy, tactics, structure, leadership, resources, and responses to show it shares many features of women's movements globally. At the same time, they describe a UK movement that has been especially autonomous and localized, in contrast to the state-sponsored gender equality of Scandinavia and the Communist Party–led "emancipation" of women in Eastern Europe or China, more pragmatic than France and Italy and more socialist than the United States.[34] Preoccupied with sexuality in contrast to movements in Africa and India, it has yet been less interested in sexual rights per se than North America, which continues to exercise the strongest influence in the United Kingdom.[35] New feminist activists now ponder what to do with a more institutionalized "gender equality" structure, alongside a newly intense set of contradictions about gender identity, sexuality, and power that infuse everything from religion to music to body hair and trade unionism. In new oral histories, the classic narrative of the WLM's emergence is joined by the voices of others, in a complex portrait of change at the end of the 1960s.

Hull, Dagenham, and Little Newport Street: Class and Women's Liberation

For those who see the WLM emerge "out of socialism," two protests are iconic: the "fishermen's wives" campaign in Hull and the Ford factory strike in Dagenham, east London. Both took place in 1968, the year of the Paris student uprising, the crushing of the Prague Spring, and violent clashes in London's Grosvenor Square, when police attacked anti–Vietnam War protestors. Lilian Bilocca, a Hull fish packer, and Rose Boland, a Ford sewing machine operator, would become famous as the faces of their protests. What, then, was their connection with the WLM?[36]

The Hull campaign was in fact not about women's rights but to improve the safety of men on fishing trawlers, after fifty-eight had died when three boats sank in quick and tragic succession in early 1968.[37] Hull member of Parliament Kevin McNamara offered sympathy, and the National Union of Seaman official John Prescott (thirty years later to become Tony Blair's deputy prime minister) talked of solidarity. But impatiently taking matters into their own hands, a group of women from the community organized a meeting at which they decided to "march on the dock. Let the owners have it."[38] Spontaneously led by Bilocca, they crowded into the owners' offices and presented a six-point safety charter. In response, the recalcitrant owners stopped pay. Undeterred, Bilocca collected ten thousand signatures on a petition calling for reform, led a delegation to Parliament, and got to see Prime Minister Wilson after threatening to picket his house. Eventually the Transport and General Workers' Union and Labour members of Parliament swung behind the campaign and new safety measures were set. Dubbed "the headscarf revolutionaries" (many women had backcombed hairstyles that required protection in factory jobs), the Hull women also fascinated the media.[39] The sight of working-class wives taking on the bosses—and winning—was novel for everyone, and inspiring for emerging feminists.

The second defining women's labour action of 1968 was the strike at Ford, dramatized in the film *Made in Dagenham* and onstage in *Made in Dagenham: The Musical*.[40] More than 360 women withdrew their labour when a job evaluation exercise downgraded their jobs as less skilled, setting pay 15 percent lower than men paint spray operators at the same grade.[41] Theirs was not a demand for equal pay in itself: their argument was whether women's work would be considered of equal value—many had been dressmakers and so were experienced machine operators. Sheila Douglas, then in her thirties and a member of the National Union of Vehicle Builders, explained in an oral history, "When Ford took over Briggs, that was when the new wage structure came in and that was when we found out that we weren't classed as skilled. . . . [We had] claims [to be regraded] that kept going in every couple of years and they were still ignoring our wants. And so we just said, 'Enough's enough.'"[42]

Barbara Castle, then employment secretary in Wilson's government, saw the opportunity to secure her long-cherished Equal Pay Act, which resulted in a deal where the women's pay was brought into line with the pay of male *unskilled* workers.[43] So on the one hand, the women's campaign must be counted as an extraordinary success: they had brought the biggest carmaker

18 • SISTERHOOD AND AFTER

Women in Hull protested to demand improved safety on North Sea trawlers. Lillian Bilocca (front row, right) was restrained by police as she threatened to leap aboard any boats putting to sea without a radio operator. The spontaneous campaign went on to lobby Parliament and force a meeting with Prime Minister Harold Wilson, after threatening to picket his house. *Photo courtesy of Mirrorpix*

in the United Kingdom and a powerful global corporation to a standstill, and the pressure this generated undoubtedly ensured the passage of the Equal Pay Act in 1970.[44] But Rose Boland, their shop steward, confirmed in a Trades Union Congress (TUC) oral history that their goal had been far more radical until Castle stepped in, and in many ways the celebration of their strike as the kickstart of the British women's movement drastically misrepresents their experience of defeat.[45] It would be another sixteen years before the machinists got their jobs upgraded to semiskilled, after a further strike in 1984. Moreover, it was not until 1988 that the principle that feminized and masculinized skills could be compared was recognized when Julie Hayward won her case that her work as an industrial cook should be paid at the same rate as that of the painters and carpenters she cooked for.

Were these feminist protests? Not according to the Hull campaigner Mary Denness, wife of a trawler skipper: "We did it on behalf of our seafaring menfolk." Though Bilocca faced misogyny, and the campaign was famously women-led, the action was primarily against heartless employers and the business and governing classes that protected them. Today, a commemorative plaque behind the Fishermen's Memorial in Hull honors "Lillian Bilocca and

Women machine operators from the Ford plant in Dagenham enjoy a cup of tea with Employment Secretary Barbara Castle (fourth from the right). Their 1968 strike for pay parity brought Britain's biggest carmaker to a standstill, helped secure the passage of Castle's Equal Pay Act in 1970, and inspired the cinema and West End musical production *Made in Dagenham*. But they felt that Castle had hijacked their cause, which was for equal status rather than equal pay. *Photo courtesy of Mirrorpix*

the Women of Hessle Road." Denness was happy to be part of this charismatic leader's group, remembering that her "plain-speaking" local accent "was part of her charm."[46] Born on Wassand Street in 1928, the heart of Hull's fishing community, Denness recalls Bilocca as a "lovely large bubbly lady," dubbed "Big Lil" by the press. She faced down threatening phone calls and was unrepentant while giving a talk at Strathclyde University the day after she had been peremptorily sacked from her fish-processing job because she had been away for three weeks campaigning.[47] Yet it seems none of the women went on to join the new women's rights group formed to support their campaign by radicals at Hull University, despite attempts to entice them with meetings in local pubs.[48]

The Ford strike, by contrast, inspired the National Joint Action Campaign Committee for Women's Equal Rights (NJACCWER) rally at Trafalgar Square in 1969. By the end of 1968 most trade unions had declared in favour of equal pay, and organizations in support of the rally included the Labour

Party, the Communist Party, the Women's Liberal Federation, the Women's Liberation Workshop, and branches of the civil rights for women movement. Their five-point plan demanded the removal of sex discrimination against women; equal pay for work of equal value; enforcement of equal legal rights for women; coordination by the TUC of a national action campaign for equal pay and opportunity in industry; and immediate government ratification of the International Labour Organisation convention on women's rights. Among the speakers was Baroness Summerskill, who had campaigned throughout the 1940s and 1950s. Rowbotham remembers that "even though it rained about 1,000 trade union women, their perms carefully covered by umbrellas, tripped smartly dressed to Trafalgar Square in high heels."[49]

Audrey Wise, an official in the Union of Shop, Distributive and Allied Workers (USDAW) in 1968, and later member of Parliament for Coventry South West from 1974 to 1979, located the beginning of British women's liberation in 1968 precisely *because* of the Ford strike. She declared it "extraordinarily important because it was the first strike since the match girls, eighty years before, which was identified as a women's strike" and because it "predated the American influence."[50] But although the NJACCWER rally built on a Working Women's Charter conceived by the unions as early as 1964, union activists did not generally frame this as a demand connected to a wider platform of women's *identities*, rather as a statement about their rights as women workers. The TUC's 2007 oral history project on equal pay activism vividly captures the distinction. An account by Maureen Jackson, a Ford employee on strike in 1984, where they finally achieved equal pay, demonstrates this approach to the issue:

> If our work built up and they didn't need so many car seats, they would say to some of the girls, "Oh, we'd like you to go over to the door panels, because they're a bit short-staffed," and the girls would go over there and get stuck in and do the door panels, or in the tank shop; they would find you work over there, but when we were very busy and there was quite a few spare machines, they could never say to the men, "Would you come over and do a bit of machining?" because, you know, the men would never have a clue how to even thread a needle, I shouldn't think, rather than do machining, and in the end the women started talking amongst theirselves and saying, "Well, this is not on; we can sort of turn our hands to anything but the men can't," which is, which seemed very unfair to us. So I think that was the start of us digging our heels in.[51]

The presence of male shop stewards alongside women recalling their days on strike in the TUC oral history is also telling, for the campaigns were more often to create alliances with men supportive of women workers' rights. But the relationship between these protests and the coincidence of working-class and middle-class women's dissatisfaction at the end of the 1960s raises a puzzle about feminism's identity as it attaches to both history and memory. One explanation is that working-class women did not share the raised, then dashed, expectations that underpinned the emergence of the WLM for white middle-class radicals. Was 1960s feminism indeed partly the response of middle-class mothers to the shock of "servantless homes," as Beatrix Campbell at first glance argued, ironically scornful of the first conference at Ruskin?[52]

For although middle-class women were horrified to discover that the sexual or marriage contract ended professional opportunities, and that domestic labour was boring and hard, many working-class women perceived housewifery to be at least as good, if not better than, the low-paid work they usually did.[53] Black women and Asian women with extended families to support were also more likely to be working in less appealing jobs.[54] Similarly, Northern Irish Catholic women were more likely than Protestants to have to work for a living because Catholic men were discriminated against in the workplace.[55] These protests were perhaps more visceral. In Hull Denness describes "an urge to do something about" a terrible tragedy, not a pleasure in activism, though in retrospect she feels pride at the thought of having possibly saved further lives.[56] The Dagenham women's demand that their skills be recognized as equal to men's implicitly challenged gender ideologies, and their attendance at the NJACCWER rally was evidence of a broader politics, as was the development of women's groups within the unions throughout the 1970s, leading to a dramatic unity in the 1979 TUC–women's movement march for abortion rights. Compared with the movement in the United States, the militant workers' movement was deeply connected and important to the WLM throughout.[57] Yet despite approaches on both sides, a political gulf remained obvious even fifteen years later, when the miners' strike again brought working-class women into contact with the WLM in large numbers.[58]

This leads to a second hypothesis as to the difference between the movements, that working-class women's protests were defined within the terms of trade union and labour organizing that went back to the nineteenth-century Chartist movement. Old and new social movements can be distinguished precisely as those focused on economic gain and those focused on lifestyle and identity issues.[59] In this approach, the women's movement, along

Protestors at the first national demonstration demanding equal pay for women on London's Trafalgar Square, May 1969. Led by the National Joint Action Campaign Committee for Women's Equal Rights, the rally was inspired by the example of the women strikers at Ford, although male trade union members also helped organize the event. *Photo courtesy of Mirrorpix*

with antiracism, civil rights, gay rights, student, environmental, and peace movements, was not primarily defined by Marxian models of class conflict but by group identity, lifestyles, and personal change, and was characterized by radical mobilization tactics: direct action, nonviolent civil disobedience, and a diffuse network rather than hierarchical central organization. These cultural movements emerge from middle-class rather than working-class constituencies, enabled by economic security and expanded civil society and democratization, even as they draw on a crisis of credibility in Western democracy, fuelled in part by economic uncertainties. In contrast, labour protests were arguably more conservative in their demands, even when allied to passionate socialism. Perhaps, as one historian has suggested, most trade union members simply wanted their fair share of the pie, in obvious contrast to Rowbotham's view that the new movement sought to "complement and to change" the old.[60]

A third explanation focuses instead on the various ways that women of different classes, races, and religions might experience sexual status and expectation. Many middle-class white women in the WLM link their feminism directly to the false promises of sexual liberation, particularly with the new availability of contraception. Sheila Jeffreys contends that patriarchy took away sexually precisely *because* women had gained economically and politically.[61] Certainly, in the Sisterhood and After (S&A) interviews, Anne Koedt's *The Myth of the Vaginal Orgasm, Our Bodies, Ourselves*, and Greer's *The Female Eunuch* were the most frequently cited texts—all classic feminist discourses on sexual liberation.

But the issue of sexual rights did not resonate as widely for working-class or black women. The usual account is that sexual rights are a luxury that comes only after people gain a minimum economic standard of living. But control over women's sexuality defines gender as a kind of "class" in itself that intersects with other differences. A deeper analysis considers how sexual and domestic respectability has been especially important for working-class and ethnic-minority women.[62] Historian Natalie Thomlinson asks "whether either black or white working-class women were able to participate in the free and frank discourse around women's sexuality so valued by the WLM without significant risk to this 'respectability.'"[63] The TUC collection shows that working-class activism was by no means reducible to economic ambition. Discussions range over the wish for control, confidence, security, and time: it is, however, true that this focused on public and work life. It also suggests why it was often more socially conservative. It shines a light on working-class women and women from ethnic-minority communities who *did* identify as feminist: Were they propelled by experiences that disenchanted them of "respectability," or denied it? It is significant that the black women's movement coalesced on issues of sexual violence even if it was ambivalent about lesbian or pro-sex demands.[64]

A final explanation for why working-class or ethnic-minority movements remained largely separate from the white middle-class centre of the WLM resonates throughout the tones and vocabularies of oral histories. Movements emerge from the pleasure of belonging, socializing, and rites of passage, especially for those leaving home or remaking themselves after some identity challenge. They reflect the friendship networks from which they arose. Questions of taste and leisure immensely influence participation. One the one hand, some WLM activists were unexcited by trade union culture, with its workingmen's clubs, beer, and pies; contrast this to Sheila Capstick's "A Woman's Right to Cues" protest for equal rights in workingmen's clubs after she had been prevented from playing snooker with her husband in 1978 (they finally succeeded in 2007).[65] Meanwhile, others were put off by the fashions and foods of the student-styled liberation movement. Mukami McCrum's tart description of the dress code at women's groups—"the donkey jacket [working-men's coat] kind of thing . . . trousers and . . . rough clothes"—appalled her, having grown up poor in Kenya, where even if you only had one dress, you washed and ironed it overnight. "To me fighting for equality did not desire me looking untidy or messy or not washing your hair," she adds. Margaret Howell, thrilled to be one of only two working-class women in the National Co-ordinating Group of Women's Aid in 1978, nevertheless insisted on maintaining her fashionable hairstyle and clothes.[66]

A more provocative example comes from white middle-class woman Erin Pizzey, who was happy with bohemian clothes and lentil stews, and shared much of the culture of the early WLM. Her problem, which later fuelled one of the most notorious incidents in the early movement, was her view of the movement as extreme and anti-men. In her tellingly named memoir *This Way to the Revolution*, she narrates her attempt to lead some (in her terms) "men-positive" women to what she considered the WLM's "headquarters" in 1969:

> Little Newport Street in Soho was insalubrious and grimy. The houses were narrow and with steep staircases. We pushed open the front door to the office and climbed upstairs. We could hear women's voices and eventually came to a door that was ajar. Alison pushed it open, and I followed her into a small room. I saw posters much like those on Artemis's walls with vengeful women waving guns. Sitting on the floor were a puddle of young women. Ensconced on the only chair was Glad. She didn't look pleased to see us.[67]

For some, the image of this "grimy" office is a fabrication: contrast it, for example, to Rosalind Delmar's oral historical account of the move from Lois Graessle's Battersea flat (apartment) to Little Newport Street, "which was where The Other Cinema had their offices." She was friendly with a secretary there, and "we rented a room from them; it was a very nice part of town to be in."[68] Having no funding and being resolutely against institutionalizing itself, the movement largely operated out of living rooms and "found" spaces. For many, this contributed to the magic of self-invention and grassroots make-do-and-mend. Delmar goes on to say that the London Women's Liberation Workshop moved from Soho to a cheap rental in Convent Garden, after the market had moved but before the area had regenerated: "it was when we were at that office that . . . some of the real arguments began to develop within the movement. And that was when we discovered that there was this woman who was coming to meetings [who] had decided that we were a, a dangerous organization, and had gone and complained to the police and, been asked to keep an eye on some of us, and, so on and so forth."[69] Though Delmar does not name her, this was Pizzey herself.

It is no surprise that many WLM activists were from fairly similar backgrounds, particularly given the networked "circuits of solidarity" rather than traditional political party structures that connected them.[70] Oral histories confirm that the Labour movement's "women's movement" and the WLM were not one phenomenon, just as the WLM was distinct from those like Pizzey who ultimately wanted to stay in the reformist tradition. What they do show is that the WLM activists still treasure the political inspiration. Campbell says that meeting Ford factory militants in the 1970s transformed her political understanding, particularly as they reflected UK Asian workers' demands for flexible working hours.[71] Eileen Evason, later linchpin of Northern Irish activism, though indifferent to the student radicalism at the University of Hull, was drawn to the Hull women's protest as a strong Labour supporter.[72] Working-class women's protests catalyzed WLM activists, in the way black civil rights worked for white feminists in the United States, even as black and working-class women were defining women's liberation in their own terms.[73] This naturally raises sensitivities about who belonged to both groups, and to political priority and expropriation.

In addition, radical feminists, largely but not exclusively white and middle class, were more interested in US influences, raising further questions as to the relationship between black power, class struggle, and women's liberation. These issues have come into new focus in debates over how we should remember the WLM conference at Ruskin College, which for some has mythic status as the moment when the UK national movement first crystallized.

Ruskin, Race, and Nation

If the Hull and Ford actions provide the first origin story of the WLM, the second is the National Women's Liberation Movement Conference at Ruskin College, Oxford, in 1970. Here at least four hundred women (some say more)—plus sixty children and forty men—gathered in an intense two-day meeting on topics from women in prisons to equal pay.[74] This undoubtedly connected sexual freedom and women's liberation in a characteristically spontaneous and largely joyous discovery of shared interests. But those outside the "charmed circle of Ruskin," wrote historian Barbara Caine, included "provincial women, who were unaware of Ruskin; women not involved in Left politics; black women; and women who were either too young or too old to be university students or young mothers in places where there were consciousness-raising groups in 1968."[75] So, while Ruskin was clearly a political turning point for the new movement, recent recordings by black and Asian feminist activists, Scottish, Welsh, and Irish women, women in the regions, and, indeed, older oral histories of Fawcett Society members contextualize the conference as only one of many important gatherings.

The conference came out of a meeting of History Workshop, a "fluid coalition of worker-students from Ruskin and other socialist historians" formed by the charismatic historian Raphael Samuel in 1967.[76] Again, Rowbotham was at the centre, suggesting in 1969 a meeting for people interested in talking about women's history, and despite being greeted "with guffaws" by the men, a group of women met to plan the event, including Roberta Hunter-Henderson, Sally Alexander, Arielle Aberson, Anna Davin, and eventually other women from Europe, the four UK nations, and North America.[77] Joined by Juliet Mitchell in a core planning group, the conference became the occasion when the first four movement demands were agreed by majority vote: equal pay; equal education and opportunity; twenty-four-hour nurseries; and free contraception and abortion on demand.[78]

The hall was packed at the first national women's conference at Oxford's Ruskin College in 1970. Sheila Rowbotham (second from left), one of the United Kingdom's leading socialist feminist theorists, helped organize the event and described how the idea initially drew "guffaws" from some of the men at the History Workshop. *Photo courtesy of Sally Fraser/Photofusion*

Sue Crockford, a member of the first Tufnell Park women's liberation group, and co-organizer of the radical film collective Angry Arts, helped to immortalize the event in *A Woman's Place*. She remembers, "It was one of those rare times in your own history where you know you're there at an occasion that's historically important . . . I personally felt terrified because I had to stand up in front of . . . 600 women saying, I'd like to film this, please could I have permission, and the majority of the crew are men."[79] The footage captures Juliet Mitchell sweeping through, hair falling across her face; Rowbotham smiling animatedly; women listening to speakers sometimes with a look of puzzlement; a blanket concealing a statue of a male dignitary. Stuart Hall, then director of the radical Birmingham Centre for Cultural and Community Studies, is on the floor of the nursery, playing with busy toddlers. This intellectual and political connection was exhilarating for the core group, for whom it expressed long-felt needs and for whom the social scene made sense. Catherine Hall recalled it as similar to a Christian conversion.

Michelene Wandor's 1990 anthology *Once a Feminist*, which gathered together transcripts of interviews with those who had been there, captures this sense of transformation. Wandor, who went on to become a playwright, described herself as the innocent abroad:

> For me the Ruskin weekend was an exhilarating and confusing revelation. It was, I think, the first time I had been away from children and husband, away from my secure home structure, operating as an individual in a collective context. Here I was, surrounded by about six hundred women, all far more politically sophisticated than I was, all seemingly articulate and knowledgeable about the role of women in history, the position of women in today's world; who could formulate profound questions about the relationship between class, gender and race, who could simultaneously quote and criticise Marx (whom I had not then read), and who seemed hell-bent on changing the world and our self-image as women.[80]

Wandor did comment that "there were parts of the psyche that even our exhilarating, all-embracing feminist politics didn't reach; art, literature and music were all pushed to one side as we concentrated on the nitty-gritty of 'real life.'"[81] Equally, race was not on the Ruskin agenda, though "third world women" and "internationalism" were. Thomlinson views this as evidence that although white activists were often involved in anti-imperialist politics, they had not connected these to the interests of ethnic-minority populations in the United Kingdom. There were few minority women present, to be sure.[82]

As with the industrial disputes and early women's liberation groups, Ruskin reflected how social movements come out of established networks inevitably based on school, community, work, and leisure. Some of the organizers were associated with the New Left —Mitchell had been at school with Raphael Samuel; Rosalind Delmar was on the CND executive committee with former *New Left Review* editor Stuart Hall.[83] Others had met through mutual friends in the counterculture—Sally Alexander and Sheila Rowbotham at the *Black Dwarf* producer Clive Goodwin's house; Jo Robinson heard about Ruskin from friends in agitprop theatre and The Poster Workshop.[84] It was precisely because these brilliant women had been so frustrated by the Left, even as they had been educated alongside its inspirational activists, that they fuelled the WLM.[85] And the conference's success undoubtedly reflected the decision to hold it at Ruskin, which, though connected to Oxford University, was an independent adult education college for those who had left secondary school early without a qualification—including Sally Alexander herself, who was studying there as a mature student and single mother. Yet it is not surprising that, despite Ruskin's extensive Labour networks and links to mothers' and wives' groups that reached beyond the ordinary university boundaries, there were few of the militant black intellectuals or activists then centred on the *Race Today* collective and other race rights groups. Their social and educational circles were still scarcely connected.[86]

Scholar-activist Gail Lewis, speaking at a forty-year commemoration of the Ruskin conference, argued that fetishizing Ruskin repeats a structural exclusion of black women who were not able to be there to define a different agenda.[87] Questioning the narrative that locates the conference as the beginning of the WLM, the Hull and Dagenham strikes meant much more to her as a young mixed-race working-class woman working in a factory.[88] The black women's movement in the United Kingdom was influenced by black radicalism in the United Kingdom as it developed during the 1960s. This ran parallel rather than subsequent to white middle-class activism, just as did white working-class women's activism.[89]

Significant dates include Stokely Carmichael's visit to London in June 1967, sparking a small British Black Panther movement, *The Black Liberator* journal, and organizations such as the Black Liberation Front, the Black Unity and Freedom Party, the Black People's Information Centre, and other new organizations in London, Liverpool, Manchester, Birmingham, and Nottingham. The British Black Panthers also had a woman leader after the departure of founder Obi Egbuna.[90] Althea Lecointe was a hardline Marxist, originally from Jamaica, who became a doctor after the end of the Panthers. She did not term herself a feminist but was seen as such by at least one male comrade for insisting on sexual restraint in party households.[91] She was an inspirational figure to young black women, particularly as a defendant in the Mangrove Nine trial of 1970, a landmark for exacting the first admission of institutional police racism in Britain.[92]

There were at least two black women at Ruskin, though—Gerlin Bean and Pat Smith. Bean says that "I couldn't really pick on the relevance of [Ruskin] as it pertains to black women."[93] She made an exception for the American Selma James, who, having come from US Trotskyism and civil rights, and married to the Pan-African leader C. L. R. James, was able to "put it all in context . . . how it would affect black women and our involvement because our struggle wasn't just about women, it was an anti-imperialist struggle about black people."[94] She was a member of women's caucuses within the socialist Black Liberation Front. It is likely that Bean was part of the anonymously documented Black Women's Action Committee, which created the pamphlet "Black Women Speak Out" in 1970. It is instructive to compare its demands to those of the white WLM: "Our demands are practical conclusions which we have drawn from the burning needs, the shameful humiliation of women in bourgeois society, defenceless and without rights."[95]

Anthologized in Wandor's *The Body Politic: Writings from the Women's Liberation Movement in Britain, 1969–1972*, this pamphlet constitutes the first widely circulated statement of black women's liberation in the United Kingdom.[96] The Marxist framework is obvious in the demands, which describe the need to influence (other) women's "backward psychology," creating "new institutions and common struggles" that will allow black women to "arrive at a new and higher consciousness."[97] But while class overrides race as the mechanism for exploitation, notably it is "because of racism" that the black woman "does not find solidarity with the working-class woman as such, but with another social group, i.e. the black national minority."[98] It foregrounds women's issues as distinct from men's—for example, the right to take control over her own body and the need for black women to have access to contraception.

Bean eventually left the United Kingdom for Zimbabwe and then returned to Jamaica; today she works in community rehabilitation.[99] However, Gail Lewis, Stella Dadzie, Suzanne Scafe, Jan McKenley, and Jocelyn Wolfe, to name only a few, went on to be prolific, recognizable figures in black women's organizing and in white women's and mixed networks. Lewis, with

Bean, was an originator of the influential Brixton Black Women's Group (BBWG), founded in 1973, which was formed by women from *Race Today* and the radical Brixton-based bookshop Sabarr. BBWG soon involved many women who had been in the black power movement, including the young Olive Morris, who died from cancer at age twenty-six and whose life has been remembered in a community-led oral history.[100] The group combined study with campaigning with West Indian Parents' Action Groups and educational and cultural youth programmes. They drew inspiration from the Manchester Black Women's Co-operative and Liverpool Black Sisters, both established in 1973, who also focused on housing, education, and policing.[101]

Dadzie asserts that black women were largely influenced by African and other anticolonial struggles, even as they were forming women's caucuses within their organizations.[102] This anticolonial inspiration is also evident in the history of Asian women's activism in the United Kingdom, as immigrant and second-generation populations discovered the reality of life in "the motherland." At the same time, Asian women's activism was shaped by language differences, and by the fact that most women came to the United Kingdom as "dependents" to join migrant men. This context meant that the first big public action by Asian women was compelling for white feminists and the white labour movement yet oddly muted on racial politics.

The Grunwick strike began in 1976, when 150 or so mostly women workers, many of South Asian origin, withdrew their labour at the Grunwick photo-processing laboratory in northwest London. It was the start of a two-year struggle in which they fought for better treatment and union recognition; the struggle ended in failure but remains a heroic collective memory.[103] The Grunwick strikers were twice migrants, urban middle-class refugees from East Africa, having already left India and Pakistan. Their expectations were different from the local working-class women with whom they shared a position.[104] As with the women from Hull and Dagenham, this was a workers' rather than a women's liberation struggle. The trade unions saw Grunwick as a cause célèbre. These perspectives are confirmed by a rich new oral history project, which reveals that the women were also largely supported by their male relatives.[105] Grunwick did not lead to activism on issues of culture, sexuality or family, but certainly challenges the stereotype of passivity with which Asian women in the United Kingdom have had to contend. Again, many commented that the strike influenced the trade union movement to become more open to issues of race or sex discrimination.

One woman who made the link was Amrit Wilson. Born into an atheist family from a Hindu background in Calcutta, Wilson came to the United

Strikers from the Grunwick photo-processing laboratory in London, with leader Jayaben Desai at front right. The strikers were mostly women of South Asian origin, and while their two-year fight was ultimately unsuccessful, it remains iconic in trade union and community history. *Photo courtesy of the TUC Library, London Metropolitan University Special Collections*

Kingdom in 1961 to pursue doctoral studies in chemistry at Imperial College, London. She married an English fellow student but found herself at odds with his family. By the time of the Grunwick strike, she had a young daughter and had become interested in women's politics in Britain, attending WLM conferences though always asserting an antiracist and anticolonial struggle.[106] Wilson's freelance articles for the *Guardian, New Society,* and *Spare Rib* grew into the first extended study of Asian women in the United Kingdom, asserting the significance of their political struggle in explicitly feminist terms. Her book *Finding a Voice* (1978) was lauded as pathbreaking.[107] Although it showed the tenuousness of even Grunwick as a meeting point for either Asian labour protestors or feminists across racial lines, it fuelled British Asian feminism.

By 1978, the London-based group of Asian women AWAZ (Urdu for "voice") had emerged, followed, in 1979, by the legendary Southall Black Sisters, which became the leader of a black women's antiviolence movement that included Brent Asian Women's Refuge, Amadudu black women's refuge in Liverpool, and Shakti in Edinburgh. This network of organizations created practical and enduring links with radical feminist antiviolence campaigns, even though many, including Wilson, remained deeply committed to Marxist anticolonial perspectives.

For black and Asian women, then, the first national conference was not Ruskin but the inaugural conference of OWAAD in March 1979. Held at the Abeng Centre in Brixton, south London, a community space more typical of activism at the time than Ruskin, over two hundred women attended, and accounts testify to the same sense of joyful surprise as they saw how many they were and realized their fluency, experience, and vision.[108] Judith Lockhart, who subsequently became a Greater London Council policy advisor, remembers it as "a real eye-opener" to see black women in leadership positions and so many black women as teachers, lawyers, and professionals.[109] Conference topics included health, education, law, anti-imperialism, and employment.[110] Yet at first, this too had been conceived for only one part of a potential constituency, as Dadzie, a key organizer, describes:

> I *always* remember . . . an Indian woman . . . from somewhere up north, she marched into [laughing] one of those meetings dressed in leathers . . . she strode in off her motorbike and said, "*And what about us?* We're here too!" . . . so *any how* we could make those links with the Asian sisters—they didn't have the same experience, we knew that . . . they may have experienced racism differently but they still experienced racism. You know, they may have experienced sexism differently but they still experienced sexism. So that began that debate and I can actually remember hand-crossing out [laughing]—we'd done all these bloody leaflets, and you see it in the archive, you know—hand-crossing out, Women of *Africa* and *African* Descent, and replacing that with Women of . . . African and *Asian* Descent.[111]

In fact, some attendees remember that perhaps a quarter of the women at the conference were Asian. Four months later, OWAAD joined with AWAZ to organize a sit-in at Heathrow Airport, protesting the scandalous testing of migrant women's virginity, and then worked together against the forced administration of Depo-Provera on women seeking advice on contraception.[112] These alliances built on a shared experience of racism, migration, and a white United Kingdom still crackling with memories of empire. Activists also shared a second-generation politics, torn between loyalty to their immigrant parents' cultural and linguistic starting points and their own evolving

Flyers from the inaugural Organisation for Women of Asian and African Descent (OWAAD) meeting had to be quickly amended by hand, changing the word *Africa* to read *Asian*, in order to acknowledge the coalition between the two groups. *Photo courtesy of Jan McKenley*

identities, which were distinct from white women's reactions to their own parents' wartime outlook.

Yet black activists worked on the same organizing principle as white feminists, building on preexisting networks and identifications. The BBWG was apparently filled with heavy-duty Marxist discussions. Yvonne Field, for example, ultimately preferred to belong to Aurat Obaa, a group for black women social workers.[113] OWAAD itself dispersed within four years over differences between straight and lesbian women, and between women of African, Asian, and African-Caribbean descent, which could include deep differences of language, culture, and political focus. The recent collection of oral histories by the Black Cultural Archives (BCA) under the heading *The Heart of the Race* (reprising the title of Bryan, Dadzie, and Scafe's 1985 history of black women in the United Kingdom) has provided a major source of memories of African-Caribbean and African women's organizing, but, following the BCA's collection policy, women of Asian descent were not interviewed, despite their presence at OWAAD. Jan McKenley's observation that OWAAD was "a conference, it wasn't a movement, it wasn't a group," shows that it has in its own way become as mythologized as Ruskin.[114]

The inaugural meeting of the OWAAD was held in Brixton in March 1979. OWAAD played a key role in protesting against virginity tests imposed on Asian migrant women at Heathrow Airport, at the direction of the immigration service, to verify residency and marriage claims. *Photo courtesy of Stella Dadzie*

Composing Feminist Memories

Oral histories confirm the diversity and variety of women's movements, which we increasingly see as crucial to any understanding of the so-called WLM. Indeed, their very provenance represents this diversity, with the TUC, the Black Cultural Archives in Brixton, the Glasgow Women's Archive, and Fawcett and Feminist Archives North and South, just to name a few, each interviewing their own constituency. Similarly, the S&A project, aiming principally to capture the self-identified WLM, sways toward a London-based intelligentsia.

Oral history methods make a distinct contribution to this history as a medium not so much of facts but of memories, subjectivities and feelings. Women respond in a range of accents, tones, genres. As Alessandro Portelli puts it, this formal, sometimes even poetic dimension is what "makes oral history different."[115] One example comes from Rowbotham, blond hair swinging as she sits in the British Library interview room, remarking, "When you're young you just want to be bouncy and [you don't want to hear] some dreary... Cassandra... going on, 'Oh, it's really bad, you know.'"[116] In 2012, as she tells this story, in her seventies, she is writing about nineteenth-century radicals, she is in love, and her voice is full of smiles.

But alongside pleasure in remembering, many interviewees convey strain, even anxiety, when asked whom the WLM represented and how it developed. This testifies to deep and ongoing personal investments in the philosophical basis of women's liberation, and to only partly healed arguments over the differences and inequalities between women. In the S&A interviews, when interviewees speak about racial, class, and national constituencies, there are often audible hesitations, repetitions, and rephrasings, as they muster the right words, confess their ignorance, or assert the unevenness or inequalities of the movement's coverage.

Here we see a process of composure in the sense that Penny Summerfield defines, by which interviewees rely on stereotypes or practiced pieces, adjusted to suit the audience, even if unconsciously.[117] The stereotypes for these activists are less about popular media images of feminism as aggressive or anti-men. Rather, they are feminist discourses of political conversion and awakening, centred on the discovery of shared struggle, coalition, and "intersectionality" as a more recent term for interconnected oppressions. At the same time, we hear where difficult memories or perceived challenges from the interviewer provoke discomposure. These include the discourse of feminist racism, class privilege, or disappointing divisions. Natalie Thomlinson eloquently described this in her experience of using oral histories to explore race relations in the movement, including inhibiting shame for white women and suspicions on the part of black interviewees about a young white woman pursuing a doctorate about them. She offers a way to think about this, arguing that discomposure in the interview might correlate not with guilt but precisely with a greater conscience, supporting her argument that black and white feminists became more politically and personally involved by the late 1980s.[118]

As interviewees approach these precious pasts, albeit at times relying on discourses of personal discovery, we also hear the other dimension of composure as a feature of oral history—where interviewees seek personal peace through the practice of narration. As Summerfield observes, this is not easy even in an oral history interview intended to accept or restore value to a version of events. When feminists are interviewed about a movement's history, we witness a struggle to position themselves on a map in which taking a position was both principle and risk, and in which the political past remains a political present. The S&A interviews especially reflect these psychic balancing acts since, at an average of six hours, they were so long and intimate.

These efforts testify to the personal relationships that all these movements inspired. But they also reveal how storytellers get caught in patterns that, although they can work emotionally or dramatically, oversimplify events. Here feminist theorists have leaned on an often unhelpful "grammar" that unconsciously shapes how we speak of the feminist past. Clare Hemmings defines this as "a series of interlocking narratives of progress, loss," driven by the wish to be politically "cutting edge."[119] These older activists are generally less theoretically concerned than the academics Hemmings is interested in, but we can still see traces of these structures in oral history interviews. Some clearly speak of progress from an initially undifferentiated idea of womanhood to a postmodern diversity, acknowledging the differences between and within genders. In contrast, others regret the fragmentation and infighting, implying that after the glory days of the WLM, we live in a depoliticized "postfeminism" that has lost sight of women's economic struggle. Hemmings identifies a third narrative structure in addition to "progress" and "decline," which she calls "return." This tries to mediate by returning to the socioeconomic emphasis of 1970s feminism while preserving later insights about gender's flexibility and the importance of identity.[120]

All three of these narratives touch on truths. The real problem is that they attach to simplified versions of who did what when, and underplay mutual influence. Thus radical and socialist feminists are "stuck" in the 1970s, poststructuralist feminists in the 1980s. Lesbian feminists are situated as helping to move a heterosexist movement "forward" at the end of the 1970s (or breaking it apart), then called to account by the pro-sex demands of the 1980s.[121] Black feminists are consistently located in the 1980s, a kind of symbolic marker of the moment when unity becomes difference, used unfairly to figure the necessary growth of (white) feminism while obscuring their own longer history. Conversely, this grammar also contributes to the overly simplistic view that lesbian feminism during the 1970s was regressively white and racist.[122] The 1990s saw the development of sophisticated queer theory, but too often such theory gets invoked as frivolously over-focused on pleasure, which leaves activists today working to return to appropriately serious, global politics. This way of organizing the narrative erases important sexual rights and problematically implies that the politics of pleasure is of only Western concern, while also forgetting that postcolonial and critical race theorists have also long argued for the importance of cultural politics.

Despite the seemingly abstract nature of these questions, in fact the templates we use to organize a historical account are filled with affect, unconscious emotions that reflect profound attachments to an idea of women's liberation. They are also problematic because "progress" and "loss" are always narrative simplifications of historical time. But even as (I hope) we avoid the temptations of either "things will get better" or "things will get worse," most of this book finds a different kind of plotting altogether, through looking at the everyday lives of generations of women who lived through times they knew were extraordinary and who did their best to make them so.

The material and the socioeconomic matter as much as the cultural. But in contrast to the opportunistic citation of lives as political positions, life narratives humanize the past, for they allow us to access the subtler time of the domestic world, learn about habits and dreams, and hear a person's contradictions. Oral history's value is the idiosyncratic as much as the typical, the person with a name, a voice, even a tone. Indeed, the ambiguous meaning of composure is part of its point, as the discovery of a past that one can live with, and that may involve discomposure en route.

The subtle drama of the domestic shines through memories of women's activism particularly aptly in the following closing example of Beatrix Campbell's memories of writing *Sweet Freedom*, which was the first history of the UK WLM. She recalled herself sitting on the stairs of an empty house, a new tenant and on strike from her job at *Time Out*. She was finding the writing process "very very painful" and was still surprised that the more established Anna Coote had invited her to cowrite the book.

Beatrix Campbell (left) and Anna Coote at the launch of *Sweet Freedom: The Struggle for Women's Liberation* (1982). The first full-length history of the UK women's liberation movement, the book's back cover demanded, in capital letters, "NO WOMAN SHOULD MISS THIS BOOK. NOR SHOULD ANY MAN." *Photo courtesy of Getty Images*

BEATRIX CAMPBELL: I think Anna was *more* generous and less sectarian than I was. I must give her a ring and ask her about that. And I'm very interested . . . that you think it was not a sectarian book. I'm very interested in that, because I, my memory of myself was that I was quite, you know, quite a sectarian rascal really . . .

MARGARETTA JOLLY: You said you think you . . . no doubt have a talent for sectarianism.

BC: Yeah.

MJ: What does that mean?

BC: [heavy sigh] [pause] Well, I think, Communist parties were always quite sectarian, and Left politics was very sectarian. So everybody was defining . . . their position *against* another position, and by reference to another position which it critiqued. [pause] And, and I *know* that I'm sectarian about Trotskyism. For example, Judith [Campbell's partner] grew up in . . . revolutionary student politics, and she was much closer to Trotskyist groups, and she and I have very agreeable dingdongs occasionally where she will happily accuse me of being . . . either reformist or Stalinist, or something like that. And her kids think that very, very funny. And she has the virtue of . . . complete political piety, in my opinion. Anyway . . . my tradition was always sectarian . . . about Trotskyists, it was sectarian about social democrats [laughs], it was sectarian about Maoists. So, I had the *habit* of sectarianism. And the Women's Liberation Movement, which was trying to find its way, is inevitably finding, defining itself against the things that it thinks it mustn't be. So, I think, you know, I was good as anybody at being a sectarian old bag, really. [short laugh] However, that said, I didn't share the . . . socialist feminist estrangement from radical feminism, and I always thought that radical feminism got at stuff that nobody else did, and I think it more and more, actually. And interestingly, since I've got to become very close friends with *some* radical feminists, they always felt that I was a *tad* radical feminist, and some of my socialist feminist friends have always *happily* accused me of being a radical feminist rather than truly a socialist feminist. So I take all of that as a compliment really, because I think, the great thing about the Women's Liberation Movement was, all of that was there.[123]

The bittersweet elements of telling feminist history evident in Campbell's memory are present for all those who grapple in turn with the enduring puzzle of ideological and personal differences between women, and the immense effort involved in conceptual construction of a containing narrative. But Campbell's joyous confession—and retrospective inclusiveness—tells too of the redemptive potential oral history can bring.

2 ORAL HISTORY AND FEMINIST METHOD

A history of living activists must navigate memories that are in every sense political. It builds on the long affiliation of oral history with feminism: a heavenly match, a natural partnership. The method of S&A was to use long life interviews to get at the inside of a social movement that was itself so committed to personal change, to probe for the people, networks, and perspectives that sustained activism. A meditation on this method is also a chance to celebrate all the oral history projects that build both the memory of activism and the community of rememberers. Oral history should be used by more people, carefully working through the challenges of what university ethics committees dryly term "research with human subjects." Yes, it is ethically knotty, but it is also fun. And it revises the grammatical clichés of feminist memory and of media stereotypes. It does this as an archive of feeling, experience, and voice, and as a record that expresses the modest surrealism of everyday life. These archives are important not only for the academic history but for public understanding—indeed, for public action.

A Match Made in Heaven

Oral history in the West has flourished as a historical and folkloric field since the 1950s, and feminists have been attracted to the method for good reasons. The history of protest enjoys pride of place because of practitioners' commitment to rewrite history from below. Coming of age alongside the WLM, the method was imbued with a belief in the class struggle of the oral against print classes, whether industrial, rural, or country folk, migrants or women who had been, in Sheila Rowbotham's memorable phrase, "hidden from history."[1] This democratizing impulse often flowers into political projects of truth, reconciliation, and justice, where the oral historian becomes advocate. Refusing the intrusive manner of journalism and the cross-cutting approach of social science interviewing, oral history attempts to interview on the individual's own terms, to listen to the whole story the long way.

Mary Chamberlain, author of *Fenwomen* (1975), felt that oral history bore a relationship to consciousness raising, enabling women to "speak for themselves."[2] The North American *Frontiers: A Journal of Women's Studies* similarly promoted oral history as "the perfect tool for the grassroots effort of interviewing ordinary women" in 1977.[3] The same year, a group of feminist historians including Catherine Hall, Jill Liddington, Elizabeth Roberts, and Diana Gittins in the United Kingdom initiated the first of what over twenty-five years would become four special issues on women in the British journal *Oral History*.[4] They were explicitly inspired by the "contemporary struggle" for a fairer division of labour.[5] In fact, feminists are associated with the method globally, from Latin America's indigenous women's testimonies to Chinese activists who expropriate state-based oral history to "affirm women's experiences, enhance their self-confidence, and thereby empower them."[6]

Such witnessing and experience make oral historical method far more than a practical means of recording lives; rather, it flourishes as an investigation of memory and subjectivity. And although this challenged traditional historians in the 1970s, who staked their professional reputation on the interpretation of printed and statistical data, feminist scholars tended to find its approach natural. For just as the WLM wished to politicize the personal, so oral history could discover and re-envision the private sphere and the shifting meanings of gendered and sexual life. Indeed, feminist epistemologies, championing the importance of knowledge rooted in experience and the body, seemed tailored to a method that could value memory in its own right.[7] Some, such as Elizabeth Roberts's *A Woman's Place: An Oral History of Working-Class Women, 1890–1940* (1984), remained carefully correlated to archives; others, such as the Hall Carpenter Archives' *Inventing Ourselves: Lesbian Life Stories* (1989), were little-mediated transcripts of voices.[8] Others took a more theoretical approach to interviews, bringing in psychoanalysis to imagine past psychologies, or linguistics to suggest what women felt they could or couldn't say.[9]

Not all feminist oral history projects went by that name: Amrit Wilson's 1978 *Finding a Voice: Asian Women in Britain*, for example, emerged from journalism, and Judith Okely's interviews with "Traveller-Gypsies" were anthropological.[10] Many prominent WLM historians—Barbara Taylor, Leonore Davidoff, Sheila Rowbotham, and Deirdre Beddoe, for example—remained primarily document-based because they focused on the nineteenth century or earlier. Yet it is notable that they were all strongly supportive of the concept.

It is therefore unsurprising that activist historians turned to oral history to trace the history of forbear activists and indeed themselves. In the 1970s, Jill Liddington, Jill Norris, and Amanda Sebestyen recorded elderly working-class and northern English suffrage activists or their daughters, much as Sherna Gluck was doing with American suffragists.[11] Admittedly, the better-known suffrage oral history was by Oxford historian Brian Harrison, who was not connected to the WLM, but his unparalleled collection of 205 interviews with suffragists, suffragettes, or their descendants was quickly recognized as a treasure of movement memory and was archived at the Women's Library in 1981.[12]

Soon activists were interviewing each other. Sheila Rowbotham and Jean McCrindle's ambiguously titled *Dutiful Daughters* (1977) presented transcribed interviews with fourteen women of working-class or lower-middle-class origin, including Beatrix Campbell's mother.[13] Beverly Bryan, Stella Dadzie, and Suzanne Scafe's *Heart of the Race* (1985) captured black women's activism in the United Kingdom.[14] Michelene Wandor's *Once a Feminist* (1990) portrayed women who attended the Ruskin conference.[15] Betty Heathfield collected interviews from women involved with Women Against Pit Closures during the 1980s miners' strike, and older members of the Women's Cooperative Guild, a mutual society important in working-class communities.[16] The Fawcett Society interviewed aging midcentury activist members in the early 1990s.[17] Miriam Bearse and Elizabeth Arlege Ross led an oral history of the radical feminist movement around Leeds and Bradford in the 1990s for the Feminist Archive North, followed by the Feminist Archive South's interviews with Bristol-based activists in the early 2000s and the Archif Menywod Cymru/Women's Archive of Wales's oral history.[18]

Oral historical representations of activism are but one part of a general feminist mode of testimonial narrative, manifest in diaries, letters, anthologies, memoirs, and photographs throughout the WLM's heyday.[19] But in contrast to autobiographically framed texts, oral history's mission is to represent others. Here, the heavenly match between feminist politics and oral history has not been cloudless, much as with the challenges of feminist biography writing.[20] If the method's invitation to explore subjectivity and personal experience made sense, it still carried the debates about representativeness, authority, and power that could divide the movement itself. Most obviously, the interview relationship came under scrutiny.[21] In the United Kingdom, Ann Oakley, a sociologist interviewing working-class mothers about their experiences during pregnancy and childbirth, gained attention with a 1981 article on the politics of academic interviewing.[22] Though Oakley was not an oral historian, her article has much in common with the "reflexive" approaches to interviewing promoted by feminist oral historians throughout the 1980s. Some, like Kathryn Anderson, promoted therapeutic techniques of empathetic listening as fairer than the traditional distant style.[23]

But by the early 1990s, others, including Sherna Gluck and Daphne Patai, argued that this did not go far enough in addressing the differences between women. Gluck and Patai's 1991 collection *Women's Words: The Feminist Practice of Oral History* in particular challenged facile ideas of universal womanhood as the basis for interview ethics and interpretation, arguing that work done "by, about, and for women . . . positioned the scholar within a complex web of relationships, loyalties and demands."[24] In an attempt to deromanticize the process, their solution was to recognize the subjectivity of the interviewer and admit the likelihood that at least at the stage of interpretation, the interviewer retains more control. In the United Kingdom Liz Stanley made a similar move in *The Auto/Biographical I*, arguing for a distinctive feminist "auto/biographical" method that begins from women's experience but stresses contingency, antirealism, collectivity—the "anti-spotlight."[25] Such influences—on the crucial effect of the interview relationship on the kind of knowledge created, the ethical challenge of oral history in contexts of difference, and the importance of considering gender in everyone's life—are why Alistair Thomson considered feminists to have forced a paradigm shift in oral history methods through the 1980s and 1990s.[26]

The feminist approach is now accepted by the academy, as indeed is oral history in general. In contrast to the 1960s and 1970s, when oral history was initiated from continuing education, trade union colleges, consciousness raising, and independent archives, it is today institutionalized as university research, school projects, or heritage community development. Indeed, some have wondered if it has become a victim of its own success. Gluck herself asked in 2012 whether "feminist oral history has lost its radical edge." She was prompted by fear that the relationship between activism and theory had withered along with the autonomous women's movements of the 1970s. Happily, her review of projects such as the Black Cultural Archives' oral history of the black women's movement led her to conclude that "despite the different political trajectories of the second and emergent generations, there is still a tradition of viewing/treating oral history narrative as a 'discourse of oppositional consciousness and agency.'"[27] Although she does not address funding structures, we might acknowledge that feminists have become part of academic and grant-giving bodies and the British Library's Sound Archive (deeply influenced by the socialist historian Paul Thompson) itself advises the Heritage Lottery Fund (HLF) as a national funder that can be pointed toward progressive causes.[28]

Institutionalization has many effects and, as with the movement itself, has enabled it to realize its aims. Consider these recent projects: the Bolton Women's Liberation Oral History and the Brighton Trans*formed oral history of transgendered locals (both HLF funded); an oral history of women in television (funded by the Arts and Humanities Research Council); and a £5 million gender empowerment project, which involved oral histories and digital storytelling with sex workers and antipoverty activists around the world (funded by the UK government's Department for International Development).[29] At the same time, we acknowledge immensely competitive and corporatized environments, and the pressures they impose on even the most delicious opportunities.

S&A: The Making of an Oral History

S&A grew out of the determination of a group of older feminists in the United Kingdom that their generation's activism should not be forgotten. A key figure was historian Sally Alexander, one of the instigators of the Ruskin conference, a participant in the Miss World protest, and an activist in the night cleaners' strike; historian Barbara Taylor and feminist publisher Ursula Owen were also catalysts.[30] Allying with a thirty-something curator-researcher at the British Library (BL), Polly Russell, and supported by Rob Perks, the BL's curator of oral history, I joined the team as a forty-something academic. A generous three-year grant from the Leverhulme Trust in 2010 enabled us to record sixty life history interviews with core activists across the United Kingdom, make ten short films, support a doctoral student, and work with the BL to design an extensive website, with downloadable packs for teachers.[31] Our primary aim was to create a permanent multimedia archive in a beautiful and prestigious library where subsequent generations can discover the work of the movement pioneers of the 1960s to 1980s. And in many ways we are delighted with the results: by late 2017, more than 477,000 unique visitors had visited the website, for example.

But our oral history did not entirely escape the challenges of power and representation.[32] Two initial decisions face any oral historian: the selection of interviewees and the method of interviewing. Who can represent a process such as the WLM? How should we select from a movement that numbers conservatively some tens of thousands? How would we justify this intellectually, and honour a movement that prided itself on its collectivity? Here we touch on a fundamental of social research, in which concerns about representation need to be addressed. The movement tends to be written about a narrow group of activists alone.[33] At the same time we knew that the life history–based nature of the BL archive and our cultural-historical frame neither supported nor required random sampling or mass approaches. We built on the foundation laid by the Women's Liberation Movement Research Network, 2008–2009, including recruiting its facilitator, Rachel Cohen, as a research fellow. This network, initiated by curators and academics at the Women's Library, ran six witness workshops with 240 women's movement activists across the United Kingdom.[34] As such, it worked as a form of field survey, the first stage of a lengthy and thoughtful, albeit imperfect, selection process. Cohen also brought expertise as a historian of Jewish feminist activism, which helped to guide the selection process.

It will not surprise anyone that our selection criteria embraced race/ethnicity, class, religion, age, sexuality, disability, region, nation, and, separately, "perspective" or "ideology." However, we sought to avoid sectarian identity politics. For one thing, interviewing someone at length erodes the fixity of categories. One example is Mia Morris's declaration in the middle of her interview that "I have never called myself a feminist. . . . We see it as a middle-class, middle-aged, white, exclusive club." At the same time, she adds, "If feminism means, you know, your right to say what you want, express what you want, have education, access, yes, I'm a feminist." Objections to the word "feminist" are not unusual, of course, and have been a particular point of debate in the black women's movement. Morris, however, brought a valued perspective as manager of the Black Cultural Archives' own women's liberation oral history. And she added that as a passionate activist she felt at odds with many black people "who live in kind of shells." "I used to feel quite lonely, you know, because I was involved in so much stuff and then I started to meet women in the women's movement."[35]

The journalist Beatrix Campbell's interview revealed a different kind of fluidity, tracing her trajectory from a working-class, communist family in Carlisle in northwest England. Raised by a Dutch mother and a Cumbrian father—they met during the Second World War—she has lived for many years between London and northeast England (people sometimes mistake her accent for Newcastle "Geordie"). Just as interestingly, her interview confirmed the crudity of histories that pose radical against socialist feminism. Though Campbell was a figurehead of Marxist/feminist campaigning in the

1970s (as opposed to "socialist feminism," in her account), her thoughts on why she turned to issues of sexual abuse and violence in the 1980s and 1990s reveal a more integrated view from the beginning.[36]

We selected people primarily by their involvement in campaigns, people whom we thought could speak to the mobilization of resources that sociologists argue is crucial to the success of a social movement.[37] However, we expanded our definition of campaigns beyond public displays or protest events to more cultural, personal, and informal forms of contention typical of women's movements.[38] For example, alongside Jan McKenley (selected because of her work in the National Abortion Campaign and the Organisation of Women of Asian and African Descent), we included Deirdre Beddoe for her work on Welsh women's history and Susie Orbach for her role in the Women's Therapy Centre and her writings on body image. We were also interested in capturing memories of conferences as a specific type of women's movement activity that melds advocacy networking with lifestyle politics.[39] A nice instance is Lesley Abdela's description of having her politics transformed by Eastern European women travelling on the Trans-Siberian Express to the Fourth United Nations World Conference on Women in Beijing in 1995.[40] We wanted to define our object of analysis above all by its actions, ideas, and lives at the core of particular areas of struggle.

In addition to campaign area, our second principle of selection, workplace, was figured by five groups: politician/public sector, academic/intellectual, grassroots/third sector, cultural activist/writer, and private sector. We did this partly to avoid simply choosing eloquent writers, though they had been formative in our own lives as women's studies graduates. There is an element of cart-before-horse, as the preponderance of creatives and academics over politicians or—the smallest category—feminist business women does reflect something important about the movement's cultural (but not necessarily practical) strength. Feminists' jobs also reflect the biographical consequences of activism. We explicitly identified those who had been political or intellectual legends—about a third of them—although lesser-known or unsung women made up the rest.[41] Almost all our interviewees would refute claims to leadership. This reflects the horizontal nature of post-1960s social movements, and the particularly fervent principles of equality and autonomy in the WLM. Although feminists sometimes worked with political parties, particularly in Scotland, Wales, and Northern Ireland, where women's liberation and nationalist causes overlapped, there was always discomfort with notions of hierarchy or even organized membership.[42]

The final result? Not a sample, but a good representation of the pattern of the movement in the United Kingdom. The denial of "leadership" left us with the contradiction that our interviewees' self-description does not square with their position at the centre of campaigns or ideas—a position for which we selected them for interviews. Juliet Mitchell, for example, explaining how she worked with others to organize the first national women's liberation conference, insisted, "I wasn't the only person thinking [about women's liberation]. These things don't happen as one person: it's a misconception of history." And she goes on to warn, "if you look for people you find people; if you want to be the only heroine of the story, then you don't find [her]."[43]

Much as this is true, we also acknowledge Mitchell's role as a formative intellectual, whose *Women: The Longest Revolution* (1966) was instantly recognized as a breakthrough in understanding the structures of women's oppression.[44] Mitchell was also, as her co-organization of the Ruskin conference suggests, an activist, an effective media-woman, teacher, and feminist influence in the male New Left. Our view is therefore that in her own right, she, and many others, are vital decision makers and inspirational organizers. Though research tends to focus on networks and groups, individuals matter enormously to mobilization, and some organizations are actually the work of a single person.[45]

All selections will have gaps and omissions and should be questioned critically, but our archive offers a broad picture of the UK movement. The groups represented range from women's centres and campaigns like the National Abortion Campaign to participants in networks such as Greenham Common Women's Peace Camp and magazines such as *Spare Rib* and *Shrew*.[46] About one-third are academics, one-third grassroots, and one-third public sector or politicians—many in all sectors see themselves as cultural activists. Two were businesswomen—from Virago Press and the Straw Works building cooperative. Ideologically, most are at the socialist/feminist end of the spectrum, but there is a sizeable minority of self-identified radical feminists and a small number of liberal feminists—and these categories included "black feminist/womanist" activists who distinguished themselves by their commitment to simultaneously conceived race and gender liberation.

We were less successful in capturing geographical diversity. We have five interviewees each from Wales, Scotland, and Northern Ireland, to reflect the political importance of the nations within the United Kingdom, but we found it difficult not to be London-centric. Thirty-one interviewees have lived most of their life in the capital, with only fourteen of the rest living today elsewhere, including Leeds, Halifax, Bradford, Hastings, Preston, and Bristol. Similarly, we did not fully represent working-class feminism. Yet geographical and class categories are deceptive, for both conceal a mobility and fluidity that is crucial to the core experience of the WLM. We interviewed fifteen women of working-class origin, a few of whom still identified as working class, and at least another fifteen from lower-middle-class backgrounds, making up half of the interviewees.

Many interviewees had travelled and settled away from their birthplaces. London was an irresistible draw for young activists. Migration histories meant that three North Americans and one Australian were included, as well as the ten black or Asian British interviewees and one British Chinese woman, though most of the latter were themselves born in Britain. Seven Jewish women are included; minority ethnic interviewees therefore made up over a quarter of the whole.

We did not select particularly for religious background, other than in Northern Ireland, but the results were interesting. Fourteen were of Catholic origin (four from Northern Ireland) and fifteen Anglican, including Scottish, Northern Irish, Chinese Malaysian, and Kenyan backgrounds. Five had a Methodist upbringing, one Quaker, and one Hutterite Christian. Two had Muslim family backgrounds, two had Hindu backgrounds, and the British Chinese interviewee described her parents as Confucian. Nine described themselves as still practicing, including three Anglicans, one of whom became an Anglican priest but converted to Catholicism in her eighties; three others are still Catholics. Two declared themselves interested in a feminist spirituality; one has been interested in Buddhism.

Sexuality was also complex; we interviewed seventeen self-identified lesbian or bisexual women but found a much greater number had had a sexual or romantic relationship with another woman.

One interviewee self-identified as disabled/differently abled, and one had experienced institutional psychiatric care; many more talked of challenges to mental or physical health.

What about those who do not appear? We decided that with funding for only sixty interviews, we would not interview those who had left the movement early on, such as the women's refuge activist Erin Pizzey, nor men, though one interviewee's partner joined the recording session briefly.[47] Happily, Lucy Delap's oral history of men involved in feminism during the period provides a source for additional study.[48] We wanted to interview transsexual women or trans men who had been part of feminist activism during the 1970s or 1980s, but no one answered our appeals. I was pleased to draw on the Brighton Trans*Formed oral history to bring in the voices of trans people. Some prominent women were either too busy to be interviewed or too concerned about publicity. Some had political objections. We found it difficult to interview trade union activists—partly, again, because of the ambiguous relationship they often had with the WLM. Again, we knew that the Trades Union Congress had undertaken its own oral history.[49]

Our decision about interview method was determined by the BL's Oral History curators, whose long life history template creates the most flexible archive and ensures that recordings go well beyond the ostensible theme or achievement for which an individual is selected. These loosely chronological life story interviews situate achievements in context but also enable an individual to reflect and connect with former selves. As Joanna Bornat states, the life story interview is "more than just an extraction of information around a particular topic, it becomes an object in itself with a shape and totality given by the individual's life."[50] Thus, though we only interviewed women who were involved at the high point of UK activism, between the late 1960s and the mid-1980s, each interview looks at growing up in the 1940s, 1950s, and 1960s, and subsequent experiences in the 1990s and 2000s, usually taking at least six hours to recount. In addition, we asked the story behind their given name, about changing feelings toward one's body, pocket money, domestic arrangements, race and national difference, and how people felt about the method itself.

For this reason, our interviews are well placed to reveal the emotional and physical relationships that help to form—and are a consequence of—the ideas, actions, and politics that are the focus of this study. The life history method also gives time to understand friendships and lovers in (and against) political networks, work at home or in unpaid, informal spheres, the ways politics is defined with and without children, sexuality, health, art, and parents. In other words, as a form of interactive biography, the oral history also allows us to see who these women were themselves—unique, ordinary, difficult, easy, and vulnerable as the next person. Less concerned about unreliability than Brian Harrison was for his suffrage interviews, we are as interested in the *ways* feminists remember as much as what they remember.

Yet we admit we wanted even more time to ask about everyday life, and also, perhaps more surprisingly, discovered how difficult it is to record feeling or experience. Interviewing, even in our unhurried and capacious manner, creates its own social expectations and inhibitions. This does not detract from the possibility of analyzing the hints and glitches of things that are less easily said. But it does mean that analysis involves exceptional ethical challenges.

I/We/She: The Challenge of Ethical Analysis and Sue Lopez's Story

Any analysis of life history interviews is ethically difficult because of their intimacy and depth.[51] It is not easy to treat them as "data" after accepting tea in someone's home and exploring personal information. Some problems were ameliorated by negotiation at the interviewing stage and by resisting more explicitly therapeutic techniques of interviewing. Interviewees could close some or all of their recording for up to forty-five years and lodge their own edited or annotated version of the transcript alongside the original. However, interviewees may want their recording to be archived but paradoxically prefer no one to access, let alone analyze it. The solution of providing only commemorative or celebratory analysis that more easily conforms to the oral historian's ideal of shared authority frankly does not satisfy the needs of scholarship.[52] Wrenching generalized meanings out of individual life stories is therefore a painful act.[53]

What methods are available for this? The first is to compare these women's lives with those of their generational peers. We move through the decades and the life courses, from childhood and adolescence in the 1940s to 1960s, to accounts of old age and dying. Other types of historical narrative provide longitudinal context. Oral history illuminates the relativity of all historical scholarship and, in the case of the WLM, the amorphous, argumentative, vital nature of the movement.

In addition to situating oral historical accounts within our knowledge of campaigns and cultures of the late twentieth century, therefore, it is prudent to look back to the women who participated in the UK suffrage movement. Edwardian suffrage activism is by no means the only forebear: the multiracial and transnational nature of feminism today draws on global activist heritages and powerfully motivated some of our interviewees. However, comparing the S&A interviews with Olive Banks's and Brian Harrison's outstanding biographical studies of suffrage activists provides a fascinating measure as to what had and had not changed in the United Kingdom since suffrage was won, for example in the surprising evidence of supportive husbands and the less surprising correlation between socialist ideologies and working-class activism.[54]

In addition to both these disciplinary tools, I made use of the lenses used by anthropologists and cultural studies scholars, such as Sarah F. Green, analyzing everyday life in lesbian London in the 1980s and Joanne Hollows's study of feminist consumption.[55] What women said about housing, shopping, and travelling, as well as liberation, campaigning, or injustice, has opened out what it meant to live as a feminist and made the most of the oral history experience.

All these techniques for analyzing interviews remain inevitably qualitative. Life history methods will never tell us how many activists there were and how resources were distributed, let alone how they were seen by or influenced outsiders, answers I have sought from elsewhere. An ideal social science study, even one focused on the biographical experience of activism, would measure the before as well as the after, capture a more strictly representative population, and provide more control comparisons.[56] But oral history allows other rewards in the individuality that our method foregrounds. One of our interviewees, the sociologist Gail Lewis, said it best when she speculated that we would pick up "patterns" flowing across "our individual biographies with their own specificity and uniqueness" and show "what was possible in terms of subjectivity . . . in this time and place."[57]

Thus, most of all, those who focus precisely on the intimacy, scale, personal networks, and bodily lives thrive on the best elements of oral history, allowing the method to act as a kaleidoscopic lens on societies. Close readings of tiny images or moments can trace unconscious as well as conscious worldviews.[58] Oral historical accounts can be interwoven to explore the individual's dependence on another. Attention to the individual therefore does not necessarily mean an individualist interpretation.

In this spirit, the history presented here merges group biography across the life course with a cultural portrait of everyday life inside and outside the movement. The idiosyncrasies of the women interviewed are moving and fascinating, even as they illuminate a collective struggle. This method involves considering where the individual narrative belies the historical, or where divisions within their account may be telling, where memory appears blocked or, conversely, overly determined. Similarly, when an interviewee talks of a turning point, we must consider how far her statement is a retrospective simplification of the actual experience. Individuals are also influenced by established discourses of identity, difference, progress, or loss. And emotions that are not "civilized" from a feminist cultural perspective—jealousy or boredom, for example—emerge when we look at the distinction between the life as lived and as it is narrated, especially in an audible account where tone of voice, pace, and mood are so very vivid.

To enhance our ability to appreciate this aspect of oral history in the limited form of text, I have annotated the archival transcriptions S&A commissioned in the "intelligent verbatim" style to bring out the nonverbal.[59] Decisions about transcription method are not merely technical: Lucy Delap's approach to the sighs and stutters of her men's movement interviewees and Luisa Passerini's "autobiography of a generation" inspired me here, as they parse oral histories not primarily to show the socioeconomic structures behind individuals but to look at collective perspectives and moods.[60] Listening for emotion precisely challenges interviewees' attempts to narrate a past that is personally and publicly acceptable, showing up contradictions, sometimes embarrassments. Julie Stephens, who has analyzed feminist oral histories in Australia, encourages scholars to be brave in pursuing this approach in the spirit of feminist activism, even (debatably) suggesting that radical anarchist feminists give more exuberantly messy interviews than those of socialist or even libertarian feminists.[61]

This raises again the point that critical analysis of emotional records may require some sacrifice of the interviewee's interests in favour of those of readers, scholars, and new activists. This risk is multiplied in the digital age where all our stories are so easily forwarded or repurposed. Today, oral history interviewees with recordings housed by the BL must consider—at least eventually—sharing with not just a tiny chosen audience of scholars or community friends, but an unknown, volatile, digital audience, where reputational risks are always present.

Such balancing acts are evident in the story of Sue Lopez, who has an important place in the history of equal rights for women in the United Kingdom as a star football (the word *soccer* is used in the United States) player in the 1970s, and an official during the Women's Football Association's campaign for better representation. She was later Southampton Football Club's Head of Girls and Women's Football and Girls' Centre of Excellence, and ceaselessly champions women's talents and rights on the playing field. Her S&A interview shows the special pleasures and challenges raised by our method. Although Lopez was named a Member of the British Empire (MBE) for her services to women's football and was inducted into the National Football Museum's Hall of Fame in 2004, she is little known in the history of feminism. I learned about her through writing to Jean Williams, an historian of women's sports, and Jayne Caudwell, a scholar in sport, gender, and sexualities, after I had been unsuccessful in identifying a sportswoman born in the 1940s or 1950s who was politically active in the 1970s or 1980s.[62] Both remarked that this "no nonsense" woman was not necessarily "overtly feminist" but was an undoubted campaigner and a rare voice from the period.[63] They were right.

My interview with Lopez exemplifies the results of selecting interviewees not by identity but campaign and sector—testing the definition of who is a feminist and what the WLM could be said to have included. It was much easier finding academics like myself to interview, despite my memories of the Hackney and Brighton lesbian football clubs (I neither played nor went). Indeed, searching for sport as a theme in the other fifty-nine interviews for S&A gives the impression that swimming, walking, or a spot of yoga is as far as many feminists will go in this direction. Interviewing Lopez therefore took me into a different history, and with it, a different social and geographical scene.

I was nervous: what I know about football would not fill a sport shirt nametag. The uncertainty was mutual. Lopez was reluctant—an indication of her distance from the WLM and the world of academic research and archives with which I'm familiar. But I relaxed as soon as I saw her, a tall, short-haired woman with a gentle voice and weathered face, welcoming me into her home in Winchester. And her story was fascinating. How did Lopez become one of England's top women footballers? She narrates a magical tale of transformation from an awkward, bored secretary who joined a charity game, to a woman

The Southampton Ladies Football Club, 1971. Sue Lopez (front left) was inspired to play seriously by watching England win the 1966 World Cup but had to battle against Football Association restrictions on the women's game. Lopez was named a Member of the British Empire for services to women's football in 2000 and entered the National Football Museum's Hall of Fame in 2004. *Photo courtesy of Mirrorpix*

dubbed one of "the most naturally gifted players of her generation," her ability spotted the first time she played an organized game, aged twenty-one:[64]

> I watched the World Cup 1966, and my . . . uncle . . . saw in the paper that this girls' team was going to play a game, and it was the Cunard Shipping Line Social Club, they arranged this match against other office girls and I thought, "Wow [intake of breath]. *Wow*." So . . . they *did* start up this league. So . . . I wrote to *The Echo* and asked for a contact and was invited to go up and play. . . . There was these girls on . . . Southampton Common all ready to play a *full* match on a *full* pitch with goals! [laughing softly] And people hanging around and getting excited. And I don't know what I did for boots, I probably had some boots by then, got some boots. So anyway, this guy said, "Okay, great, go and play on the right [back]." I thought, "Right back, mm, I like scoring goals." So anyway, started off, whenever I got the ball I just ran up the field and had a shot at goal, and I think I scored a few goals or made them. And at the end of the match he said, "*Oh, yeah, would you like to play every week?*" "Mmm!!" So that was the start of it. And from then on this became a regular thing, a regular league of local girls. . . . It wasn't just this group that played in this charity match against the Cunard, there obviously were a lot of *other* girls that wanted to play, and once the word spread—on Southampton Common on a Sunday morning if you wanted a game—there were teams! So, it was amazing where all these women came from.[65]

I do not understand the meaning of positions on the football field, but Lopez is laughingly telling me that by running "up the field" she had ignored her role as a defender. She also did not know anyone, unlike the others who had joined through their workplace; she was just desperate to play. However, as she implies, England's World Cup victory in 1966 had the unexpected effect of opening a door to women. Seven local teams sprang up in the Southampton area alone, mostly young women working in companies such as Cunard or Southern Gas. But even when the best of these formed the South Hants Ladies Football Association (FA), trained by supportive men such as Ted Bates, the football authorities remained indifferent if not hostile to women, either as players or fans. Even the best, like Lopez, were regarded as novelty players.

As she explains in her 1997 book *Women on the Ball*, after female munitions workers began to play during the First World War, sometimes to huge crowds, the Football Association (FA) opted to ban women from their pitches in 1921, stating that "the game of football is quite unsuitable for females and ought not to be encouraged."[66] Lopez describes playing on Southampton Common without goal nets, a dripping cold-water tap for cleaning their boots, no expenses paid, and less respect. When the new players received modest sponsorship from Butlins (a chain of seaside resorts) and ITV, they realized too late that the real agenda was to provide "sexy" copy. Lopez tells a pitiful tale of *The Daily Mirror* promoting a match in 1969 by using a photograph of one of the best players, Joan Tench, simply because her shorts were falling down as she jumped to head a ball. Lopez remembers thinking she had gotten rid of a journalist from the high-circulation magazine *Tit-Bits* only to read a distorted, sexualized version of her account, shaming her as she arrived for her next match. The "final straw came" when they were prevented from playing even a prematch on the official Southampton pitch, and when the Cunard team manager Dave Case was "reported" to the FA for working with women—men were not supposed to waste their time on women's football. As Lopez puts it, "Basically, again we were given the red card, if you like, and *told*."[67]

It seems that this experience turned a fundamentally shy and unpolitical woman into an activist. In 1969 she went with a group representing women's clubs to a turning-point meeting at London's Caxton Hall with the intention of forming the Ladies Football Association of Great Britain. The venue was poetic as the meeting place of the militant suffrage movement, but WLM activists at the time were too busy with so many initiatives to either know or care about female footballers demanding equal rights. Their champions were Arthur Hobbs, a carpenter working for the town council at Deal, on the southeast coast of England, who gave his spare time to lobbying and fundraising, and Olive Newsome of the Central Council for Physical Recreation, who declared to the group that "*ladies* play . . . netball . . . but it's *women* play football, so it's got to be the Women's FA." "And we said, 'Hell, yeah, that sounds better than the ladies.'"[68] Thus began the Women's Football Association (WFA), with forty-four member clubs. Lopez still has the newspaper cuttings and remembers "2nd of December 1969 *The Daily Express* said 'FA say okay to girls.'"

Lopez's dry "Oh, jolly good" suggested that the struggle was far from over. Not only was the WFA an English association, like the men's, thereby not extending to the whole of the United Kingdom (and Scotland seemed particularly resistant to including women), the FA's inclusion of women, announced in January 1970, was only *recommended*.[69] As the 1970 Equal Pay Act allowed businesses five years to implement it, so local football associations in a highly decentralized structure could drag their feet. Thus, although the FA rescinded the ban on women playing in 1971, it was 1984 before the FA granted the WFA the equivalent of county FA affiliation, and nine further years before the FA acceded to the Union of European Football Association's (UEFA) recommendation to manage the women's game.[70] Lopez sees the struggle of UK women football players in international competition as a direct consequence of this delay.[71] The FA also refused women the right to become registered referees or coaches for years. One of the few fully qualified women referees, and the chair of the WFA, Pat Dunn, resigned over the issue. Lopez talks eloquently, meanwhile, about male referees who refused to penalize women for breaking rules, thus ensuring they would never create decent competitors; international star Flo Bilton sewing and laundering their sports kits; and the amateur "softly softly" approach of the WFA to allowing women due recognition.[72]

Her frustration was heightened when she experienced the contrast of playing in Italy for nine months in 1971. Joining FC Roma was her chance to give up secretarial work, and she smiles at the memories of Italian food and company and, above all, of being a respected sportswoman playing in front of thousands of fans:

> I loved the feeling of running with the ball, going past a player, doing a bit of trick to get past someone, little dodges. I loved the feeling of scoring goals, which, when I was a kid I'd practiced at when . . . my mum was with her second husband, I made this goal and I used to practice on my own if I couldn't play with the two lads up the road. I used to practice penalties, so, for me to score goals, either as a penalty or in regular play was—it was a thrill! And I like, loved the camaraderie of ten other players, you know, working together to beat eleven others. And, *yes*, I liked the acclaim . . . it was nice when you did something well that . . . you'd get an applause. So I suppose it's a bit like being on stage, if you like.[73]

Lopez had evidently always loved football, and she describes it as a joy when much else was hard. Growing up an only child in Wiltshire, she never saw her father, who had returned to Jamaica after a wartime marriage. Her mother was usually out at her factory job. Early on Lopez lived with her maternal grandparents, tenant farmers. Though she loved the outdoor life of the farm, she was belittled at school, in part, she thinks, because she was deaf in one ear. Eventually she was pushed into the "Shorthand Typing and Office Practice" stream. But in a village without television, football was hugely important to the community. In the cold farmhouse, she buried her nose in her favourite football comic, *Roy of the Rovers*, to read about the fictional Roy. Her mother was a Marchwood fan, and when they won the Hampshire cup, she took Lopez as the mascot (the club's lucky child) to the Isle of Wight. Stepfather, grandfather, and gran's brother were equally avid fans.

Unlike today, it would never have seemed possible then for a woman to make football her career, but it was that chance to play in a charity game, and the recognition of her abilities by a sympathetic man, that allowed her to escape from the expected life course, combined with her willingness to seize that chance, to campaign, and, perhaps, though she is reticent on this, to sacrifice the option of a family life. After her glorious year in Italy, she returned to England (having been threatened that if she did not, she would never be able to join a new national WFA team). The 1970s saw her touring, eventually playing for the English national team twenty-two times and winning eight FA cups. But again, the FA and UEFA moved so slowly that it was 1991 before they organized a major women's tournament, and by that time she was too old to play professionally.

As I listen again to her interview, I sense an isolation poignantly at odds with the team life she represents. Football, as she puts it, became her "family," but not always a supportive one.[74] She made her living as a head gym teacher and eventually became one of the first recognized women's football coaches, with captivating comments on how to win the respect of boys, how to head a ball safely, and more. This culminated in running a Girls' Centre of Excellence in Hampshire and a Women's Premier League team for Southampton in the 1990s. But when Southampton's men's team finished at the bottom of the men's Premier League and was therefore relegated to the league below in 2005, the whole women's programme was cut, and she is now a freelancer. Her untrained leap into football also incurred early injuries, which she feels have left a lasting legacy. Her vegetarian diet, which she adopted in the 1970s, set her apart from her peers: "I think they think I'm a pain."[75] In response to my questions about relationships, she talks of being seen as an "honorary man."[76] Her life, at the time of our interview, was dominated by her concern about her elderly mother. I wonder how she would have fared today, as women's football comes on apace.

It is striking that she speaks so little of feminist community or the WLM despite the precise contemporaneity of its development. Clearly, one reason is her dislike of "extremes," a repeated theme. She did not take a strong position about racism in football, despite the well-publicized experiences of black male football players and of racism in the stadia when she was in her playing prime.[77] She speaks about her love of the royal family and praises Queen Elizabeth II as an example of female leadership. Though in some ways we can analyze this view as an equal opportunities politics of fair play, her perspective seems to reflect a cultural distance from a world in which she could might have found more support. But few WLM activists at the time would have shared her passions, proving the point that solidarity is ironically easier to cultivate in work than in leisure contexts. We might also contextualize this cultural conservatism, and the fact that sexuality was not a prominent part of our interview, in the ambivalence of many working-class women toward women's liberation as a movement that seemed to threaten their respectability. Historically, such women have been subject to particular sexual judgment and control, and sportswomen have had to defend themselves against both sexualization and prejudice, where being lesbian risks further ostracism and ridicule.[78]

We might also speculate that Lopez's approach reflects growing up in conservative Wiltshire—her parents voted Tory—where women in sports had often come from private school field hockey clubs, in contrast, at least to some degree, to the bolder style of the munitions-factory worker culture of her footballing forebears. She jokes that her mother observed that if she'd been as good at tennis as she was at football, she'd be living in luxury.[79] But that is all she says on the matter of class inequality, though in her book she clearly states that football has been a "working-class game for men—controlled by middle-class men at the FA."[80]

Yet Lopez has been as courageous and consistent in her campaigning as any self-identified WLM feminist, and she acknowledges having gone to Canada to find out about a feminist football network after another disappointment where a job with the FA did not materialize. Interestingly, *Women on the Ball* was published by Scarlet Press, a feminist nonfiction publisher. It includes an account of the Theresa Bennett case in 1978, the first time that the Sex Discrimination Act of 1975 had been used to challenge the FA. Twelve-year-old Theresa had been banned from a local boys' team. The judge overturned the FA's decision on the grounds that it failed to provide her with recreation facilities. But ironically, the FA could appeal successfully under Section 44 of the Act, which even today states that sex discrimination is not unlawful where "the average woman" seeks to take part in a game, sport, or other activity of a competitive nature where physical strength, stamina, and physique put her at a disadvantage with "the average man."[81] Lopez points out the fallacy of judging athletic girls against the "average woman," particularly at the age of puberty. For her, these are clearly "outmoded biological beliefs."[82]

And then there are the llamas. I find myself profoundly touched by the sheer unexpectedness of their appearance in our conversation, but as the following excerpt from the end of our interview records, they are an important clue to how Lopez sees herself:

MARGARETTA JOLLY: What about the llamas?
SUE LOPEZ: [laughing] Oh right, that's out now, is it? I'm out as . . . a llama aficionado, yes, I love them. I go down to this place near East Grinstead and walk them. And they're, they're *so* relaxing, walking a llama, I recommend it. [Smiling voice] They're beautiful, calm animals. And you can walk along with them and you just glance to your side and there you are, you see this, the most *beautiful* eyes and eyelashes. And they're just—so chilled out. It's . . . so far away from the madness. And it's in the beautiful Sussex Downs. . . .
MJ: This may be a difficult question because we've talked about the . . . the quite different worlds, in a way of grassroots women's liberation activism and the kind of *politics* you were involved in in football, but I'm wondering if you could just, as we come to, to the last few questions, reflect on whether you think the Women's Liberation Movement did have any effect on your life and, and work?
SL: Well . . . that was in the Sixties, wasn't it?
MJ: Mm. Sixties, Seventies.
SL: Yeah.
MJ: Eighties.
SL: Yeah. [long breath] I was aware of it and aware of the constraints on some women, but it never seemed to actually impact on my life. You know, I, I read the papers quite avidly, and [am] always aware of the news. . . . I think I'm, yeah, I'm very supportive of it, but I don't think I actually want to do it, 'cos I know a friend of mine went up to Greenham. I don't like this active—what's the word? Kind of, *action*, if you like. So . . . I've done my bit in my own way, I feel. I'm a bit like the llamas [laughs]: I like it calm. And I don't like it when people get angry. [pause] I don't like to see *discontent* in people. I like to think that it can be sorted out in a calm, in a sort of pleasant way, if you like, for want of a better word. So it's not my scene, really, to have a lot of people, and . . . because I *am* deaf, I realize now that noise, and so people get noisy and shouting, or, which I think could happen in those environments where you're protesting—it's quite a turnoff.

MJ: How did you cope with the noise of *football*, and shouting and matches? I'm *imagining* it was noisy?

SL: I think . . . when you're on a pitch it's all a bit further away, but I guess I was in my own bubble so—totally focused. And in control, you know, I, I felt safe, I felt *good*. I was with colleagues. So it's this, it's this purpose, you know, you were there to, to work together and it suited me.[83]

I left, wondering what liberation is to Lopez, about sports, but also about animals, love, and teams. For her, competitive football is more peaceful than the protests of the WLM. What kind of team life did the WLM offer, after all? The WLM's ideals have been to work consensually, to refuse leadership altogether, living out the egalitarian community we hope to create. Yet the limits and disappointments of such prefigurative politics are evident in many of our interviews. The very memory of the movement is contested. How hard it is to create a team without a captain, even if the aim is not to defeat an organized opposition? While Lopez was never skipper, she led young women's and indeed young men's teams, as well as the Girls' Centre of Excellence. She speaks of the complex balance between controlling egos and nurturing girls in particular, who seemed uneducated in how to work together, whose lack of self-esteem, in her view, often fostered rivalries or grudges that male coaches did not understand. Lack of leadership in the United Kingdom, for her, was part of what had held back women's football for so many years.

And even as I ponder, I realize that I am wondering about my own sense of responsibility to this oral history. Privileged as I am as principal investigator, this is a history that is in every way far more than mine. By the third year of S&A, our own "team" included myself; Polly Russell, the key BL curator; Lizzie Thynne, my filmmaker colleague at Sussex University and her assistant Peter Harte; Rachel Cohen, busily cataloguing those precious interviews; Abi Barber from the BL Learning Programme, writing and rewriting the copy for the website; and Sally Alexander, as advisory board member, sweating with us over how to pull a narrative together. We were not facing the legendary blazers of the English FA, nor centuries of prejudice as to whether women could play competitive sports. It has been our pleasure to have instead been faced with the different challenge of living up to the expectations of our interviewees, and our sense of feminist history in all its diversity. And here, Lopez's story raises the further intrigue of how she dealt with the pressure of performance, where for her, the concentration of the game created a bubble that could protect her. What skill, what method, what team does feminism create that can also sustain performance?

In returning to the question of ethical method, I turn finally to one further analytic resource for feminist oral historians: autobiography itself. Autobiography at least tells you who "I" am in this relationship, and turns the experience of publicizing the personal around. On this principle, the members of the project team interviewed each other and have archived the recordings. If you were to listen to our own, somewhat startled, self-interviews, you will hear how personally committed to feminism we are, though we are of different generations, genders, sexualities, nationalities, and ethnicities, and have different ideological histories.

And you will hear us ask each other the same question with which we concluded all our interviews, "How do you think your life compares to your mother's?"[84] As Lizzie posed this question to me, I remember hearing myself exhale. My mother was a rock for me, and she was then ill. Yet my breath also expressed the difficulty of explaining, in that self-imposed moment, the way that feminism was my way to stand up to my parents' wonderful but impossible example. Meeting the WLM changed me—when as a sixteen-year-old my women-only excursions, to clubs, to Greenham, marked my rejection of prescribed femininity. It became my passion, nurtured on feminist theory at university, moving predictably to London in my twenties, learning more and more about the visions and demands of the movement as a society.

So this oral history has been more than a personal dream come true, as I saw the women whose voices I'd listened to for so long materialize in front of me. In writing this book, I've even dreamed I had a spare rib growing on me, curved bone inside soft flesh—an inverse birth not so much bursting out but digging in. I thank Sue Lopez for her lifelong campaign against prejudice and inequality, a woman whose achievements must be partly measured by the fifty-five thousand people who watched the England-versus-Germany women's match at Wembley Stadium in 2014.[85] But I also thank her for her personal story, which includes lessons in coaching that any feminist would be impressed by, and the unexpectedly wonderful image of the llama, gazing through beautiful lashes, walking at her side. I thank her for having agreed to be part of an oral history in which she clearly tests the boundaries, yet to which she has added a unique and invaluable element where more established feminists missed the importance of women's participation in sports. And I thank her, along with all the interviewees, for reminding me that liberation is singular as well as collective.

3 FORMING FEMINISTS: GROWING UP IN THE 1940s, 1950s, AND 1960s

Even in the 1980s, it was standard to educate girls to be "conformist, helpful and to wipe the tables," while boys were encouraged to be "independent, adventurous and unruly," concluded Marsha Rowe, surveying reports on the UK school system in the WLM magazine *Spare Rib*.[1] Feminists wanted to dramatically rethink the whole of childhood, through girls playing sports and gender-neutral toys, to the incest survivor movement, or radical psychoanalysis. They also critiqued the inadequacies of boys' upbringing and the class and ethnic biases of Britain's educational system.[2] They believed that gender was not destiny but could be reshaped through feminist nurture. Their own childhoods incubated their later activism. Oral histories show that activism does not necessarily evolve out of personal discontent, and that the WLM did not grow simply from the disappointment of unfulfilled girlhood expectations. Rather, the potential for activism came out of early investments of time and resources in girls, and immersion in powerful social networks, especially through education at home and school.

Socializing Girls in the Century of Childhood

A child's life is shaped by home, school, and peers, and the women interviewed for S&A were no exception.[3] But the landscapes in which they grew up have changed dramatically. Our oldest interviewee, Una Kroll, born in 1925, remembers living in Stalinist Russia; our youngest, Pragna Patel, born in 1960, had a daughter still in her teens at the time of interview. The largest age group within our interviewees comprises early baby boomers, born between 1943 and 1954, aged at the time of interview in their late sixties or seventies.[4] Their girlhoods were most obviously defined by the fact that, if they were born in the United Kingdom, they grew up in a society where the new welfare state introduced by the first postwar Labour government introduced free "cradle to grave" healthcare and free education up to the age of fifteen.[5] S&A interviewees often felt their mothers' lives, although stymied, were a step up from those of their poorer grandmothers. Yet they still critiqued postwar family ideology, stoked as it was by new consumer markets and the inequalities still present in social reconstruction, nicely exemplified by the fact that the 1944 Education Act was not complemented by equal pay for women teachers.

Even if one did not believe in the perfect family, with Mum fussing at the breakfast table, the baby boom transformed domestic life. Peaking at just over one million (1,025,427) births in 1947, a third higher than the 723,779 births at the beginning of World War II, more children, more housework, and a starker gendered division of labour redomesticated mothers.[6] At the same time, as markets targeted teenagers as a new category, youth cultures flowered as never before. Siobhan Molloy began her interview by stating that she felt lucky to have been born in 1948: "We were the first generation to have secondary level education for free, in Northern Ireland. Also we were the generation of the Beatles . . . and all those exciting things. I think if I'd been born maybe ten or fifteen years earlier life probably would have been very boring in some ways."[7]

Older women also joined the WLM.[8] Some of them felt marginalized, but others with greater political experience rose to prominence: S&A interviewees include pioneers such as birth activist Sheila Kitzinger (born in 1929), anti–male-violence radical Jalna Hanmer (born in 1931), mining community campaigner Betty Cook (born in 1938), and New Left intellectual Juliet Mitchell (born in 1940). From those whom we did not interview, we might add Selma James (born in 1930) and Germaine Greer (born in 1939). Their early lives were defined by economic depression, war, and, typically, the expectations of marriage.[9] Jalna Hanmer contrasts the "grit and gumption" she was expected to develop as a child in rural America to the education she felt her English peers had received. She also says that she "lived in another world, a world that died with the Second World War."[10]

Their sense of being older strengthened as younger women joined the movement. The late baby boomers born between 1955 and 1964 include activists such as Kirsten Hearn (born in 1955) from Sisters Against Disablement, Jan McKenley (born in 1955) from the National Abortion Campaign and Hackney Black Women's Group, and Valerie Wise (born in 1955), chair of the Greater London Council Women's Group.[11] They were too young for the antinuclear march to Aldermaston or the Cuban missile crisis, but not for Greenham, all-night antiapartheid sit-ins outside South Africa House, or the protests demanding "troops out of Northern Ireland." They were in their late twenties or thirties when the Berlin Wall came down, in their forties or fifties at the time of the financial crash of 2008. As with their older sister boomers, they were also shaped by the postwar era of reconstruction and vision, though increasingly of anxious disappointment. They too were benefiting from better standards of living and new possibilities for education. They came of age as the birth-control pill ("the Pill") was said to propel a sexual revolution, though for the six years after it was introduced in the United Kingdom in 1961 a woman had to be married (or at least pretend to be) to get it on the National Health Service. If they were teenagers in the 1970s, they could benefit from the semi-legalization of abortion in 1967, of male homosexuality in 1967 (which indirectly helped to normalize lesbian relationships), and divorce in 1969.

This later tranche of baby boomers shaped a women's movement blown by the winds of postcolonial change. The historical imprints of war, depression, and reconstruction interwove with major migrations, from Jews escaping 1930s fascism on the continent, to African Caribbean people responding to postwar calls for labour in Britain, and East African Asians driven out of Africa by the Africanization of the 1960s.[12] Minority ethnic women interviewed for S&A situated their parents within a generational consciousness framed primarily by diasporic identity as well as memories of violence or conflict. Virago Press founder Ursula Owen (born in 1937) and writer Michelene Wandor (born in 1940) spoke vividly about the Holocaust and family relationships with Israel. For them, childhood was often defined by a sense of repression, silence, and loss.[13] Writer-campaigner Amrit Wilson (born in 1941) grew up through Indian independence and Partition, while photographer Grace Lau (born in 1939), daughter of a Kuomintang diplomat, tells of her family's exile from Mao's China.[14] The "Troubles" in Northern Ireland from the 1970s to the 1990s and emerging questions about Scottish and Welsh devolution also shaped distinct generations.

Across this diverse group of activists, almost all benefited from the growing acceptance that children are not expected to work, new educational opportunities, and better health. With the important exception of religious minorities, families were getting smaller and more mobile. And as the century continued, living standards rose for the majority, such that today the wealth gap is less between middle and working classes than between employed and unemployed, old and young, couples and single parents.

Most important of all was the lengthening of childhood itself in the twentieth century, "the century of the child."[15] It universalized the nineteenth-century European Romantic ideology of childhood as a special, determining time of life. But even as children were idealized as innocent and vulnerable, new state and professional resources were brought to manage their upbringing, guided by postwar concepts of rights and by Freudian, Bowlbyan, and other psychologies. These ideas of children's rights and needs helped fuel the new investment in education and care that nurtured our interviewees, but also ironically tied their parents—especially mothers—to the parental role. They often recalled with relish childhood's ambiguous gifts of protection, investment, and educational opportunity, particularly as it perpetuated notions of girls' dependence and, in turn, their anticipated role as servicers or caregivers to their own children. But others whose families were not conventional or simply where children were expected to start earning young, speak powerfully of the sense of exclusion or stigma, of having to get by without.

Some of these ambiguities are revealed in interviewees' memories of the "eleven-plus" test that determined which type of school a pupil would attend in the system established under the 1944 Education Act. Children either "passed" and went to the more prestigious grammar school or "failed" and went to the local secondary modern school. This system effectively separated children by class at the beginning of adolescence, as middle-class children tended to do better, and perpetuated gender inequalities, since grammar schools remained single sex, with far fewer places for girls than boys. Moreover, because it was deemed that girls were more mentally advanced than boys aged ten, boys who took the exam early were marked up, something that Siobhan Molloy, who remembers the "nasty remarks" when she failed on her first try, points out.[16] Sandie Wyles, born in 1957, whose mother was a school secretary and father a plasterer in Aberdeen, commented:

> I think it's a self-fulfilling prophecy, isn't it. If you're encouraged and you're seen as bright and the teachers look for *you* for the answers, you respond and the groups that were more kind of, maybe their houses didn't have as many books as we did or their parents weren't as talkative or as encouraging, there wasn't the stimulation to encourage these kids on. I think they were left very much, well, you'll go to the secondary modern. That was your . . . path and . . . I felt I *had* to pass that eleven-plus. I think I would have died of *shame* and humiliation if I hadn't. That was the way you were made to feel.[17]

When Wyles took the test in 1968, she had good reason to be anxious about passing or failing. By 1970–71 the university education participation rate had still reached only 8.4 percent of the population. In 1970 there were 51,189 graduates from English universities, more than double the 1960 figure, with 15,618 women (around 30 percent of the total).[18] The low expectations for women in Wyles's age group reflected their expected futures primarily as wives rather than "career women." In 1975, as the Equal Pay Act came into effect, the average age of a woman at marriage fell below twenty-three for the first time since the war. Moreover, though their aspirations were different from their mothers—they expected to work for more than pin money, and enjoy sexual satisfaction and emotional fulfilment—the terms of the marriage contract remained markedly unequal.[19]

The 1969 Matrimonial Proceedings and Property Act had guaranteed the wife a share of family assets on divorce based on her labour as either housewife or wage earner, while the Divorce Act of the same year allowed marital breakdown as grounds for divorce in addition to adultery. Yet a married woman still gave up her right to a mortgage without a man's signature, or to child custody in the event of divorce. Pensions and child maintenance payments went to the father and, with only 8.4 percent of children born out of wedlock, illegitimate children did not gain inheritance rights until 1975.[20] Neither domestic violence nor marital rape was considered a crime. And the option of a lesbian future, let alone marriage, was shrouded in ignorance and stigma. Perhaps as important, the script of "working in a bank, getting married, having two kids and going to Blackpool on my holidays," which Wyles described as her destiny should she fail the eleven-plus, was extraordinarily generic.

Of course, the eleven-year-old Wyles did not know this. But her own life story—studying librarianship (no thanks to a distracted career guidance counselor), falling in love with girls, forming a feminist Scottish trad and punk band, and becoming a radical youth worker—suggested how activism opened up new possibilities. Ironically, this was in part because most of our interviewees, like Wyles, passed the dreaded eleven-plus and benefited from the system. Retrospectively, most feel uncomfortable or frankly guilty. Anna Davin (born in 1940) won a scholarship and worried that she thus deprived a working-class girl of a chance.[21] Rosalind Delmar (born in 1941), daughter of a building labourer in a steel factory, felt divided from her siblings who did not pass.[22] Though it is common for young people to feel like outsiders, in the 1950s and 1960s this aspect of childhood was dramatically enhanced by the school system, combined with other large forces such as slum clearance, new industries, urbanization, and migrations.[23]

Racially and religiously segregated education systems intensified feelings of marginality. Molloy (born in 1948) spent unhappy years at boarding school because there were few Catholic grammar schools in her part of Northern Ireland, while Jan McKenley (born in 1955) remembers her parents getting "a lot of stick from local people about why she—who did they think I was and who did they think they were that the local school wasn't good enough," as well as the punishing costs of the school uniform at Tottenham County.[24] Beatrix Campbell (born in 1947) is one of those who did not pass the eleven-plus. Her experience was by far the more representative at the time:

> I feel . . . privileged to be part of the majority who failed, *because* 75 percent of children of my generation and before failed the eleven-plus, and so I'm located with *them*. I know *exactly* what that feels like.
>
> It's . . . almost in the *DNA* of, a majority experience in, working-class culture—To. Have. Failed—and to have been disappointed.[25]

Campbell's Communist Party parents fought for her education and were proud of her achievements anyway. She initially hoped to become a hairdresser, and then a teacher, like her sister who did pass the exam. Instead she worked in a shop and then, after leaving home, "worked in an office as a typist, and then met Bobby, who said, 'Ohhh, get a job at the *Morning Star* [Communist Party daily newspaper].' He was an engineer who had been . . . a fitter in the John Brown shipyards in Glasgow, and had been part of the folk revival in Scotland and played the fiddle."[26] The Left became her way out—at least at first.

Of course, education was by no means the only challenge that girls had to negotiate as they grew up: menstruation, sex education, and the first sexual experience also loomed large. Several interviewees recalled relief when tampons and menstrual pads without loops and belts became available. Many remembered their sex education as no more than a pamphlet provided by the school to parents, usually discovered under their pillow. Karen McMinn, born in 1956, whose family ran a post office in Belfast, received hers around the age of twelve:

KAREN MCMINN: No, Mummy couldn't, no, no. No. No. Couldn't talk about that. [laughing] And, I remember getting my period, and . . . it was a bank holiday weekend. And I just woke up and my, you know, pajamas were full of blood and, there was all this . . .

RACHEL COHEN: How did your mum react? Did she, was she supportive?

KM: Och, yeah, but it wasn't, you know, it was like . . . [laughing hard] It was more like, "Oh!" [high-pitched sound of embarrassment], you know, rather than, do you know, "Don't worry." It was all a bit of stress really, you know.[27]

Lesley Abdela (born in 1945) received a "textbook-y thing" from her awkward father (her mother died when she was fourteen). She talks about her later naiveté in relationships, including a violent early marriage. Though primarily a campaigner for parliamentary representation, Abdela today also stresses the importance of providing menstrual pads to girls and women in postconflict situations.[28] Rebecca Johnson (born in 1954), who received the pamphlet from her (former Hutterite) Christian mother, only after she got her first period, aged ten, remembered the physical distress of growing breasts and menstruation—"I just saw the whole thing as a curtailment . . . a real restriction of who I was." Her school's sex education involved a film of "a couple getting married and then walking around a lake holding hands and then next minute she seemed to be having a baby."[29] Gail Chester's version was a school film of a man in a dressing gown bringing a breakfast tray to a woman in bed. "I hadn't an *idea* . . . how all this happened!" she chuckles.[30]

Our interviewees, as the daughters or even granddaughters of 1930s and 1940s families who did not openly discuss sexual issues, were unsurprisingly ill prepared for reproductive agency or sexual pleasure.[31] Despite the popular narrative linking sexual liberation with the Pill in the Swinging Sixties, two-thirds of the population still declared sex before marriage as immoral (whatever they actually did).[32] Even by 1970, fewer than one in five young married couples used the Pill—typically, affluent young professionals, because at that time it was the only drug for which doctors were allowed to charge.[33] Abortion was not legalized until 1967. Jo Robinson remembered a "horrifying" experience of helping one friend to get an illegal abortion, while another "had a slush fund with money in it for emergencies, for the abortion." When Anna Davin got pregnant at school, she chose to have her child, but the consequences of motherhood, despite being married to Luke Hodgkin, who became an influential New Left academic, set her up for a life course strangely like her mother's. But perhaps Gail Lewis's story best measures the ongoing struggle. Aged seventeen, she got pregnant the second time she had intercourse, "ridiculously really," in 1969. This was two years after abortion had been legalized, subject to psychiatric approval, but she was still treated abusively in the hospital, was not given painkillers, and was put next to a woman who had miscarried. Her mother, who had endured seven illegal abortions, was horrified and furious on her behalf.[34]

Such conditions evidently helped frame the connection between sexual and women's liberation, though lesbian feminism questioned how far heterosexual sex in any form could help. Campbell tells of reading Anne Koedt's 1970 *The Myth of the Vaginal Orgasm* a year after she married Bobby Campbell and "throwing it across the room":

> I did, I threw it! Because it was *so* challenging. The story it was telling me about my sexual life—detonated it, it was a detonator. And so, a married heterosexual life that was sexually *actually* very disappointing, unacknowledgeable... how to say the word? You know... Unspeakably so, both because it was so painful, and because it wasn't *speakable*, and was put down for women in my generation to us being, there's something wrong with *us*.[35]

Even girls from the late baby boomer group were troubled by the terms of heterosexuality, despite the new availability of contraception. Jan McKenley (born in 1955) tells of fears she could not be penetrated, and her struggle to claim sexual pleasure as a young black woman who had always been a "good girl."[36] Gail Chester relates rueful stories of her Orthodox Jewish-Irish mother sending her to non-Orthodox youth clubs, where she endured the ritual of waiting for a boy to ask her to dance the Twist. When one finally did, she was flabbergasted: "Oh, it was just a torture. It was a torture, honestly.... I'm sure books have been written about the torture, not only I, but somehow it felt like it was worse for me because my mother was blooming Irish [chuckling]."[37]

The choreography of new teenage sexual cultures could be depressingly old-fashioned. Those, like Susie Orbach or Grace Lau, who were punished by parents or schools for being more heterosexually confident, could only later integrate this confidence into a sense of identity. Such pressures were of course acutely felt by lesbian or gender-atypical girls. Once they showed signs of sexual difference in adolescence, they were treated as ill if not dangerous. Most still assumed they would get married—one large-scale study of lesbians aged sixty or over in the United Kingdom reveals that 52 percent of them were once married to men, rising to 63 percent for the over-eighties.[38]

Many interviewees laugh at the memory of their rites of passage. Chester remembers practicing dance moves in front of a mirror with a school friend as a quiet example of getting control. Mary McIntosh (born in 1936), a pivotal figure in gay liberation, talked about crushes on her teachers.[39] Kirsten Hearn (born in 1955) narrates in strikingly dry tones the frightening experience of losing her sight. Sent away to a school for children with visual impairments, she had to navigate an entirely new social scene, miles from home. However, she audibly refuses a victim narrative, chronicling her escapes to a local disco where she pursued various acne-ridden youths, and an insistence she be allowed to do an art exam. Defying predictions by progressing to Goldsmiths College to study art, she continued to pursue unsuitable men until she encountered the women's movement and turned the same energy to relationships with women, alongside setting up Sisters Against Disablement.[40] Young women could turn the now mainstream cultures of teenage rebellion to their own interests. Rosalind Delmar spoke explicitly about being inspired by the James Dean film *Rebel Without a Cause* to define herself as an "angry young woman," and playing Fats Domino in her room after going to Mass.[41] Sheila Rowbotham remembers wearing black sweaters to look "beatnik," while Jenni Murray's longing to have Joan Baez's hair showed how glamorous the counterculture could seem.[42] A decade or so later, Gail Lewis was wearing a "long, blue leather coat," double-breasted in Mod style, to her further education college (an alternative to university), where she surprised everyone with her poetry essay, delivering a defiant message: "They could go fuck themselves."[43]

Not-So-Dutiful Daughters: The Family Behind the Feminist

Growing-up stories thus help explain why some activists later focused more squarely on economic security and civil rights, others on sexual and identity liberation, and how these were expressed in the differently focused WLM, the trade union/working-class women's movement, and black/Asian women's movements. At the same time, such stories raise the question of whether experiences at home or with siblings and peers were as, or even more, formative of later feminist consciousness. Certainly many interviewees say so. As parents put sex education pamphlets under pillows, gave preference to brothers, or, in worst cases, hit or sexually abused their children, they helped motivate later protests. Even stories of mild family conflict, loss, or pressure can support the thesis that feminism is a response to suffering in the household and family.

Jalna Hanmer intriguingly tells of coming to a primal sense of injustice in these terms: "I was twelve or so, that really started—*it's not fair*—about other people and other things in the world around me. Now my father . . . I think thought it rather amusing and I think he admired it too, a bit, this *it's not fair*. But he told me I'd grow out of it . . . which I never did, actually."[44] Her parents were liberal, though not especially political, struggling as modest businesspeople in their unhappy marriage. Her printer father felt he had "never got started" and drank; her mother dreamed from the outset that her daughter would go to university. She attributes her strong sense of injustice to an unconscious deprivation of love, a realization she says came only in her seventies.

Parenting styles and the possibilities for attachment help define gender identities as well as capabilities.[45] The WLM obsessed about this, particularly in its love–hate relationship with Freudian psychoanalysis, at the time typically crude and sexist.[46] In fact, the focus on reforming the family, especially maternal relationships, helped differentiate the WLM from liberal or equal rights activism. Jean McCrindle and Sheila Rowbotham paid respect to midcentury feminist Simone de Beauvoir's *Memoirs of a Dutiful Daughter* (1958) in their book *Dutiful Daughters* (1977). Yet they remarked that women of those generations appeared bitter toward their mothers: "We were surprised by this hostility until we realized that teaching a daughter her role as a future housewife can all too easily develop a sadistic quality when the mother herself is tired, over-worked and oppressed by her own existence."[47]

The mother's hopes for her daughter are played out against the ironic loss of her own financial and legal power in marriage, due to the circumscription of wifehood in the 1950s and 1960s. For migrant families, or where the daughter migrated alone, the mother–daughter tie is often refracted through a language of duty not just toward the family but toward the nation, the culture, or the race. Pragna Patel's mother, struggling in London after arriving from Kenya in the 1960s, tried to whisk Patel into an arranged marriage.[48] In contrast, fathers are often remembered as more respectful of a girl's ambitions, while absent fathers or male lovers embody early fantasies of omnipotence and strength.

The account of Jenni Murray (born in 1950), the voice of BBC Radio 4's "Woman's Hour," typifies the soft version of this memory of parents. Always skeptical of the "loony" and self-defeating elements of the autonomous WLM, she presents her childhood in direct lineage from de Beauvoir, wittily calling her 2008 autobiography *Memoirs of a Not So Dutiful Daughter*.[49] Where Murray's mother was content with a bit of secretarial work alongside her primary role of wife and household manager, Murray's ambition led from the BBC typing pool into local television in the 1970s. Her small-town Yorkshire mother pursued respectability after marrying down, and disapproved of those choices, even when Jenni became famous. Murray was miserable and could not solve "the Oedipal triangle," her terminology for a lifelong competition between mother and daughter for father's attention. The pain calls on her mother's tale of giving birth in stirrups without anesthesia, in such agony she refused to have more children, and a childhood of being primped to her mother's liking while her father was out at work.

"When did my feminist lightbulb first come on?" Murray muses, before recalling, aged about fifteen, she persuaded her mother to take a job as a receptionist, but saw her still doing all the housework. Why didn't her father? And why did he offer to "help," instead of taking responsibility?[50] But the centre of the struggle is her mother's cold control and preference for her husband over her daughter. Going to Hull University in 1965, Murray is breezily confident, disliking the uncool girl from the South with whom she initially has to share a bedroom, and getting the Pill by pretending to be engaged with a "wedding ring" from Woolworths. She recounts with extraordinary honesty being raped by a sleazy actor after a Drama Society party. Yet her mother's meanness was clearly far more painful. Murray describes her parents driving straight past as she waited for their visit, because they did not recognize

A young Jenni Murray with her mother on vacation on the Isle of Wight, wearing her school blazer, complete with top-pocket fountain pen. In her S&A interview, Murray said that she was unable to please her mother but concluded that while her mother's life had been happier, her own had been more interesting. *Photo courtesy of Jenni Murray*

"this long-haired, rather fat girl." She finally got their attention, only for her mother to attack her for her appearance.[51]

Many of the oral histories continue to testify to the painful inadequacies of patriarchal structures of the 1920s, 1930s, or 1940s: structures mediated by mothers. And many employ psychological, indeed explicitly psychoanalytic, language to strengthen the case for how maternal more than paternal socialization constructed an unconscious inferiority, injustice, and anger that fuelled their feminism. Here is Cynthia Cockburn, whose family dynamics were very like Murray's, responding to my invitation to talk about her mother: "[Pause] My mother. I don't remember my mother talking to me about very much at all, ever. . . . But also, I've always thought that the exceptionally large breasts somehow kept her at a distance from me. I don't remember a great deal of cuddling. Maybe she was shy about her body, I don't know."[52]

Stories of siblings are also presented as sources of later rebelliousness, with resentment against favoured brothers and more conventional sisters. Where interviewees talked about sexual abuse or violence, the family's role as political incubator was even more direct. In abusive scenarios, mothers who apparently "chose" fathers over daughters can be seen at their most cruel. Beatrix Campbell again is eloquent. Having amicably separated from her husband to become a heartthrob of the WLM's lesbian scene, Campbell's relationship with her mother remained complex. Her mother in fact encouraged her to join the WLM, after Campbell "rubbished it" in a review of the Ruskin conference for the *Morning Star*: "a movement of middle-class people who haven't got servants anymore." (She hoots at the memory.)[53] And her mother went on to set up her own women's groups and feminist weekend schools, annoying her distinguished daughter by continually inviting her to speak: Campbell "dutifully went."[54] Indeed, Rowbotham and McCrindle interviewed Campbell's mother for *Dutiful Daughters*, and she spoke about her own struggles as a mother on a low income. Campbell tells this story often.

But she has talked far less about her father, a working-class patriarch, who made homelife like living in a hurricane. A cruel tempest, he was abusive to everyone, including his wife and his children, bequeathing his own traumatic childhood and wartime horrors wantonly to his own family. Working originally cleaning the railways, he became a maths teacher to troubled boys like himself. Campbell's account of her subsequent campaigning for child rights and empathy for victims is moving, and her feminism and her writing has led her to explore violence generally and sexual violence specifically, including working as a writer with women and young people who have suffered abuse and young violent men serving long prison sentences for rape and murder, learning about their lives and their own troubled childhoods and fathers.

Such experiences show why feminists argue so strongly against romanticizing the family in ideologies of marriage and home. As Cockburn puts it, "I was married in the Fifties, but we were making ourselves anew as we went along; there was a different spirit in the air—you know, rock 'n' roll was beginning to happen and things like that. So, although I remember the grip of that kind of patriarchal family, I was not finally caught by it." Yet, as the debate following Mary McIntosh and Michele Barrett's 1982 *The Anti-Social Family* proved, family was also the subject of intense theoretical and political disagreement.[55] McIntosh and Barrett's concept was that "people paid too much attention to the family and that took you away from the wider society" and that "women were subordinated within the family first and foremost."[56]

But McIntosh and Barrett's analysis provoked a thorough critique from sociologists Kum-Kum Bhavnani and Margaret Coulson, who argued that the book universalized the meaning of family and ignored the experiences of women for whom family unity was an aspiration.[57] People divided by migration, poverty, or racist state immigration laws, for example, or historically split by slavery, could make family a cherished inheritance. Black women's campaigns combined mothers' and children's rights, often focusing on black boys. This seems exemplified in S&A by Mukami McCrum, born in Kenya in the late 1940s, who spoke intensely of missing her mother and sisters after moving to Edinburgh with her Scottish husband. Indeed, her sense of responsibility to her family was not so much a problem for her feminism as a condition of it. She would not marry unless her husband-to-be understood this:

> I wasn't forced to do that; it was by choice, I wanted to do that and even when I got married, one of the things that I explained from the beginning to my husband is that my family is part of me and I have responsibilities. And he was willing to be *part* of that and to help me.[58]

Evolving analyses of family and sexuality within black feminism now consider the original black feminist critique of *The Anti-Social Family* as overstated.[59] Certainly some who led the critique, such as Gail Lewis, tell deeply ambivalent family stories, balancing loyalty to a mother they could see was doubly marginalized with their need to escape. But such protests emphasize that family remained a positive idea not only for the more traditional black community but in general; marriage was still extremely popular in the 1970s, despite rising divorce rates.[60] The stakes became even higher once child abuse became a more central concern for feminists, exploding with Esther Rantzen's launch of a telephone helpline, ChildLine, in 1986 and then in 1987 with allegations of large-scale sexual abuse in Cleveland in northeast England. It was at this moment that Beatrix Campbell, among others, began to think that mothers sometimes could be "perpetrators" as well as "victims," "enlisted as the lieutenants of dangerous men."[61] Mary McIntosh intervened with a 1988 article that acknowledged the civil liberties of mothers but described how feminists could not support a totally "hands-off" policy toward families where child abuse was suspected:

> Many of us would argue that, if the battle lines are to be drawn up as State versus Family, we should side with the State, even with a white bourgeois state. Black women as well as white have wanted to call in the police to protect us against a violent husband, though we have preferred to set up our own refuges and networks; and we have wanted an independent right to social security benefits rather than dependence on a well-paid husband.[62]

Is the family to be reformed, dispersed, collectivized, abolished? Our oral histories reveal that the answer still eludes these feminists. In the context of other struggles, even the nuclear family against which the white middle-class core of the WLM fought in the 1970s has emerged as a place of comparative comfort and stability. McIntosh's own part in creating a new kind of family precisely at the point of writing *The Anti-Social Family* is striking. She was then the partner of her coauthor Michèle Barrett:

> ... and at the time Michèle said she wanted to have a child and I said, errrmmm! I've decided *not* to have a child and by that time it was probably too late to have a child anyway and I didn't really want to be a mother, but as soon as Duncan was born, of course I fell in love with him and I *did* want to mother him or whatever... So I did *completely* change when he was born, when he was there as a physical fact from how I'd been in *theory* in relation to having a child.[63]

Later, she resisted the suggestion that they would have considered this "a family," but added, "I think it's *true*, if you plotted my life it's been quite couple-ish and so forth. I mean, I think one thing to be said for gay people: we invented serial monogamy and in a way straight people have followed and that is now the pattern among a lot of straight people."[64]

Yet she does not ultimately repudiate her early critique, even of the extended family, so much as note the irony that even a lesbian couple in a powerful network of friends, ex-lovers, and children may find themselves isolated in old age, even through choice: "And also, people don't necessarily, in the European context, want to live in the same household and so forth that they, again, probably ideally think they used to live in when they were a child or that their parents used to live in. I think a lot of this business about the extended family is a kind of fantasy of how it *should* be rather than an actuality."[65]

For Sara Ahmed, feminists should challenge the emotional blackmail of parents who say "our happiness depends on your happiness" yet tie this to a restrictive life plan for marriage, children, grandchildren.[66] But duty and family itself is not so easily banished. Indeed, what is most striking about feminist mother–daughter narratives is the ongoing connection, even in anger, and the sense that family itself is not ultimately given up in the mid- or late life of activists, but reemerges in postpatriarchal forms. Older interviewees are also more able to appreciate what kinds of girlhoods formed their own mothers. Murray goes back to de Beauvoir herself to make this point, appreciating her mother's Edwardian upbringing: "So I try to have as much as I can a politically centred, forgiving nature towards my mother." Indeed, Murray's final candid assessment of her own life in contrast to her mother's is that though hers has been more interesting, her mother's had been happier.[67]

Feminists are moving from the "father quest" that dominated early life narratives, exemplified by Germaine Greer and Sylvia Plath. We now see life from the mother's perspective, too.[68] This is obvious where interviewees become mothers themselves, constructing their own generational chain. But even when they do not have biological children, the daughter has a sense of herself as a caregiver now—corresponding also to late-life remembering and inheriting.

Feminism may have been a wish for love or approval, a means of sibling self-assertion, or precisely a way to differentiate oneself from a mother who had been successful, or just happy with her lot, as much as unsuccessful or unhappy. Family structures were crucial to the form the WLM took—both in the majority who were reacting to the midcentury nuclear family, and in the minority who were trying to balance critiques of family backgrounds with other needs that kept them loyal. In many ways, the long lives of all our interviewees suggest that this latter position has proved more typical of how feminists balanced their need for family in relation to its possible risks and dangers.

Catalysts: Aspiration, Inspiration, and Susie Orbach's Story

The puzzle remains as to why our interviewees became feminists when most of their peers did not. Successful women such as the television cook Delia Smith (born in 1941) or singer and TV personality Cilla Black (born in 1943) might have identified with those arguing for more professional ease; senior police officer Alison Halford (born in 1940) fought fiercely against sex discrimination but was never interested in the movement and eventually shifted from Labour to Conservative party politics in Wales. Margaret Thatcher herself is an extreme case (born in 1925), but even Labour's Barbara Castle declared that she had "no use for the sex war and all the nonsense about encouraging women to believe they could only feel big by making men feel small" and was "irritated by the Women's Lib trivia."[69] Then there are the many other housewives and mothers who agree on common frustrations but who never joined the WLM.[70] There are many explanations, of course: off-putting ideas of what a feminist is; misdirected or misconstrued feminist campaigns and analyses; the lure of respectability; the sense that housewifery or motherhood is satisfying and better than many alternatives. The WLM occasionally called these positions "false consciousness," but political innocence might be a more suitable explanation.

In fact, feminist identification may arise not out of anger, deficit, oppression, or frustration, but because of a political education, social network, or moral inspiration. Social movement theorists, who notably have found little correlation between activism and particular personalities, argue that becoming an activist depends on a range of conditions, some structural, others cultural.[71] "Biographical availability" is a good place to begin this analysis: Does the person have time and resources? Is she plugged into appropriate networks? Students and others at a stage of life with the time, means, and structures became the core activists. In the WLM, the vital clusters of women who met at university, or travelling, through the New Left or the counterculture, those associated with *Race Today* and the British Black Panthers, and the Communist Party breakaways all testify to this.

But there are also important predictors of activism that attach to an earlier life stage. These include being raised by political parents and given a strong moral education, including in religious settings that may be retuned toward political ends. Half of our sixty interviewees grew up in left-wing or anti-imperialist families, and seven had mothers who were or became activists. Notable examples include Valerie Wise, chair of the Women's Committee in the Greater London Council in the 1980s, whose mother, Audrey Wise, was a leading parliamentarian in support of women's rights, and Amrit Wilson, whose mother was a human rights activist in India. The Communist mothers of Beatrix Campbell and Barbara Taylor became so interested in feminism that at times their radical daughters were irritated with their interference.[72] Jean McCrindle speaks of her Communist family as being like a Christian or a Muslim one—and though she overthrew her "righteous sect" after the Soviet Union's invasion of Hungary in 1956, her feminist activism remained indebted to it.[73]

As much as it seems that the mix of an unhappy childhood and political parents fed later activism, feminism as the outcome of positive education or social appeal is perhaps one of its best-kept secrets. The pleasures of friendship and belonging as well as the excitements and spiritual conviction that activism can offer are as important as explanations as those of unhappiness, especially when life is dull.[74] The early lives of WLM activists often show what—or who—inspired them. As divisive as the eleven-plus experience was for our generations, many remembered charismatic or beloved teachers, including a surprising number who directly introduced them to feminist ideas or texts. Sheila Rowbotham read *Look Back in Anger* in secondary school, and Juliet Mitchell recalls when, at just twelve, she was taken to hear Margaret Mead lecture.[75] Murray was introduced to de Beauvoir's *The Second Sex* at school.[76] Wilson remembers her mind being opened by *The Well of Loneliness* as a lonely teenager in Calcutta, while in Kenya Mukami McCrum felt privileged to be in school in the first place and recognized education as essential to her personal and professional successes.[77]

These memories are important not only to the formation of a more rounded feminist identity but also to its functioning as a social movement.[78] Many activists gain organizational affiliations, as well as values, from their parents, which are then reinforced by the experiences and skills gained through education.[79] Such foundations, when nurtured through university, correlate to leadership in social movements.[80] Although this pattern has often meant that middle-class men continue to dominate these movements, such personal and educational connections are also critical to leaders from less privileged backgrounds; Malcolm X turned himself from street hustler to black power icon, in his own account, through self-study while in prison; Rigoberta Menchu, icon of indigenous Guatemalan rights, drew on extensive activist family networks.

The work of WLM activists who went into education themselves matters in several ways. On one level, this pattern reflects the feminized nature of education as a career. It marks the grassroots and third-sector domain of the WLM, in contrast to the suffrage movement's focus on Parliament, trade unionism's focus on industry, or liberal feminists' focus on business and management. Yet teaching was also as an intervention in the life course of future generations, a form of cultural change within schools, and within the family through feminist parenting.

Sheila Kitzinger (born in 1929), Anna Davin (born in 1940), and Sandie Wyles (born in 1957) represent three generations of activists who have directly focused on younger women's chances in this way. Kitzinger, known for her irreverent reenactments of giving birth at conferences, was influential in creating the National Childbirth Trust and challenging the medicalization of birth. Clearly a forebear more than a WLM activist, Kitzinger had five daughters who are all passionate feminists, and Jenni Murray credits Kitzinger for her own insistence on taking control when she gave birth.[81] As a mature student with three children, Davin wrote beautiful academic histories of working-class childhood, informed by opposition to the corporal punishment of children. Davin's family life surely informs her insightful question as to how new levels of children's empowerment can be squared with increasing management of their lives.[82] Finally, Wyles narrates her pleasure in proving that girls love to play pool as much as put on makeup, connecting with the Scottish National Organisation of Girls' Work to fund girls-only sessions across Scotland.[83]

The story of Susie Orbach is key to thinking about feminist childhood. Orbach was a central figure in the WLM and, as a psychotherapist as well as a girls' rights campaigner, interested as well in child development. Her own childhood was certainly conflicted, yet she talks with evident pleasure of youthful outings and love, friendships, rebellions, and the opportunities offered through political circles from her parents onwards. Above all, she gives insight now as a catalyst, hoping ultimately to inspire a sense of justice and liberation without endless personal suffering.

Orbach's critique of the beauty industry and women's self-image has made her a media go-to for questions about teenage femininity, but her political background is less well known. Born in 1946, in her S&A interview she describes socialist secular Jewish roots. Her father, Maurice, was born in Cardiff to a large family that had emigrated from Poland and ran a corner shop. He left school at thirteen. He was loud, clever, enterprising—at one point trying to get a business going through his new design of menstrual pads, of all things—and a committed trade union member who eventually became Labour member of Parliament for Willesden East. He lost his seat in 1959—a dreadful moment for the family, Orbach remembers—because his support for Nasser's Egyptian nationalism and the Soviet Union alienated the local Jewish vote, but he was reelected in 1964 in Stockport South.

Orbach describes her mother as frankly "mean."[84] Ruth Huebsch, a first-generation educated Jew, had dreamed of becoming a lawyer. But she "married down," having met Maurice when he was on a trade union speaking tour in New York. A "modern New Yorker," she "never should have been transplanted to another country," says Orbach.[85] In war-impoverished London she worked part time as a language teacher to immigrants, receiving care packages from her friends back home and feeling bitter and frustrated.

She forced her children to attend private schools, North London Collegiate in Orbach's case, from which Orbach was expelled. Anti-Semitism in such schools can be measured by their unofficial restricted entry quotas for Jews. Maurice and Ruth were "contemptuous" of religion as they were of the frivolities of sports, romance, and fashion. Orbach says her family "kept *schtum* [silent] about everything," a "postwar generation of parents who were dealing with the post-Holocaust situation."[86] This was combined with the classic "distant" mothering style—"You were put out in the pram [stroller] . . . and left there"—and she remembered Huebsch's doctor telling Huebsch that the more intelligent woman doesn't like babies.[87] In addition, despite rare but wonderful spaghetti-eating competitions in the small Formica and check-patterned kitchen, Orbach's "tiny" mother forbade them to eat potatoes, rice, or bread at a time when these were rationed anyway. Strikingly, considering Orbach's later work, her mother would go on the Mayo Clinic diet (eggs, grapefruit, steak) twice a year to maintain a weight of 100 pounds: "I just took it as that's what you do when you're a grownup. That's the way to be a proper woman: you *go on a diet*."[88]

Treated as "problem children," Orbach and her brother rebelled: "our intelligence got honed in an oppositional sense." Her self-portrait at thirteen is "hair over one eye, probably trying to iron it, bright but sad eyes . . . precocious looking, Lolita-ish."[89] She fell in love with a nineteen-year-old friend of her brother, got pregnant, dosed herself with quinine and gin, and went to the hospital saying she would kill herself, because abortion was permitted on mental health grounds. Her father, a trustee of the hospital, soon found out, and, while her mother slapped and screamed at her, he took her to Switzerland for the termination.

Orbach's family was also intensely political. Acting as "father's date" on his many evenings at Soviet-bloc embassies, she observed his work for the

London County Council, Jewish Trades Advisory Council, Movement for Colonial Freedom (of which he was chair), plus undercover work "getting Jews out of the Soviet Union and Iran and Iraq."[90] Her mother was involved with socialist Zionist women's organizations and drama groups, including the Unity Theatre, while her brother Laurence's initiation of a magazine styled on the *New Left Review* when he was just sixteen allowed Orbach at fourteen to be "secretary" to a network including Doris Lessing, Marghanita Laski, Eric Hobsbawm, and Christopher Hill. Driving his sister to school after the abortion, Laurence defended her when she was expelled, phoning the headmistress, Kitty Anderson, to complain she was keeping the "sheep" and getting rid of the "leader." Secretly reading romance magazines, she also remembers,

> When I was fourteen or fifteen I read Sartre and de Beauvoir, I'm sure I didn't understand a word, but I knew it was really groovy. And I wanted to *look* like [all those French intellectual heroines], and I'm sure I did, by ironing my hair and wearing lots of white lipstick and black stuff around my eyes . . . I would have identified with all of the *men* in the books that I was reading. I didn't even know that there was anything wrong with that. I think I would have . . . been male-identified, which meant that I would have wanted to make myself into a pretty young thing![91]

Male-identified, perhaps, but being able to see the Existentialists as gorgeous was as much the point. The only teacher she remembered fondly from the hated school was the one with smeared lipstick and runs in her stockings—the wife of a relative of leading Labour politician Tony Benn. At Camden School for Girls, where she was happier, she was taught by Margot Heineman, a legendary Communist and feminist. And clearly formative was her very much older American cousin Eleanor, whom she was close to when she moved to the United States. Eleanor, aged fifty to her eighteen:

> was full of life and generous and bought me things and told me the world was my oyster and believed in sex and all the things my mother didn't. . . . She was just so full of bravado. My mother was, too, you see, but I didn't get to see it. [Adopts urbane American accent] "Honey! It's a tonic. It's a vitamin pill. That's what it is. That's *all* it is, it's just a tonic." Well, *she'd* been probably . . . fifteen, sixteen, seventeen during the war. She said, "Honey, sex was really different then."[92]

Then there was her mother's best friend's daughter (now her sister-in-law) bringing a Joan Baez record and the catalogue from the New York Museum of Modern Art exhibition *The Family of Man* from the United States (much debated by the Left),[93] and her uncle, Edward Huebsch, a screenwriter blacklisted under Senator Joseph McCarthy, going underground. The Orbach family boycotted South African and Spanish and Portuguese goods. And her gap-year job with the United Nations Association in London, organizing talks in high schools, for fifteen pounds per week, enough to buy Tube fares and black stockings and to afford weekend visits to her boyfriend at Lancaster University.

What "saved" her, having dropped out of the conservative School of Slavonic and East European Studies at London University, was a transformative trip to New York for her own summer of love in 1968. Finding a job in the city planning department, she soon joined Urban Underground, Teachers for a Democratic Society (through her leftist teacher boyfriend), and Students for a Democratic Society (SDS), and became involved in the political upheavals of the time, seeing herself as a "full-time revolutionary." SDS were linked to the Black Panthers, revising the anti–Vietnam War

A smiling Susie Orbach (left) in 1966, aged twenty, sells sandwiches at Portobello Road market in London. In her S&A interview, Orbach happily recalled the relationships and rebellions of growing up in an intensely political home, though she also recounted her mother's maxim that to be a proper woman, "you go on a diet." *Photo courtesy of Rex Features*

struggle toward anti-imperialist ends. Though she is clearly critical of some of her youthful actions, her account is fascinatingly honest about the appeal of social movement life:

> I think what happened is you—were suddenly living in a collective situation—there were various collective houses in New York—and you were engaged in political education all day long and you took that model of criticism, self-criticism sessions. So you would, if you raised the issue it would be *answered* by people arguing with *brilliance*, actually. So that it wasn't that your doubt was suppressed, it was that you were *convinced*. And I think they were brilliant enough that they would be able to turn around what you saw and what you felt into—I'm not saying I was being conned, I mean I think this is what a good political thinker can do, it can say the image of the person who's represented as a victim that we feel X and Y for can be understood in this way . . .'[94]

By 1970 she had moved into other radical scenes. With the New York Law Commune, she helped develop legal defence cases for military deserters, Black Panthers, and women seeking divorce. Under Veronika Kraft and Carol Lefcourt, she evolved the concept of back pay for women instead of alimony, and parental leave for men: later her husband was the first to take it, from his job at City University of New York in 1984, on the birth of their first child. Aspiring to train as a lawyer, she returned to university but quickly changed to taking and then teaching at the first women's studies programme in the United States, at Richmond College, Staten Island, led by Phyllis Chesler, Dorothy Riddle, and Carol Bloom. It was there she met Luise Eichenbaum, who, with Bloom, became a lifelong friend and colleague, and Joe Schwarz, a physics professor, her partner for thirty-four years.

Her inspiration for *Fat Is a Feminist Issue: The Anti-Diet Guide to Permanent Weight Loss* (*FIFI*), which put her name on the map when published in 1978, came from attending a workshop on body image with Carol Munter at the Alternate U in 1970.[95] Thinking it would be about "First–Third World food distribution," she was fascinated that Munter focused instead on the attendees' own identities, including the idea that giving up dieting would not only liberate but possibly enable women to lose weight. *FIFI* was one of the most successful books of the British WLM, breaking into the US market—despite her insistence on keeping "feminist" in the title (the publishers wanted it to be "feminine," and forced the subtitle). Its success came partly from its accessible, self-help formulation, drawing on the human potential movement in growth therapies and gestalt and visualizations as well as the women's movement's emphasis on "women speaking their own experience."[96]

She began with the principle that compulsive eating and anorexia are individual and unconscious protests against patriarchal sexuality, including the way femininity in patriarchy is transmitted intergenerationally through the mother–daughter relationship and the way in which complex messages are expressed through the management of children's eating. She then developed a how-to manual for self- and group-analysis, with exercises that included directed breathing to connect the disowned fat thighs with the "wrist that seems so much more acceptable" and guided fantasies to bring back and analyze memories of "The Family Meal."[97]

The book was an instant success, sold out its first printing within a week, and remains an iconic text. *FIFI* did annoy dedicated Fat Liberationists who had begun to organize in Los Angeles in 1973 and were in London by the 1980s and some found the populist style underplayed class and race differences and economic structures.[98] Moreover, the method did not always work: Cynthia Cockburn, for example, turned to *FIFI* to deal with a life-long struggle with overeating, agreeing she had been undernurtured by her mother and school, but confessed that she found that Weight Watchers had more practical effects.[99]

However, Orbach's interests proved prophetic as questions of size, troubled eating, and poor self-image mushroomed alongside the fast-food and beauty industries and the growing consumer power of young people at the stage of identity formation. Today, the diet, food, beauty, style, and fashion industries remain a target. Troubled eating stalks women of all sizes. Orbach maintains that the "discourse of control" is ideological, a displacement of problems that need to be solved through improved parental and peer relationships as well as pleasure in food. Her messages, while still controversial ("the worst thing [is] to be on the wrong side of size as though it were the new class issue"), have gained more mainstream acceptance than many feminist ideas, and Orbach has advised government, schools, and industry on eating and body literacy.[100] This included a high-profile consultancy with Dove soap's high-profile "Real Beauty" marketing campaign, and grassroots work with her pressure group Endangered Bodies and AnyBody, promoting body diversity and confidence. She persuaded the UK government to set up a summit at UN Women to recognize the colonialization of women's bodies and the "sell" of Western body hatred around the world as a form of "unseen violence against women." There were delegates from Sudan, South Sudan, Europe, Indonesia, and Latin America, all confirming that girls and women are being robbed of civil participation because of this new horror of body obsession.[101] Her treatment of Princess Diana, who developed bulimia in 1991 after learning of her husband's infidelity while she was pregnant with her first son, measures the extent of her success. Diana's life as the celebrity victim of an arranged royal marriage seems far from the WLM, but Orbach comments that "as a fairy story and a princess who's lost and then does something *with* that, I think it was a very interesting modern fable."[102]

Orbach's robust approach also supported her other outstanding initiative, The Women's Therapy Centre, set up in London in 1976 with Luise Eichenbaum, with whom she had trained in psychotherapy at the Stony Brook progressive health services centre in the United States.[103] It first met in the basement of her house in Islington, and Orbach remembers the pot plants, cigarettes, plainly furnished rooms. To their astonishment, two weeks after they had sent off a home-produced press release with the help of Orbach's brother, they were flooded with would-be clients, some wanting help after treatment in mental hospitals, others simply seeking therapy at a time when there was little advertised, including feminists who wanted individual rather than group attention. (Lynne Segal mentions that the members of her household went to the centre to sort out rivalry over a man.)[104]

Indeed, as well-known feminist clients grew in number, Orbach and her colleagues had to withdraw from their local activist scene in Islington. Men were not prohibited in principle, but once it was clear so many women wanted their services, they were sent away. Interestingly, this was also when Red Therapy, a mixed socialist group from 1974 to 1977, became an alternative destination for "men's movement" men. The Red Therapy group in turn sent Sheila Ernst and Lucy Goodison to the Women's Therapy Centre.[105]

In the early days, the therapists worked part-time for £15 or £30 a week, and clients paid on a sliding fee scale from nothing to £10.[106] Orbach secured local government funding to make up the difference: she rejected as "complete nonsense" the edict that paying for therapy was psychologically important, particularly since women "couldn't then offload the issues around dependency by paying for it."[107] And they analyzed themselves, especially their class backgrounds; all appreciated the importance of class and being Left-aligned. Yet Orbach and Eichenbaum saw the centre as democratically run, rather than as a collective. She argued you cannot be a collective unless all agree to equal responsibility and most people at the centre worked one or two days, whereas she and Eichenbaum were full time. Again, her ability to resist pressures from the community of different kinds marks her out as willing to take a risk. Within a year they were running group therapy on "women in power or envy or competition or women and anger," which became a joint book with Eichenbaum, *Bittersweet: Facing Up to Feelings of Love, Envy, and Competition in Women's Friendships* (1987).[108] The book maintains their optimistic approach to women's problems, rooting rivalry and overexpectations of each other again in patriarchal unconscious mothering practices where women "bind each other's ambition and desire" in ways that can be changed.[109] Orbach has never felt that therapy is a retreat from activism, either for the client or, perhaps more surprisingly, for the therapist. This is surely part of her agreement to give an open oral history.

Orbach's own midlife was one of partnership and two children with Joe Schwarz. In her account, he supported her politically and shared the emotional and domestic work—their arguments were more in the vein of Old Left (he) versus New Left (she), Russia (he) versus China (she), and "whose chicken soup was better" (hers).[110] Unsurprisingly, she was determined not to parent as her mother had, fighting her daughter's "battles with her at school" and throwing a champagne celebration when she first got her period. Still libertarian, she attempted to manage teenage "separation" behaviour like sexuality and drugs by "asking to know about it," though she drew the line at her daughter using a chemical depilatory on her legs. A small story of her daughter's wish to put "X" instead of "male" or "female" on a form in support of transgender rights shows that she has passed on her politics, even as they change with new times. While being interviewed for her oral history, news arrived of youths rioting in London. She commented on her sympathy with the rioters, despite wishing their anger was "targeted in a political way, in a way that my generation would have liked," holding another segment of her generation responsible for selling "consumer goods and bling as a form of belonging."[111]

Yet Orbach's seduction by the writer Jeanette Winterson in 2009 has torn up a possible final chapter as wise old feminist advice columnist. Winterson, a star in her own right, is, in Orbach's words, her opposite: a Christian country "hermit-hobbit" and flamboyant lesbian icon, in contrast to her as sociable urban Jew and post-heterosexual therapist. One thing they clearly share is concern for unhappy girls as they themselves had been, and a belief in what Orbach calls "hyper-variety" as the answer to "this global brand called woman and soon to be global brand called man or boy."[112] Orbach presents their marriage in 2015 as a part of a life and identity still changing.[113] She shares her startlingly frank oral history as a therapist who has committed to a philosophy of self-change and healing, and someone used to giving interviews.

This version of feminist agency is obviously optimistic in contrast to more orthodox psychoanalysts, including in the WLM. Though Orbach comments that it can be "overwhelming" to think about the political problems for young people today, she concludes that "you just have to keep trying to make interventions."[114]

If remaining a believer is easier when organizations, family, friends, colleagues, and partners agree, becoming one clearly is too. While Orbach's history is unusual in many respects, in others, it exemplifies the point that WLM activists did not simply grow from unhappy mothers, abuse, or even a divisive education or stymied opportunities in adulthood. Rather, it demonstrates the equally important effects of a rich political inheritance, and a youth constructed not simply in opposition but in harmony with a large, international, exciting set of peers convinced they were remaking the world. She says that feminism gave her "my best friends . . . and it gave me a place to stand from."[115]

Looking at Orbach and other feminists' stories confirms the particular opportunities these generations enjoyed, and social movement theorists' predictors of activism. Studies of these generations in the United Kingdom and the United States suggest that while those born in the tough times of the early twentieth century have been more likely to follow traditional paths, those born midcentury have been more willing to adopt an alternative lifestyle, aided by factors including postwar peace, secularization, easy contraception, greater opportunities, and equalizing of incomes.[116] Many consider that economic and social growth allowed the baby boomer generation to privilege self-expression and quality of life.[117] But we might also observe that many responded to these opportunities without questioning the status quo. Perhaps it is the more recent years of a stagnant economy that has prompted alternative lifestyles, "delaying entrance into adult roles."[118] A more sympathetic interpretation holds that the easier postwar years allowed activists to reject normal life-course trajectories as a conscious choice.[119]

Activists' lives in this way appear to be an extreme version of a generational shift from a focus on material goods and family fortunes to individual and collective self-realization.[120] Many motivations for feminism that were attached to childhood or adolescence were activated, perhaps sometimes even invented, retrospectively, stimulated by consciousness raising, movement literature, women's studies, or therapy. These motivations then fed into feminist parenting practices, typically libertarian, as well as attempts to refashion partnerships and family structures. In one sense, the WLM rode on the back of a macro-move to youth as the cultural age for everyone, an age of self-making, of leaving home. The conservative version of this concept is that the baby boomers were and remain permanent adolescents, joyriding about. But the teenage period continues to be prized by those with little power precisely because it is one of self-determination before the responsibilities of adulthood close in.[121]

4 CAMPAIGNING AND COMING OF AGE IN THE 1970s

The decade of the 1970s remains vivid in the memories of many activist elders of the WLM, for it typically coincided with their coming of age, the time of life that often shines brightest in reminiscence.[1] Many S&A interviewees were then students, young workers, and/or mothers in their twenties when the WLM was itself youthful. This decade provided a charmed opportunity to combine self-realization with protest. From the disruption of the Miss World pageant in 1970 to the Southall Black Sisters' march against domestic violence in 1980, activists' memories challenge the conservative interpretation of a time sometimes described as Britain's Weimar: a grim decade of inflation, strikes, and strife in Northern Ireland. Feminist oral histories join a counternarrative to stress that this turbulent decade actually saw historically high employment and income equality levels.[2] The so-called Winter of Discontent of 1979 was also paradoxically an exciting time for many feminists. The National Abortion Campaign involved hope, pride, and pleasure as well as anger at the threat to women's precarious reproductive rights and the election of Margaret Thatcher. Personal experience reinvigorated conventional politics in a campaign that tried valiantly to bridge the WLM, the unions, and party politics, personal experience reinvigorated conventional politics. Yet memories of this campaign in turn open difficult questions about women's longer-term hopes and desires, as activists challenged conventional scripts of fertility, sexuality, and motherhood without knowing exactly what would replace them. Oral histories help to unearth what they were feeling at the time, and they reveal that interviewees today see liberation and choice as bringing new challenges. Nevertheless, women's ability to question and choose our destinies stands as a permanent gain from the WLM.

The story of Karen McMinn, coordinator for Women's Aid Northern Ireland for over ten years, beginning in 1976, tells of a dedicated campaigning life in Belfast at the height of the Troubles. At the same time, it highlights the narrow political opportunity structures that shaped the activism in this period in other parts of the United Kingdom as well. These contexts lead us to "mainstreaming" tactics, integrating feminist ideas within state or public- or private-sector policies and jobs, in the 1980s under Thatcher's government—when, as new activists were joining the movement, others were beginning to retreat from it.

What Do We Want and When Do We Want It?

A quick reminder of what women were up against even in the 1970s: they still required a man's permission to borrow money from the bank; jobs were advertised by gender; only 26 of the 650 members of Parliament (MPs) were women in 1970, and fewer still (only 19) in 1979, the year Thatcher was elected as prime minster; domestic violence and marital rape were not considered crimes; doctors (most of whom were men) were often ignorant of women's health; husbands often got child custody; and marriage—allowed only to heterosexuals—was still idealized as the high point of a woman's life. It was not until 1975 that the Sex Discrimination Act was passed and, as with equal pay, its changes were phased in over subsequent years.

This scene underlay the WLM's seven demands. The first four, set out at the Ruskin conference and passed at the national conference in Skegness in 1971, were equal pay; equal educational and job opportunities; free contraception and abortion on demand; and free twenty-four-hour nurseries for children. Demands five and six, passed at the 1974 conference in Edinburgh, called for legal and financial independence for all women and the right to a self-defined sexuality, including an end to discrimination against lesbians. The seventh was added in 1978 at the last national conference in Birmingham: freedom for all women from intimidation by the threat or use of violence or sexual coercion regardless of marital status; and an end to the laws, assumptions, and institutions that perpetuate male dominance and men's aggression to women.[3]

From today's perspective, these demands are relatively uncontroversial, if unachieved, particularly equal pay, equal opportunities, legal independence, freedom from violence, and an end to discrimination against lesbians. Others—free twenty-four-hour nurseries, abortion on demand, and the right to a self-defined sexuality—seem overly simplistic. Yet they provide a

The national women's liberation conference in Birmingham in April 1978. The conference adopted the seventh and final demand of the WLM—freedom for all women from intimidation by the threat or use of male violence. An end to the laws, assumptions, and institutions that perpetuate male dominance and men's aggression towards women. *Photo courtesy of Val Wilmer/Photofusion*

measure of the movement's imagination at the time. Asking for the moon—as the night cleaners' action group playfully did—did not seem pointless.[4] Discussions about pay were part of transforming what counted as work, what class meant, what "success" itself was. Yet it was difficult to translate such ambition into the limited political framework of the time.

The night cleaners' campaign of 1970–73 to improve pay and conditions for women bearing the double burden of low pay and the responsibilities of unpaid work at home demonstrates these difficulties.[5] The campaign was initiated by May Hobbs, a cleaning supervisor who was, unusually for someone in the cleaning trade, a union member. The WLM got involved when she approached the Dalston Women's Liberation Workshop (of which Sheila Rowbotham was a member) and the International Marxist Group for help. Sally Alexander and others spent two years picketing, leafleting, publicizing, and socializing with Hobbs and her husband, with shop steward Jean Mormont, and with the thirty-five or so other cleaners.[6] The campaign was initially successful—the women received a substantial pay raise and gained the support of MPs such as Lena Jager and Joe Ashton.[7] However, these gains were lost when the cleaning contract changed hands and the new contractor was not bound to the terms of the previous agreement. The Transport and General Workers' Union, to Hobbs's and others' fury, was largely unsupportive of workers they considered unskilled and unorganized.[8] Hobbs barely mentioned the WLM in her witty autobiography of 1973, and the Berwick film collective's avant-garde version of events failed to impress the cleaners as any kind of campaigning tool.[9]

But if we think about the 1970s as a time when *concepts* were developed that reevaluated the centrality of childbirth, caregiving, and maintaining the home—central to economies and nations as well as to personal psychologies and relationships—then the picture looks much more compelling. Campaigns around women's domestic labour were at the heart of the movement. This drove the thinking behind the demand for unlimited childcare (women work flexible shifts at all hours because of their responsibilities to care for children) and a reformed benefit and legal system in which women would not be dependent on a male breadwinner and lack reproductive rights.[10] The links between class and gender struggles fed the fifth demand, the campaign for financial and legal independence, popularly known as YBA (Why Be A) Wife. Mary McIntosh, a key formulator, explained that this campaign grew from a married friend's objections to paying tax as part of a couple in light of the long assumption that women would be kept by men.[11] But this grew into a larger analysis of the marriage contract—playfully proclaimed on the badge "Don't do it, Di!" as Diana Spencer prepared for her marriage to Prince Charles in 1981. McIntosh, who had shifted from the Gay Liberation Front to the WLM, enjoyed this moment of lesbian solidarity with a very heterosexual problem. What united so many was that women took care of the house and family, always and for free.[12]

Feminist body politics pushed existing political frameworks still farther. For some, the notion of a "self-defined sexuality" was absurd from a psychological perspective, as Ros Delmar, a member of the Feminist Psychoanalysis Group, immediately argued.[13] Yet the sheer weight of feminists who remember affairs with women within the movement suggests that sexual liberation was fundamental, and fundamentally different from the masculinist sexualities whether of Masters and Johnson or Mick Jagger. This led, by the end of the decade, to "political lesbianism," controversially staked out by the Leeds Revolutionary Feminist group, and particularly by Sheila Jeffreys, comparable in approach to Andrea Dworkin. They stood in contrast to versions of heterosexual liberation championed by the equally controversial Germaine Greer.[14] Not all appreciated her 1970 *The Female Eunuch* because it blamed women for their sexual inhibitions, rather than patriarchy or capitalism.

Juliet Mitchell criticized the book as "written from the anarchist individualist stance, the Hippie 'my life is the truth of your life' . . . It elects to be alone when people are coming together in a social and political movement, so that despite the book's many pertinent insights it dates itself as it appears."[15]

However, Greer's audacious invitation to pleasure and self-realization inspired many: Zoë Fairbairns remembers practically "leaping out of [her] chair crying *Yes!*" on reading Greer's pronouncement that

> "if women are to effect significant amelioration of their lives they must refuse to marry"—because it had never occurred to me that you could *refuse*. It seemed to me that it was something that either you achieved, in which case you would be miserable for the rest of your life, or you *failed* to achieve it, in which case you would be miserable for the rest of your life—the idea that you could just *walk away* from it was tremendous, that was a real moment of epiphany and liberation for me.[16]

This fizz is audible too in the S&A interviewees who disrupted the Miss World beauty pageant at London's Albert Hall in 1970. This widely publicized action was the United Kingdom's answer to the Freedom Trashcan protest outside the Miss America beauty pageant in 1968, when women symbolically discarded bras, girdles, curlers, false eyelashes, wigs, and issues of *Cosmopolitan, Ladies' Home Journal,* and *Family Circle*.[17] Jo Robinson, in retrospect less angry than excited about her role in the protest, describes herself as "longing for" the action, her new identity "bursting through":

> I dressed in clothes that I thought looked as though I was going to Ascot and I got, probably [from] secondhand shops, I got a pink corduroy coat and a big pink floppy hat. No idea what was on the legs. And I had my arsenal of equipment packed tightly inside a leather satchel on my shoulders, and my hair was, like, huge and all over the place, hanging out, but I think I tied it down, because I thought, "I've got to get in there and I've got to look *normal,* I've got to look acceptable," so that's why I decided on the Ascot image to cope with the natural hippie style I had adopted that was bursting through. I had to, like, damp that down.[18]

Robinson, with Jenny Fortune, Sue Finch, Sarah Wilson, and others, coproduced the action's iconic pamphlet, which had been written by Sally Alexander, Mary Kelly, Laura Mulvey, and Margarita Jimenez in a typically

Activists, with Jo Robinson wearing the floppy hat (centre), disrupt the Miss World beauty pageant, then one of TV's most popular shows, in London's Albert Hall in 1970. Hurling flour bombs, stink bombs, and leaflet, shouting slogans, and blowing whistles, the protestors were quickly ejected, but within ten years the BBC had dropped the show from its schedule. *Photo courtesy of Leonard Burt/Central Press/Getty Images*

collaborative production.[19] Lynne Segal, another movement mainstay, read it after helping in the nursery that her son attended with Robinson and Fortune's children:

> "Why Miss World?" was literally the first women's liberation pamphlet I read and I thought it was very, very good, you know [laughs] ... I remember reading it, for some reason ... in the bath thinking, "You know, we're not ugly, we're not beautiful, we're angry and women are more than people who want to be stared at and have their bottoms pinched." Everything [that] was in that resonated with me, so I suppose I became a feminist through those first—through meeting those women from

Grosvenor Avenue. I would have become a feminist anyway, I *imagine* [laughs] . . . because I was a single mother by this time.[20]

Later that year, a much smaller Scottish action sparkled in its own dramatic way when Sue Innes entered the St. Andrews University Charities Queen Contest on a platform of being "neither more nor less beautiful than any other woman in the university," and promising, if elected, to abolish beauty contests everywhere.[21]

These issues—time, work, sexuality, love, bodies, peace, self-expression, the idea of gender itself—felt distinctively fresh. In sociological terms, the women's movement was becoming identity-oriented, or expressive, in contrast to instrumental or strategy-oriented.[22] Although participants campaigned, organized mass meetings and rallies, and promoted petitions and civil disobedience, the WLM lived more productively in the health and sexual rights movement, theory groups, women's centres and refuges, rape crisis helplines, booths in Saturday shopping precincts, aesthetic experiments, women's studies, dances, and discos. O'Sullivan, originally from the United States, by then a key member of the London WLM workshop, who later went into feminist publishing and HIV/AIDS awareness, explains:

> The whole way that I wanted to be involved politically was not focused on *particular* demands . . . So I wasn't wildly involved in the National Abortion Campaign, I went on the demos [demonstrations] but I wasn't—that was not what I was in. I was *much more*, I think, focused on grassroots, coming together of women of all sorts . . . and trying to figure out how we could press forward with the whole notion of being involved in a movement . . . so, yes, if somebody could get involved by getting—going into the National Abortion Campaign, great—but there was *also* a way of—of trying to address women's . . . *daily lives*, and be able to do that from your own experience of overcoming contradictions and so on.[23]

O'Sullivan's emphasis on "your own experience" is telling. Experience was not only a source of insight into the forces that oppressed women (but had never been considered worthy of recognition) but a form of participatory change in contrast to party politics, the hard-left centralism, and the domination by men of civil rights and other allied groups.[24] For this reason, there were soon no men at meetings or conferences, and specific jobs, such as media spokeswoman or chair, rotated between women on a principled basis.

The WLM's method was fluid and egalitarian, embodying the society it wanted to create, in the way of the New Left.[25] But this approach cost it the ability to mass mobilize. An early attempt to create a unifying structure, the National Coordinating Committee disbanded within a year of its establishment in 1971 because of infiltration by hard-left activists wishing to take over to promote their own (and quite different) political objectives. Newsletters linked the groups, especially *Shrew* in the early years and *WIRES*, set up in 1975 after the Manchester national conference to act as a national referral service, though still with a rotating editorial and a distinctly Leeds-based radical bent.[26]

A 1971 "operational guide to Women's Lib groups" by Sheila McNeil in the *Sunday Times Magazine* lists groups in forty-five locations in the United Kingdom and Ireland, excluding London, with membership ranging from 3 (Loughborough) to 150 (Oxford, contact Hilary Wainwright).[27] Dublin (outside of the United Kingdom, but extremely active), Liverpool, Brighton, Bristol, and Oxford all feature as having more than five groups each—but even so, my admittedly rough membership count suggests not much more than a thousand individuals all told. Ten years later, the number of explicitly named women's liberation groups had likely reached some three hundred across the United Kingdom, with an informal membership of ten thousand.[28] We could arguably multiply the number of supporters by at least three on the basis of subscriptions to the most popular movement magazine *Spare Rib*, and it should be said that there were other, more formalized women's pressure groups reinvigorated or inspired by the WLM: three hundred bodies responded to the Conservative government's consultative document "Equal Opportunities for Men and Women," published in 1973, including the Fawcett Society, Women in the Media, the National Council of Civil Liberties, and the National Joint Council of Working Women's Organisations.[29] After Labour returned to power in 1974, there was a major campaign in Parliament against sex discrimination, as women from both sides of the House as well as these outside groups testified to a newly powerful women's lobby. Yet the WLM generally distinguished itself from such groups.

The WLM did include organized lobbying, but unevenly. Ellen Malos, a Bristol activist with a background of Communist Party organizing, remembers speaking at a Church of England women's society lunch, when two artists from her WLM group, Pat Van Twest and Jackie Thrupp (notorious for wearing a shared hat), suddenly appeared in maids' outfits, flinging alphabet noodle soup letters about the room and declaring, "Eat your words!"[30] While Twest and others in the situationist Sistershow group are inspirational in their own way, Malos was clearly tired of such behaviour as a political strategy.[31]

Malos focused instead on characteristically grassroots social work, intellectual inquiry into domestic labour, and early Women's Studies teaching. Similarly, Harriet Harman at the National Council for Civil Liberties went from legal advisor in support of the Trico women's equal pay strike and Grunwick in 1976, to winning landmark cases under the Sex Discrimination Act (defending a woman firefighter, a part-time worker who had been laid off), to becoming the first "women's movement" MP in 1982, also the first pregnant sitting MP, and eventually the most senior feminist in any UK government as Deputy Leader of the Labour Party in 2007.[32] Harman sees herself as passionately "enlisted" in the women's movement. But she also sets herself apart from the radical feminists and their consciousness raising; she felt "uncomfortable sitting in a group discussing sex."[33]

Arguments about the movement's demands themselves were indicative, for although they provided (and still provide) focus, many found them reductive and redolent of the kind of hard-left politics the WLM was trying to escape. Rowbotham says the idea of having demands came from the Maoist Mr. Manchanda, "who we thought was a crashing bore, I'm afraid, at the time, because he was inclined to lecture us."[34] (He, Harpul Brar and his wife Maysel Brar, and another "officious" man were subsequently ejected at the Skegness conference by the Gay Liberation Front breakaway women's group, the moment the movement went "women-only.")[35] For many, the demands were not that important. Gail Chester comments: "The question is, who are you making those demands of? . . . The point is that all the demands up to that point [of the fifth] were demands of the *state*, and . . . I suppose that . . . what made me a radical feminist, in a way, was like, "Well, *actually*, you know, we, we need to make demands of *men*.'"[36]

Chester adds that "what I was fighting against then, intuitively, and what I would still fight against, is, as it were, the parliamentary road." Few from the autonomous movement were on that road at the time, but the divisions, particularly between socialist and radicals, certainly inhibited anyone who might want to be. Rosalind Delmar remembers Pat Thorne's struggle to interest anyone in an equal rights bill:

> During conferences, I would always go round and look and see how many people were attending which bit. . . . And her workshop was *always* tiny, and I thought it was *so* interesting that women were not interested in this kind of bill for Parliament or anything like that. . . . The

hot subjects were relationships with men and sexuality . . . [and] after Skegness, could men be a part of a women's liberation conference?"[37]

Activists were similarly ambivalent about engaging with the mainstream media. They were dismayed at the unnuanced press coverage of the Miss World protest, for example, though its visual spectacle still makes it one of the few tangible WLM stories. They subsequently had little to do with journalists, but actively tracked media sexism. A survey of national newspaper coverage reveals that in fact the conservative *Times* as well as the left-leaning *Guardian* gave largely positive coverage of the movement in the early years, though the populist-left *Daily Mirror* was hostile. But despite sympathetic headlines such as "Let's face it. A housewife's job is bloody awful" to a raft of 1975 coverage pegged onto the Sex Discrimination Act, the narrative increasingly framed the story as "good reformers versus bad revolutionaries."[38] The WLM's refusal to try to control such frames, in contrast to lobby groups such as Women in Media (chaired by Mary Stott of the *Guardian*) again came at a political price.[39]

Oral history, even with its documentary limits, supports the thesis that the WLM's ideas and cultures were its key contribution, while the Labour Party and the trade unions developed the organized women's movement. WLM literature spanned agitprop to Barbara Burford's *The Threshing Floor*, coolly conceptual Mary Kelly's *Post-Partum Document* to Jacky Fleming's cartoon feminist girl (outsize hair bow, naughty smile), and *Spare Rib*, launched in 1973 as the WLM's answer to *Cosmopolitan* and *Ms*.[40] An inspirational grassroots intelligentsia spread ideas through extramural adult education networks in the face of resistant British universities (far more closed at the time than in the United States).[41] *Red Rag, Feminist Review, Trouble & Strife, Women's Review, Outwrite*, and *FOWAAD*, and the array of feminist presses and radical bookshops were activist hubs.[42]

The WLM's cultural activism also tackled prejudices and fears, particularly about lesbian visibility, just as US feminist-inspired lesbians challenged the National Organization for Women (NOW)'s view that "the lavender menace" would threaten mainstream acceptance. While lesbians certainly had to fight the case within as well as without, the WLM clearly emerged on their side, first when the stigma of lesbianism was used to discredit Women's Aid, and again when the first "out" lesbian MP, Maureen Colquhoun, was asked in 1980 to leave the platform at the launch of an all-party campaign for 50 percent representation of women in Parliament.[43]

Yet even within the WLM proper, "experience" as the basis for political knowledge was more complex than is sometimes admitted. Oral histories are most revealing on the subject of consciousness raising (CR), a method of political education through sharing experiences in small groups. CR was "the backbone of the Women's Liberation Movement," claimed one popular flyer inspired by American Kathie Sarachild and distributed by Gail Chester.[44] Wandor's account, published in her pioneering collection of early movement writings, *The Body Politic* (1971), gives a beautiful picture of how CR worked in theory:

> The pattern of development within the small group is that the more you discuss and analyse, the more appears to be discussed. Gradually a complex and comprehensive picture of social and political structures builds up, in which, as you constantly refer back to your own life and experiences, a basic tension and interaction appear: that between the individual life and the collective life of the society. Because women have been caught between the two—expected to embody as individuals collective political and psychological images (in paid work to support industry as a collectively underpaid and exploited group, and in the family to contain and transmit youth, love, comfort and sex), we have a basic comprehension of the way our lives are fragmented and isolated. But perhaps because women rather than men have become symbols of emotional qualities, we have lost touch with our internal selves.[45]

Many women still contend that CR was a revolutionary method for "releasing themselves from 'the inner and outer bondages,'" drawing together women across classes in mutual political education—much as Susie Orbach argued in her "Fat Is a Feminist Issue" workshops.[46] But for others, CR was a luxury for a movement that had not yet discovered the more urgent needs of those facing direct discrimination or poverty. Others simply found CR socially awkward. Sandie Wyles, a youth worker in Aberdeen, described it alongside "taking your clothes off, face painting, jewelry making, dancing in the rain, hugging trees . . . writing poetry about menstruation, about their wombs"—the activity of "middle-class Edinburgh women," even as she "saw the point of it, I suppose."[47]

Listening to these accounts, the question is how women see the developmental nature of both movements and individuals and what they considered the movement to be for. Delmar remembers that "there were great chunks of the movement ... not at all interested in consciousness raising."[48] But she was deeply committed, since she enjoyed an intellectual group and was working to become a psychoanalyst. Jalna Hanmer, however, was clearly bored as a seasoned activist interested in practical policy change, joining simply because it was "the only way to get into the movement" in London.[49] Even Wandor herself, a member of the Belsize group, said that although initially it was "fantastically helpful,"

> there was also a point where I just thought, "I can't go on doing the same thing week after week." The thing about consciousness raising is that the initial discovery of other women's experiences in the group was exciting and it was revelatory, but there then comes a point where it becomes like a way of being. And it wasn't that I stopped wanting to complain about things, but it begins also to become collusive and the group begins to set up its own dynamic.... And I probably talked too much! [laughs] ... Oh, at one point we talked about being a campaigning group because, you know, with small children at school the idea of having after-school activities and using school premises seemed like a very good one. So ... I was quite keen to campaign for that. But there weren't enough, I think one other woman had an au pair, there just didn't seem to be enough enthusiasm from the other mothers in the group.... And after a bit I, I just ... dropped out, really, and one or two other people dropped out. And then the group continued—some of them, I think, still meet fairly regularly.[50]

Nadira Mirza, an activist working to support British Asian Muslim women at the University of Bradford in the 2000s, tellingly situates CR at a particular historical moment but recognizes the parallels between CR and subsequent programmes designed to build young women's confidence:

> Consciousness raising! I haven't heard that term mentioned for a *long* time. But I think we consciously used to do that in the seventies, eighties, and very early nineties. And there was quite a lot of public funding available to run programmes specifically for women and young women. And I actually developed some education training programmes around that, and I think—I could probably say now that a lot of my work with students at the university involves some consciousness raising, because we talked yesterday about ... different types of *confidence* in young women and how that's ... impacting on

behaviour.... I think some education programmes in higher education are consciously doing that, but it's very much seen now in the sector by other educationalists, academics, as being slightly passé.[51]

CR could be useful for those new to politics.[52] Equally, some of our interviewees use it today to explore the contradictions of old age, though groups have long been closed to newcomers and are as much about friendship as anything else. Our oral histories show tension between self-discovery and campaigning, political youth and maturation. This tension was paralleled by divisions in priorities. Younger women focused on questions of separation, individuation, and sexual autonomy, while questions of time and pay dominated for women who had children. The media seemed the obvious target for the former, the law and the unions for the latter. Many activists were in an intense process of identity making, but CR was less interesting for those who were joining the movement as older, already experienced activists, like Hanmer, James, Malos, and Mitchell. The latter sometimes used CR more as a debating group or a campaigning cell. This is not to dismiss the contribution of youth—it was mental youthfulness that allowed so many to question the status quo and, in particular, the expected life course of heterosexual marriage and motherhood. Nevertheless, these memories point out the complex relationship of experience to activism, its change as women grew politically older, and how far a group could stretch to campaigning for others once its own needs were satisfied.

All social movements go through these processes: they spark, grow, consolidate, and then make decisions about maintenance versus recruiting, lobbying versus integrating.[53] Concepts of cycles, waves, or campaigns all attempt to explain periods of intensified protest, and a recurrent dynamic of ebb and flow in collective mobilization.[54] As movements demonstrate authorities' vulnerability, they lower the cost of collective action for other people and also provoke countermobilization. To accept that social movements have their own life course suggests that whether a movement succeeds or fails, it eventually dissolves. A movement's core cannot survive institutionalization, even though this may be an objective.

The National Abortion Campaign in the Winter of Discontent

Although early 1979 is remembered largely for dispiriting clashes between unions and the Labour government, helping to pave Thatcher's election victory in May, at the same time a different political battle was unfolding over women's bodies. Conservative MP John Corrie presented a Private Member's Bill to drastically restrict the availability of abortion, challenging the 1967 Abortion Act, which had largely legalized it.[55] In reaction, the feminist National Abortion Campaign (NAC) sought allies in the wider Labour movement to stage one of the WLM's most successful campaigns, culminating in the bill's defeat in 1980.[56] The NAC worked locally and nationally, picketing the offices of health authorities in areas where abortions were difficult to obtain, holding conferences, pressuring union branches, and working with the broad-based Committee in Defence of the 1967 Act (known as Co-Ord) to lobby across the political parties and medical associations. When the Corrie Bill passed its second reading in the House of Commons by a large majority, the NAC organized a rally and immediately launched the Campaign Against the Corrie Bill.[57] Crucially, it also worked with the Trades Union Congress (TUC) to mobilize a march on October 31 of some 100,000 people.[58] According to *Spare Rib*, this "was the largest trade union demonstration ever held for a cause which lay beyond the traditional scope of collective bargaining; it was also the biggest ever pro-abortion march."[59]

The feminist-led defence of abortion intriguingly challenges conventional accounts of a political period that focus on economic crises and the welfare state.[60] In itself, the TUC's support of reproductive rights transforms the right-wing narrative of unions driven only by irresponsible, self-interested pay claims.[61] Indeed, the unions were in the process of being transformed by women's and black rights groups, notably with a breakthrough TUC Working Women's Charter in 1974 whose demands repeated those of the WLM.[62] Here the initiatives of feminist doctors in the British Medical Association, and of Terry Marsland, deputy secretary of the Tobacco Workers' Union, who had previously worked as a dinner lady preparing meals for schoolchildren, had resulted in the first pro-abortion resolution at the TUC conference in 1975.[63] In hindsight, 1979 represents a significant milestone in a new alliance between the masculinist Left and the new, autonomous feminism, forged over the issue of abortion.[64]

This breakthrough came when the national mood was much less certain, at least as represented in the media, Parliament, and medical bodies.[65] Although it did not altogether back Corrie, the *Daily Mail*, a conservative, middle-brow paper known for its "women's interests," featured stories of aborted fetuses "fighting for life" and the moral dangers of new "quickie" abortions in private clinics. There was public anxiety about a "surge" in abortions following the 1967 Act, with Conservatives worrying about new sexual promiscuity, particularly among young unmarried women, who had gained free access to the Pill. Parliament, for example, seemed to have significantly underestimated the potential demand for abortion, expecting to see 10,000 procedures per year; by 1973, there were 169,362.[66]

All of this reflected concerns about teenage sexuality. The *Times*'s medical correspondent in 1978 dubbed teenage pregnancies "the problem that will not go away," noting that thirty thousand babies were born to unmarried teenage mothers in 1977, with twenty-eight thousand teenage abortions (thirty-five thousand by 1979). His answer lay in sex education and birth control.[67] Some believed young women were treating abortion as a quick and easy form of birth control, a viewpoint refuted by feminists such as Jan McKenley, who became a NAC national coordinator in 1979. McKenley's own story is one of sexual inexperience, an interpretation confirmed by one 1972 study, "Abortion and Contraception: A Study of Patients' Attitudes."[68] Whatever the truth, more women were having more sex, and by 1979 the average (median) age at first heterosexual intercourse for women was eighteen, three years lower than in the early 1950s. Virginity before marriage was becoming largely less relevant. More people having more sex meant there were more chances of contraception failure; it was simply a matter of arithmetic.[69]

Feminists struggled to reshape the debate by appealing to a principle of women's bodily autonomy. Even the alliance with the TUC was by no means easy. Anna Coote and Beatrix Campbell's analysis in 1980, as with many in the WLM at the time, was that they had little to thank the unions for, and that the October march was one of their *"few, major, tangible achievements for women"* [their emphasis].[70] Part of the problem was that though the TUC clearly supported the 1967 Abortion Act, it resisted the feminist policy of free abortion on demand, as did the Labour Party. The NAC demanded "a woman's right to choose," a much stronger demand than the TUC's "Keep it legal, keep it safe." The march itself was the scene of an angry clash; a few hundred radical feminists carrying the London Women's Liberation and Women's Aid banners delayed everyone as they argued that they, rather than the TUC General Secretary, Len Murray, should lead the procession. The NAC's efforts to mediate reflected its difficult position, too extreme for most of its affiliates (Co-Ord had nearly expelled it the previous November) but too moderate for parts of the women's movement.[71] The campaign was internally divided, as it tried to combine the foundational position of women's autonomy with the much narrower focus on defending the 1967 Act in an attempt to win over an apparently volatile public opinion.

The political pressure also affected the NAC's methods. Based at Gray's Inn Road near London's Kings Cross, a large ramshackle activist hub, the campaign generally followed the WLM's fierce principle of decentralized and autonomous local groups, including separate chapters in Scotland and Wales.[72] McKenley's memory of her appointment on a one-year, minimum-wage job-share captures its voluntarist and collectivist ethos.[73] She saw the work as an "active gift," driven by her personal experience of an unfortunate pregnancy. Aged twenty-two, a recent graduate of Essex University, involved in black politics and punk, she remembers

> looking in the mirror at the clinic in Brighton and saying it was *never going to happen to me again* and that . . . something so *profound* had happened from being so *frivolous* that I was going to kind of *wake up*.[74] . . . And through that I joined the National Abortion Campaign and . . . that was the year I became a feminist through my own experience. And within the year I was its part-time coordinator.[75]

Yet others claimed the NAC was losing touch with its WLM roots. Sheila Rowbotham, not known for intemperate views, said, "We found it difficult

National Abortion Campaign coordinator Jan McKenley (fist raised, left) leads the singing at the NAC march in 1979. McKenley saw the work as an "active gift," driven by personal experience of an unwanted pregnancy and termination. *Photo courtesy of Steve Sklair*

to carry over the experience of the women's movement in discussing abortion in relation to our personal experience of our sexuality, our relationships, our attitudes to having children, or childcare.... [We] could not make these connections in relation to the National Campaign for Abortion."[76]

The relationship between experience and activism was thus tested—but here, nine years after the Miss World protest and the night cleaners' campaign—and the NAC was in a difficult position, given the highly emotive politics of abortion. On the one hand, there was the inchoate public "opinion," as far as it could be understood in the press and the media. Then there was the bittersweet experience of working with the unions and allies in Parliament. It also faced an organized opposition that occupied the emotional high ground in the Society for the Protection of Unborn Children (SPUC). Formed in 1966 to oppose the moves to legalize abortion, SPUC and a splinter group, LIFE, worked with MPs throughout the 1970s, trying four times to repeal the 1967 Act or restrict abortion to the truly "deserving." Indeed, the Corrie Bill had been drafted by Sir George Crozier, the chairman of the pro-life coordinating committee. It had a clear strategic aim, and its methods were highly "expressive."[77] Michael Litchfield and Susan Kentish's 1974 book *Babies for Burning* was one example of grisly, mostly false, stories of aborted babies crying, recycled in the *News of the World* and *Daily Mail*.[78] Such coverage undoubtedly influenced MPs and stoked the debate in the run-up to Thatcher's 1979 election victory.[79] In contrast, NAC feminists stuck to a rationalist approach.

Such currents coalesced at an emotional public meeting at the end of 1979, during which women shared their abortion experiences in a way that campaigns—and apparently CR—had not allowed. McKenley described it as a cathartic turning point, not only personally but also for the WLM; she cried desperately. Talking about women testifying to sadness, guilt, loss, and shame as well as relief, she highlights complexities not captured by headlines such as "Abortion on Demand—A Woman's Right to Choose" and "Our Bodies, Our Lives, Our Right to Decide," still less the "potty [daft] slogans" that Polly Toynbee remembered of women chanting, "When do we want it? Now!"[80] Later McKenley wrote to a friend about hearing a child "screaming," a grief exacerbated by her fear she would not be able to get pregnant later. All of this suggested that the reality of choosing oneself as a woman over another life could be agonizing. Abortion was not any old choice, but a solution when motherhood was too hard or unappealing, and where men dodged responsibility for contraception.

It seems that despite clichés of the women's movement's emotional style, public sharing of emotion was uneven. In fact, sharing of *feelings about feelings* was sometimes a more accurate description of what happened. Feminists had to guard against appearing overly emotional about political demands, especially abortion. In addition, internal ideological objections controlled emotional practice. Indeed, 1979 was the year when a new constituency of lesbian feminism, the Leeds Revolutionary Feminists, first lobbed its infamous "Political Lesbianism: The Case Against Heterosexuality" paper at a movement already uncertain as to the emotional case for heterosexuality. Chiefly inspired by Sheila Jeffreys, this paper had nothing to say about abortion, seeing it as a mere consequence of penetration, a "tedious/dangerous form of contraception."[81] Also inhibiting were Marxist arguments on the individualism of emotional discussion or therapy and the greater priority of materialist struggle.[82] Though longstanding, these arguments were rejuvenated by black and working-class activists throughout the 1970s.[83] The 1979 agenda of the London-based United Black Women's Action Group gives a sense of the competing priorities, as set out in *Spare Rib*: housing, education, employment, and police mistreatment of black youth.[84]

The emotional public meeting McKenley attended took place a month or so after the Revolutionary Feminist "Love Your Enemy" conference. Gail Lewis was there as well as McKenley, and offers a bravely reflexive account of the deep feelings involved, with a different emphasis from McKenley's, though they were both black women willing (sometimes) to work with the white-centred women's movement. A charismatic founding member of the Brixton Black Women's Group, Lewis describes feeling uncomfortable and angry, and challenging the white organizers, including *Spare Rib* editors, for an agenda that did not address the testing of the contraceptive Depo-Provera, the right to have children, and other issues of reproductive control pertinent to poor, black women. "Feeling," as she smilingly narrates it for S&A, "was petit-bourgeois indulgence." She mentions also that she was never in a CR group.[85] This was little different from the position expressed in the first widely circulated statement of black women's liberation in the United Kingdom in 1971 by the Black Women's Action Committee of the Marxist-Maoist Black Unity and Freedom Party.[86] Though this statement provided an important defence of black women's right both to contraception and to fertility, it also defined consciousness as something to be attained through new institutions and common struggles, far from feelings.[87]

Emotional performances did not capture, or fully repress, more personal emotions about self, body, opportunity, and status. Lewis now says that she has completely changed her mind and has qualified in psychodynamic psychotherapy. She chuckles at her former self, asking, "What was I defending against? Well, we won't go there now." She comments that what she now wants to know is this: What "is in excess, what does the focus on structure not encompass, leave out?" She muses, "Even then, I think, there was a miniature person wondering this."[88] What indeed was Lewis, and many others, defending against? One answer is power and position within the new feminist scenes. But Lewis's question suggests that feelings of status and belonging were not the only "excess."

Indeed, perhaps it was precisely feelings about sex and reproduction and race that she found intolerable, particularly in a setting that would have been all too familiarly white-dominated, despite McKenley's presence. Lewis's writings and S&A account reveal what she perhaps could not say then, that her white mother was ashamed of her black daughter, yet attracted to black men; that her mother's seven illegal abortions reflected her wish not to bring more children into poverty and racism; that her mother did not want to have more children with violent partners she both loved and hated.[89] She remembers her mother's empathy when she herself had an abortion, at age eighteen, in 1969. Lewis agreed with her mother that she would ruin her life having children at such a young age, but retains a "what if?" today.[90] Suzanne Scafe, who with Stella Dadzie and Beverley Bryan produced one of the most respected books of the autonomous black women's movement, *Heart of the Race* (1985), reflected:

> Some, though not all, that is missing from the book is the personal dimension, a category we defined as "Self-consciousness: Understanding our Culture and Identity." The title of the chapter is telling in its omission of a "self" and the use of "our," and I think it's interesting that some of those omissions are addressed by the women who have contributed to the S&A project. In the years that Gail Lewis and I were in the Brixton Black Women's Group, I had never heard her talk in personal terms about her mother, and indeed I don't suppose I ever spoke about mine, though we all spoke about our mothers' cultural and public roles, as employees, as migrants, as women who held families together.[91]

Kirsten Hearn's portrait of confrontational meetings between Sisters Against Disablement (SAD) and the NAC in the early 1980s also illuminates the "mood work" that abortion rights evoked. A militant for disabled rights, Hearn called for able-bodied women to be less "afraid of the anti-abortionists'... emotional kind of arguments" and admit that sometimes they were having abortions simply because it was inconvenient to have a child at that time, or that they did not want a disabled child. Indeed, SAD's tactics were to argue "in a very unemotional *but* emotional way." As Hearn puts it:

> In the end I would find myself standing up at National Abortion Campaign meetings and going, "You're talking about killing babies, or killing fetuses or ending fetuses who might grow up to be someone like me." [short laugh] And whilst that's true, it's a rather hard way to do it.... I think we made our point. And I think... that our intervention helped the National Abortion Campaign be a bit *clearer* about their ethics around what they were advocating, actually. And in the end *I* think it actually really helped them take on the crap that was coming from, you know, the pro-lifers...[92]

Hearn suggests this "hard" challenge to simplistic feminist demands for "abortion on demand" reclaimed some of the ground that SPUC controlled in dealing with the unglamorous realities involved in reproductive choice. Yet how far could it encompass disabled women's own emotional ambivalences? In her S&A oral history, this account is entwined with a more fulsome story of growing up as a twin, losing her sight, with a mother who had to abandon her ambitions to be a doctor because of her children's needs. Inevitably this offers a much softer picture as to Hearn's own eventual decision not to have children.[93]

Such memories can undermine McKenley's optimism that, for a moment, abortion rights cut across differences of race and class, uniting older with newer women's movements—though clearly in contrast to many feminist demands, they *did* constitute one of the few issues capable of rallying mainstream support and were an important unifier in the Irish WLM (North and South).[94] But on another level, they support her different argument that the movement was beginning to mature emotionally:

> When we were active in the seventies... feelings were considered to be *indulgences*... they were considered to be areas that would make you weak, not strong. And that's come to be [seen], through the seventies, eighties, nineties, [as] not a strong position. You are strongest when you understand your own weaknesses and your own fears, and I think... much of the... fundamentalism was out of *fear* and a fear of change and... not really being clear what it would mean to change, what change would mean and all the relationships would have to

change, not just somebody else's set of relationships, *your* relationships would have to change.[95]

McKenley is surely right that "feelings around abortion, pregnancy and fertility get more complex and deep as you get older."[96] She situates her own abortion in this light, where her sexual relationships as a young woman reflected her protest against her Jamaican immigrant working-class parents' limited opportunities and her mother's conservative morality. Even as she berated herself for having conceived pregnant through something so "frivolous," she conveys a life-long sense of responsibility to family and community. This is expressed in her later work as an inspector for Ofsted, the body that inspects and regulates schools and services that care for young people, trying to improve education for black children. McKenley spoke later of her joy in becoming a mother; she never regretted, or abandoned, her profound commitments to "a woman's right to choose."

Behind these discussions, therefore, lay a different, more complex set of feelings. These were not always admitted or even understood at the time, but their operation was not necessarily destructive. In the long view, the turbulent feminist self-exploration did more than protect women's right to choose. Even as activists managed their conflicted reactions, it explored the dramatic social and psychological consequences of controlled reproduction in ways that the mainstream evaded. This dynamic is apparent in the development of advice on "feelings about unwanted pregnancy" for the 1978 British edition of *Our Bodies, Ourselves*, written in part by Angela Phillips, who worked at the NAC alongside McKenley.[97]

Feminist "mood work" is also captured in Zoë Fairbairns's striking science fiction novel of 1979, *Benefits*. Published by the feminist press Virago and set in a future of decaying tower blocks full of squatters, not dissimilar to the United Kingdom at the time, it was based in part on Fairbairns's experiences volunteering for an "abortion charity" in London, in which she "listened to women who felt unable, because of poverty, to continue their pregnancies."[98] As a gender- rather than class-framed dystopia, "the dying welfare state" of an imagined post-1984 United Kingdom poisons the water with fertility drugs and uses the welfare benefit system to punish rebellious women through its political "Family" party.[99] The feminist journalist-protagonist becomes pregnant unexpectedly, delighting her sympathetic "new man" husband but causing deep ambivalence for her, heightened when the child is born with a chronic illness. As with all the novel's characters, the child is somewhat manipulative, neither victim nor heroine. Fairbairns's novel captures a profound psychocultural shock at the recognition that maternity is passing from instinct to conscious choice, along with other feminist novels of the time.[100] Yet it also looks at where women cannot and may never be able to choose, and how a feminist community can only respond imperfectly to forces that include biology, the state, big business, but also love, mortality, stupidity, and pride.

Even as the national WLM conference of 1978 combusted into bitter divisions over sexuality, 1979 proved an extraordinarily creative year for feminist activism.[101] The NAC's work to defend the 1967 Abortion Act, with the TUC and others, marked a breakthrough in understanding how gender and class interests could align. But the winter of women's discontent was also a renewal in diversity, ironically galvanized by Thatcher's election. The lesbian feminism that upset the NAC's mainstreaming attempts fed an antiviolence movement that was highly influential in the 1980s; liberal feminist initiatives included the beginnings of the anti–nuclear war protest that led to Greenham and ongoing equal opportunities activism; socialist feminists responded to the new challenge of Thatcherism by joining the Labour Party and initiatives such as Rowbotham, Lynne Segal, and Hilary Wainwright's *Beyond the Fragments*.[102] 1979 also saw the formation of Southall Black Sisters and the first national conference of the Organization of Women of Asian and African Descent (OWAAD), as well as the first black women's centre in the United Kingdom, Mary Seacole House, founded in Brixton three months later.[103] Pertinently, a high-profile and successful sit-in at Heathrow Airport against the "virginity test" examinations of Asian women arriving to meet their fiancés built a broader and subtler understanding of reproductive rights beyond the question of abortion.[104]

Just as creatively, Belfast Women's Collective engineered a surprising coalition of dissident Nationalists and Unionists to help them send every MP a package containing a coat hanger strung with a mimeographed British Airways ticket and the message "These are the two ways women in Northern Ireland can get abortions." Marie-Thérèse McGivern explains that they secured the support of the speaker of the House of Commons, George Thomas, but the campaign still failed because they would not "force legislation on Northern Ireland." But, she said, "I don't believe it is wasted energy; it was *hugely* important to do it at that time, but you don't win all campaigns."[105] Despite the peculiar pressures involved in the politics of the NAC, it helps to challenge the racial, sexual, and national biases of a narrative that holds that 1979 saw the end of the British WLM.[106]

The question remains as to whether there was a broader public change of mood about abortion, and more generally about everyday life in the United

Kingdom (excluding Northern Ireland). According to opinion sampling, the conventional approach to measuring mood, the public has remained supportive of the abortion rights set out in the 1967 Abortion Act, although it has never come close to endorsing a fully feminist position of abortion on demand: the NatCen social research agency found that in 1983 just 37 percent endorsed what might be regarded as a women's right to choose.[107] Yet equally, and in contrast to the United States, the public has resisted SPUC's demands as well. Perhaps for this reason, MPs did not back the Corrie Bill, nor was Thatcher prepared to commit government time. Although she voted for the second reading of the bill in July 1979, she only supported its more modest parts, which would have allowed medical staff to "conscientiously object" and reduce the time limit from twenty-eight to twenty-four weeks. So too did the *Daily Mail* reject Corrie's much more radical proposal that abortions would only be permissible where the mother's life was at "grave risk."

Perhaps the dissociation of sex from reproduction and marriage proved too useful to the leisure and consumer industry to be curbed, not to mention the sheer pleasure it offered to men, perhaps more even than women.[108] Along these lines, the Revolutionary Feminist had argued that abortion rights are a very weak challenge to patriarchy. An alternative explanation is that the endurance of abortion rights in Britain lies not so much in the power and interests of men pursuing "free" sex, so much as a more comprehensive influence of New Right ideologies of liberalization and choice, combined with the need to push women into the workplace.[109] Consider the disappearance of the 1950s and 1960s dramas about backstreet abortions (especially 1968's *Up the Junction*), replaced not so much by tales of abortion as a choice—that was still too difficult—but by *The Joy of Sex* (1972), an instant bestseller; *Cosmopolitan* (UK launch, 1972); the *Sun*'s "Page 3" (featuring a daily photo of a topless woman; started in 1970); and the first British porn boom.[110] 1979 itself saw the opening of the first official nudist beach in Britain; the YMCA suing the Village People for "gay-ifying" its reputation with their hit song "YMCA"; the US television show *Dallas*; and disco queen Donna Summer. Fringe right-wing groups captured the fears of those who could only see their place and power threatened by Mary Whitehouse's "rising tide of filth": the SPUC comprised not only older white Christian men but women who had given their own lives to an identity and "job" as mother.

Feminist protest, on the other hand, can be read as a dissident and radical version of a mood in which both men and women associated reproductive choice with freedom and autonomy. This insight may be one of the enduring contributions of the WLM, as much as the brilliance at gaining support from the doctors and the enduring political coalition between feminists and the Left.[111] Its perceptions made a minority movement become meaningful for the majority.[112] The Labour MP at the forefront of defending the Abortion Act, Jo Richardson, compared her revelation about sexual politics to having a cataract removed.[113] The *Daily Mail*'s editorial in July 1979 concluded, "The members of Britain's Parliament—the overwhelming majority of whom are men—must endeavour to penetrate beyond the organized and sincere passion of the pro- and anti-abortion lobbies and try to evaluate for themselves the profound complexity of feeling that moves so many women these days when this sad debate is raging."[114]

The passion of the two lobbies betrays hidden structures of feeling.[115] On one side, the anti-abortion portraits of extreme vulnerability and mortality in the iconic dying fetus spoke to a longing for innocence and safety in a world of threatening change and new choice. On the other side, the debate over the deeper feelings within the women's movement stirred by the fight to defend and extend abortion rights brought out an unglamorous but terribly realistic ambivalence about what choice over fertility meant and felt like, the adult responsibilities of allowing women as much as men the burden of free will, and the difficulty of making the absolutely "right" choice.

Women's Aid in Northern Ireland: Karen McMinn's Story

The WLM's campaign to protect abortion rights remains an enormous achievement; even more so has been the movement to protect women against violence, and the Women's Aid organization that came out of it. Karen McMinn's work as coordinator for Women's Aid Northern Ireland illustrates how this campaign took root amid militarized violence, yet managed to create a network that could contain, support, or spin off such very different groups in the four UK nations, in white, Asian, Black, Jewish communities, and for men (cis and now trans) who were victims of violence, too. The history of Women's Aid also charts the move from autonomous to state-funded organization, and the ideological dimensions of how to interpret men's violence. In this effort, a politics of empathy and coalition, as much as experience, was needed. And this is something McMinn has in spades.

In Northern Ireland, the narrative of the grim 1970s holds, which perhaps explains the lyrical urgency of Derry punk group the Undertones' *Teenage Kicks*. The precious abortion rights that people lobbied to defend in England, Wales, and Scotland were still denied in a country dominated by conservative Christianity.[116] The divorce law of 1969, which for the first time allowed a "no-fault" basis for separation, did not apply in Northern Ireland until 1978, and contraception remained hard to access. These were just some expressions of the politicized religious state that exploded into sectarian strife in the late 1960s, heralding a period of escalating violence that peaked in 1972, the year that saw thirteen civilians shot dead by British soldiers in Derry on Bloody Sunday (a fourteenth later died of his injuries). The decade ended with a double attack on the same day in August 1979 by the Irish Republican Army against the British: Lord Mountbatten and members of his family were killed while on vacation in Mullaghmore, while eighteen British soldiers were killed by remote-controlled bombs at Warrenpoint. Things would not begin to improve until the first paramilitary ceasefires in 1994.

Karen McMinn grew up during these years. She was sixteen at the time of Bloody Sunday, perhaps busy at home helping her mother, a Protestant, brought up in a Protestant area of Belfast only a few streets away from Catholic neighbours. Both parents had come from poor farming families, though her father had set up a post office and shop after having endured military service in the Second World War, including as a prisoner of war. He died when she was six, leaving her mother to manage the business as well as four daughters. When asked in her interview about the Troubles, she says:

> I remember being in Northern Ireland during the [1980s] hunger strikes, and you just [softening voice] ... think what a lack of ... political skills in terms of the British Government's handling of that. And ... living in Northern Ireland was really tough, you know, it was like, the most *horrific* acts of violence perpetrated against ... individuals. ... whether, you know, ranging from Bloody Sunday, of course, to something like the Kingsmill massacres where, like, twelve workmen were just taken out of their, their work van on their way home and, you know, put up against the wall and, you know, mowed down. [pause] So, it was ... a place of ... great despair at times, because there was just ... all the clichés of ... people behaving in such an inhuman way to each other. And ... I suppose I felt very disempowered about how I could do anything to influence that. So ... that was another reason ... I chose to put my political effort and energy into supporting women, which was an area I ... was committed to, and I felt that actually *could* really change attitudes.[117]

McMinn's life changed when she discovered Women's Aid. She had already "moved away [from a] Unionist identity" at Queens University, where she had studied sociology. Temping as an A-level sociology teacher, she enjoyed political debates and considered going into social work. After a boyfriend told her about Audrey Middleton, founder of Northern Ireland Women's Aid, she went to a meeting in Belfast in 1977 without knowing what to expect. Immediately, she was attracted to the group's practicality and charmed by what was new for her then—women-only organizing. The refuge had been operating informally since 1976, in the way of Women's Aid at the time, moving into any available abandoned house, staff and residents living together, with no staff-only meetings. The concept, typical of the WLM, was that any woman could be the victim of violence and therefore mutual self-help, consciousness raising, and political as well as practical solutions were appropriate. But a fire in the refuge had prompted a focus on professionalization and safety, and it was in a huge renovated building (funded by the local government) that included a playroom and two kitchens that McMinn began to serve as a refuge worker in 1978, in her early twenties. She joined two other women and a volunteer group.

So began ten years' work, during which she became coordinator of Women's Aid Northern Ireland, in charge of four hostels, living and breathing the work. She spoke happily of early days of roundtable meetings of fifty women; the amazing solidarity between the women who came in overwhelming numbers in the first year, two families per room, thriving support groups and their own management of the building at night. After 1981, Women's Aid expanded to six or seven refuges with annual residential events of 120 women. A Women's Education Project in 1981 enabled residents to access adult education.[118]

Working across the sectarian divides was the question—although the way she tells it, this was not really a question but the starting point. There was "no political support for women's issues because power struggle between Unionists and Nationalists dominated political space." Repeating Eileen Evason's description for Northern Ireland at the time as an "armed patriarchy," McMinn goes further to say that men's access to weapons in the Troubles fuelled the problem, remembering trips into dangerous areas to pick up women wounded by armed husbands.[119]

The police were uninterested in domestic violence—"security" was their priority—and indeed would refuse to respond to women's calls in Nationalist areas for fear of ambushes. Nevertheless, Women's Aid was committed to working with the police, indeed seeing the imperative to educate and influence a macho force and brilliantly involving the refuge users to do so. Conversely, their policy was to ask each woman if she wanted police involvement (unsurprisingly, some did not); their priority was getting women into safe spaces and explaining their rights—which were few, if they left their husbands. She adds that a policewoman was herself once a resident.

While feminist theorists were wrestling with the conceptual question of what women really shared, the limits to notions of sisterhood were more than obvious in this scenario. Tension between feminist and Nationalist politics ran through all Northern Irish women's groups at the time.[120] McMinn explains how the refuge managed this, with a principle of taking women across sectarian divides—deliberately mixing residents—and of protecting Women's Aid's reputation as accessible to all women by avoiding public statements on divisive political issues, from jail protests to abortion. There was to be no formal discussion of the Nationalist question; women were accepted whatever their politics—and she emphasizes that women of all classes as well as religions used the refuge.

There were also positive expressions of this kind of coalition. The highest-profile one was the successful campaign for the release of Noreen Winchester, who was sentenced to seven years' imprisonment for killing her sexually abusive father in 1976. McMinn helped look after her children, and with many others from Women's Aid, including Sarah Nelson and Barbara Harvey, joined a rally, bravely held in Belfast city centre despite bomb threats, with the Belfast Women's Collective, Northern Ireland Women's Rights Movement, Women Against Imperialism, the Coleraine and Derry Women's Aid groups, and Women's Aid from England and Wales.[121] She remembers men showing support on the street, as well as the joy at Winchester's pardon—joy not only for the sense of justice, but the unity between women across such divides. Here she pays tribute to the Northern Ireland women's rights movement as equally committed to inclusive campaigns, such as childcare provision, and campaigning against public cuts.

Is violence against women a unifying issue? McMinn certainly thinks so, even as she adds that respect for Women's Aid helped, as did the close community in Belfast. Women's Aid has been instrumental in putting women's private trauma on the map—which was key to a feminist critique of the idealized family. Relating domestic violence to street or military violence has also been the means for getting women's rights recognized as human rights. The 1993 United Nations World Conference on Human Rights in Vienna was a key moment in promoting new understanding of the connections between masculinity and violence from rape in war to rape in marriage, and in December 1993 the United Nations General Assembly adopted the Declaration on the Elimination of Violence Against Women.

Karen McMinn (fist raised), coordinator of Women's Aid Northern Ireland, celebrates the news of a royal pardon for Noreen Winchester, who had been jailed in 1976 for killing her sexually abusive father. The protestors rallied in Belfast city centre despite a bomb scare—a serious threat given the scale of Northern Ireland's Troubles at that time. *Photo courtesy of Derek Speirs*

But in some ways male violence is too obvious a cause. Women can bond over the terribleness of men without any broader feminist platform, and indeed male violence can too easily join with a regressive view of programmed aggression that leaves no room for political change or gender fluidity. Activist Erin Pizzey, from whom Women's Aid split early on, talked problematically of abused women's "excitement" over violent relationships.[122] But clearly desire brings its own questions, while the image of the vulnerable abused woman is too quickly co-opted by patriarchal causes. McMinn stresses the practical. She comments that more women went back to partners than not—but refuges offer the means for temporary time out of a relationship. They disempowered men and, through that, educated some. And ultimately she argues that men are also vulnerable—something the Northern Ireland conflict makes plain. Here, she departs from some versions of radical feminism, which have little to say on men's own vulnerabilities to male violence. But her interview does not engage with the tension in Women's Aid, and radical feminism in general, between a "systemic analysis of domestic violence, on the one hand, and their uncompromising account of perpetrator responsibility on the other."[123]

Even by 1985, McMinn could comment in a piece she wrote for the Belfast political magazine *Fortnight* that "to many people, Women's Aid has become 'the acceptable face of feminism.'"[124] It is certainly striking to see that Women's Aid survives when so much else has not. The Crown Prosecution Service for England and Wales reported that the number of violent offences against women, including domestic abuse, rape, and sexual assaults, rose by almost 10 percent to a record high of 117,568 in 2015–16, while acknowledging that historical underreporting of offences such as stalking, domestic violence, rape, and sexual assaults meant that the number of cases being charged represented only a proportion of the offending taking place.[125] Women's Aid, today recognized as expert consultants, suggest women are becoming more confident in coming forward—violence against women inside the home is now clearly accepted as a crime rather than a domestic issue, and indeed psychological and online violence have now gained political recognition.

In contrast, the NAC spent fifteen years campaigning just to defend the 1967 Abortion Act, and it looks as if there has never been any chance of success in allowing abortions after perceived fetal viability.[126] It is not all bad: a 2017 survey by the social research institute NatCen showed that 70 percent of respondents supported abortions if the woman did not wish to have the child, almost double the percentage in the early 1980s.[127] But feminists, in obvious contrast to SPUC, still have to walk a delicate line between reason and emotion in their publicity. The lobbying group Abortion Rights, created in 2003 through the merger of NAC and the Abortion Law Reform Association as the national grassroots campaigning body, has as its key demands the extension of abortion rights to Northern Ireland and the removal of power from doctors as gatekeepers. The tone of their advice is coolly neutral and they avoid American pro-choice tactics in the 2010s of using "coming out" stories as campaign tools, keeping their case studies anonymous.[128] Abortion remains a litmus test for ideologies of gender relations but also questions over self, body, and life chance, in a time of even greater reproductive and gender choice, yet sexual pressure and social uncertainty. The success of the campaign led by Labour MP Stella Creasy to enable women from Northern

Ireland to get free abortions in England, a surprise consequence of the British government's weakened position after the June 2017 general election, will add to the complexity of the debate in Northern Ireland, where an ultimate decision on abortion law lies with the Northern Ireland Assembly.

Compared to "choosing" a woman's life over a (potential) baby's life, Women's Aid's message that women should not be abused by violent men is far easier to sell. But Women's Aid has another element that ensured its endurance: its willingness to work with institutions in a form of "professional radicalism."[129] Once the principle of crime was accepted, resources became available from the traditional structures of social work, charity, and policing, resources that can be used to maintain social control and manage the weak or disruptive. Women's Aid's ability to work within these structures is a remarkable example of a radical feminist group working largely within the state.[130] Today Women's Aid is a federated network of more than three hundred local projects and more than five hundred refuges in England, where local groups are autonomous but have a headquarters in Bristol. English, Scottish, and Welsh Women's Aid Federations are entirely autonomous but cooperate.

Is this because its message was acceptable enough for those doors to open? Or that it was canny enough to use the resources that were there? This was no simple or naïve negotiation, and often the move to "professionalism" was a painful one. McMinn remarks on the resistance of some women to shift from a democratic collective management structure to a more decision-focused, professional management in the mid-1980s, appointing team leaders, fundraising, and educating emergency medical personnel, lawyers, and police. An interesting comparison from the S&A interviews is Mukami McCrum's comment on a similar process for Shakti, a black women's refuge where she worked in Edinburgh in the 1980s: she flatly states that professionalizing was the only sensible thing to do to reward those who had been there for the long haul.[131]

McCrum was not atypical; many refused to take on explicitly "feminist" structures in wishing to develop "fair and equitable leadership."[132] Jane Hutt, who was coordinator of Welsh Women's Aid, considers that the group was the WLM's general opportunity for women to develop more professional managerial skills.[133] Hutt is today one of the most institutionally powerful feminists in Wales, and for a while finance minister in the devolved administration—so perhaps she would take this view. But though a "professional feminist" identity remained taboo for many British activists, Women's Aid helped show the way the wind was blowing.[134] As activists all over the United Kingdom soon discovered, Thatcher's government smashed the postwar consensus and ushered in a far harsher climate for social progressives. Local Labour politics provided a shelter—indeed, the saving grace for a plethora of social movements—and feminist municipalism became a major new strategy for the previously "autonomous" activists.

Sheila Gilmore (born in 1949) is a lawyer who was elected to the City of Edinburgh Council, served on its women's committee, and went on to be elected as Labour MP for Edinburgh East. She explains how Scottish feminism was little different in content in the 1970s to English feminism and, indeed, was largely indifferent to the (unsuccessful) 1979 referendum for Scottish devolution.[135] But the sense of distinct Scottish interests strongly grew in the 1980s, feeding into a distinct kind of feminism there, as Thatcher's government alienated the Scots, particularly by introducing in Scotland a new form of local taxation, the poll tax, a year earlier than in England and Wales.

And what of McMinn herself, in Northern Ireland? For her, the 1980s process of professionalization seemed not to faze so much as exhaust her. As she managed the expansion of services and refuges, her own life grew yet more different from her mother's and sisters'. Although they too benefited from a grammar school education, upward mobility, and professional jobs, they married, had children, and stayed out of politics. Why did McMinn take a different path? The women's movement mobilized more Catholics, she contends, since many Protestants believed that radical activism would be disloyal to the state. McMinn's motivation could be attributed to her mother's poverty or to her sense of women's challenges; but as she narrates it, it came as much from the personal liberation and political education she received at university. She tells a touching anecdote about going to a professor's party wearing a Laura Ashley dress, shares and remembers not telling her family about living with her boyfriend in the 1970s, which was unacceptable in Northern Ireland back then. But her years of work soon took her beyond her own struggles and joys. While she, as any feminist from the WLM, would utterly refute the terminology of charity, there is public service as well as political identification in her life story. In different terms, such service expresses the feminist ethics of care in addition to the ethics of justice, as a political principle.

And here, despite the idea of mutual self-help and CR, the question was how this worked personally when the job was mostly helping others. Out of the sixty S&A interviewees, only two disclosed domestic violence from a former partner of their own, but many knew of a member of the family who was abused, and the strong identifications they felt. McMinn did not. Rather, as she put it, she became aware of the meaning of power and its abuse all around her, and how understanding injustice was part of living a bigger life than running a post office. The problem comes when care for others comes into conflict with care for oneself. McMinn was depressed by the late 1980s. She felt she had not achieved an acceptable work–life balance, and, when asked about not having had children, remarks that "the political work does have a cost, can have a cost at times to your, to your personal life, and I think there's, there's probably a lot of women who, who, you know, have paid that cost in some, some way."[136] She had chosen not to have children in her twenties, concentrating on work and not wanting to end up a single mother, like her mother. She was single for much of the 1980s.

Her narrative makes plain how good it was to take a break, travel, and meet and marry her now husband, a Spaniard, who then settled in Belfast to run a restaurant, in her early forties. Acquiring two teenage stepsons brought new challenges, but she reflects on this as a new form of care and family, along with the "family" she gained in Women's Aid. Revealingly, she reflects that "where you become so [pause] entrenched in the collective, and . . . you begin to feel that you're indispensable, which of course, it's, you know, not true. [smiling voice] You know, everybody is . . . dispensable in, in some way. But then, you know, you begin to have a sense of your own self-importance within your role or your work, and, you know, that level of dependency, you know, can, can play out in a very negative way."[137]

Although the campaign against domestic violence showed some of the "genius" of radical feminism in its insistence that women were not so much victims as survivors, its ideal of self-help and autonomy for activists who make their lives on this principle can be extremely demanding:

> I think in the end that's part of what happened for me, but, you know, that there's great *learning* in that as well. So, you know, I'm in a stage in my life where I'm, I'm *very, very* lucky to be able to say I'm . . . *content* with my life, and, and, you know, very lucky, you know, to have had the experiences that I've had.[138]

The campaign family can falter, just as can marriage, family, and state care. Yet just as quickly, she returns to her sense of privilege. It is no accident that McMinn went on to work in conflict resolution, as have many S&A interviewees. Liberation, personal as well as political, remains an ongoing quest. But there is no doubt that women's activism over the 1970s, in its methods, ideas, and cultures, changed the political agenda for good.

5 GUILTY PLEASURES? FEMINISM AND EVERYDAY LIFE IN THE 1980s

Judy Chicago's "The Dinner Party," hosted in Edinburgh's Victoria Hall in 1984, was an epic feast, for 1,038 guests.[1] In its first European showing, this legendary artwork of the US women's movement featured a triangular trestle table dressed for diners who included Sappho, Boudicca, Sojourner Truth, and Virginia Woolf. Chicago had decorated ceramic plates with vulvar butterfly designs. The banquet was to be followed by sexy dancing. Thousands saw the piece in Edinburgh and then in London, with much critical as well as delighted discussion, but one element remains unconsidered: What was on the menu?

Cooking is only one element of an uncharted history of feminist everyday life. Little is known of the habits and homes of feminists. As Ann Oakley theorized in 1974, housewifery was the most alienating form of work under capitalism—monotonous, fragmented, isolated, unpaid.[2] Yet having a comfortable, secure home, even doing the housework, can offer unique pleasures. If feminists start by saying that everyday life needs to be transformed, it is also obvious that home can be a domain of retreat and renewal.[3] In the United Kingdom of the 1980s, this puzzle was exacerbated by the New Right's ideologies of privatization, including in the housing sector of home ownership as the goal to strive for. Ask UK feminists what characterizes the decade, and they will quickly talk about Greenham Common, the murder in 1981 of thirteen young black partygoers in the New Cross fire, black uprisings, the miners' strike, the Cold War, war in 1982 with Argentina over control of the Falkland Islands in the south Atlantic, anti-apartheid demonstrations, AIDS, and Section 28 of the Local Government Act 1988, in which the government prohibited the "promotion" of homosexuality. Depressing times and, in their bitter way, galvanizing. But push the conversation a bit, and they might talk about relationships, home life, and guilty pleasures. Such conversations are equally revealing about what happened to the WLM in the reign of Thatcher.

With almost no money for offices and a powerful commitment to decentralization, activists turned their houses into spaces in which to organize and to experiment with new forms of domestic life. At the same time, women's attachment to their homes tested some of the simpler feminist arguments about equality and collectivity, showing the need to develop feminist ideas of privacy as time went on. Similarly, shopping choices and leisure habits can also tell us about changing preferences as WLM generations hit their middle years and navigated expected rites of passage, which, by the 1980s, included career, home ownership, childbirth, family, health, and beauty. Yet while questions of lifestyle remained fraught for activists dedicated to socialist as well as feminist and antiracist ethics, the story of Barbara Jones offers an unusual yet inspiring solution. Her quest for radical new ways to live saw her join Women and Manual Trades, a body supporting women to develop careers in the building industry, and become one of the few women builders in the United Kingdom. Her life as the owner of an eco-building business in the lesbian-friendly market town of Todmorden in Yorkshire illuminates the need to rethink production as well as consumption to fulfil WLM's high ideals.

These aspects of everyday life offer clues to the fun and comforts of feminism, in regeneration at home and through play, as well as its anxiety, anger, and shame.

Where and How We Lived: Owning, Renting, and Sharing

Houses for activists in a social movement are far more than places in which to live and recuperate. For feminists with typically few resources, they are places for planning, consciousness raising, or even action, such as when women collectively confront violent men. It was at Lynne Segal's rambling Victorian house in Islington in north London, around the corner from Mary McIntosh's, that the occupation of the post office in Trafalgar Square in 1972 was planned. They were demanding that family allowance, a social security payment to help with childcare costs, should be paid directly to mothers rather than as a tax deduction for a husband (achieved when the Labour government brought in the Child Benefit Act 1975).[4] Close by, the notorious Grosvenor Avenue collective housed Jo Robinson, Sue Finch, and Sarah Wilson, among others, who were central to the Miss World protest in 1970. All the children there were given the last name Wild, avoiding patrilineal markers.[5] Virago Books began in Carmen Callil's house.⁶ Val Hart's home became a meeting place to help sustain the first Birmingham WLM group; Al Garthwaite's did the same for a WLM group in Leeds.⁷ The hubs of the black women's movement included Carol Leeming's and Donna Jackman's houses for Leicester Black Sisters, where the Ajani Centre was planned; Abina Likoya's was at the heart of the Manchester-based Abasindi Pan-African Drummers and Dancers.⁸ In London, in addition to legendary shared houses in Brixton and Haringey, Jocelyn Wolfe's flat (apartment) in west London and Ama Gueye's in the East End brought activists together.⁹ In Belfast, Bronagh Hinds turned her living room into a nursery: it became a "rent-a-crèche" for the Northern Ireland Women's Rights Movement, the unions, and Gingerbread, the campaign for single mothers.¹⁰ The lesbian cooperative in Stanley Road, Edinburgh, fostered raids on patriarchal art galleries.¹¹

In Bristol, Ellen Malos found her flat so taken over by the nascent Bristol women's movement in 1972 that "we moved specifically in order to have a place where the women's movement could happen that was not in the middle of our lives, so it was down in the front room of the basement, of . . . what's now the garden flat. And the back room was . . . where . . . the Gestetner [duplicating machine] was . . . and a silkscreen printing frame. All *kinds* of things happened in our basement, you've just no idea."¹² It soon became known as a temporary refuge for women in violent relationships, and it received phone calls at all hours from social services, police, and "safe" contacts. Malos suggests her house became a focal point because she did not have paid work, so she was more available than others; she had a baby, so she was at home more; and she had access to a car, and a husband who did not mind the living room being taken over by nightly meetings. But obviously she was up for it, raising the deeper question of who was motivated to activism. Malos was fascinated by the politics of housework; she was the wife of an academic, struggling to continue her own PhD, and the mother of small children, and she had been told she would never get an academic job. Similarly, the nursery that Bronagh Hinds set up in her Belfast home was in part because she herself had no childcare. Carol Leeming gave the same reason for why her house was the main meeting place. Houses did not make the movement; people did. Yet remembering houses reveals important questions of place and resource, as they morph from social and moral hub to workplace or sanctuary.

Interviewing in women's homes reveals much. Malos and I sat in a generous but old-fashioned kitchen in a house that seemed too large for an elderly woman, without extravagance or pretension, decorated with purple and green suffragette colours, posters, and badges, some of which were ready to be sorted for the Feminist Archive South. Similarly, Gail Chester's flat, owned by a not-for-profit housing association in Stamford Hill, north London, summarized everything about her ongoing activisms and her inability to throw stuff away. Both homes also spoke of children, now gone, of partners (Malos spoke sadly of her husband's death; Chester's was typing in the other room), and of ordinary comforts: kettles, mugs, rugs; photos of pets, families, friends, vacations. Liz Armstrong's home was bright and tidy, free of memorabilia she had recently given to the Glasgow Feminist Archive, with a huge sigh of relief, after her move to the suburbs. To think of the house is to think of the bases not just of movements but of life's rhythms.

Feminist homes mattered as organizing hubs and foundations for personal security, choice, and care. The UK women's movement included women from all backgrounds, but it was most widely represented by white working/middle-class women baby boomers. Many began life in private rented accommodation, some moving to publicly owned ("council") housing as it became available. This was true also for first- or second-generation immigrant women who often had significantly more difficult memories—ironically, first houses often situated in low-income areas were lost when urban redevelopment disregarded immigrant businesses and communities.[13] Pragna Patel, whose family came to the United Kingdom from Kenya in 1965, remembers looking after her four younger siblings, surviving on toast, while her parents were "trudging through snow, looking for somewhere to live."[14] Stella Dadzie's painful memories of homelessness reflected the difficulties of her parents' mixed-race marriage: her white mother had been ostracized by her family for marrying a Ghanaian pilot who had come to study in the United Kingdom after the war.[15] Activists from middle- and upper-middle-class families were more likely to have grown up in family-owned homes, though not always, and almost invariably, these properties were not in the mother's name. Moreover, women's inheritance was tied to caregiving duties for elderly parents, especially if the daughter had not married.

In their own adult years, then, a secure place to live was important to feminist activists. Postwar UK governments prioritized local council–owned housing, and the Labour government promised relative redistribution of wealth through an inheritance tax. But by the 1970s, tower blocks nationwide were a byword for misguided planning and poor-quality housing, described in Fairbairns's novel *Benefits* as "like a pack of chewing gum, upended in a grudging square of grass on the side of a hill."[16] At the same time, swathes of rundown Georgian, Victorian, and Edwardian terraced houses ("rowhouses" in the United States) in cities across the land were in poor repair, had fallen empty, or were rented by older "sitting tenants" who had to be bought out or allowed to stay until they died. Activists, who typically lived in low-income urban areas, often bought such homes, which in today's terms were astonishingly inexpensive. London's Islington then had some of the worst housing conditions in England: now it can be a prestigious location. By the early 1970s, just over half of all homes in the United Kingdom were owner-occupied, almost twice the proportion two decades before.[17] But few people could buy outright, and mortgages, until the 1976 Sex Discrimination Act, were not available to women, as BBC journalist Jenni Murray found out:

> "Well, yes, you've got the deposit you need, but we can't loan you money without the signature of your father or your husband," and I was just *demented* with fury about that and there was *nothing* I could do about it, and so luckily the house I wanted didn't sell until the Sex Discrimination Act came in and I went back to the one that had the best rate and I said, "Okay, you're discriminating against me because I'm a woman, and I will take you to court if you won't give me the mortgage"—and they gave me the mortgage straightaway [gleeful laugh]. So that was another... real lightbulb moment.[18]

The story continues. When Murray objected to the solicitor's description of her as "spinster of this parish" on the house deeds, he replied:

> "Well, I haven't got any alternative. That's what you put on legal." "*Find another way of saying it!*"—I was a bit stroppy in those days [laughs]— "Find another way of saying it" and he rang me a couple of days later and said, "How does 'feme sole' suit?" and I said, "That suits me just fine." He said, "Well, it's obviously from the Norman and it's f-e-m-e s-o-l-e so it's not quite FEMME SEULE," he said, "but it's an old English Norman way of expressing a woman alone and it's legally acceptable still."[19]

The right to own property in a woman's name has been central to women's equality in all parts of the world. Yet activists were acutely aware of the link between housing tenure and inequality.[20] Alongside experimental domestic arrangements, there were also campaigns for housing rights, targeting landlords who refused to rent to black or Irish people; housing associations that would not allow young "excluded" women or, in the 1980s, Muslim women; local councils that refused to recognize that women escaping domestic violence had not "voluntarily" made themselves homeless or that a woman might want to live with a man but not be considered his dependent and thus forgo benefits. Malos counts the inclusion of abused women's rights to council housing in the 1977 Housing Act as one of her proudest moments. Jenny Lynn describes working with the Claimants' Union in Swansea in 1972 to get women rent money.[21] Pragna Patel explains the long and eventually successful campaign to reform Immigration Law in 2002 to allow an emergency housing benefit to be paid to abused women with insecure residency status.[22] Others tackled discrimination against accommodation for lesbians when very few owned their own homes (in contrast to gay men) or themselves worked in housing services.[23]

There were campaigns for the rights of Gypsy/Roma/Traveler communities and homeless women, which Siobhan Molloy describes as particularly vibrant in Northern Ireland.[24] In response to the Housing Act of 1972, which forced local councils to increase rents, feminists supported protests against soaring costs and tenants who refused to pay. Alongside the celebrated rent rebellion at Clay Cross in Derbyshire in 1972–73 was a dramatic campaign led by the women's branch of Big Flame, a Trotskyist organization in Liverpool, which supported a fourteen-month rent strike, initiated by three thousand council housing tenants in Kirkby, a deprived neighbourhood on the outskirts of the city.[25] Indeed, feminists have consistently highlighted the vital importance of good-quality homes at affordable rents as a cornerstone of safe and stable communities, especially for low-income mothers, who often face particular difficulties in caring for their families. Such factors emerged again with the Focus E15 Mums' protest in 2013, in which a group of young mothers resisted attempts to evict them from their east London homes close to the site of the 2012 Olympics and relocate them to towns and cities far from the capital because of a shortage of affordable housing locally.

In such situations, the notion of owning one's own home can be seen to test the collectivist ideals and the antimaterialism of the late 1960s and 1970s. Sheila Rowbotham tellingly writes that the best thing about her first house, bought with a small inheritance in 1966, was "a gray tumbledown shed which backed on to the garden wall which reminded me of those faded-out shacks on my blues records."[26] Many activists squatted, pooled resources in collectives, or rented from housing associations, which offered nominal rents for poorly maintained properties that at some stage they would repossess for refurbishment. Barbara Jones comments that she did not know anyone who owned their house in the early 1980s, nor did they aspire to, as "part of the capitalist system," while Fairbairns actually felt sorry for two gay men who had secured a mortgage: all that debt! Those who owned tended to feel inordinately guilty and turned their houses over to collectives. Rowbotham recalls:

> I considered rent irrational, so each week we all paid £1 into a common fund for bills and rates and £1 to a political fund of our choice. The economic flaw in this theory of rent was that we never covered the cost of repairs, and the house disintegrated gradually around us.... I eventually cracked when a notice in red print, threatening legal proceedings about "nuisances," arrived from the council. I might have been fighting the state in general, but I was terrified of the state in particular. I went to see Bill Fishman at Tower Hamlets College in tears towards the middle of May [1968]. I was going to sell the house; I couldn't bear the responsibility any longer. I put it on the market at the estate agent's at Lebons Corner.... the daily troubles look unbearable in retrospect and my delay in acting absurd. Desperation, however, finally made me ruthless. I swept everyone out of the house except Stevie and Helen on the grounds that it was to be sold. Brian had left and Kathie and Mary were away. Peace fell. Life suddenly felt better again and I had second thoughts. The "For Sale" notice was taken down.[27]

In 1979 Rowbotham was still not charging rent, however, living by then in another shared house in Bristol, still having nightmares that it would collapse.[28]

Such questions gained new urgency for feminists during the Thatcher years. One of her government's significant early reforms was the 1980 Housing Act, which obliged local authorities to sell council houses to tenants at a discount. This served to increase the rate of home ownership but reduced the number of houses available to rent, as the houses that were sold were not replaced. And throughout the 1980s, Thatcher used the tax system to reduce the costs of mortgage borrowing, a policy that subsidized home ownership but tended to push up house prices. Pressures on housing were exacerbated because people were living longer: often three or even four generations of a family survived and wanted to live near but not necessarily with each other.[29] The context was divisive: the decline of the industrial regions and economies of northern England coincided with the growth of services and finances in the south. These "tore apart and obliterated" an assumed social welfare consensus to a degree unimaginable to older activists, as Rowbotham saw it, looking back.[30] Many joined the Labour Party or nationalist parties of Scotland, Wales, or Northern Ireland. Some took jobs in regional and local governments that were still under Labour control.[31] On a personal level, the 1980s ate away at collective living experiments and the counterculture's irreverence toward authority. Insecurities intensified when house prices rose sharply in the late 1980s. They then slumped in the mid-1990s, trapping people in negative equity alongside a volatile rental market, as happened again after the financial crash of 2008, fuelled similarly by unregulated bank bets on housing. But those who held on to homes they had bought earlier found themselves unexpectedly and immeasurably better off.[32] For feminists who benefited, this good fortune remained deeply uncomfortable.

The dislocation that the Thatcher years brought to housing as a foundation of everyday life is described in Valerie Wise's oral history. One of the best-known feminists of the 1980s, Wise was chair of the Greater London Council (GLC) Women's Committee, the first strategic body of its kind in the country, which sensationally showed what "municipal feminism" could achieve and inspired women's initiatives in local government across the United Kingdom, including in Manchester, Liverpool, Leeds, Birmingham, Cardiff, and twelve of Scotland's local authorities by 1990.[33] Wise's mother, Audrey, was a Labour member of Parliament (MP) and a prominent socialist and union activist, instrumental in the National Joint Action Campaign Committee for Women's Equal Rights in 1968 and the Leeds garment workers' wildcat strike in 1970. As such, Valerie Wise bridged the Left and the WLM. Under her direction, the GLC women's unit championed better childcare and being able to breastfeed in public, fought against female genital mutilation, and employed nearly a hundred people in its nurseries and as caregivers. *Spare Rib*, Wages for Housework, Reproductive Rights, Lesbian Line, Sheba Feminist Publishers, the Women's Health Information Centre, and Southall Black Sisters, among many others, found their fortunes transformed through public investment of one sort or another, from direct grants to advertising in their publications. Wise remembers: "You name it, we funded it. We funded everything in London. I mean, we just—it was—it was absolutely fantastic because we had this money."[34]

This was a particularly good moment for black and other ethnic minority women's groups in London, who made up nearly three-quarters of the four hundred women's groups that received GLC funding between 1982 and 1985.[35] However, the new money brought inevitable tensions, in the wake of black uprisings in 1981 over extreme racial division and inequity, and the ensuing promotion of "multiculturalism."[36] Beatrix Campbell laments that the black women's movement, which had suddenly expanded thanks to local government funding, was left high and dry when the money ran out, giving black and white women too little time to understand each other better.[37] Also controversial was the GLC's experiments in combining representative with participatory democracy, "an alternative to the pro-state and anti-state split which had for so long divided the left, as Rowbotham astutely analysed it."[38] Much of this was done through reinventing the "Planning Unit" that dealt with housing and transport design. Wise remembers one memorable occasion when five hundred people crowded into an open consultation meeting of "Women Plan London."

When Valerie Wise explains how, as the twenty-five-year-old chair of the GLC's Women's Committee, she found herself in charge of a £7.9 million budget (far bigger than the national Equal Opportunities Commission ever had), she mentions that her mother, Audrey, had bought a one-bedroom flat in London's Barbican—as MP for Preston in northern England, Audrey needed a London base for when Parliament was in session. Valerie relocated to London after university to work as her mother's assistant and then for the workers' alternative technology unit, CAITS.[39] She and her husband shared the Barbican flat with Audrey, sleeping on a sofa bed in the living room. As an example of Brutalist architecture, the Barbican was widely derided at the time: today it is a celebrated and glamorous apartment complex and home to a world-renowned performing arts centre. Wise felt that its central London location and spacious living room made her home an "obvious place" for Labour Party planning parties. It was where GLC leader Ken Livingstone, whose own flat was tiny, convinced Valerie to run for office. Wise felt "not posh" but well connected, and she glows when remembering serving her trademark trifles. In her words, "one should always have food at a party." However, when she was nominated to stand in a local election in Battersea in south London, several miles from the Barbican, which she might not win, Wise and her husband "took a *huge* gamble . . . and we bought a house," relocating to be near the area:

VALERIE WISE: We couldn't afford Battersea South, we couldn't afford Battersea, but we bought a house in Tooting, which was the next constituency, which was then Tony Banks's constituency, so I knew Tony. I got to know . . .

FREYA JOHNSON-ROSS: What was the house like?

VW: It was a terraced—so it was our first house. It was a terraced house [a rowhouse] but it was a three-bedroom house. And yeah, it was fine. It was—yeah, it was just a little terrace.

FJR: How did it feel to have your own house? So that must have been the first time you'd had—

vw: Yeah. Well, it felt good. And of course, I was right near Battersea, so it was good. And *luckily* I won, thank God.[40]

Being able to buy her home, albeit in a modest part of the capital, was in its own way as magical as feminists' fairy-tale capture of the GLC's imposing County Hall headquarters on the South Bank of the River Thames, almost directly facing the Houses of Parliament, where Thatcher reigned imperiously. Wise remembers entering County Hall through the doorway reserved for the elected council members on a hot day licking an ice-cream cone, much to the disapproval of the porter.[41]

The moment did not last, for in 1985 Thatcher's government abolished the GLC along with six English metropolitan counties effectively to quash Labour-run municipal strongholds. Thus ended a golden age for state-supported feminist initiatives and Wise's own personal "best years," as she describes them. Domestic life, however, was good. In 1987, Valerie's mother, Audrey, regained her seat in Parliament, and, having earlier sold the Barbican

Valerie Wise in January 1982 outside County Hall, then home of the Greater London Council (GLC), with GLC leader Ken Livingstone and John McDonnell, chair of the Finance Committee (foreground, left to right). Wise chaired the Women's Committee, which demonstrated what "municipal feminism" could achieve and inspired women's initiatives in local government across the United Kingdom. *Photo courtesy of REX Shutterstock*

flat, helped Valerie buy a bigger house in Tooting. In addition to her obvious pleasure in having her mother with them, Valerie also, after seven years of trying, had her first child and combined motherhood with freelancing, including a consultancy on equalities for retail chain Littlewoods in Liverpool. Her second son was born in the bath of this second Tooting house in 1988, with the help of a friend and a radical midwife, while Audrey slept soundly upstairs after a long session in Parliament.

Eventually, Valerie Wise moved back to Preston, becoming a council member, leader of the council, and later chief executive of Preston Domestic Violence Services. Her mother died in 2000. Today she lives in a rural suburb, not far from where she grew up. The interview records some of her trials and her undimmed political convictions. Wise certainly faced media hounding as the feminist face of the "loonie left" GLC, and her time in local politics has been turbulent. But her homes suggest ongoing domestic pleasure, entwined with memories of her mother as political example and best friend. This in its own way conjures a feminist dream. Her memories of their organizing refreshments for Labour Party gatherings bring this together, as does her pleasure when musing on baking cakes and setting up a charity shop for domestic violence services: "*I* think it would be a real opportunity, to have a *cheap* café offering homemade simple foods and cakes and things. It might be what I do when I retire; who knows [laughing]!"[42]

Domestic cultures in themselves can support social change. Yet the private sphere, as feminists were the first to point out, reflects the inequalities of the public sphere. These divisive economic conditions also emerge in Betty Cook's narrative. Cook was a founder-member of Barnsley Women Against Pit Closures (WAPC) and the Barnsley Miners' Wives Action Group, which, as with the GLC Women's Committee, became legendary for women's activism in the 1980s.

A shop steward for the Union of Shop, Distributive and Allied Workers (Audrey Wise's union) at her mail-order factory in the 1970s, Cook identifies strongly with working-class struggle but remains tentative about identifying as a feminist, citing the much-repeated poem of the time, "Where women's liberation failed to move, this strike has mobilised."[43] However, she is upfront in criticizing women's economic dependence on men, domestic exploitation, lack of opportunity, men's violence, and men's control of public life, including in the unions. Born in 1938, the only child of a mother who had given up service when she married a mining foreman, Cook's early years in a company house were relatively comfortable. She also loved living in student digs as a trainee nurse, having left school at sixteen. However, after a little-wished-for marriage at eighteen, accidently pregnant, she found herself denied the chance to complete her training and living in an isolated two-up, two-down "pit house" without electricity, running water, or telephone but with rats in the cellar. Her husband, out to work at the mine at 6 a.m., returned late at night after drinking in the pub. She remembers putting her three young children on the council office counter with the words, "You look after them; I can't." The family were moved to a council house, but this did not solve marital inequality; her husband only agreed to her finding paid work after she pointed out she could then pay the rent. When she finally got up courage to leave, her son said,

> "Oh, Mum, you should have left him years ago." And I said, "Yes, but years ago unless you were married you couldn't get a council house." I said, "The only way I could get around it was to put you in [foster] care, get a job, get somewhere to live and then fight to get you back and, I'm sorry, I just wasn't prepared to do that. Although we didn't have a very good life, it would have been a worse life if we'd have had to split and you go into care."[44]

Cook immediately supported the March 1984 strike call by Arthur Scargill, leader of the National Union of Mineworkers (NUM) against the National Coal Board's pit-closure plan. One of ten thousand women who converged on Barnsley in south Yorkshire two months later, Cook became a frontline activist in the WAPC network, taking part in soup kitchens, pickets, confrontations with police (resulting in a smashed kneecap at one point), arrests, and public speaking. Later in the 1990s, with Anne Scargill, who became a close friend, she led Greenham-style sit-ins in mines against a new round of pit closures. She stood up to the local union in opening soup kitchens to the whole community rather than just for picketing men, and opposed middle-class students when she felt they were taking over organization.

Political awareness also led Cook to study for a diploma at Barnsley's Northern College, encouraged by Jean McCrindle, who taught women's studies there and had become treasurer of WAPC. In 1988, she moved into a college residence and by the following year had begun a degree in sociology and social policy at Sheffield University. As a forty-nine-year-old, her "leaving home" narrative was shaped by midlife perspectives alongside a thrilling discovery of her potential and the wider political scene. When she was still working part-time, looking after her aging and often disapproving mother and her grandchildren, and avoiding her angry husband, one teacher tried to persuade her to take a year off. By this time, the strike was over, but Cook was not going back to her old life. Asked what she would like to include in a life story interview, she replied: "Mainly that I realized quite late on in my marriage that I didn't have to be just somebody's wife or mother, and that there was a life out there. And although I'd been told previously I wasn't capable, I found that I *was* capable, but it was just the experience of [the] '84, '85 miners' strike that gave me that confidence."[45]

Cook celebrates a domestic liberation that she clearly connects to her political awakening. Barnsley, in south Yorkshire, is a former industrial, mining, and market town now working hard to attract new businesses and move away from an overreliance on the public sector. It has also become, like much of the formerly industrial north, a place of cautious opportunity for migrants from South Asia. But Cook says: "People build these new industrial estates [corporate parks] and we've got an estate at Cortonwood, where Cortonwood colliery [coal mine] used to stand and we've got shops like Morrison's and Next and Asda and B&Q and local councillors will say to us, 'But look what we've got instead.' But they're all part-time, low paid-jobs."[46]

Cook was sharing a house when she took voluntary redundancy (a "buyout" in the United States) from the mail-order company in 1999. By then she was sixty years old, the state retirement age for women at that time. It is not clear in her interview whether she chose collective living, nor whether she owned, part-owned, or did not wish to own the property. She describes taking another job at an educational call centre in 1999 to protect her savings (though she also loves the job), and she explains the challenge of becoming an "unwilling carer" when one of her housemates became seriously ill.

The miners' wives' action emerged from union activism, but it learned from and taught the WLM, and was connected too with black and global women's movements.[47] In this sense, despite the strike's crushing defeat it arguably measures the diversification of 1970s feminism, as does the growth of municipal feminism and the greater connections between women's movements across race and ethnicity. The Barnsley Wives' richly coloured banner, which Cook designed, portrays a dove of peace to reflect the Greenham Common women's peace camp as well as the coal miner's pick and shovel. On the reverse, giant daisies grow in front of distant pit machines, each petal bearing the name of a local pit community, while the leaves of the daisy represent forces who nurtured them: the WAPC, the NUM, Jean McCrindle, and local fundraiser Percy Riley.[48]

But these alliances were not always easy, as with negotiations between black and white women's movements during this time. Cook talks fondly

The richly coloured banner of the Barnsley Miners' Wives Action Group. Designed by Betty Cook (left, with her friend Ann Scargill, right) and created by David Andrassy (behind the banner), it displays daisies blooming in front of coal pits, underpinned by the defiant message "they did not starve," attesting to the massive community mobilization in support of striking miners and their families. The reverse depicts emblems of the coal industry—the pick, shovel, and lamp—while the dove of peace references the Greenham peace camp. *Photo courtesy of Mark Harvey*

of McCrindle, who had brought a wealth of experience from Oxford and London contacts including the Thompsons, Raphael Samuel, and Sheila Rowbotham:

> Jean was—was very supportive as the national treasurer, but also I think we were just a revelation to Jean as well and these working-class women who sat and smoked continually through a meeting and Jean always used to be coughing and her eyes running 'cause she couldn't cope with cigarette smoke. But I found her to be a very gentle person, but again although we loved her to bits we realized that she hadn't had the struggles that we'd had, she didn't know what it was like to be a working-class woman, and often I think her education [laughs] was broadened by mixing with us and going with us. And she often used to go on the picket bus with us and if we got pulled up and the police used to say, "Are you a miner's wife?" she just used to look at them and she'd say, [middle-class voice] "Officer, do I *look* like a miner's wife, do

I *sound* like a miner's wife?" so we used to find that quite amusing, yeah [laughing].[49]

This audible class difference, playfully acknowledged by McCrindle, can naturally be heard in the oral history interviews. McCrindle's own narrative, which complements Cook's in her tribute to the bravery of mining women, tells of moving to London when Northern College became politically inhospitable, to buy into Hermione Harris's house in Highbury Hill, pursue a midlife PhD on the miners' strike, teach, and return to her parents' world of theatre and the arts.[50] This was not a narrative of financial wealth, nor indeed of the rootedness Cook describes, but of other resources that inevitably shape domestic lives. Cynthia Cockburn, who came from a business family in Leicester but became a freelance academic, puts this plainly:

> Telling you this story over the last few hours has made me realize how much I've been able to make my own choices about where I put my energies, and that applies to work and activism. So, it's been a self-*chosen* career, if you like. . . . I *owe* that to certain factors which it's important not to forget, it's important to me not to forget. . . . The . . . security that has derived from my middle-class status . . . I just don't think we can forget that. Compounded by being white in a majority black world. But the middle-class thing, what that amounts to, really, it's not a *huge* high status or great wealth. What it is simply—owning your own home, not being paralyzed by the fear of the future and your old age, because there is that little nest egg there somewhere, the little bit that you're going to inherit which will make the difference between poverty and deprivation and a basic living. So that, we *can't* underestimate, I think, what a middle-middle-middle-class kind of status gives you.[51]

Cockburn tells me this as we sit by the fire in her splendid study, a library of feminist books surrounding a busy desk, her photographs of women on the wall. She bought the house in 1966, then in a rundown area of London, with £3,500 from her parents and £3,500 from her then-husband's parents.

Perhaps it was asking saintliness to resist domestic security on principle, particularly in later life. Una Kroll, militant in the Movement for the Ordination of Women, got nearest, selling her family home in 1988 to live as a hermit in church housing at age sixty-three, to the dismay of her children.[52] We might also consider the women who left home to live at Greenham Common in tents, benders (shelters made from branches), or simply sleeping bags, to protest against the siting of American nuclear missiles in England. Nevertheless, even older women who dramatically gave it all up for the cause eventually had to create sustainable domestic lives. Many continued to live collectively because they had not been able to get onto the property ladder or into rent-controlled housing, or had not realized how critical such housing would be.

Michele Roberts's 2007 memoir *Paper Houses* turns on this exact problem, making the rented shared house the metaphor for her floating life. Roberts tells a story of colourful but unsettling collectives, and appealing but ultimately disappointing relationships. She presents herself in retrospect as naïve. Because she does not own her own home, she misses out on the boom in house prices. A born romantic, yet somehow unsettled from the start with a French mother and English father, she was a class migrant, falling repeatedly into unsatisfactory relationships with men, her feminism an awkward fit. Although she loves women for a chapter, that does not endure. The book's final section seems to promise resolution when she meets her soulmate, another white working-class exile, another hedonist and poet, another renter rather than buyer. They make their home in the attic of a friend's house in Islington, cosy with love, but she denies her readers the expected resolution with an account of their breakup. She finally gets to own her own home, a cottage in Normandy, which she bought with the earnings from a literary prize. The purchase is a vindication of her choice to give up her intended career as a librarian for the ups and downs as a writer of feminist novels—indeed, for her earlier lack of economic focus. "Paper houses," as the title suggests, can be flimsy but perhaps in the end provide better security than relationships.[53]

To conclude that housing inequality divides women would be reductive. Roberts's memoir raises the question of whether she did not get a house because she lived for relationships, or whether she never sustained a relationship because she did not stay put. Both forms of freewheeling were, in her view, feminist. Though the happy ending turns out to be a home of one's own, love feels more important. Most of our interviewees spoke this way. Housing is, in this respect, entangled with feminist ideas of dependence, independence, care, desire, and partnership that are at the centre of everyday life. While Cockburn and I talk, a young woman arrives back from a trip home to Mexico: she is a student at the London School of Economics, one of many young women who have lived here. Cockburn's house has done far more than support low-paid, uncertain, if fascinating, scholarship on masculinity and technology and conflict resolution. It has sheltered an international feminist community, her single daughters, and their daughters, and meetings of Women in Black, a women's political choir, and other such groups in which Cockburn, now in her eighties, has been involved.

This is not so different from Betty Cook's everyday life of meetings, outings, poetry writing, and protests. Cook also lives as a single woman in her late seventies by choice, supporting her extended family members and grandchildren. Her committed volunteer work, organizing food and leisure activities with the Salvation Army, is reminiscent of the soup kitchens she ran during the strike.

Kirsten Hearn, who was the GLC Women's Committee Disability Outreach officer from 1982 to 1986, tells a similar story. Initially living with her girlfriend in a shared house, getting work allowed her to move to her own rent-controlled flat in central London. Even as she judges herself for becoming a "wage slave," her meticulous home has evidently nourished Hearn through nearly thirty years of disabled rights activism, fat liberation, LGBTQI choirs, and more. Sometimes she dreams of giving it all up

> but actually then I think, "No! But I like my place!" [mock wail] . . . I can close the door and it's entirely mine, [it's] *fantastic*, but it also stops me from doing some of the other things I might like to do and, you know, every so often I'd run away and I'd go and live in a community for a few weeks, which is great, actually, and I like it for a few weeks and then I get heartily sick of there always being people around, and I run away again back to my little home here.[54]

But there is another reason Hearn abandons her communal living impulses: "Oh, but what will I do with my thi-i-ngs! What will I do with my *possessions*? Because I have possessions now, you know."[55]

Feminist Shopping: Pleasure and Shame

Just as the S&A interviewees shy away from discussing real estate, they rarely mention shopping, despite its connection with crucial areas of feminist concern. Valerie Wise comments that she and her mother loved looking for clothes together in shops such as Debenhams and C&A, and Betty Cook remembers wearing unsuitable red leather heeled boots on her first picket.[56] The consumer boom was well under way during the WLM years. Despite or perhaps because of inflation, strikes, and national economic bailouts, the Access credit card was launched in 1972, foreign vacations became cheaper, and home decoration became a serious leisure pursuit, while fashion, music, and football flourished as entertainment industries.[57]

Women, as always, were targeted as the prime household spenders, but now were likely to be earning money themselves. Delia Smith's *How to Cheat At Cooking* (1971) showed the nation's favourite television cook advising busy mothers to turn to new already-prepared foods and supermarkets.[58] Shirley Conran advises, "What to do with the time you've saved" at the end of her bestselling *Superwoman: Everywoman's Book of Household Management* (1975): make yourself more beautiful, healthy, and educated; take up crafts; volunteer for a charity; get a job such as a florist; or meet men.[59] For some, the book presented the newly spirited wife who makes "no secret of the fact that I would rather lie on a sofa than sweep beneath it." However, the vision is tiny: she proposes women use better domestic appliances (like stockpots for easy casseroles) and clever cleaning methods (apparently wood ash is a good scouring mixture). She recommends replacing "the au pair" with a refrigerator-freezer and dishwasher as a family business investment, quipping, "I'll never have to do the freezer's homework and the dishwasher is hardly likely to have an affair with my husband."[60] He clearly was not a gadget man.

Unsurprisingly, the WLM scorned the idea you could shop your way out of the double burden. However, feminists were experimenting with their own version of consumer politics, protesting price increases, setting up food cooperatives, and promoting fair trade initiatives. Griselda Pollock (better known as a pioneering feminist art historian) explained in *Spare Rib* how she and her housemates cooperated with ten other shared houses to shop for each other, and the "joy" of "learning to buy in large quantities, . . . to compare prices and get a good bargain." She noted that, since many women live in households with men, it would be impossible to have segregated "feminist" food, but naturally they ensured men participated equally in the project.[61] Nottingham WLM ran a successful food prices campaign when the Finefare supermarket was accused of profiteering from inflation. The East London Big Flame Food Cooperative, from March 1974 to late 1975, bought items and food cheaply in bulk, trying to make staples affordable while also sharing labour and saving time. Initiated by middle-class women, this also represented an attempt to create cross-class and working-class–led feminism. The concept that underlay it was to empower women as consumers and to reclaim shopping from capitalist exploitation, inspired too by Maria Della Costa's theory of the housewife as a revolutionary figure.[62]

These efforts were of a piece with collective living experiments, represented by Lynne Segal's house, in which a succession of single mothers and their kids lived for over a decade. The photograph on the cover of Segal's memoir features her smiling from her kitchen table, reading a large newspaper. In front sits a huge jar of Maxwell House coffee, what looks like some marmalade, and an enormous wooden salad bowl, behind which a wooden spoon rests on the lip of another bowl. A large saucepan is on the gas stove, further large bottles on the sideboard, and she is happily keeping up with the news in the midst of domestic life. Instant coffee was clearly a sustaining pleasure.[63]

Sue O'Sullivan's 1987 *Turning the Tables: Recipes and Reflections from Women*, the first WLM cookbook published in the United Kingdom, gives clues to feminists' food cultures. Its menu, from soda bread to "rush rush curry," still tells of thrift and collectivized work. Each recipe is accompanied by an autobiographical commentary addressing everything from eating disorders and vegetarianism to fair trade, though notably it was too early for organics. Kum-Kum Bhavnani's contribution queried whether it had been ethical to eat out while the miners' were on strike and declined to offer a recipe. In more recent

Lynne Segal, in her north London kitchen in the 1970s, looks up from a newspaper resting against a jar of Maxwell House coffee. She is surrounded by the everyday items of a kitchen—jars, bowls, and pans—though the books at her elbow hint at the life of a writer and activist. *Photo courtesy of Lynne Segal*

years, she has made a film promoting ethical cocoa cultivation.[64] O'Sullivan's oral history reveals that her mother was a "lousy cook" whose advice when O'Sullivan got married was "Now, Susan, what you really have to remember is that all you have to do in cooking is to make sure you have plenty of... canned condensed soup, mushroom, and you can use that as a sauce to put on top of anything, chicken, meatloaf, anything" (both the interviewer and O'Sullivan laugh).[65] She elaborates an upbringing in which her youthful diet was shaped by her parents' belief that fatness exposed a person's moral weakness and a lack of healthy control in regard to food. Slimness was pleasing, especially in a woman. It was something a future husband would always find attractive.

In contrast, the cookbook celebrates women's eating in sometimes erotic tones. Perhaps inevitably Angela Carter's fantasized alternative career as a cook turning out "hearty fare" involves "potato soup, beans with sausage, braised oxtail, cabbage pancakes, chili... all the things I know best how to cook, due to a life spent on a relatively limited income in mostly northern climates"—though she noted the chili came from a stint in Texas.[66] (Carter was characteristically naughty in choosing not just meat, but such a phallic cut.)[67] In the UK context this resonates with vivid memories of postwar rationing, described by Cockburn, Campbell, Kroll, and others. O'Sullivan's recipes, however, foreground migrant and mixed heritages more prominently—reflecting her expatriate North American circles and the objective of Sheba Publishers, for which she then worked, to publish writing by lesbians and women of colour. Shaheen Haque and Pratibha Parmar's recipe for tamarind mango pickle and bhajias, for example, is lyrically nostalgic. There are three versions of groundnut chicken. Linda Bellos, sometime accountant for *Spare Rib* and infamous leader of Lambeth Council, offers a recipe for salad Niçoise, which she notes is best accompanied by a glass of dry champagne.[68]

This manual of feminist taste turns the tables on hidden snobberies. A clever introduction by Dena Attar challenges the genre of the cookbook itself and encourages women to cook from experience instead of written recipes.[69] Conscientiously reclaiming bodily pleasure for women by making the kitchen a creative space, feminist everyday life met consumer culture more directly than it had in the 1970s. It might seem today that this pioneering book presages the "lifestyle" drift that has ended in Nigella Lawson's "five rules of feminist cooking." (These are unobjectionable and comprise men doing 50 percent of domestic cooking; women having equal opportunities in the professional kitchen; women being allowed to eat meat; dissociating women from cupcakes; and breaking the binge/guilt cycle. The difficulty is their co-option as promotion for Nigella's business and image as a "domestic goddess.")[70] But O'Sullivan's book—her oral history too—tries to enjoy consumption without insisting women do the domestic labour or glamorizing shopping, asking "women to stay out of the kitchen as much as possible" at the same time as reclaiming it for themselves. It chimes with Rachael Scicluna's anthropology of older lesbian feminists living in London for whom "the 'kitchen table' emerged as a feminist and democratic symbol, as powerful as that of the Arthurian 'Round Table.'"[71] Yet these modest experiments in ethical consumption might again be measured by Cook's memories of soup kitchen fare for miners' families (largely supported by donations) of "liver or stew meat, Yorkshire puddings, potatoes and vegetables, and always a sweet [dessert], something with custard or rice pudding, something like that, 'cause it was important that they did get a good balanced meal, it really was."[72] Cook's banner design conveys the pride involved: "They Did Not Starve 1984–85."[73] Perhaps Bhavnani was right in her own way for declining to give a recipe to O'Sullivan's cookbook.

Joanne Hollows perceives that the real challenge for feminists was that they wanted women to consume less even if they were not trying to influence what women bought. But this underplayed women's pleasure, pride, or care in shopping, especially where they wanted to shop for a family or husband. The solution of shopping for ourselves was also problematic. If you were buying your own food or other essentials, this hardly took away the work. If you were "treating yourself" (for example, with new clothes, beauty products, or adornment), you risked fuelling an industry based on women's objectification and appearance. Yet many women enjoyed dressing up. Rowbotham loved clothes and reminisces over outfits with great precision, particularly the mini-dress she wore when she was laughed at by the left-wing men for suggesting the Ruskin conference in 1969.[74] Jocelyn Wolfe remembers her Biba coat as "just heaven," though it cost her "an arm and a leg": "It was brown, and it kind of overlapped with buttons, quite large buttons... roughly to the side here, up to about here and then it kind of opened, and it was full length. [sighs] Bliss."[75]

Biba, the brand for "swinging" London of the sixties, was known for women's clothes that signified modern power and independence. But even Laura Ashley's floral retro maxi-dresses, clearly not a feminist style, as punk Viv Albertine scornfully points out, were happily remembered by Karen McMinn, who dressed up inadvisably to go to her radical lecturer's party: "We had long Laura Ashley dresses, like, maxi-dresses. And we hitched from . . . Carrickfergus up to Slemish, about twenty miles, got . . . a lift in a bread van. And arrived, it's in the middle of nowhere, and [laughs] he had . . . home brew, and we were drinking out of jam jars."[76] And especially ambiguous are accounts of dresses bought for early weddings, ritualistic purchases sometimes forced by mothers, often long out of date with current values or relationships. Beatrix Campbell's was "chosen by my mother, and it was a mauve, long, A-line item with a silver motif down the front." She missed the legendary anti–Vietnam War confrontation in Grosvenor Square to marry Bobby Campbell in Carlisle, but he did wear a silver mohair suit.[77] Anna Davin got married when only eighteen, pregnancy seeming to require this even in her bohemian family. Her sister made the dress, feeling guilty she had not told Anna about contraception (Anna knew, in fact, but had not followed her mother's advice). The dress was "cyclamen-coloured heavy silk with an A-line, no waist." Without nostalgia, Davin remarks: "It was a pretty dress actually. At school they said, 'Have you heard Anna Davin got married in red because she's a Communist?' [laughs]."[78]

Generally, activists avoided conspicuous consumption, preferring recycled, handmade, jumble-sale clothing styles that built on the values of "health, the natural, economy and craft production."[79] Most women made at least some of their own clothes; sewing was still required in girls' education. Wise had crocheted her white and red election victory jacket. But feminists positively embraced the self-help approach. And although Nadira Mirza points out that Asian women's movements were more focused on "livelihoods" and were wary of being stereotyped as traditional, self-help also expressed itself in minority ethnic fashion.[80] Wolfe, who loved her Biba coat, also bought African prints from Brixton.

Natural hairstyle was a major element of the "black is beautiful" movement for women of African or African Caribbean descent: Manchester's Abasindi Cooperative offered a hairstyling service for this reason as much as a source of income.[81] Jan McKenley interestingly comments that her "commitment" to wear her hair in dreadlocks (achieved finally in her late thirties, grown surreptitiously while working as a schools inspector) went with a decision to go vegetarian/vegan and to live more spiritually.[82] Gail Chester welled up during her interview, remembering how her feelings about her shamed "Jewish" hair were transformed on first seeing Afros in the early 1970s.[83] Conversely, the pride in veiling so prominent now among young British Muslim women was almost absent at a time when Iran's new fundamentalist government had imposed the hijab.[84] The Gay Liberation Front had also inspired new looks, most spectacularly "radical drag," which rejected conventionally gendered (or transgendered) drag. But most revealing here is how much more important drag was for the men (Stuart Feather thought that all men being made to wear dresses was "almost the answer" in itself).[85] "We weren't very interested in shopping," Mary McIntosh explains, remembering secondhand shops as favoured destinations—though, admittedly, during that part of the interview we were talking about wearing velvet loon trousers (exaggeratedly wide "balloon" bell-bottoms)![86]

Many feminists became even more critical of consumer culture by the late 1970s, when, for example, *Spare Rib* abandoned its responsible consumer articles for campaign-focused items.[87] But a distinct feminist market was nevertheless emerging. The *Spare Rib* cover of March 1982 features a young woman wearing a studded belt, tee shirt, punkish zips, black clothes, lesbian badge, and spiky hair.[88] She seems to be at a "women say no to male violence" demonstration and listens respectfully to an older woman who has stopped to talk—the latter in her wool coat, scarf, stockings, skirt, and furry hat. Unlike a mainstream women's magazine, these outfits are subservient to a story, here of female solidarity. Yet somehow the punk is obviously the feminist.

Other stylistic choices are modelled inside, where alongside articles on "Life in a Soviet Nursery," a history of race legislation, an article on shop work, and a short story about incest, there is a letter about a knitting pattern and a cartoon-strip-style advertisement from Ragged Robin Ltd., in which "Cinders" is refusing to wear her ball gown. "Sweaty nylon rubbish [. . .] too tight around my waist," she grouses. Happily, the Good Fairy arrives to offer "drawstring dungarees navy or paprika cord" (£12.50) "or in green & white striped ticking" (£9.00). Cinders purrs: "That's better—I can move in these" while a mouse at her feet squeaks, "Much more you!"[89]

Ragged Robin also offers "straight-legged drawstring trousers" and "warm & comfy" tracksuits, in sizes S, M, L, and XL. Such clothes are designed to maximize free movement, grounded feet, and comfort (no need for a prince). Yet Cinders is obviously still up for accessorizing, as seen in the advertisements alongside for knee-length leather and natural crepe rubber lace-up boots from Adams & Jones, silver jewelry, a mohair waistcoat decorated with a woman's sign, and "Happy Hands" floor-length bathrobes in terry toweling made by a Women's Co-op in Port Talbot.[90] Kirsten Hearn again entertains, remembering how she left behind her "colourful artist" clothes of the 1970s to "embrace the dungaree with rapture." She appeared on the front cover of *Spare Rib* sporting "lesbian earrings."

RACHEL COHEN: What are the lesbian earrings?
KIRSTEN HEARN: Oh, double women symbols. They were mustard-coloured, enamel ones, I suspect. I probably had some badges on my chest as well. So in the eighties . . . I dressed like a scruffy feminist, mostly. And then in

Advertising feminist fashion in *Spare Rib*, March 1982. In a cartoon depiction, Cinderella rejects her "sweaty nylon" ball gown in favour of "drawstring dungarees navy or paprika cord (£12.50)" produced by Ragged Robin Ltd. Other advertisements on the page offer leather boots, enameled feminist earrings, floor-length bathrobes, and "what every woman should know about vibrators." *Photo courtesy of Ragged Robin/Lesley Arrowsmith*

1990 I was, you know, contemplating leaving the Lesbian and Gay Unit and going and getting a job in the real world. I realized I had to put, I had to dress up a bit more corporately, so I . . . got into, you know, suits and shirts and all that kind of stuff, which I quite often like, actually. So I have many different costumes I might wear. I can brush up quite nicely actually, but happiest in my jeans. Still . . . I see all those as role plays, you know. Because in the '90s I was, you know, becoming quite senior in local government, it was necessary to wear a suit or something similar and I would put the uniform on . . . and be corporate Kirsten, you know, and behave in a different kind of way, actually.[91]

Hearn's knitting needles, clicking companionably in the background of the recordings, suggest that "corporate Kirsten" is not generally at home. However, her description of dress as "role plays" suggests how consumption could be rethought as a feminist choice. Elizabeth Wilson's *Adorned in*

Dreams, published by Virago in 1985, did just this. Rejecting theories of conspicuous consumption and dress as language, Wilson argued explicitly against "the feminist condemnation of fashion," suggesting that "it is inappropriate to see fashion as a moral problem, or as evidence of inauthenticity, 'false consciousness' or subjection to false values. We should rather see it as an artistic or political means of expression, albeit an ambiguous one."[92] I remember being dazzled by Wilson's red lipstick at a talk at this time; Wilson, McIntosh's ex, by then partner to leading gay rights activist Angela Mason, was no longer in the C&A tweed McIntosh describes as their sixties getup. Janice Winship, writing in 1988, went further to suggest that clothes shopping itself could be feminist, describing a sisterly outing in Brighton that involved clothes swapping and identity experimentation across class and sexualities.[93] More mainstream was Liberal Party activist Lesley Abdela, who was by then organizing "how to put on makeup" workshops for aspiring women politicians. Abdela describes an outing to Oxford Street with a prominent human rights activist from the former Yugoslavia, who went on to become a government minister in the 1990s:

> We were talking about who's going to be the new prime minister there and she mentioned this chap . . . and I suddenly said, "But . . . didn't I meet him with you last time I was there . . . You know him, don't you?" "Of course I know him," she said. I said, "When are the negotiations on?" She said, "Today." I said, "*Get on the phone and say he'd better make some women ministers.*" She said, "That's a good idea." So we're—picture it—we're still standing in our underwear, music blaring out in . . . either Zara or Mango or one of those stores [laughing], and she gets him on her mobile and she's telling him, "Make sure that you choose good people, honest people, and make sure that there are some women amongst them." And she comes off the phone and we just both collapse in giggles because . . . obviously he didn't know the setting.[94]

But Abdela begins her story by stating that this was "perhaps a very sort of odd feminism in a way."[95] She could only identify the chain store as a borderline feminist space. The same held for shoulder-padded deals clinched in mainstream women's magazines.

Shopping for sexual goods was even riskier, yet it also expanded in the countercultural 1980s. Ann Summers launched its women-only "parties" in 1981, pyramid selling by and to housewives.[96] But *Spare Rib*'s advertisements for vibrators signal that a culture of sexual consumption was present within the women's movement, though whoever wrote the copy clearly was not quite sure how far to push it. Sold by Orion Scientific, based in Long Ditton, Surrey, the Harmony Personal Vibrator (£7.95 in the April 1984 issue) was introduced in the guise of a short educational article:

> The most important thing to remember is that they do work—providing the woman has no violent prejudice against the use of artificial sexual stimulation. Some women find the shape off-putting. The phallic symbolism, deliberately created by the makers to emphasize its sexual usage, gives them the impression that it is meant to be used as an artificial penis, and indeed it can and is so used. Some women, however, find the effect—when used in this way—to be more numbing than stimulating. The vibrator is designed and is far more effective when used for clitoral stimulation and its undoubted value for this purpose has been well established by Masters and Johnson.[97]

Erotica and fetish gear also began appearing as "feminist" products. SH!, the UK's first "women's sex shop," was opened in 1992 by arts graduate Kathryn Hoyle, "out of passion, rather than business acumen," according to the website, to enable women to discover "*our* pleasure." Launched on "a budget of £700 and a large tin of playfully ironic pink paint," the shop says men "were welcome when accompanied by a woman."[98] Grace Lau, photographer for the fetish scene magazine *Skin II*, ran workshops for women who wanted to photograph male nudes, and celebrated her mixed heritage at a British Chinese women artists' exhibition in 1990 with a leather cheongsam art piece.[99] Sue O'Sullivan, ever the mediator, tried a gentler approach with the egalitarian and culturally diverse collection of lesbian erotica *Serious Pleasure* (1989) and *More Serious Pleasure* (1990).[100] These sold well, though O'Sullivan was much criticized for them.

The antiporn movement took a bleaker view of the expanding commodification of sexuality. "Off the Shelf" campaigns in which women complained at local newsagents that stocked porn magazines (or smashed sex-shop windows) gained mass support when MP Claire Short introduced a bill to ban "Page 3 girls" (photographs of semi-naked women published in daily tabloid newspapers).[101] Barbara Jones remembers her "disco collective" instituting a dress code in Todmorden in 1986, with a notice on the door saying

> "All women welcome, dress to *im*press not *o*ppress. Please do not bring weapons, handcuffs, dog collars into our disco." And some women chose to challenge that and we thought, how are we going to deal with

it if we see somebody who is in the disco and they're breaking our dress code? Two of us will go up to the woman and we'll ask her very politely to remove the handcuffs or blah, blah. And maybe she will, which will be fine. If she doesn't, then we will *not* make a scene, we will just close the disco immediately and everyone will go home and we'll make an announcement and we'll say that we will come back at a future date and we will all discuss this, but we will *not* discuss it now.[102]

This policy resulted in one couple leaving with "a big fuss" and "other women who just said, 'Ooh, sorry,'" and stuffed it in their pocket or whatever." But the strenuous effort to reason with each other—presumably after at least a day had passed—showed the high feelings being channelled through dress codes, display, and leisure.[103]

Sexual consumption clearly tangled complex desires and rebellions inside and outside a growing feminist constituency. No longer dressing to emphasize women's commonality in practical "masculine" clothes (or long skirts), younger dykes wore black clothes, platinum-blond crewcut "gender-bending" styles, as well as a minority "feminine" "ethnic" look. This emphasized the increasing diversity and malleability of women's identities and self-presentations.[104] Those who blamed S&M clothing and the desires "tied" to it as perpetuating the patriarchal system did not share the idea that subversive dressing could express women's liberation in a different way. At the same time, the liberal position that clothing was simply a matter of personal choice does not fully satisfy, either. The deeper question was what kind of civic law was appropriate for a feminist community.[105] The issue of dress codes certainly conveyed a tension, where feminism resisted any explicit arguments about submission to discipline, still less a uniform, yet also invited it. Feminist local government could not answer this problem. Wise agreed to rope off part of an art gallery because it was "dangerous" to women, at the request of anti-S&M lesbians who arrived at her office.

But could the rest of the world follow this model? While feminists chilled in radical bookshops and cafés, reading Virago Modern Classics, vacationing at the Hen House, or taking acrobatic workshops with Cunning Stunts, they also shared in the nation's favourite pastime: watching television.[106] Miss World, which the WLM had disrupted in 1970, remained one of the highest-rated TV shows throughout the 1970s, and Germaine Greer naturally declared she enjoyed it precisely for its ridiculousness.[107]

Remembering feminists' leisure, like their diets and dress, helps to restore a missing history of everyday life as well as combatting stereotypes that feminists were "killjoys." Moreover, it responds to the primary feminist demand of women's right to equal time as well as equal pay, and, indeed, to time off, bodily pleasures, and sharing fun with women without a marriage plot in sight. The importance of leisure activities became more meaningful and obvious as activists grew older and settled, whether employed or not. But what happens when you need time off from politics itself? Guitarist Alison Rayner's comment that her band Jam Today offered the "light entertainment" where "everybody could get terribly drunk and dance with each other" at feminist conferences is suggestive.[108] Pragna Patel talks about sharing a love of cricket with her husband—a pastime that their kids hate and none of her feminist friends appreciate.[109] Feminists' shame about consumption and sexual play is the byproduct of a politics that unavoidably scrutinizes everyday activities that reify—abstract and conceal—exploitation. But such shame entwines with compensatory control and release, envy and desire.

One answer was to meet feminist consumption with feminist production, as with the growth of small food, clothing, and sex toy businesses. But housing was perhaps the most fundamental purchase underlying everyday life, and thus more ambitious and inspiring still are feminist businesses involved in building and making homes.

A Builder's Business: Barbara Jones's Story

Barbara Jones arrived at the Bernie Grant Arts Centre in Tottenham, north London (named after one of the UK's first black MPs), for her interview with me on a chilly Saturday in April 2012. She shook my hand and regarded me with large blue eyes set in a face that had evidently seen the weather. She is a woman who works outdoors, on roofs, in muddy pits laying foundations, in crop fields looking for materials, and on the moors in Todmorden, where she lives in a Yorkshire farmhouse that she is rebuilding with her civil partner and friends. The interview had been arranged in London because she was a consultant to the construction of an environmental centre in Haringey.[110] Her practicality was evident from her clothes: loose, warm, easy to move in, several pockets, yet strikingly coloured in primary red, green, yellow, and turquoise panels, her ears decorated with small silver studs. Although I had never met her, I felt pleased that I had chosen to wear my red jeans and blue checked jacket (lapels needed for the microphone), along with flat shoes. When the Bernie Grant Centre closed, we moved to her friends' house nearby where, nearing midnight, I did not want the story to end. There was the dog, and her flirtatious friends, and the temptation to see and hear more of someone whom a friend had said was "living the life."

Articulate, funny, modest, and strong, Jones exuded the self-possession that feminism at heart must be about. She is also used to giving interviews. As one of the UK's tiny number of women builders and vanishingly few exponents of strawbale construction, she was given a Lifetime Achievement Award by Women in Construction, and also honoured by the UK Resource Centre for Women in Science, Engineering and Technology. It is for this reason too that we chose to interview her, since she explains her work as a direct result of WLM philosophies and her experience of Women and Manual Trades (WAMT), one of the signature municipal feminist initiatives of the 1980s. Jones trained in 1981, acting on a mixture of instinct and a momentary but pleasurable attempt at carpentry, jettisoning a conventional career as a feminist child social worker. She loved WAMT, especially its women-only policy, holistic approach to skills training, and deep political connections. She remembers "meetings, newsletter, drinks in the pub, talking about current political issues, talking about the *London Women's Newsletter*, you know, we didn't confine ourselves to manual trades, we talked about everything, because . . . it's like *everything* is open to us and the manual trades route was just one of the things that I was doing that was an avenue, a vehicle for discussing feminist and radical lesbian separatist politics."[111]

WAMT was set up in 1975, in the wake of the Sex Discrimination Act, as a campaigning body by and for tradeswomen influenced by the WLM.[112] By the early 1980s, within an emerging network of feminists that included Women's Education in Building and groups in Edinburgh, London, Leeds, Manchester, Nottingham, and Sheffield, it had persuaded some local authorities to fund entry-level training for women in traditionally men's trades, including electrical, plumbing, carpentry, and building.[113] The courses were women-only and provided childcare as well as basic skills in English, math, and computing. Sustained mostly by radical Labour local governments—Jones comments of Valerie Wise that "for the first time we felt somebody was taking us seriously"—WAMT lobbied for further funding from business and the European Social Fund (which allowed women-only projects) and the programme eventually ran in cities around the United Kingdom.

Jones revealingly comments that WAMT trainers were politically motivated women who had trained through the government Training Opportunities Programme (TOPS), upper-working-class women or, as she describes herself, the "dregs" of the lower middle class. Trainees were often working class and were trying out new skills, unlike the handful of independent tradeswomen whom Jones suggests learned through working alongside their building-sector fathers. Indeed, WAMT's template, the Lambeth Women's Workshop where Jones trained, had originally been created by

Barbara Jones in the film *On Tools*, directed by Lizzie Thynne, S&A, 2013. One of the UK's few women builders and even fewer exponents of strawbale construction, Jones received a Lifetime Achievement Award from Women in Construction. Jones exemplifies the feminist principle that manual and intellectual labour should remain connected, speaking frequently about her love of the physical work of building. *Photo courtesy of Lizzie Thynne*

Women's Aid specifically to help women who had experienced domestic violence get paid work after leaving a refuge.[114] Attempts to attract and support women from minority ethnic groups were prominent—and Lambeth's programme eventually closed itself to white women to prioritize this goal. Jones presents her own training as a unique opportunity that changed her life.

Having discovered that she loved carpentry, Jones went on to TOPS. Six months of intensive training under industrial conditions followed by eighteen months of continuous employment and/or attaining a City and Guilds Certificate enabled TOPS trainees to be classed as skilled workers. But initially Jones still assumed she was only going to learn to put up shelves rather than make a living: "that's the level of . . . internalized prejudice we all carry."[115] And if WAMT represented the vision of what women could do, Jones's TOPS experience made vivid what stopped them. On applying to TOPS, it was suggested she switch to hairdressing. Persisting, she found herself one of only a handful of women among three hundred men. Jones loved the technical elements, which included making parts of a large staircase, a tongue-and-groove garage door, and tusk tenon joints for shipbuilding. She describes one instructor as very supportive, but his gentlemanly treatment of her and the one other woman as "special daughters" caused resentment among the men. Her other instructor was "really misogynist," forcing the women to wait for his attention, then making them repeat exercises unnecessarily. Knowing she could not show her anger overtly:

> I went up to him with my second joint that was done right, just like the first one was, and I took my axe with me and I put it on the desk in front of him and there was a few other lads gathered round as well, and I said, "How's that, then, Mr. whatever his name?" and I looked straight at him and I had my axe in my hand and I just went *whack*! like that, with my axe into the wood on the table just as though it was a normal thing to do. But I was looking straight at him and he knew *exactly* what my message was, and he didn't bother me after that. But it was like, I thought I have to do *something* that lets him know that I am *not* going to take this [breathing out laugh].[116]

The other men "all went 'whoa', although nonverbally," she adds. Though "on the whole the guys were fine," she had to "go through that whole banter thing"—teasing, tricks, and proving she could be "laddish with them." Walking into the cafeteria for lunch—where ruder plumbers and mechanics joined the carpenters—involved "walking the gamut," silence followed by whistles and innuendos. Her friend challenged them over their lewd talk and sexist jokes. But, discomfited, she eventually left.

At that stage, TOPS courses had effectively been available to women for only six years, forced open by the Sex Discrimination Act. Although the construction industry makes up around 8 percent of the labour market in the United Kingdom, the percentage of women involved remains tiny and clustered in painting and decorating, despite the much-lauded recruitment of women into the trades during the Second World War.[117] Census returns show the total number of women in the building industry in 1971 was only 971.[118] Patriarchal unions were partly to blame. Even in the war, these unions ensured that women were paid much less than their male counterparts. In addition, the business operated on an apprenticeship system, so that getting a job required the patronage of a company. This system shut out anyone who had come through a government training programme, effectively women and minority ethnic workers. The unholy alliance between the unions and the private building sector may help explain why so few women are in the trades today. But it was not only the unions, for construction workers are often self-employed and not unionized. It was as much the deeply masculinized and macho culture that made it so difficult, and why WAMT argued for women-only training classes.

Nevertheless, Jones survived and went on to get a City and Guild certificate, using subsequent experiences building houses in Hackney and Halifax to qualify. Her first jobs were with Strawberry Building Collective, with which she worked until 1984 (including installing double-glazed windows at the Campaign for Nuclear Disarmament offices). She left to set up the United Kingdom's first women-only building company, Hilda's Builders. Although this soon foundered, she was gaining experience fixing up the house in east London where she was squatting. The building had been smashed up by Hackney Council to make it uninhabitable to squatters, a standard policy for local governments unable to afford renovation. It was infested with vermin and the ceilings caved in after a squatter ripped out the sellable wiring and pipes. But Jones, living with another woman with building and plumbing skills, and helped by an elderly man apparently pleased with his practical new neighbours, saw it as an adventure. She loved figuring out how to restore the piping, create a shower with a watering-can head and garden hose, rehabilitate a boiler, plaster walls, connect the gas fire with a bicycle inner tube—creative solutions that demystified the skills involved. This also allowed her to live on a pittance as a carpenter, topped up with the government's "Enterprise Allowance" of £40 a week.

Life was sweet—she by then in her mid-twenties, out every night at a meeting, gig, party, or trip to a lesbian feminist house. Coming out, which she described in our interview as an epiphany, had literally brought colour into a dutiful life, from her yellow dungarees, white shoes, and pink hair to a bedroom splashed with paint and sporting a gold-and-maroon line around the baseboard. Lesbian sexuality here indeed was feminism's magical sign.[119] However, by 1985, she could see the writing on the wall for this way of life; local governments were evicting squatters and she was never going to earn enough to get a mortgage or the free way of life she enjoyed. She and her partner Carol, a carpenter who had also trained through TOPS, thus sought to buy derelict houses outside of London, having saved £4,750 between them. Visiting friends in the market town of Todmorden in West Yorkshire, they learned they could buy two small terraced workers' cottages, which became their homes for the next decade.

Working on these, and connecting with the handful of lesbians who had similarly moved to Todmorden because they could afford to buy houses there, laid the grounds for her second attempt to create a women's building company, and this time it worked. Amazon Nails grew out of a job in 1990, fixing the roof of an elderly lesbian couple's house. Jones soon became agent and manager of a team of self-employed tradeswomen. One big commission was back in London, roofing the Southwark Women's Aid Hostel, the first all-women building site that was put out to tender, despite difficulties competing for established local government contracts with men's companies. Jones tells a story of how she managed the heavy timbers involved:

> and the guy who'd actually been saying, "You know, women can't do this, women aren't strong enough," when he came on site you *should* have seen him: he was a little weed, honestly. If we couldn't have lifted it, neither could he. [chuckling] ... You know, it's a *terrible myth*, this one about women aren't strong enough.... It might be true that I can't physically lift the same amount of weight as a bloke can, but I've got more stamina than they've got and I can go up and down ladders faster and I don't stop. Whereas, you know, you watch blokes on site and they go *phuh*, very fast at something, and then they're done in and they stop! And they have lots of breaks. You know, if you actually observe how men work, that's very often what they do and it's the tortoise and the hare, isn't it. You know, we might not be able to carry, I can't carry twenty slates, I can carry fifteen, so I have to do more loads, but I *can* do it. And you *do* become very physically strong anyway. I was really fit in those days, I had lovely muscles, you know, and I *loved* it, I loved being able to use my body like that. But, there you go.[120]

These foundations supported a still more ambitious project, when Jones discovered strawbale building in 1994 on a trip to California. The natural properties of straw, with traditional building materials of cob, lime, and wood, complemented a technique she insists anyone can learn. By 2007, she and her colleagues had designed and built over three hundred strawbale buildings, from council houses to garden retreats, an abalone shell–shaped house to an auctioneer's warehouse, while also running hundreds of training courses. Such work also fulfils the socialist goals of enabling affordable housing. Her company's current manifestation, Straw Works, codirected with Eileen Sutherland, pointedly features on its website free downloadable designs, such as a two-bedroom version that "can be built by a self-builder for £50,000."[121] "That little pig story is a good one," she comments, "but when people tell the story of the Three Little Pigs and the house of straw and sticks and brick, what they don't tell you is the ending, which is that the wolf worked for the brick company."[122]

Jones also holds to the feminist principle that manual and intellectual labour should remain connected. She speaks frequently about her love of the physical work of building, the "meticulousness" of making a perfect dovetail joint, using her body to be "skillful," the views from roofs. This helps explain why she is a builder, not an architect, even as she brings teaching into a job. Most of Straw Works' buildings are part-built collectively through ongoing open courses.

Her trajectory parallels that of Anne Thorne Architects, which designed the Haringey Eco-hub that Jones was working on at the time of our interview. This all-women business also grew out of the WLM; Thorne was a founding member of Matrix Feminist Design Collective, where she was architect for the Jagonari Centre, founded by Bengali feminists in London's East End in 1987, and one of her firm's partners, Fran Bradshaw, was a bricklayer and friend of Jones at the time.[123] Inspiring as these and other feminist initiatives in the world of construction are, Jones's story represents an unusually holistic answer to the relationship between feminism and housing. At every level, it seeks autonomy—technically, physically, intellectually, and emotionally. Jones also frames her work in spiritual terms, creating a ritual circle for the team at the beginning of a job (a Muslim man saw them on the Haringey building site and asked sympathetically if they were praying), and believing that strawbale construction enhances the "soul" of a building.

Jones's everyday life is continuous with her work; as she puts it, "Your home life feeds the rest of your life." She chooses wool over synthetic fleeces, favours vegetarianism, lives collectively. Perhaps most of all, she is prudent. In these ways, she addresses the politics of consumption so important to the feminist critique of capitalist patriarchy. Even more, her work as a self-employed builder arguably represents the power of taking the means of production back into women's hands—the missing element of the ethical consumer movement that has exploded into prominence since the 1980s. Jones's choices clearly express a radical, lesbian-centred, ecofeminist philosophy, one that often clashed with "socialist-feminism" throughout the 1980s, especially in the so-called sex wars. But just as clearly, she assumes that any feminist is anticapitalist. She even argues against anyone profiting by selling a house she has worked on and proposes she should not be paid very differently from her team. Jones confesses that her business has a small turnover, allowing payment in kind or at very low rates, while her personal income is modest.

Jones has undoubtedly been successful, not simply by making her way as a builder in a man's world, but by driving an ecological method and business that is increasingly respected by the mainstream. She insists that her successes are simply the result of "chance of birth." However, it is surely no accident that of her six siblings, four have gone into small businesses. Is it also coincidental that they have done so from a low-income background where her parents pushed them to aspire? Jones was the first generation to get into higher education, her father a working-class man who had got into the civil service, her mother giving up work to look after the children. These deep impulses behind Jones's business acumen are perhaps even more shaped by her intensely Catholic upbringing, along with her parents' own socialism. As she explained: "We were quite poor, had no extra money for luxuries and only one of everything, so learnt to be frugal. My parents were very sincere in their religious beliefs and their socialism and from them I learnt egalitarianism, generosity, to believe that God (I now would say 'the universe') will provide and *not to be addicted to money* [Jones's emphasis]."[124]

Yet it might be argued that Jones's story contains elements of free enterprise as much as of socialist production. The transformation of Californian hippies into Silicon Valley yuppies is the most dramatic example of how the counterculture became consumer culture: Steve Jobs picked the name Apple from his days as a fruitarian orchard worker. But Kirsten Rennie and Susan Grimstad's *New Woman's Survival Catalogue* of 1973, with its chapter on "Women and Money: Jobs, Feminist Enterprises, Alternatives," signals where US women's movements also intersected with countercultural economies.[125] The settling of rural plots as "lesbian or womyn's land," moreover, build on longstanding patterns of utopian, separatist communities striking out to create their own society and economies, free from federal tax and control. In the United Kingdom, such experiments are less obvious, because it is less easy to go off the grid and because more consistently socialist perspectives have prevailed in the WLM. The view that alternative enterprises did not take root in the United Kingdom was played out in my attempt to find businesswomen to interview for the S&A oral history. Although there were women who smashed through the glass ceiling, from Penguin director Gail Rebuck to Body Shop founder Anita Roddick, I consistently heard that there were no businesswomen in the WLM.

Yet we must surely acknowledge the business elements involved in Jones's history and the women suppliers, distributors, trainers, and builders with whom she works. Equally, there are the examples of Sue Boots the shoemaker, Gwenda's Garage in Sheffield, and the craftswomen and small traders who produced the dungarees, lesbian earrings, food services, and holiday packages advertised in *Spare Rib*: itself a business, even as it struggled to stick to the principle that all contributors should be paid.[126] Further, we might consider the self-employed printers, designers, filmmakers, therapists, publishers, educational consultants, and even shareholders, for example of Virago, the most business-minded of the WLM publishers. To survive, all must market themselves, even where payment involves exchanges in kind or alternative currency systems. Or indeed, where no profit is made.

As the history of feminist everyday life shows, capitalist economies shaped the WLM, especially in comparison to women's movements working within state socialism during the same period, such as in Eastern Europe and China. But capitalism can take many forms. Consider whether a business refuses to outsource to cheap and unprotected labour overseas and whether it redistributes profits and maintains long-term investors; which ones are owned cooperatively and locally? Consider as well whether working practices allow parental leave and flextime, as well as whether hiring practices allow equal opportunities or even positive discrimination. Feminist businesses attempted these things, with price controls, egalitarian pay principles, local investment, ethical materials, nonsexist and nonracist marketing, and usually a size limit (mostly sole traders). And others, like Liz Armstrong, seeded such perspectives into existing cooperative and credit unions, promoting hens' egg collectives and women-friendly meetings in the Scottish Highlands and Islands.[127] Consider the career of Sheila McKechnie, a member of the Marxist feminist group Red Rag in the early 1970s, who moved from being a pioneer for health and safety demands in the unions, to directing the homeless charity Shelter, to heading the UK Consumer Association and *Which* magazine—maintaining her socialist and feminist agenda throughout.[128]

Ventures such as Jones's also illuminate the mixed relationship that WLM feminists had to the state, especially to local government. Sex worker lobbying groups have seen feminist partnerships with the police as devilish, for example, because such collaboration restricted their own form of women's trade. Black groups had resisted the injustices of police and immigration law. Yet all such groups drew on state resources. Feminist small business was often sustained by state funding, and feminists have disproportionately worked in the public sector. In relation to women in the construction industry, state funding and employment were vital, in the face of the patronage approach of the private sector, just as local government funding for adult training programmes was essential, as Jones testifies. Hackney had the best representation: by the mid-1980s it was running one of the largest training programmes for building workers in the United Kingdom, backed by the Union of Construction and Allied Technical Trades, and over half its trainees were women.[129] Yet despite all of this, in 2017 women still only make up 11 percent of the workforce engaged in construction and just 1 percent of workers actually on site.[130]

Even as feminist initiatives depended on state protection and often direct sponsorship, they have been sustained by private donations, in money and in kind. *Spare Rib* was initially funded this way.[131] Such resourcing was mostly in the form of modest inheritances, feeding into houses that were used as bases for meetings or rent-free accommodation, feminist publications, speakers' tours, and the participation of those on low incomes at feminist conferences or the Greenham Common Women's Peace Camp. Feminist investment also enabled commissions from feminist artists or builders such as Straw Works. Juliet Mitchell remembers, somewhat guiltily, advising Diana Gravill, who was taking Mitchell's pioneering women's studies class at the Anti-University in 1968, to spend an inheritance of £2,000 on founding a bookshop rather than a refuge for women.[132] But Compendium, as the bookshop became, was a radical hub.

Yet this history is even more hidden than that of feminist business, and it proved just as difficult to find women willing to be interviewed on these topics for the S&A project. The concept of feminist philanthropy remains almost unheard of in the United Kingdom, in stark contrast to the United States, where the Ms. Foundation for Women was established in 1973 and where the Michigan Womyn's Music Festival in the 1980s included workshops on how "women of wealth" could manage their guilt by productive giving. In Europe, Mama Cash established the first international women's fund in 1983, funded largely by anonymous feminist donors. Personal subsidies of projects, as with state funding, risked reactivating class or other hierarchical relationships, furthering "power trips" and dependencies. Indeed, WAMT had split in 1979 over whether it should become a charity to raise money (thus being able to pay its volunteer workers) or whether this would create a hierarchy.[133] It would seem money itself is a shameful subject. Susie Orbach comments:

> You cannot have lived through the '80s and the '90s and not had your position on money change in this culture . . . and social democratic ideals have really been *destroyed* in Britain and I think . . . so I've got very conflicted attitudes towards money, as I think my whole generation has, and I think a lot of people cover that up by not wanting to have money or only wanting to have so much money that they don't have to deal with the conflict.[134]

In the "turbocapitalist" twenty-first century, many consider that the only way to curb unethical consumption is to produce and consume less. This too was a feminist hope. Jones's website boldly explains that "Straw Works gives me the opportunity to continue designing great houses and buildings, work on roofs, teach on real buildings and work part time," adding: "It's too easy to lose sight of what's important in life—living and loving, giving and growing."[135]

Yet even in the 1980s such attitudes were difficult to maintain. Everyday life rolled on, and even as feminist ideas of consumption and domesticity grew more sophisticated, permissive, and varied, the conditions under which they lived grew still more unequal. These inequalities were exacerbated by the professional opportunities that some feminists enjoyed. Juliet Mitchell's assessment of the movement in 1986 argued that whereas ten years previously the problem was unconscious rivalry in "sisterhood," now it was complicity with a longer-term change in capitalism that set middle-class women's new employment against working-class women and men's redundancy.[136] On the other hand, feminists of the period were both critics and participants of a new urban lifestyle associated with early gentrification in the towns in which they lived. In their small "colonies" in Islington in London or Totterdown in Bristol, they also widened the constituencies of people able to afford modest house ownership. These generations of activists pioneered new life-course trajectories in which the alternatives they represented in local places and subcultures of opportunity such as campuses, low-rent neighbourhoods, and upper-middle-class suburbs eventually influenced civil society at large.[137]

As with the 1980s ideal of "Greenham women are everywhere," the feminist revolution can be understood in small acts of care as well as protest on the street, making and tending sustainably beautiful homes, bringing up children (or pets?) differently, and learning to draw, saw, or sew. The darkening contexts of Thatcherism and the New Right demanded a response, yet simultaneously, feminists were evolving approaches to everyday life on their own terms. Houses, as with shops, offered pleasure, privacy, and comfort, without in any way losing the zeal for justice and equality.[138]

6 FRIEND OR FOE? MEN AND FEMINISM THROUGH THE 1990s

How did I come to interview John Petherbridge? The S&A team had decided not to interview men. In a way, this was absurd: men were involved in women's liberation, for better or worse. And what, after all, is a man? Gender is a construct, performance, moving target, fantasy, game, relationship. We knew that from feminist theory. And trans liberation, exploding around us, made women-only approaches to history look naïve, even cruel. Surely as oral historians we would anyway be interested in outsiders' perspectives, even when the insiders were feminists? Would it be strategic to show the men who supported feminism? No. It would be even more absurd to prioritize men when we had funding to interview so few of a movement that numbered thousands and that so fiercely wished for every woman to speak for herself. We would, however, try to interview a trans woman. Or a trans man who had been part of the WLM, despite the uncertainty of mutual understanding during the 1970s and 1980s. But we could not find anyone willing—perhaps confirming, regretfully, that uncertainty. Yet there I was, interviewing John Petherbridge.

I was visiting Zoë Fairbairns, novelist and activist, at her home in south London. We were talking about her work as editor for the Campaign for Nuclear Disarmament (CND) in 1973. One of the editorial board members was "him out there." Funny, socialist, interested in writing, she quickly knew "he was the one," and they moved in together in 1975, and he soon began working for Chiswick Women's Aid as a nursery worker.[1]

"I have to ask a bit more about him... because I haven't yet had any, very many people telling me about men who actually were actively involved in campaigns," I encouraged.

"Well, do you want me to bring him in? I mean, rather than have me sit here and speak for him."

"That would be great. Maybe we... shall I pause it?" I replied.

So down he came, Zoë left, and off we went.

The difference between men and women, perhaps the biggest "difference" of all, is feminism's starting point. Feminists are so often said to hate men, but oral histories show this is rarely the case. Rather they confirm the goal of transforming men and women's relationships and how gender itself could be rethought as a behaviour that could be changed over time. Women disagreed, however, over whether to work with men, and if so, how. At the same time, interviews also show some men trying to engage with the women's movement, rethinking masculinities in ways that became prominent in public debates about men's roles in the 1990s.

The politics of voice, central to the WLM's articulation of women's right to speak and to oral history, here parallels with the politics of looking. Who looks, who gets looked at, and how, became a preoccupation of antisexist men as well as feminists. But even as it became easier over time to create "queer" alliances of people exploring progressive genders and sexualities, men's violence and sexual abuse was a sticking point for any easy deconstruction of gender. Here, oral historians are part of a broader politics of memory that has become a powerful tool for survivors' advocacy since the late 1980s. Such memory politics remains contentious inside and outside women's movements, wavering over gender, race, and sexuality as they form not just the basis of liberation campaigns, but activists' reputation within them. It is important, therefore, to hear as well about successful conversations and coalitions across differences. Catherine and Stuart Hall's marriage is one intimate example. Recounted through two independent oral histories, we appreciate their growing relationship and their love and understanding across decades of activism.

The Voice and the Gaze: Men, Masculinity, and the Question of Difference

John Petherbridge grew up sharing the domestic work in the family guesthouse, and it was his sister, rather than him or his brothers, who was sent to private school. He exemplifies a small but significant group of men who allied themselves to the WLM, politically and personally:

> Well, I was fully supportive of it. Supported the seven demands and things, the issues. And, you know, working with women who'd been on the receiving end of being hit and battered and tortured by men,

it wasn't very difficult to take a feminist position [small laugh], I must say, on it. And I guess I still, I mean, I'm not sure whether it's legitimate for a man to call himself a feminist or not, but I still . . . hold those *values* and they're important to me.[2]

Petherbridge worked at the Women's Aid nursery in the mid-1970s, first at Chiswick, then Wandsworth. He had, he emphasizes, "already worked . . . as a primary school teacher." His job involved setting up a playgroup and accompanying women to court or to offices to get orders restricting the actions of abusive husbands or partners. "Also, I was actually a member of the National Women's Aid Federation on the publicity committee, so I worked on that with various other people and we published a pamphlet . . . I think it was '76, probably. And I also contributed to the report on domestic violence, a parliamentary report."[3]

Men could be allies, and not only as childminders, which freed up women for political or professional work. Petherbridge sought to be "a role model for the boys," demonstrating a new form of masculinity. Yet he admits it was "quite weird" that he was on the publicity committee: "It's almost as if people didn't *know* I was a man."[4]

How far "good" men might be trustworthy is more dramatically illustrated in his account of holding off angry men determined to attack former girlfriends and mothers of their children. However, by about 1977–78, he says, "There was a feeling of actually not employing men any longer." He wonders if men doing this work were given too much praise simply for doing what women do ordinarily. He also suggests maybe women could better discover their own skills if men are not present. He ends by saying that women should be entitled to decide the nature of men's involvement: "I mean, you really have to ask women who worked with me about what *they* thought, you know, because it's . . . *I* just accepted it, I didn't actually find it a problem at all."[5]

His sensitivity perhaps explains why, despite the new women-only policy, Petherbridge was invited back to help with the summer children's playscheme about 1981. He went on to write a prize-winning play based on his experiences, *Passing Through*; it was criticized by some feminists, he says, because it "showed some of the women had flaws," made worse that a man had written it, though the refuge residents appreciated it.[6] However, he is clearly proud of his refuge work and felt he learned personally from it.

Petherbridge talks slowly, his deep voice soft, with "maybe this, maybe that" cadences. From his ordinary sound, we can hear a history of men who have responded to feminism, reshaping how they spoke and listened to women. Paul Morrison, a film editor who became a central figure in the men's movement, conveys why this was necessary: "There were a lot of really basic things like how you talked, language, and kind of assumptions that you held at the back of your head. I think I always thought, you know, that, erm, in a conversation I would have a bit more to say than [my partner] Lucy would have."[7]

Feminists were fighting hard to assert that *they* had "a bit more to say" and that when they spoke, they would be listened to. "Finding a voice" and "breaking the silence" are constant tropes, but also physical truths. This was especially so for public speaking. Squeaky is out. Deep is in, whether for boardroom or bedroom. Ensure you drop, not rise, at the end of the sentence.[8] Out there, on the podium, the danger is stammering, constricting, or swallowing. French feminist Hélène Cixous prescribed learning to laugh like a Medusa as a means for women to refind the bodily self-possession needed for public speaking.[9]

But it was not always easy to laugh. The BBC refused to hire women newsreaders because they did not have enough authority; Jenni Murray broke through, having erased all traces of her working-class Yorkshire accent.[10] Una Kroll managed to persuade a few radical priests to let her give the Eucharist as one of the few (unpaid) women deacons in 1970—but many churchgoers were affronted by hearing a woman's voice. (She never backed down, loving especially to think of performing religious service when she was menstruating.)[11] Preparing to challenge Prime Minister David Cameron in the House of Commons in 2010, acting Labour leader Harriet Harman knew that she "couldn't go in there with a quavery, uncertain voice."[12] But it was hard for women to speak up, even in alternative scenes like the Gay Liberation Front (GLF)'s meetings.[13] And interviewees talk of the relief and pleasure when men would listen. Lynne Segal even found love with a man with one vocal cord, whose "very soft voice," alongside his brilliant philosophical mind, helped distinguish him from "that tough or aggressive masculinity."[14]

Notorious acts of betrayals by men whom women had assumed were political allies provoked the WLM. Jean-Luc Godard wanted Sheila Rowbotham to walk naked up and down stairs while he filmed her speaking "words of emancipation."[15] Black power leader Stokely Carmichael quipped that the best position for women in the movement was "prone."[16] Farrukh Dhondy dismissed feminism as "mindless abuse, rubbish."[17] Maoist Harpal Brah told the lesbians at the 1971 Skegness WLM conference they were "a bourgeois deviation" that would disappear under socialism. As he was saying this, the miners were also in Skegness for their conference and were intent on enjoying a striptease act, which the feminists "zapped" with a spontaneous protest, although rather uncomfortably.[18] The unions failed to support the night cleaners' strike.[19] Men on the Left philandered, as acidly memorialized in Malcolm Bradbury's cult novel of 1975, *The History Man*.[20]

Yet men were very much involved throughout the WLM as supporters and partners, foils and adversaries. Indeed, some women discovered feminism through men. Barbara Taylor, Sheila Rowbotham, and Gail Lewis first heard the term from a male friend, lover, or teacher. Susie Orbach's boyfriend "said to me, 'Well, of course every woman should be a feminist,' and I had absolutely *no* idea what feminism meant, and I remember trying to keep the conversation going enough so that I would understand what feminism was."[21]

Male political allies were also significant, from Liberal member of Parliament (MP) David Steel's sponsorship of the Abortion Act in 1967 to traditionalist Labour MP Harry Lamborn, helping Harriet Harman succeed him as the candidate for his Peckham parliamentary seat in 1982.[22] The Ford women's strike was crucially supported by shop steward Bernie Passingham.[23] Male shipyard workers actually applauded Julie Hayward into Cammell Laird's shipyard at Birkenhead in 1984, when she took the employers to an industrial tribunal to argue that her work as a cook was of equal value to their shipboard painting and joinery. Her victory in 1988 secured the principle of equal value as well as equal pay.[24] Many British Asian women's husbands supported their wives' legendary strike at Grunwick.[25] Similarly, fathers and brothers were significant early inspirers of feminists, and feminists classically rebel against undereducated or overly invested mothers instead of their male relatives.

But the subtlety of the problem is revealed in the early days of *New Left Review*, which in 1966 published Juliet Mitchell's groundbreaking theory of women's oppression, "Women: The Longest Revolution." The magazine's editorial board included only one woman, Mitchell herself, and refused her wish to do a special issue on women because, the other members said, "women are not a subject."[26] Catherine Hall, whose husband, Stuart, had earlier been editor, explains that the *New Left Review* made her a feminist, because "the [men] were the group who talked and the women would listen."[27] Some, such as E. P. Thompson, were quite antagonistic.[28]

In the first years, then, the relationship of feminists to men and men to feminism was varied. Some black men supported black women's initiatives from their inception, organizing music, caring for children, operating as drivers, decorators, and sponsors for funding applications.[29] Jan McKenley remembers that at the second Organization of Women of Asian and African

Descent (OWAAD) conference, "black men, most of the partners and brothers of women who were active in OWAAD, ran the crèche [nursery] and did the cooking for the conference. That was... a *big* thing... that they weren't men who were in men's groups, they were men who were active in mixed campaigns, but they came and it was a very, very big thing to do that."[30]

But the majority-white WLM also encouraged men to seek a place as ancillaries. The kind of men who did this were typically left wing, active in other campaigns, and involved with feminist partners or friends.[31] Lucy Delap found forty men willing to be interviewed for an oral history on this basis. From across political wings, and all parts of the United Kingdom, her predominantly white, heterosexual, and middle-class sample reflects the membership of men's groups. However, working-class men and men from minority ethnic groups were not entirely absent. One interviewee was the comedian and actor Lenny Henry, former husband to feminist comedian Dawn French.[32] Stuart Hall was another luminary who staffed the nursery at the Ruskin conference.

The men's movement—self-declared supporters of feminism—involved a notably high proportion of Jewish men: as UK Jewish feminism gained

Stuart Hall (right), one of the twentieth century's leading cultural theorists, helping at the nursery at the Ruskin women's conference. In his oral history, Hall suggests that although men cannot be feminists, "they can become sympathetic to it, and understand it from the inside, and try to change their own practice." *Photo by Sally Fraser/Photofusion*

identity, it was sometimes explicitly supported by Jewish men's groups.[33] Such men went on demonstrations, including the national women's liberation marches. They fundraised. There was even a group called Cash Against Sexism, and there were attempts to get men to give 12 percent of their income to feminists. They picketed sex shops, did typing, supported women outside abortion clinics, painted graffiti, taught women manual trades, and worked with violent male offenders to get them to control their behaviour. They took on childcare or other domestic labour, and supported mothers' political involvement.[34] Men also read feminist literature—many cited Kate Millett's *Sexual Politics* and *Spare Rib*.

But this cautious alliance would be stretched to the breaking point. Following the WLM's decision to organize as "women-only," such men also began to work autonomously. They created men's groups, networked as Men Against Sexism, and created publications, prominently *Achilles Heel*, which was launched in 1978 and was "intended as a cousin to *Spare Rib*," with a mission to change masculinities and "give up power."[35] *Achilles Heel* distributed four thousand copies an issue, according to its editor, Paul Morrison. Lynne Segal estimates that there were twenty or thirty men's groups in Britain by 1975.[36] For some, "men-only" spaces could seem as suspicious as "white-only" or any other privileged group perpetuating exclusivity, from El Vino's refusing to serve women at the bar, to football, to workingmen's clubs.[37] Men therefore initially met under the negative concept of "antisexism" rather than "men's liberation." Paul Smith, a member of Liverpool's Big Flame in the 1970s, characteristically refutes the term "men's liberation" as a contradiction in terms.[38] Another way that men justified men-only groups was in the idea they were sparing women from the emotional labour of transforming masculinity (including in rewarding them for being so good).

One example comes from Colin Thomas, who resigned from his role as a BBC producer in 1978 over censorship of his reports from Northern Ireland.[39] Thomas set up a Bristol men's group with friends who were similarly involved with feminist women. After reading Doris Lessing's *The Golden Notebook*, he saw that he was just like its sexist white Communist revolutionary character. Why *should* men be thanked for staffing the nurseries at women's conferences? (He did, at his girlfriend's instigation.) Was it terrible for women to mount the soapbox to talk about bad husbands? (He wasn't sure.) Should he share childcare and cleaning duties? (Of course—but difficult when he was the breadwinner.) Was there any connection with gay liberation? (Not in his group, but he remembers the shame of heterosexual men's treatment of gay men.) The Bristol group became a valve for "men reeling under the impact and trying to adjust . . . their own lifestyle. But also expressing resentment as well, even anger."

As Thomas suggests, these mostly straight men were also challenged by emerging gay rights. As with black power, the GLF had its own priorities, fighting stigma, an unequal age of consent, and police repression despite the partial decriminalization of homosexuality in 1967.[40] Gay men's and lesbians' interests were not always the same: gay men in the GLF were preoccupied with the right to "cottage" (have anonymous sex in public) and "presentation of self," which were less important for women. The eventual split between most lesbians and gay men was also over anti-imperialist class politics.[41] However, not only did many lesbian or bisexual women remain allied to gay liberation, but a minority of gay men became involved in antisexism.[42] John Chesterman used fake Metropolitan Police stickers to warn fellow gay men off cottaging on the grounds of "objectification," while Jeffrey Weeks condemned "role playing" alongside "owning" people through monogamy.[43] The GLF developed a "radical drag," donning outlandish, camp outfits to poke fun at gender binaries. A few hardy souls even followed the American "Effeminist Manifesto" (1972), written by Robin Morgan's (gay) husband Kenneth Pitchford and friends, which demanded that gay men abandon S&M and masculinity along with patriarchy. Further ideas came from Andrea Dworkin's (gay) partner John Stoltenberg's 1974 "Refusing to be a Man."[44] Gay men also challenged the straight men's movement, notably in a fracas at a conference in London at the end of 1974, and gay men's militancy put an end to the men's movement's national conferences from 1977 to 1980. The flavour of this clash can be gathered from an anonymous letter in the magazine *Brothers Against Sexism* (1974), which fuses a feminist demand for men to stop using women with encouragement for straight men to "make it with men":

> If, on the other hand, you are not prepared to abolish your gender role, then you are merely playing—devising more and more subtle ways of "treating your women right"—they're still *women*, they're still *yours*— and you're still *men* . . . ADMIT TO YOURSELVES that gay men make you freak and run for reassurance to your women and to your own particular world of straight men. Admit that you freak and then we, together, can deal with it . . .[45]

Some remember the "queer undertone" of seemingly straight men's groups, the sexual experimentation and close physical relationships. When one male interviewee mentions he's "bisexual anyway," his friend retorts, "You bugger, I didn't know that!"[46] On the other hand, the concept of gender choice was hardly conceived of, let alone considered. For trans men, trans women, and even transvestites and bisexuals, the 1970s and 1980s were a time of political oblivion despite a quiet presence in the GLF and WLM.

It is the emotional shock of women's and gay men's demands, in which joy, relief, and excitement were accompanied by anger, uncertainty, and anxiety, that oral history particularly helps to uncover, and it is palpable in the sighs, groans, and hesitations in the interviews. Men's gestures and recollections in their interviews reveal panic about how to relate to feminists, and how they sometimes did not literally know how or where to look. One describes keeping his eyes down when protecting women entering abortion clinics from the religious right protestors.[47] Another, Misha Wolf, remembers reading *Spare Rib* while travelling "and a woman sitting next to me smiled at me, so I shut my eyes and I kept my eyes shut for the rest of my journey 'cause I just didn't know, I had no idea, how to deal with that."[48] When Delap interviewed firefighter Dave Baigent, he said: "I don't know whether to look at you or look away, I'm not sure. I don't like looking away, it's not my way."[49] Not knowing where to look manifests men's uncertainty about what it is to be male and how to properly recompense for their oppressive gender. It is not surprising that men's groups often became therapeutic; being good seemed to require changing masculinity itself.[50]

The men's movement combusted when three hundred men gathered in Bristol in 1980, and Keith Motherson (who changed his name from Forrester-Paton) called for men to subscribe to "Ten Commitments," ranging from "consciousness raising done rigorously" to "learning from gay and feminist culture."[51] Motherson's proposal was inspired by the artist Monica Sjoo, his then partner, who wished to reconnect men and women to matriarchal spiritual traditions. Daniel Cohen recalls "so much argument that we could never get anywhere," including the first commitment to "being able to count on each other to do what they say they'll do between meetings." He goes on, "There isn't a monolithic women's movement and there never was, so at the minimum you have to say, 'Well, who am I accountable to? The ones who say "X" or the ones who say "Y"?'" This crisis of accountability ultimately ended the men's movement.[52]

It is ironic that during the 1980s, while the women's movement was expanding outward into public sector policy and service delivery work, networking across ethnic groups, and debating the politics of sexuality, the men's movement retreated into a search for masculinity. *The Anti-Sexist Men's News* changed its name to *Man*, and the Men for Change network was founded. *Achilles Heel* looked at personal growth. Cardiff-based anarchist-socialists Pete 6 and Five Cram, editors for the 1983–84 issue, proposed "masculism" as feminism's partner, inspired by American and Buddhist ideas, and the concept of "enlightened self-interest," where men could continue, for example, wishing to "sleep with feminists," so long as they were fully aware of their motives.[53] Therapy, dancing, hugging, and friendship were prioritized. The Cambridge men's group (which is still active) banned discussion of sports, cars, and television in favour of relationships and work. At its extreme, this bore little relation to feminism; for example, John Rowan led rituals and spiritualist workshops that allowed men to discover their inner "Horned God."[54] Other men thought more directly about the relationship between ethnicity and masculinity, particularly Vic Seidler, Paul Morrison, and Daniel Cohen, who analyzed their Jewish inheritance and allied with Jewish feminists.[55] However, as with the latter, it seemed as if they came to this position after initial politicization around gender, in contrast to black, Asian, or Irish activists, who initially politicized around race. The first black gay men's group was founded in 1981.[56]

By the 1990s, the antisexist men's movement was a matter of weekends and retreats. Meanwhile, other campaigns created new spaces for men to rethink their position. The Greenham women's peace protest and Women Against Pit Closures had their male supporters, while the trade union movement supported sexual harassment training and pensions for part-time workers, realizing it could only survive with women's membership.[57] LGB alliances were galvanized by AIDS, and the infamous "Clause 28" of the 1988 Local Government Act, which banned the "intentional promotion" of homosexuality in schools.[58]

But most generally there was the public discourse over a "crisis of masculinity" in the context of dual-earner economies and men's unemployment. If women gained, did men automatically lose out? Like Susan Faludi's *Backlash* (1992), Lynne Segal, Ann Oakley, and Juliet Mitchell challenged this deficit model, arguing that all genders gained from women's liberation.[59] Julia Sudbury's *Other Kinds of Dreams: Black Women's Organisations and the Politics of Transformation* (1998) analyzed the "backlash in blackface," unpicking the conditions behind some minority ethnic women's social mobility, challenging black men and women to avoid being pushed into old, racist sex wars in the so-called multicultural Cool Britannia.[60] From queer theory and masculinity studies to poststructuralist and postcolonial theory, there was a new appreciation that we all possess many identities, and the value of building coalitions to facilitate change was recognized.[61] As Pratibha Parmar concluded in 1989: "Critical self-evaluation is a necessary prerequisite for all of us engaged in political struggle if there is to be any movement away from intransigent political positions to tentative new formulations."[62]

The emergence of a more complex way of doing politics demanded new ways of thinking about whose voices were heard. "Can the subaltern speak?" asked philosopher Gayatri Spivak about the Indian women whose perspectives were overlooked, even by well-meaning advocates.[63] This was true within the field of oral history too. Gluck and Patai's 1991 *Women's Words: The Feminist Practice of Oral History* soberly argued that "recovering the voices of suppressed groups" requires much more than "asking appropriate questions, laughing at the right moment, displaying empathy."[64] Oral history involved multiple negotiations across what the authors termed the "linguistic event," to show the social translations involved even if interviewer and interviewee spoke the same language.[65] People often mocked the rarefied terms of deconstructive theories, and yet a more plural vocal representation had entered the public sphere, in the varied accents of the 120 "New" Labour women MPs elected in 1997 and the northeast England ("Geordie") burr of Marcus Bentley announcing the ups and downs of the first *Big Brother* reality TV contestants.

As for the gaze, in 1988 Laura Mulvey herself revised her theory to emphasize that the politics of spectatorship was certainly not the prerogative of men alone, and, indeed, that cross-gender identification and an unstable sexual identity is par for the course.[66] Among the S&A interviewees, photographer Grace Lau represents this move. After being told by the feminist photographic agency *Format* that "I like your photography but we're not ready to address sexuality yet," by 1992, Lau, with Rosie Gunn, Robin Shaw, and Del LaGrace (formerly Della Grace) Volcano, had set up *Exposures for Women*, with projects that attempted to reshape the gaze. Workshops for men to photograph the "female nude" and for women to photograph the "male nude" anticipated Volcano's 1999 trans photography of drag kings.[67] Black artists explored related approaches, notably Kobena Mercer, who argued that the eroticized, racialized black men in Robert Mapplethorpe's photographs could offer positive images for black gay viewers.[68] Radical sexual rights activists sought to harness sexual popular culture and encourage more playful approaches to gender relations.

For some, feminism changed in the 1990s so that pro-feminist men and women were newly able to connect across sexual and gender liberation movements. The "liberal feminist" edges of this alliance were debated in terms of the "third wave" of UK feminism, often represented by Natasha Walters, a journalist and founder of the charity Women for Refugee Women; her 1999 book *The New Feminism* criticized the dungaree-wearing image of Greenham and welcomed "new men" and choice-based feminism.[69] Perhaps Prime Minister Tony Blair, hand in hand with his lawyer and "out" feminist wife Cherie Booth, with a working-class "glottal stop" catch in his voice, was not welcomed by all. Yet by 1999, British men were active in a vast range of initiatives: in social work, therapy, disability activism, black pride, HIV prevention, working with violent men in the criminal justice system, progressive boys' clubs, schools, and autobiographical writing. Many if not most were directly influenced by feminist approaches to power and control.[70] And for the old hands, Daniel Cohen's quip is a nice indicator:

> My friend Asphodel [formerly Pauline Long, described by some as a grandmother of the Goddess movement] . . . once said at some point, "Well, I wouldn't trust any man absolutely. Come to think of it, I wouldn't trust myself absolutely."
> LUCY DELAP: [Laughter][71]

Trauma and Memory: Men's Violence and Movement Identities

One of the most prominent of the WLM demands—the right to freedom from violence—grew out of a response to abuse overwhelmingly by men. Tied to another prominent and related demand—the right to a self-defined sexuality—the two remain the arena for a more confrontational gender politics. Among the S&A interviewees, there are two accounts of incest by fathers; four of rape and more of attempted rape, including rape in marriage; two of domestic violence; and one of an attempted forced marriage. Everyone could remember experiences of sexual harassment, always by men. Their experiences parallel the national picture. In the 2017–18 Crime Survey for England and Wales, 1.3 million women and 695,000 men reported incidents of domestic abuse. Women were four times as likely as men to have experienced sexual violence by a partner in the year and nine times as likely since the age of sixteen: 6.3 percent of women as opposed to 0.7 percent of men. The survey showed a significant decrease in the proportion of women reporting such incidents to the police.[72] The deconstruction of gender, the trials of masculinity, and antisexist men's commitments fit uncomfortably with such statistics. Oral historians, moreover, must interpret interviews about such topics in the context of a highly politicized field of memory.

WLM antiviolence campaigning helped shape the 1976 Domestic Violence Matrimonial Proceedings Act, which introduced civil protection orders, and the Sexual Offences Act of the same year, which began to improve the treatment of rape complainants at trial.[73] However, the appalling crimes of the "Yorkshire Ripper," Peter Sutcliffe, who killed thirteen women in West Yorkshire between 1975 and 1980, galvanized the cause. As a serial rapist and killer stalked the streets, and as media reports drew meaningless distinctions between his sex-worker victims and "respectable" women, feminists looked at the links between domestic violence and street violence. Jalna Hanmer, a university lecturer working in the localities where Sutcliffe committed his atrocities, honed her view that the problem "was in individual men's behaviour to women whom they knew; that's where the problem was. It was about men, fundamentally, not about marriage, not about the family." Much like American lawyer Catherine McKinnon's theories that sexuality was to women what labour was to the working class, this became a plank in the UK version of radical feminist theory, in which "men as a social category benefited from violence against women."[74]

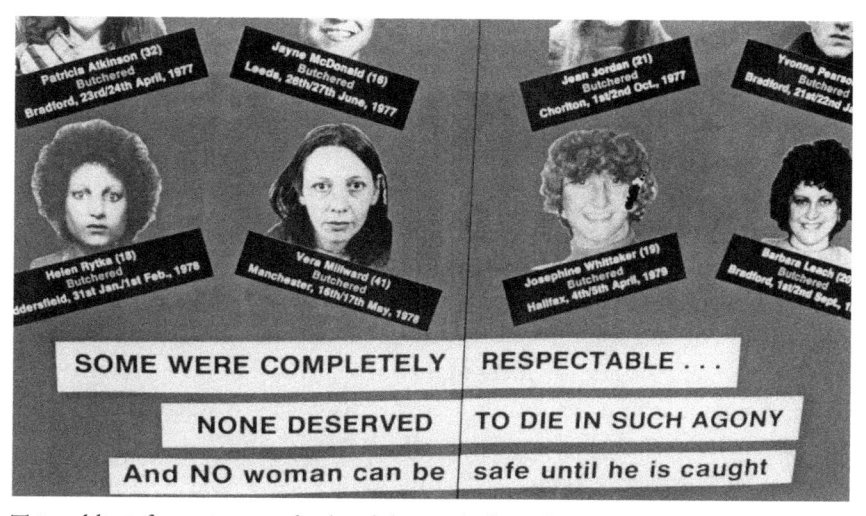

This public information was displayed during the hunt for Peter Sutcliffe, the Yorkshire Ripper, who murdered thirteen women between 1975 and 1980. Many people were outraged when the police, lawyers, and parts of the media drew spurious distinctions between "respectable" women he attacked and women sex workers. *Photo courtesy of Photofusion*

Such arguments stoked the binary view of gender and masculinity with which the men's movement was grappling. Yet men's violence could be a powerfully unifying platform that also recognized the different contexts of race, class, and culture, as the campaigning of the Southall Black Sisters (SBS) on the issue makes clear. Pragna Patel, SBS director since 1982, is upfront about the challenge their "intersectional," multi-issue approach posed for black and Muslim as well as white feminists who did not want to admit to violence in black communities or to work with white activists. She justifies their tactics as borrowing from Indian feminist traditions alongside strategic involvement of white women precisely to counter stereotypes of "barbaric" Asian patriarchy. Their first major campaign in 1984, which stemmed from their outrage over the suicide of Krishna Sharma after years of domestic abuse, set the template: they protested at the inquest and arranged a march to the house of her abuser, "turning around the whole notion of shame and dishonour and who should feel it," as Patel explained. Nervous about going outside the principle of black autonomy, she says nevertheless that "the issue of violence against women is a universal issue, and by *joining* us on the demonstration you're helping to break . . . that stereotype that this is only pertinent to Asian communities. . . . And in the end a lot of women came, and . . . [laughs] I still remember to this day, Mary [McIntosh] helped to . . . run the crèche [nursery] while we went on the demonstration in Southall."[75]

The translatability of campaigns against violence seemed even stronger by the early 1990s, when SBS secured Kiranjit Ahluwalia's freedom after her conviction for murdering her husband was overturned on appeal. The further cases of Sara Thornton and Emma Humphreys "allowed the inequities [of the law] to shine"—that is, men could be acquitted on charges of violence by using the defence that they were provoked—a law finally abolished in 2010.[76] For Vera Baird, who made her name as a barrister defending striking miners and Greenham protestors, the opportunity to represent abused women who kill violent men took her into the women's movement from the hard Left. Just as Hanmer strategically focused on police behaviour in the early 1980s, criminal justice approaches pulled together Rights of Women, Rape Crisis, and Women's Aid with feminist social workers, lawyers, and police.[77] In 1993, a 2,500-strong conference in Brighton, organized by Hanmer, journalist Julie Bindel, and others, took place after a decade in which it seemed no feminist conferences of scale were possible.[78] The same year, the United Nations responded to testimonies of women with the Declaration on the Elimination of Violence Against Women, thus accessing, in the language of the conference abstract, "a universal and seemingly uncontested ethics of cross-cultural relations, an inevitable and natural moral grammar."[79] This was ratified at the 1995 Beijing Fourth World Women's conference, an extraordinary gathering of six thousand delegates and a further thirty thousand activists.[80] As Bea Campbell puts it, "Not even a Tory can happily do away with a Women's Aid refuge."[81]

Indeed, the language of human rights has been applied specifically to remembering as well as the doing of rape, sexual abduction, and other gender-based violence, through the Right to Memory and the Right to Communicate initiatives.[82] Joining marches and discussions, but also viewing artworks, performances, memorials, and archives, creates solidarity and resilience between those who have and have not been abused, stirring a bodily identification and public remembering across generations and groups in the way first theorized by children of Holocaust survivors.[83] The importance of these activities is obvious in the context of the 2010s, where the 1950s is systematically misremembered as a time of sexual innocence and safety.[84]

The "revival" of feminism in the United Kingdom in the 2000s used these forms of collective remembering to powerful effect. Public testifying about gender-based violence, pornography, and sexual abuse has been at the centre of the London Feminist Network, founded in 2004 by Finn MacKay, a charismatic Scotswoman who grew up "obsessed with Greenham Common" and who helped relaunch Reclaim the Night marches.[85] This has grown into thousand-strong annual meetings that end with the annual Emma Humphreys Memorial Awards for service to anti–domestic violence campaigns, organized by Bindel and solicitor Harriet Wistrich. In 2014, awards were given to a woman who had been sexually harassed by her local council member, to whom she had gone with mental health support requests, and an asylum seeker who had been abused while in detention. Hanmer appeared, aged eighty, as an honoured pioneer.

Yet there are risks to orchestrating survivor-based rights campaigns, as they can troublingly play into traditional ideas of gender, good and bad women, sexually forced versus sexually willing.[86] The S&A oral histories, especially when compared with those of adjacent social movement histories, show more complex accounts of sexual violence. Such violence emerges as only one axis of gender relationship, and not the basis on which most WLM activists identified with each other. We can see this in the different ways that S&A interviewees speak of rape: one testimony becomes traumatically mixed up with a "trashing" by other women at the Greenham women's peace camp, suggesting a more complex set of gender relations where women's cruelty is as painful as men's.[87] A different complexity comes when Jenni Murray speaks of being raped after a party in the late 1960s:

> Once I had a—a guy who tried to rape me, you know, I was hitchhiking and he drove off down a side street but I managed to fight that one off. I was raped by another guy which was—I really look back on that experience now with interest because [pause] . . . I mean, whether I'd been taking the Pill or not, he would have done what he did, so that—that the fact that I was on contraception made no difference, it was *not* the worst thing that's ever happened to me, and I was *daft*.[88]

While neither condoning the crime nor the culture of police scepticism that prevented her from reporting it, she refuses a narrative of vulnerability that could be taken up by feminists as well as conservatives determined to control women's sexuality. Jan McKenley, with almost mantric repetition, describes being "full of the fear of rape when I was younger" from her mother's own

> fearfulness about that great unknown outside, outside being a dangerous place, you know, sexual liberation being something *fearful* and sexuality being fearful. I mean, she managed to have five kids and gave an impression of kind of virgin births, really. And the body being something slightly nasty and not nice to touch and not nice to be seen touching yourself and all those sorts of things. So I think those were some of the powerful self-images that the sort of "Black is Beautiful" was trying to kind of work against.[89]

However, while McKenley found sexual confidence in feminist circles, Marie-Thérèse McGivern remembers that the "rape debate" divided and upset women's groups in Northern Ireland in the 1980s when the political lesbian argument that all penetration was rape began to circulate.[90]

Oral histories with pro-feminist men show different uncertainties over how they should relate to campaigns against sexual violence. Jeff Hearn, a colleague of Hanmer's at Bradford University, a socialist with a strong sense of "working-class masculinity," got into the men's movement through feminist literature in the early 1970s. When Hanmer, Hilary Rose, and Sheila Allen set up the United Kingdom's first Applied Women's Studies MA as a "semi-women-only space" in 1981, he started a parallel module on masculinities for the social work degree, which looked at "things like child abuse, and violence, and [inhales] stuff like that—boys and things."[91] This attracted the interest of women's studies students. "And it was a mixture of these women's studies students, who were—you can imagine—and... these Social and Community Work studies, both men and women, who were very different. Especially the men. And then some of the feminist Social and Community Work students were kind of in between. [laughs] Anyway, these were very heavy sessions!"[92]

Hearn published a number of academic papers with Hanmer on the agreement that each worked autonomously, and the work remains one of those most allied to a gender–class analysis, even rejecting the focus on "masculinities" as a theoretical evasion of the actual trouble with "men." Yet Hearn describes an incident when his "town men's group" learned that one of their members was being violent to his partner:

> I mean, he never came again to the group because he was so, I think, shamed, I think, but the issue was that some of the men in the group thought he should be thrown out of the group, and other men in the group thought... um... he shouldn't be thrown out *necessarily*, because there were probably many things, actually, that men do, I mean, that were not necessarily physical violence, but you know, like, okay, to use—perhaps this is an unfair example—to totally avoiding childcare. Now that's not necessarily directly physically violent, but you understand. So this became a sort of divisive issue, and that actually—in fact the group stopped after that actually, in fact.... I thought, well, he shouldn't be expelled but he should be confronted, if you like, and dealt with. And of course you can criticize both positions, obviously. Anyway. Sorry.[93]

BBC engineer (now therapist) Five Cram and his friend Pete 6 (Peter Goodridge), a potter/art-handling company director fond of capes and purple hair also remembered awkwardly responding to other men's violence. Particularly difficult was their effort to act as a referral service for Women's Aid Cardiff, who would send women's violent male partners to their men's group. Not only was this ironic for men who had joined the movement partly because they felt so uncomfortable with other men, but it also showed the social and cultural differences between men; the abusers had "all their worst fears confirmed—when they—when they met us, yes... um."[94]

Many have identified the 1980s as a time when, perhaps perversely, radical feminism gained the upper hand in the UK movement. Lynne Segal opposed its arguments in *Slow Motion: Changing Masculinities, Changing Men* (1990). She addressed "the belly of the beast" by contextualizing the vast majority of rape and domestic violence in impoverished communities, male-on-male violence, shame, financial stress, overcrowding, and heavy policing. The book also considered how the "masculine mystique" compels men denied other forms of expected masculine fulfilment and damages themselves as much as women, in terms of addiction, suicide, and homicide.[95] Segal differentiated between domestic, "date," and psychotic forms of rape, suggesting that the more brutal forms require economic and political as much as judicial or cultural change. Fuelled partly by her sadness at Israeli army violence toward Palestinians, she also compared the obvious violence of poor men with the indirect forms of violence wielded, for example, by white women, and the outsourced violence of capitalism, especially in Central America, the Caribbean, and the Middle East. Finally, Segal explored the unconscious elements of masculinities and femininities within each person, even homicidal Sutcliffe, as products of cultures that equate sex with sin and women.[96] Remembering the book's reception, however, Segal said:

> It was just seen as beyond the pale. I was really criticized. I'll tell you the *funniest* situation. I was swimming up and down in my local pool and the lifeguard saw me and recognized me and jumped up and said, "Are you Lynne Segal?" I said, "Yes." He said, "I think you're too soft on men!" [laughing heartily] He'd been to Essex [University]... [laughs] obviously done some feminism... So this idea I was soft on men was *so* much the main response, not from my friends, it's not what Sheila [Rowbotham] or Mandy [Merck] or Mary [McIntosh] or anyone thought, and indeed I think they thought I was rather bold to write it there because I would be criticized—and I *was* criticized.[97]

Queer theory was to push the argument farther, as Segal found out when trans female masculinity theorist Judith Halberstam confronted her:

> I didn't realize not just that women could be *violent* but women could be *masculine in toto* [hooting]. So she was right, I—that was not something I could encompass at that time pre-queer, and of course my book comes out the same time as *Gender Trouble* that *I'd* yet to hear about... actually Judith Butler [who wrote *Gender Trouble*] had yet to be invented.[98]

Feminism's relationship to traumatic memory becomes even more tangled in relation to child sexual abuse. As with violence and rape, it has been the subject not only of global feminist protest but nineteenth- and early twentieth-century feminist activism.[99] Scotland Rape Crisis's Oral History (2009) shows how the issue emerged often spontaneously, where activists running helplines found they were increasingly contacted by women who wanted help with childhood experiences.[100] But allegations in 1987 of widespread child sexual abuse in Cleveland in northeast England propelled the issue into the national spotlight. The evidence provided by two pediatricians at Middlesbrough General Hospital, Marietta Higgs and Geoffrey Wyatt, helped the authorities remove 121 children from their parents on the grounds of abuse. A subsequent formal inquiry in 1988, chaired by Lord Justice Elizabeth Butler-Sloss, condemned almost all the agencies concerned with the protection of children, including the local MP, Stuart Bell, for his defence of furious parents.[101] Higgs and Wyatt were restricted from working on child abuse cases.[102] Higgs did not describe herself as a feminist, yet the debate galvanized the women-led incest survivors' and child rights campaign in which feminist ideas of sexuality as power were influential. Liz Kelly spoke of a spectrum of sexual violence, which expresses men's sexual socialization through patriarchal family, school, and work structures.[103] Beatrix Campbell prominently took up the cause.[104]

Surviving abuse has involved an epic personal and public form of remembering and of combatting shame. In feminist circles, self-help groups nurtured women to remember forgotten or repressed experiences. Unsurprisingly, the survivors' campaigns encountered resistance, especially from fathers and sections of the media. In the United Kingdom, the British False Memory Society emerged in 1993, patterned on US models, primarily to defend men accused of child abuse and mothers or others who do not accept an accusation.[105]

As arguments about the instability of memory were honed, the conclusions of a 1994 government-commissioned report by a professor of anthropology at the London School of Economics, Jean La Fontaine, that allegations of "satanic" abuse were unfounded, reinforced doubts about testimonies. It is notable that in her Cleveland report Lord Justice Butler-Sloss did not comment on whether children were or were not abused. In the meantime the reactionary pressure group Families Need Fathers, which formed in 1974 to lobby against feminism and gay rights, argued that children benefit from seeing even violent fathers and that male violence is "a final response to violence inflicted in other forms, especially by women, verbal violence."[106] Today it is joined by the militant Fathers 4 Justice, which goes further in attacking, for example, the Fawcett Society, the Labour Party, and even Tory "betrayers" for being brainwashed by feminists.

Beatrix Campbell continues to be critical of La Fontaine's work. She has written extensively about sexual abuse and violence, specifically about "who does what to the body of a child," but rarely talks about herself in this context:

> I don't want anybody thinking about me that way. [pause] And . . . it's hard enough to manage the shame of your own story without that. And . . . I might be wrong and I might be right, who can tell, but I know for sure that even if it did me good, it wouldn't do the story any good, because, it would be enlisted as, Ah, well, you see, all the stuff about masculinity is because she hates men. I don't. All this stuff about sexual abuse is because she's been sexually abused. It's not.[107]

Fathers' rights groups typically reinvent the battle of the sexes that in principle feminism has tried to refute. Yet they raise difficult questions. Feminists themselves drew attention to the constructed nature, if not the falsity, of memories of all kinds, indeed to the unreliability of oral histories. In particular, cognitive psychologist Elizabeth Loftus has suggested that *The Courage to Heal* (1988, UK edition 1990), an immensely influential book in self-help groups, can be a source of false memories. Her approach uses guided imagery to access repressed memories and elaborate details and emotions, while discouraging doubts. The book was certainly comforting to individuals living with memories of abuse, but questioned the effect it would have on people who do not have such memories.[108] Similarly, Janice Haaken argued for the need to engage with ambiguities of stories, the mythic and historical aspects of memory, to prevent a seemingly returned memory from gaining power over the more ordinarily remembered.[109] The growing numbers of boys and men who today testify to abuse forces a more intersectional understanding of how and why institutions such as churches, children's homes, and celebrity culture have permitted and ignored abusive behaviour.

Fathers' custody rights also emerge as a point of uncertainty for feminism, which has long argued that men should share childcare, and for a reformation of masculinity. In contrast to activism around violence and sexual violence, the 1980s saw a disappointing failure in galvanizing action around childcare, despite or perhaps because of a feminist baby boom, as activists hit their thirties and forties.[110] Feminists were also unsure of how to respond to the

Cleveland case. More generally, although feminists thought children should be separated from abusive fathers, they thought fathers, not children, should be required to leave—yet they did not trust the state to save children, or social workers not to blame mothers and the "family system."[111] Campaigners also failed to respond to the 1989 Children's Act, a landmark in recognizing "the child's welfare shall be the paramount consideration," although it proved the Thatcherite "Victorian family" ideology was neither monolithic nor all-powerful.[112] The introduction of the Child Support Act under John Major's premiership in 1992, which forced absent fathers, rather than the state, to pay for their children's upkeep, was also difficult for feminists to respond to. Wages for Housework allied with aggrieved men through a "Payday Men's Network."

But should the state mediate between parents, or indeed mothers and sperm donors? And if so, how? The desire to be good fathers and caregivers, and how to be good, is a major theme in the men's movement—often, for white middle-class men who recall distant and authoritarian fathering. Hearn, a "radical feminist" of the movement who clarifies he is "not pro-fathers," is surely right to argue that we need an ethics that challenges men's control of women through children after the end of marriage, but that also enables men to learn "how to relate to children, women and other men in ways that do not draw on the traditional power of fathers and husbands."[113]

Here, black women had more to negotiate than white women did. Black activists typically rejected white feminists' attacks on the nuclear family as ignorant of the role of family in minoritized communities, and the variety of family structures. But minority ethnic women's movements, especially African Caribbean ones, were also maternalist because of discrimination against young black men. This was exemplified by Mavis Best's (formerly Clarke) lobby, supported by Paul Boateng, then an elected member of the Greater London Council and later a Labour member of Parliament, against the notorious "sus" laws, which allowed police to stop, search, and subsequently arrest a "suspected person."[114] The 1981 repeal of the legislation, though a political triumph, was too late to prevent the uprisings in London, Liverpool, Birmingham, and Manchester in which again young men were victims as well as fighters. The murders of three black men in separate incidents in the London borough of Greenwich in the 1990s, most prominently of Stephen Lawrence in 1993, catalyzed a critical alliance of mothers with sons and fathers.[115] Stephen's mother, Doreen Lawrence, emerged as a campaigner against institutionalized police racism, and twenty years after her son's murder was made a baroness for her charitable work. All the black and Asian interviewees in S&A mentioned this case, none of the white interviewees. Complex families are the global norm, the product of unemployment, migration, and relying on extended families for childraising.[116] The vulnerability of minority ethnic men as well as women underlines the difficulties in formulating children's rights and men's caring in communities already under siege. One S&A interviewee's excruciating experience of having to call the police on her alcoholic partner captures the pain: "For a black woman to call the police on a black man is a *huge* thing. My son was traumatized by it; psychologically it was just a *nightmare*."[117]

Gay rights further complicated a feminist revision of fathering. The GLF generally criticized the nuclear family, partly because many gay men's families, especially fathers, had rejected them. A 1995 oral history of the GLF said nothing about childcare.[118] Yet the men's movement oral history shows fathering was on the agenda of gay as well as straight/bisexual men by the 1980s. Chris Heaume got involved in childrearing when the lesbian couple to whom he had donated sperm separated. Actor Nick Snow loved coparenting with a feminist friend in a gay and lesbian housing cooperative, but painfully lost contact with the child in the 1990s after disputes with the women involved.[119] These memories show the struggles that gay caregivers faced before they gained adoption rights in 2005 and before lesbians became eligible for in vitro fertilization in 2002.

While far from the radical communitarianism of GLF, these changes legitimized a form of parenting that challenges not only gender but sexual models of reproduction. MP Harriet Harman, briefly Secretary of State and Minister for Women under Tony Blair, sees such legal breakthroughs as part of the belated fulfilment of many women's movement demands after Labour's reelection in 2001. This included more state-funded childcare, lone mothers' right to work, and paternity as well as maternity leave (still far better in the United Kingdom than the United States), all within a model of the family that does not presume that a nuclear family or a father's presence is essential or benign.[120]

Remembering such dilemmas is tied into the difficulty of campaigning on many interconnected fronts. Memory, even when traumatic, must be kept *conscious* in order to challenge violent inequalities and sometimes the inequality of violence itself. Conflict resolution tries to achieve this goal, and it is no coincidence that several WLM activists became involved with this, particularly in Northern Ireland, the former Yugoslavia, and South Africa in the 1990s.[121] Rape and child abuse survivor movements also include rituals of personal forgiveness. But the recent difficulties of the UK government's commission into historic sex abuse shows how much survivors also want punishment for perpetrators.

Oral historians, on a different scale, have their own tradition of work with survivors, arguing that "deep listening" can support a processing, even if not a full articulation, of wounding experiences.[122] But it is not obvious how to respond to hearing or sharing past traumas. Consciousness raising's functions were semiprofessionalized in feminist therapy and health practices for some of the same reasons, although some argued that such processes depoliticized earlier models of collectively sharing difficult experiences as a catalyst for action. The history of feminist oral history indeed has also become professionalized to make clear it is not ersatz therapy, nor indeed legal testimony or qualitative research.

Moreover, movements create their own traumas, even as they reactivate old ones. Ironically, the most audible shame in our oral histories reflects fears for reputation *within* movement communities.[123] S&A interviewees shifted uncomfortably when asked whom the movement represented, slowing their speech, searching for justifications, or worrying they could not remember names. These are not the traumatic repetitions of someone recovering from abuse, nor of someone who risks legal judgment. Rather, these are symptoms of remembered arguments and accusations between supposed allies. As such, they pose questions of how social movements manage relationships not simply between victims and perpetrators but between oppressors who are the most eager to relinquish inherited power and those wishing to discover their own, or indeed, between individuals who are simultaneously oppressor and oppressed.[124]

The dynamics here are similar to those between white and black feminists, Jewish and Gentile, Protestant and Catholic, heterosexual and lesbian, and currently, cis (people comfortable with the gender assigned at birth) and trans feminists, or any other deeply politicized relationship in which differences are hammered out within a social movement. Black and working-class women clearly did not want white, middle-class women to become subservient, needy, and apologetic, either; they wanted allies. Yet guilt and shame were ever-present in women's movements as well as men's, in a perplexing spiral that included feeling guilty about feeling guilty.[125] Some of this emotion reflected the United Kingdom's endemic class consciousness, and socialist critiques of consumption merging with embarrassment over material pleasures and inequalities, especially around house ownership. Guilt also motivated political action—a "Trotskyist trick of the trade," Rowbotham suggested.[126]

From the late 1970s, however, WLM activists were clearly testing their own racial identities in ways they had previously tested class identity. This development was not because there had previously been no black women's activism, although racism was becoming more visible to white people. Rather, the timing of the race debates in the WLM reflected the fact that black women became more interested in (white) feminism, having initially found it irrelevant or off-putting, while white women from Jewish, ethnic minority, and the Celtic nations were becoming more interested in their own different identities. Further, as the WLM came to blows over lesbian feminism, the "second" big test came to take the responsibility for some of the first. Heterosexual memory is often enigmatic in the feminist record, including the S&A interviews, although almost two-thirds of interviewees were married or had relationships of more than twenty years with men.[127]

Natalie Thomlinson shrewdly attributes part of the psychological shock white women felt over being challenged on race to the small group structure and intense ethic of care within the WLM, which led many women to expect self-valorization alongside taking on each other's traumas.[128] Amrit Wilson, an Indian woman involved in the bitter arguments over race relations in *Spare Rib*, evokes the messy results:

> You *always* felt excluded, you *always* felt like an outsider who was somehow being given space. So there was a lot of that, but having said that, I *did* stick with *Spare Rib*, and I *did* write, and gradually *Spare Rib* became more open to things, and there's absolutely no doubt that it changed its approach. So I suppose we had an impact in that sense. At broader conferences, I mean, there was always the issue of "what can we do for you," right, "you poor, poor things, what can we do for you?" So there wasn't any understanding of the notion of struggle or of solidarity. And ultimately, we felt that maybe we couldn't get *through* in many of these meetings, that it was just too much, you know. We'd have women *crying* in meetings, or often I was particularly notorious as somebody horribly aggressive because so many women *cried* when I spoke.[129]

White women's tears seem to result from being criticized as much as their "extreme pity" of British Asian women's imagined lot, but their upset again could lead to further pointless self-examination as opposed to useful political action. And Wilson, too, was anxious about being represented accurately.[130] She tells of how, at the office of the *Observer* newspaper, she tore up a draft spread featuring *Finding a Voice: Asian Women in Britain*, furious that it focused only on the issue of arranged marriage. The newspaper got word to Wilson's husband, asking, "Can you stop your wife from doing this? She's gone berserk."[131] Wilson, dropping back into her "own" voice as she recounted the story, adds, "To his credit, he said, 'I don't stop my wife from doing anything.'" Although Wilson redirected the paper's orientalizing focus (the *Observer* promoted her chapter on isolation instead), this anecdote shows how concerned she was about not being quoted out of context.[132] Indeed, *Finding a Voice* was criticized later by Pratibha Parmar, who, though it made her cry, felt it would play too much to white stereotyping.[133] Here the politics of the voice is again less obvious than it seems—as Wilson conveys, as she herself tried to fit in with the British Asian community:

> But I *did* make an attempt to fit in with them, you know, in terms of dress, in terms of attitude, because I knew that I was so used to.... So I did do all that, admittedly, but I thought I should be sensitive to the other person.[134]

As with men's movement groups, white women sometimes created therapeutically infused antiracist consciousness-raising groups that avoided demanding anything from black women but were often agonizing affairs comparable to men looking for sexism in themselves. Again, there was a performative aspect here, as the groups perhaps even encouraged women to admit to greater feelings of racism than they possessed.[135] Moreover, they contributed to the small group culture that would further discourage people less ready for this kind of display, although others, such as Beatrix Campbell, relished the fray:

> I speak as a white woman: one of the *great* privileges of feminism was that we just got knocked about, and I think that was an amazing privilege, to have access to very challenging black women, who were prepared to *be* with white women. I mean, how precious was that? And so, I know that some people felt a bit bashed up by it. [Breath.] I just felt that, you know, we had to be challenged, we *were* challenged; we had to get off our knees and not be *craven* in the face of that challenge, and take responsibility for it, and do our homework. And, and many people *did*. And we all benefited from that *very, very, very* tough dialogue.[136]

Listening to memories of schisms, factions, sectarian or personal "bashing," especially as they connected to guilt over prejudices or advantages, reveals the extent to which an activist's reputation matters within movements. In the WLM, maintaining a good reputation had less to do with men's violence than women's. Many have related aggressive competition to unconscious relationships with mothers, to daughterly rebellion against control, particularly of sexuality. As Barbara Taylor put it, "Very dark emotion flow[ed] around the women's movement" in this respect.[137] But though this rings true, the fact that there were similarly emotional splits in every other movement suggests what Freud described as the "narcissism of small differences," or the competitive impulses that attach precisely to those closest to us. Taylor is fantastically honest about her destructive approach to the *New Left Review* when the men *did* try to include a decent number of women on its editorial board in the mid-1980s, "maximalizing" demands to the point where all the women left. This is the deep secret of "difference"—by the time it plays out within a movement, it is usually exceedingly narrow.[138]

Yet this aggressive rivalry also expresses an equally powerful political conscience. The signs of discomposure in white feminists' memories of race are not evidence of proven guilt so much as heightened concern.[139] Similarly, the "inner voice" that reverberates through men's movement accounts, Colin Thomas's for example, wondering what his wife would think if she were a fly on the wall of the oral history interview, represents an internalized political morality.[140] For this reason, there is evident relief when the interviewer appears to accept the sinner, audible in Delap's interviews with men, who move from low, slow tones to joking, laughing, sometimes crying, later sending effusive thank-you emails, as their past efforts seem validated by an informed, respectful Cambridge feminist historian. In contrast, when the oral historian has nothing to forgive and may indeed wish for pardoning acceptance, the interview's scene of conscience may be marked with distrust.

Jeska Rees met with extreme suspicion when interviewing eight of the most prominent "Revolutionary Feminists," who asked her directly whether she was a lesbian. She decided that younger generations of scholars might be owed a little more trust.[141] S&A's all-white interviewing team were concerned about our ability to engage fully with questions of racism, particularly with minority ethnic interviewees, although Rachel Cohen's knowledge of race relations in the movement brought an informed perspective.[142] Differences within the oral history interview thus gesture to the narcissism of small differences that grip social movements in their attempts to right the wrongs in bigger differences. Yet in this echoing, they also capture, though often only in the cracks and slips, the interviewees' grounds for activism—care and conscience, anger and hope.

Together in the Time of Transgendered Liberation

A focus on what differentiates us still commands discussion in social movement activism.[143] This partly arises from unformalized power structures, competition to attract limited funding, political opportunities, past traumas, and the psychologies of social movements that magnify expectation and disappointment. However, it also reflects the context of postmodern needs and demands, which prioritize identity and cultural recognition as much as equality. The logic of postindustrial and digital societies indeed leads to ever more diversifying claims by groups, though met with unprecedented inequality of opportunity to make them.[144]

The basis of feminist politics in this context is complex. Indeed, the tension over womanhood as something to defend or transcend, prioritize or contextualize, remains central. The ongoing appeal of radical feminism is that it addresses primal fears of sexual violence, alongside equally primal pleasures in women's community, desire, and love. It responds to the sexualization of youth culture and internet porn and the ever-troubling questions of body image for the young. Its achievements are reflected in new legal and human rights, party politics, academic activity, subcultures, markets, medical practice, popular culture, religious groups, and victim–perpetrator programmes.

But more "intersectional" forms of gender politics have their own political influence, in academia, niche identities, internet communities, minority ethnic, leftist, and liberal groups. Revived national feminist networks such as Rights of Women and the Fawcett Society attempt to mediate, the latter including explicit appeals to men and partnership with Fathers Direct, a government-funded think tank promoting fathers' interests in gender equality. Here, neoliberalism can in its own way help undermine absolutist models of gender difference promoted by backlashing antifeminists. Gender equality remains a distant goal, but men and women—albeit within often disconnected class/ethnic groups—are converging in their attitudes, activities, and life-course patterns, with dual-earner families, shared domestic work, urban living and working, mixed-gender schooling and adolescent rebellion, and sexual rights for girls as well as boys. Further, the greater presence of young men in women's movements, alongside a growing number of young people identifying as LGB (30 percent between ages 18 and 26), suggests that gender means something changeable and political for them as well.[145]

Most of all, the explosion of the transsexual and transgendered liberation movement in the 2000s is revolutionizing gender identities, relationships, and philosophies, with obvious challenges to earlier feminist premises. If those assigned male identity at birth desire to be women, what does this say about male power, and might it be a welcome abdication of it? If people designated female at birth desire to be men, what too does this say about feminist (and lesbian and queer) models of alternative womanhood? If feminism draws on women's oppression, how does it respond to the experiences of people whose histories are usually so different from those of ciswomen? How are ideas of sexuality and reproduction, as well as equal pay, time, and representation, reworked from the point of view of cisgendered privilege? More fundamentally, how does a newly biologized understanding of gender, in which body shape, chromosomes, hormones, sex organs, and brain are all engaged, relate to an equally insistent emphasis on the changeability and fluidity of gender, through technology but also conversation and touch? EJ Scott, a trans man interviewed for the Brighton Trans*formed oral history in 2013, encapsulates the puzzle for many feminists, themselves included:

> My brother doesn't have a problem with my trans status at all, but he doesn't understand why I had to transition. Because when I was a young, radical queer "dyke," for want of a better description, I was a raging feminist; I still am. And my brother was brought up by me lecturing him, you know, "Women can do anything. Women are strong." I instilled that feminist ethic that he still holds today. So he didn't understand why I needed a male body to be me and why I needed to do what I needed to do.
>
> I still don't have a lot of the language surrounding having to explain that. I don't have the answers for that. I don't know why I have such a deep-seated problem with my own physicality that I literally had to change gender, because I don't believe in gender binaries, so why on earth did I need to be a man? I don't know, and my brother doesn't know either. But I just have to say to him, "Look how much happier I am" and every time we have this conversation that's where he stops and he's like, "Absolutely, there is no denying that; you are happier since you transitioned."[146]

And this, from Michelle, a trans woman, underlining the seeming irrelevance of sexuality for most deciding to transition:

> I'd lived in Brighton for twenty years, but in a relationship, and I'd eventually married and had children. Then last year I found myself questioning what was going on in my head. I'd met some cross-dressing

people and some people that were ambiguous and androgynous and things. I was very pro-androgyny, and I was very pro-feminism, and very pro-queer, and lots of things that weren't typically heterosexual male-orientated things. Yet I couldn't grasp my sexuality because I didn't know if I was gay or not. I didn't think I was, so the whole thing was very puzzling in my mind.[147]

It is unsurprising that trans activists largely feel unconnected to the feminism of the WLM period that was based on reclaiming pride for a ciswoman's body, on the one hand, and on detaching gender from biological determinism on the other. The 1978 UK edition of *Our Bodies, Ourselves,* so central to the feminist health movement, contains nothing on gender variance and discusses hormones only in relation to contraception, for example.[148] But feminist and trans movements both propose gender as a system of violent control and inequality. Both demand reproductive and sexual choice, nondiscrimination in paid work, safety—far worse for trans than ciswomen, statistically—and political representation, nicely captured when Brighton & Hove City Council removed "Mr. and Mrs." from its paperwork after a Trans Equality Scrutiny exercise.[149]

Even as a trans feminist politics emerges, however, the distrust and rivalries seen in other movements are evident, amplified, and accelerated, in large degree by the internet. Few feminists now argue that trans women are really men attempting to infiltrate the women's movement. But radical feminist Finn MacKay represents a larger group who believe that, despite so much shared oppression, "male supremacy" continues to afflict ciswomen differently from trans women and that, particularly in relation to sexual abuse, alliances should not preclude separate spaces.[150] Jacqueline Rose, by contrast, a long-time psychoanalytic feminist in the WLM, puts it that once again this is a question of fear of identifying, of an unconscious closeness within difference: "The bar of sexual difference is ruthless but that doesn't mean that those who believe they subscribe to its law have any more idea of what is going on beneath the surface than the one who submits less willingly."[151]

Rose encourages cis-feminists to take up Kate Bornstein's proposal to realize the "seams and sutures" we all have, literally in a world of cosmetic surgery and hormonal treatment for non-trans people. Indeed, the non-trans person has arguably greater responsibility to challenge gender stereotypes and acknowledge newly claimed trans identities.[152] Meanwhile trans movements are themselves diversifying, with arguments between male-to-female, female-to-male, those who want to be visibly trans and those for whom that is their last wish, essentialists and constructionists, minoritarians and universalists, straights and queers, celebrities and now some de-transitioners. Equally, the danger of being only identified through victim narratives is repeated—including at the annual Remembering Our Dead ceremony for those killed out of fear or prejudice, founded in the United States in 1998, which takes place now in many countries. Just as with initiatives to combat violence against women, this ritual also risks covering up complexity, for example about race: trans people of colour are more likely to face persecution.[153]

It is intriguing to imagine what might have happened if trans liberation had mobilized at the time as the WLM and whether its passionate desire for gender would have modified the WLM's critique of gender. In some accounts, trans liberation was indeed the "missing" movement of the 1970s and 1980s: even more stigmatized than sexual minorities and dependent on a still clunky medical service, some trans activists had been tentatively organizing from the late 1960s. We can glimpse a few in Lisa Power's 1995 oral history of the GLF, where Rachel Pollack (subsequently a figure in the Goddess movement) was ironically welcomed more by the separatist women's elements than gay men; in Ros Kaveney's 1988 novel (not published until 2015) about trans street life in the late 1970s, in which a feminist character heartily disapproves of the seeming conventionality of her trans friend; and in Stephen Whittle's accounts of radical feminist activism, transitioning in the late 1970s, and becoming a global leader in trans legal rights.[154]

But trans liberation was "delayed" in the United Kingdom by the 1971 court ruling that the marriage of April Ashley to Arthur Corbett was illegal because Ashley was "really" male—denying the legal status of transsexuals until the ruling was overturned with the 2004 Gender Recognition Act. Now transsexuals can marry, on condition that they first obtain a Gender Recognition Certificate, forcing some already married couples to divorce in order to remarry if one or both transitions. Despite the ongoing binarizing and stigmatizing that this implies, trans activists insist that gender is important, pleasurable, nontranscendable for most people. This is changing the territory for feminism, refuting the pessimistic vision of gender as essentially "oppressor and oppressed." It returns us to the question of how we can live with, as well as challenge, differences.

Two people, at least, suggest a kind of answer within a marriage cemented before the WLM but transformed by and through it, in which the question of gender proved neither more nor less important than that of race. Catherine and Stuart Hall were intellectuals who devoted themselves to the politics of identities in the widest sense, as part of the histories of subjectivities and cultures as well as racial, gendered, and capitalist economies. Their ideas, students, texts, and institutional groupings have entered the stream of radical education that itself has been one of the most important achievements of the social movements of the 1960s through to the 1980s. Both were committed to adult and working-class educational opportunities. They were involved in activist initiatives in Birmingham, which in the 1970s and 1980s was experiencing the rising pressures for African Caribbean and Asian settlers, most visible in the Handsworth uprisings of 1981. Birmingham was also the site of the final National Women's Liberation conference in 1978, which Catherine Hall helped organize. Both enjoyed excellent educations and other advantages that made them unusual even within the social movement circles of the time. Yet both were in characteristic ways initially isolated by histories that they were later able to challenge. Drawing from two separately undertaken oral histories for two different projects, I interweave their words to suggest that part of the burden, but also the means of solution, came from their relationship itself.[155]

Two Lives and One Marriage: From the Oral Histories of Catherine and Stuart Hall

CATHERINE HALL: I was born Catherine Mary Barrett.... And I got married when I was nineteen, and that was in 1964, before the women's movement. And so I took my husband's name without finding that in the least problematic.... I had vague thoughts about whether I should go back to "Barrett," and I never thought it made any sense because that was my father's name, and why was that any preferable to my husband's name?

STUART HALL: I was born in Jamaica in 1932 ... into a coloured middle-class Jamaican family. My father had been from a lower-middle-class family, but he had been quite well educated, and he got a job ... with the United Fruit Company. He ... was the first local Jamaican to hold every post he had, and finally ended up as the chief accountant.... My mother, however, came from a *very* different background. Her mother was a postmistress, and her father was, I think ... "Jamaican white"—you'll understand what I mean! [smiling voice]

CATHERINE HALL: I was born on 18th February 1946 in Kettering.... I must have been conceived ... very close to the end of the war, when things looked a bit more—hopeful.... My mother's maiden name was Hipkin.... Her family were ... millers, who'd lived in the Peterborough area for several generations.... She went to a girls' grammar school ... and ... to do [study] history at Oxford in the late 1920s.... If she hadn't married my father, she would undoubtedly have become an academic historian. She did [studied for] a DPhil in Oxford, which again she got a scholarship for. But then she married my father, and being a clergyman's wife was a fulltime occupation.

STUART HALL: My father's family lived in Old Harbour.... It's the less interesting, less picturesque part of Jamaica.... My mother, on the other hand, came from ... this Grosset family, who were a very prominent family in Port Antonio ... definitely part of the Port Antonio elite ... and we've since discovered, through Catherine's work on slave owners, that John Grosset, in the nineteenth century, was a plantation owner, active pro-slaver.... My mother was brought up ... *as if she* were an estate girl.... You know, she drove the buggies, and she gave commands. [smiling voice]

Apocryphal story.... When my sister looked into the crib and saw me, she said, "Where did you get this coolie baby from?" Because ... within that family, there was every shade! My mother was the fairest, my brother was almost as fair as her. My sister was a bit darker. I was *distinctly* darker, much closer to my father and my father's family.

My mother really thought ... some sort of some genetic error had occurred to make her not English! Indeed, her mother's name was "Hopwood" [gentle laugh], and she became convinced, at one stage, that this was a derivation from *Hapsburg*! So ... this is the Freudian Colonial family romance.... My father wasn't quite like that.

CATHERINE HALL: My father *never* talked about his adoption to us and didn't talk to my mother about it until well after they were married. And it was clearly a shameful matter for him.... It seems that he was in fact the biological child of the man who adopted him but that his adopted mother was not his biological mother.... My father was, for *us*, a very open, honest person.[156] So discovering these aspects of his own background has been very [pause] troubling.

STUART HALL: I would have Christmas at home—deathly ... ham and turkey, and two kinds of hot Christmas puddings! [Chuckles] Temperature outside 95°! ... Boxing Day, we went to Old Harbour. *Completely* different. The place teeming with people ... always invited was the Anglican priest and the Catholic priest, because my father's family was divided between the two.... And my grandmother said, "There are only three things I will not have discussed at the Christmas table. One is religion. Two is politics. And three is the abdication of Edward VIII." [Laughs] So I just adored her. I wear her wedding ring.

CATHERINE HALL: Baptists started as dissenters in the full meaning of the word. They believe in adult baptism . . . only through adult choice can you really become part of the Christian community. . . . My brother, my sister, myself never did. . . . There's always been a kind of radical progressive wing, and . . . a . . . reactionary wing. . . . My father was *absolutely* attached to the radical progressive wing. . . . He had a very sunshiny presence. . . . I was his little sunshine [smiling voice]. . . . I often remember him with his dog collar on.

My parents had very little money all through; you know, Baptist ministers don't earn very much, to put it mildly. And my mother had—my mother had long hair, which as a child—when I was a child she wore it in plaits, plaited round her head.

STUART HALL: I went to Jamaica College—one of the . . . schools that the educated middle classes go to—by that stage, black boys on scholarship had come to the school. . . . Mother would *not* allow me to bring a black boy home. . . . So my life was divided between people that they liked—including girls that they thought were appropriate for me, about whom I had no feeling whatsoever [laughs]—and my underground life with my friends at school.

CATHERINE HALL: [My sister] was the older one. She had to fight lots of battles that I then didn't have to fight. . . . I was not identified as a clever child in the way that my sister was [smiling voice], so there was less pressure on me. . . . My mother's identification with my sister was very, very strong and she was destined for Oxbridge from a very early age.

STUART HALL: My sister went to work and [pause] fell in love with . . . a black Barbadian student, medical student—very educated, etc., etc.—but black. My mother said, *No!* . . . They broke it off. My sister had the most *tremendous* mental breakdown within two months. She was given shock therapy. . . . And I suddenly saw that the whole . . . macrocosm of Jamaican society and its problems and intricacies, were being mirrored inside the family culture, you know? . . . And that's when I decided, if I get the chance to study, I don't want to go to the University of the West Indies and live at home, I want to go elsewhere.

CATHERINE HALL: I *know* why, given the kind of background I had, I got involved in the women's movement. . . . middle-class background, radical dissenting background, strong mother, grammar school girl, new university . . . it's completely classic. . . . I understand all that historically and psychically, that emotionally I really was *looking* for . . . both a political and a personal identity—and an intellectual identity.

STUART HALL: We had a tuck shop [candy store near the school], imitation *Tom Brown's Schooldays* . . . you will find these schools throughout the Caribbean.... I did [studied] Latin; history was principally the history of England. Empire, was not, as far as I know, ever mentioned. I never was taught anything about slavery in my *entire* life formally in school.... We were the subalterns. They were going to leave eventually, and the place had to be left in safe hands.

CATHERINE HALL: Going to a single-sex school had terrible disadvantages.... There was no ease of mixing with boys.... The [atomic] bomb became a very present fear and so YCND [Youth Campaign for Nuclear Disarmament]... I got involved with [it] and the Young Socialists.

STUART HALL: I arrived on ... a banana boat and passenger ship, and my mother was with me ... with a huge steamer trunk, to deliver to Merton College, Oxford. [Chuckles] ... It was all, in some way, uncannily familiar.... On the other hand, ... the dark sombre colours, ... the drizzly wet of August.... We went to the Festival of Britain—1951, we went to the Houses of Parliament ... went to [the play of Agatha Christie's] *The Mousetrap*! [Laughs]

I walked past Paddington Station one day, and I saw this *stream* of ordinary Jamaican people coming out ... and I thought, "Who *are* these? Where are they going?" [wondering voice].... It was only two years after the arrival of *The Windrush* [passenger ship that brought one of the first large groups of West Indian migrants to the United Kingdom], which is 1948.... *There* was my problem! [Laughs] ... In their brimmed felt hats and their brightly coloured dresses, and their baskets—an incredible sight! And I thought, "Can they find work that isn't available in Jamaica?" ... "What sort of Jamaicans will they *be* in ten years?" ... This experience would transform them.... In that sense, they, and I, couldn't *really* go home again.... So for the first time, their fates and mine were sort of the same! That's where I learnt to see life as a diasporic subject.

I went to Oxford to read [study] literature.... There were no black students in my college; there were a few Indian students.... [Hugo] Dyson once said to me, "Oh, well, Stuart" [imitates clipped English voice] ... "When you go back, you'll be governor, won't you, or something like that," and I thought, "What *are* you talking about? You don't have a *clue* who I am. You don't know where I come from, where I'm going back to. I've been sitting in this bloody room with you, week after week after week, *pouring* out my heart and my mind, and you just don't know who I am!"

CATHERINE HALL: I went to Sussex [University in 1963] but ... I was in a pretty bad state.... My mother was *incredibly* depressed. My father was still very, very much an invalid. Sussex ... was already sort of north London by the sea.... I ... felt like a kind of northern provincial girl, ... didn't have the right clothes, I didn't know the right things.... I was in emotional turmoil.... I'd met Stuart, it had become already a very serious relationship. You know, I was very young and he was much older.

STUART HALL: What was I to do? [Chuckles] Oxford—no. MA, hoping to be a DPhil, but meanwhile not a social skill in the world! [Laughs out loud] Could I drive a milk float [milk delivery truck]? No, I didn't have a license then! Well, I could be a secondary school teacher.... So I got a job.

CATHERINE HALL: I met Stuart ... on an Aldermaston march [antinuclear bomb protest in 1962].... My sister ... and her boyfriend, who she then married, Michael Rustin, were both involved in the student part of the New Left in Oxford, and Stuart at that time was very heavily involved in the New Left. So Margaret through Michael got to know Stuart.... So I met Stuart ... again when I came to London the following summer, because they were doing lots of things together.

Well, he's a very beautiful man, very charismatic, surrounded by ... young followers of both sexes. Very intellectually powerful, already, you know, very established as a public figure. Strong physical presence ... and I was very young.

STUART HALL: She was eighteen—I'm fourteen years older than she is—so I was already a kind of established figure, you know. We met after an Aldermaston march, and two Aldermaston marches after that I spoke in Trafalgar Square, she was on her way to Sussex to do her undergraduate degree. So there was a *big* disparity between us ...

It wasn't a good period of her life ... and not a very happy period of mine, because I'd, by then, taken [made] the decision to stay, but not fully reckoned what that meant. You know, what did it mean to live in England for the rest of my life, rather than in the Caribbean? So we were both at odds, in a sort of odd situation. So we got together.

CATHERINE HALL: [My parents] really liked him, from the beginning. And there was never an issue about him being black. They were worried about—until they got to know him, about him being so much older than me, but really he completely won them over from the very beginning.... Of course, we'd ... absolutely been brought up to think of everyone as equal, ... but when my sister first had a Trinidadian boyfriend it caused ructions [a fuss]. So I think ... my mother worked through some issues there and it was really never an issue with Stuart.

And then in the autumn of '63 ... Richard Hoggart got some money from Penguin after *The Uses of Literary* to set up some research in Birmingham and asked Stuart to go, and that ... was the origins of the Centre for Cultural

Studies. And in the first year and a term that I was at Sussex, we were travelling up and down... I was never settled in Brighton at all. And then we decided to get married because—partly because of my father and not wanting him to be distressed about the idea of our living together when we weren't married. So in December '64 we got married and I... transferred to Birmingham University.

STUART HALL: It took a long time to equalize that balance, between me as a more established figure on the Left, in his early thirties, and an eighteen-year-old trying to learn how to become a historian. It took a *long* time. There was a big imbalance, and I'm afraid, in my characteristically masculinist way, I thought this was right! [Chuckles] We have love letters in which I in entirely D. H. Lawrencian language, see planets circling around the moon! [Laughs] Ridiculous nonsense! But when you look back at them, they weren't at all antifeminist or anything; one just assumed that the man led, and was experienced and knew things, and talked well, and did theory.... And it's quite a while before our interests began to converge, and then, really, we were able to learn from one another, though *she* said she always learned from me. But I didn't think, in that area, I had much to learn, I learnt that, and then I learnt from *her!* [Laughs]

CATHERINE HALL: I didn't feel in awe emotionally; otherwise it could never have worked... but... it was... pretty [pauses] scary basically for such a young woman.... We'd go and stay with Edward and Dorothy Thompson and I just felt like an ignorant little girl.... It was completely opaque to them why the wonderful Stuart should have chosen *me*. But I knew *emotionally* why he'd chosen me and why I'd chosen him, so there was a... confidence... from the beginning in what I could give him. But it took me a *very*, very long time to establish... intellectual equality with him.

Until I got my degree I really didn't know what I was going to do.... Then I got... a first [highest grade for a university degree] and I got a grant immediately, so... I was very, very happy to... become a postgraduate.... I chose to do [study] medieval history, which was because I thought that [Rodney Hilton] was such a wonderful teacher, but it was a foolish decision really because my Latin was just not good enough.... So that didn't last very long, but it gave me—it gave me a base. And then in '68 I had Becky.

STUART HALL: The Centre for Cultural Studies... became very involved in the 1968 occupation of the Main Hall in Birmingham, as a protest about the increase in overseas students' fees. Indeed, the Centre published an issue of the Birmingham University magazine, addressed to the Vice Chancellor, called "To Sir, With Love" . . . times are changing, you know—it's a very undemocratic place—reflecting the sixties.

CATHERINE HALL: I was very far pregnant by the time of the occupation. . . . I can see myself completely clearly. I had this wonderful turquoise corduroy—it wasn't a maternity dress at all but I wore it as a maternity dress. It was just like a little tent. So I had this huge bump and this turquoise—brilliant blue, you know, with a high collar. It was a lovely dress. But of course I was completely different from everybody else. Nobody else was pregnant, nobody had children. But they were very nice to me . . . they wouldn't let me stay overnight . . . but again, you know, it was the men who were dominating—and a lot of women's politics came out of that.

STUART HALL: Well. Now she's locked up at home with a young baby, starting a medieval history PhD, and I'm teaching my life out at the Centre. So she was ready-made for . . . feminism. And lots of other people like her—those mothers with academic husbands, or people who worked elsewhere, who are locked up for the first time, at home, with children—got together. So Birmingham started a crèche [nursery], and a school, and jointly parents looking after other children, and the whole neighbourhood became a kind of feminist network. . . . This is a very difficult period for us, because that rubbish about moons and planets just had to go! It had [laughing], it had to go! [Laughs]

CATHERINE HALL: I knew almost nothing about babies and young children. . . . All my friends were students. . . . The birth wasn't straightforward, and I was in labour for a very long time, so I was very, very exhausted afterwards. . . . I had to adjust to being at home with a baby and . . . I had to learn how to look after her. . . . From the moment she was born, Stuart completely fell in love with her. . . . I think he thought he wouldn't have a child, and it really was like magic. So it changed our relationship obviously. . . . And the absolute assumption was that I would look after the baby and Stuart would go on working. I mean, it never occurred to us to question that. . . . And it was with one of those new friends [Val Hart] . . . also completely discombobulated by . . . all her political life disappearing and thinking, well, who am I now, what do I do, how do I make this new kind of life with a baby? So we just started talking and that was the origins of the first women's group that we started.

STUART HALL: And what I discovered from it is that you change your ideas, but your practice is much more stubborn. . . . I was in favour of this equality. Of course! *Obvious!* . . . Men bossed them about and tell them what to do, as I have done with Catherine, so this has to stop. But what was an alternative way of relating to one another? I didn't believe [men] could become feminists; I still don't believe that. I think they can become sympathetic to it, and understand it from the inside, and try to change their own practice [smiling voice]. In any case ... the early stages of second-wave feminism, they didn't want to *hear* from me! "Shut up! We're going somewhere else. Have our conversation, listen to our *own* voices for a change!" So that has been another big transformative moment for us. It took quite a long time, and by the end our relationship was very different from the dependent/independent thing that it started out.

CATHERINE HALL: We [the women] were certainly supposed to look after the children. . . . [The men] tended to think that they were the group who talked and the women would listen. And ... even ... very strong women like Juliet Mitchell had trouble kind of establishing a presence as a political and intellectual equal. . . . I think the New Left men were ... a *major* factor in making me a feminist, absolutely! [Laughs]

You know, the frustrations of motherhood, the sense of isolation, the boredom, the—being at the beck and call of somebody else, the loss of independence ... sharing it was just so fantastic, actually. . . . "What do you do?" "Oh, I'm a housewife." You know, it's—it wasn't an identity to be proud of. It was ... being a non-person, really, in a world where ... people were teaching and writing books. . . . Obviously everything that's encompassed in saying the personal is political, thinking that, you know, it was perfectly reasonable to say, "You do the washing up [the dishes]" or "Why don't you cook tonight?" or, "You know, you should pick up your clothes when they need washing," or "You should put the washing machine on," even. . . . We were all middle class. We'd all been brought up to think that, you know, our job was to look after our husbands and children in whatever—many varied versions of that, but nevertheless a powerful imperative about what it meant to be a woman.

STUART HALL: I just *assumed* our inequality, and after that I couldn't assume it. I ... therefore had to tolerate—you know, if she'd have friends I didn't particularly like—okay. We had to decide what sort of marriage it was: an open marriage—whatever that is—or, we're going to try to remain monogamous. What did *that* tell you about men and women, and about marriage, as a kind of contract, a binding contract on women? Then there's the sexual politics. So it's a period of huge turbulence. And because Catherine was involved in all of that—very actively involved—it was a matter of in the home as well. How do you bring up the children? Do you give the boys guns? I had *always* had guns, I grew up with holsters and air rifles at home! . . . What about the girls, read them cowboy stories, etc.! [laughs] . . . Were we going to stay together?... And eventually there was no question, we decided to do so, but after that we couldn't live the old relationship. Not possibly, inconceivably.

CATHERINE HALL: I was bisexual for quite a long period ... and that was absolutely to do with the kinds of friendships and emotional connections that I developed in the women's movement.... I think friendship with other girls had always been very important, but then the friendships through the women's movement... they were so close because ... often it was about collective childcare, which was so close to our hearts, and, you know, sharing our emotional lives, sharing our political lives. They were ... foundational to my life.

STUART HALL: She started to change, almost with their birth.... She's there in ... one of the first feminist play groups ... they've written a pamphlet called, "Out of the Pumpkin Shell."... A lot of our friends were involved, and the men were all helping, while the women had discussions, the men were helping with the kids, and helping at the school. [Happy voice]

CATHERINE HALL: The very first ... campaign we tried to do was about housewives, and we leafleted streets and invited women to come and meet and talk, but I can't say that resulted in any great transformations. [laughs] ... Obviously there were the four demands which ... gave ... shape to what we thought we were doing. But ... childcare was always at the top of the list because that's where we were.... The Women's Liberation Playgroup ... survived for many, many, many years and ... they just recently had a ... memorial for it.... The men would pick up the children and ... sometimes cook for them.... We all lived very close by.... In those ways we were very privileged.

We wanted a women's centre for a long time and eventually ... some people ... who were ... into communal living gave us ... a whole house in Balsall Heath. And Balsall Heath was ... next to Moseley and was one of the areas of heavy South Asian settlement. And that's where the playgroup was as well, in Balsall Heath Park. And we had many hopes of involving—they were mainly Pakistani and Bangladeshi women, but we were ... not very successful in that and it was a very white-dominated group of women at that stage in Birmingham.

... By '76, '77 ... there was an abortion campaign, Women Against Racism and Fascism, the Women's Centre, women involved in Women's Aid, women involved in Women Against Violence, a Marxist feminist reading group, a socialist feminist reading group, a Women in Ireland group, a women in social work group, a women in health group, local area groups, consciousness-raising groups, a homeworkers' campaign, a lesbian feminist group, a women and film group, the women's history group, women involved with Rape Crisis, a women and art group, a theatre group, and the women who ran the newsletter, which passed from group to group to group.... The labour involved in producing this material was very, very considerable [laughs].

There was a lot of discussion about sectarianism.... So many tensions, many, many tensions, around lesbianism, around theory versus practice, consciousness raising versus activism, class questions—not race questions in the '70s, they hadn't really—they hadn't hit in the '70s, in Birmingham at least. It was the radical feminist versus socialist feminist that was the most difficult issue, and I was very identified with socialist feminist groups and they were very strong in Birmingham, very strong.

STUART HALL: My feeling about feminism was very complicated ... because of my involvement through Catherine and people in Birmingham.... I encouraged the work on women's magazines, and I even tried to get one or two feminist scholars to accept an attachment to the Centre for a year.... So *I* thought, "I am as usual in advance of this move." I didn't really like to be told by younger women, "I'm afraid you should shut up," "Why don't you take a back seat?" [pause] "Dear Stuart, because it's not your time any longer," in that unmediated way. They were quite *right*. Quite right. But it's an old habit that I couldn't learn at that stage.

It taught me a *very, very* important lesson about the distinction between change in *theory* and in practice. Men can be as *feminist* as they like in their orientation, beliefs, what they subscribe to, their ideology, their politics, but their *actual practice* remains stubbornly fixed [chuckles] in older gendered modes. I didn't like being thought of as believing that theory was masculine, but, well, I suppose I [pauses] sort of did.

CATHERINE HALL: Then in '78 Lee [Davidoff] and I got a grant to do the work that became *Family Fortunes* and I was full-time on a research project for four years ... so I was defining myself increasingly through that work rather than through involvement with the movement.... The book was very much shaped by the two of us in dialogue.... I think it came as well from how both of us were working out things about our own families.... Making an argument about family as central to nineteenth-century and indeed twentieth- and twenty-first-century social structure was ... a pretty unusual thing to do, but ... insisting on the centrality of women to the organization of capitalist production was an even more unusual thing to do.... The ways in which women contributed labour, reproductive powers, money, to the development of family enterprises ... were absolutely at the heart of new forms of capitalist production in the early nineteenth century.... Limited liability doesn't exist until the later nineteenth century, so partnership and family, family and kin, were absolutely central to the whole thing.... The first third of the book is about, quotes, domestic ideology and the development of domestic ideology. The second third of the book is about the centrality of... women and family to capitalist production in this period, looking at... patterns through wills... the transfer of money through women was absolutely central, how marriage is critical to it all, how family labour is the key to all these enterprises, etc., etc.

STUART HALL: I'm perfectly comfortable in England, I feel I know the English like the back of my hand—I'm married to one, I'm friends with so many English people—and anyhow, what *else* am I? But I can't ever forget that I am... different from other people, and the mixture is partly race and colour, but it's then also... about quite another history. That which is still present in *me*, came into the relationship through me, and makes me a different person.... And I'm sure Catherine, as a young eighteen-year-old Yorkshire lass, was completely—I mean, I don't know [hesitates], I've never talked to her about, the early times we met and started to go out, what on earth she thought? A mixed [middle-class] couple was much rarer then, as you can imagine.... Amongst New Left people, I was the only black person... but it didn't stop us. And she, I think, would say, "Well, I just grew into it. I met him before I really understood what I was doing, and after that my life has just been as a mixed couple."

CATHERINE HALL: The first time I went to Jamaica was incredibly shocking because of the... what it means to be looked at and identified in a way that you have absolutely no control over, that you are fixed in other people's minds as something that you don't think of yourself as at all.... And then obviously there are... racist episodes around the children and so on. But I... hadn't really critically thought about myself in terms of the privileges that I just assumed as a white middle-class woman until challenged in very personal ways in the *Feminist Review* collective in the early '90s.

STUART HALL: When we went to Birmingham, we had to find a place to live—very difficult. Birmingham atmosphere was declining significantly after Powell and all of that..... People shout terrible things at us... often nastier things at her than at me, for going out with a black man. But... our relationship has never been structured around that as an emotional focus. It's been structured around that as a *cognitive* focus because, of course, I was always interested in it, and we went to Jamaica all the time... and she became a Caribbeanist and now she knows much more about the Caribbean and about Jamaican history than I do!... We are, therefore, conscious of racialized and colour differences, but it has never been the subject of trouble, or difficulty between us. There have been all sorts of other things, like in every marriage have been, but I don't recall that that ever was. I don't think I ever felt, "She would like out of this relationship *because* it's a mixed one." *Never*.

CATHERINE HALL: Profoundly difficult questions of competition and rivalry were very, very rarely addressed. The consciousness-raising groups . . . talked about a whole lot of things, but there were a whole lot of things they didn't talk about that were off bounds . . . really addressing the more difficult areas of female subjectivity . . . weren't in the forefront of our minds in the '70s. . . . But there was a lot of blaming of men . . . and, of course, . . . the very critical moment for me . . . was in relation to black politics in the late '80s and early '90s when . . . the whole question of . . . the privileges of whiteness became very—extremely preoccupying for me, both personally and politically, and . . . led to a huge change in terms of work as well as thinking much more critically about my own practices.

The only possible way that it was going to shift was by having a group of black women who had come at the same time. So that's what we did, and that really did change things, as it needed to. But it was a very, very difficult experience. . . . It was absolutely about our practice in meetings, you know, who got listened to, how people spoke, what happened to different kinds of articles. I mean, it was at every level, the unthinking forms of assumptions of white superiority, to put it at its hardest. And some—I mean, some women couldn't stomach it and left and those of us who stayed, I mean, turned the [*Feminist Review*] journal into something else, which is what it has remained.

STUART HALL: It's not that I'm antihistorical in any way, but . . . I didn't see why somebody like me, born in Kingston, should not aspire to live a modern life. I didn't *see* why I should go on being a native, primitive, and consigned to the margins of the intellectual and philosophical and literary world—this is how I felt as a boy growing up. . . . I wanted to know who the hell Paul Klee *was*, and who was James Joyce? And, you know, why did Eliot write what he did? . . . "Go on," you know, "find out what is at the leading edge of the world, and *claim* it." I think *loads* of West Indian writers and thinkers, at that point, without having it as a particular project, *did* just that. . . . It's, "I *will not be shut out* of future history because of what has happened in the past." . . . What is it like when some of the primordial social divisions—like wealth and property and so on—are compounded by *new* issues around sexuality, or around feminism, or around race, which is, after all, *more* primordial than class, but had never been given serious attention?

CATHERINE HALL: The book of essays that I did . . . *White, Male, and Middle Class* . . . there is a long autobiographical essay in there, which was a . . . working out for myself of the shift I made from working on gender and class to working on questions of race and ethnicity as well as gender and class, and placing that politically and historically. . . . That shift . . . had a . . . double dynamic, because obviously, from being with Stuart . . . I've always had a relation to black politics through him and to Jamaica. . . . But then . . . I began to think . . . what the impact of empire had been on Britain . . . to work on Jamaica, to work on slavery and emancipation and to do that through Birmingham. . . . It was a way of putting pieces of my life together as well . . . and challenging the view that . . . is so common in . . . Britain that . . . black people arrived . . . post-1945, whereas in fact there's been this historic connection over centuries that has been . . . effectively erased. . . . And . . . it was about my father, . . . too. . . . Well, . . . the whole thing began with me being in Jamaica with Stuart and the children and driving through a little village called Kettering, which was of course the place where I was born, and thinking, you know, why is this place called Kettering? And then working out why and the extraordinarily close relationship that there was between Baptist missionaries in Jamaica, Kettering, Birmingham. . . . All the places I know suddenly getting linked up in this . . . cross-Atlantic relation that was so intimate to people in the nineteenth century. . . . I just was very sorry that my father never knew I'd done that. . . . So, I mean, that book just came from my heart really. It did.

STUART HALL: Ends and beginnings are resting points, not teleological things built into the real world. When you write history, it has a beginning, middle, and an end, because *books* have a beginning, middle, and end, but *history*, well—when does history actually start and finish? [chuckles] . . . It's hard to think of a spectrum that doesn't have a beginning and an end, so you have to have one. But that's not what's important. It's the passage from one differential position to another which really is the thing to go for.

CATHERINE HALL: We've been through all sorts of things together, but we've absolutely stayed together. . . . And I think that . . . having a partner where you share children, you share a very rich and large friendship group, and you share your intellectual and political commitments. . . . So it does feel like—I mean, a partnership is the right . . . description of it. We made a life together. We just made a life together.

Catherine and Stuart Hall together on holiday. Their long marriage combined the white majority women's movement, black rights, and gender identity, but above all, it exemplified a powerful sense of family, love, understanding, and growth across decades of activism. *Photo courtesy of Stuart Hall estate*

STUART HALL: Personally, the great boon of my life is having married Catherine. . . . I was a pretty lost soul by the time of my thirties. I'd chosen to stay, I was going to stay. I didn't feel at one with England, I didn't feel English, so I wasn't going anywhere. [monotonous voice] . . . I was in a bad way, really, and she *absolutely* saved my life. Fourteen years younger than me, not yet gone to university, I imagine she can't possibly have *known* what she was doing. What would an eighteen, nineteen-year-old girl, just done wonderful A-levels [high school exams], going to Sussex, pick up with a thirty-two-year-old Jamaican man from the Left, why would you do it? But she *did*. She rescued me—which is a funny way round, you know [happy voice]. But she rescued me.

CATHERINE HALL: The biggest turning points in life [are] having children, and I think retirement's another one. . . . Now [I have] issues . . . not for myself but for Stuart, in relation to ill health . . . a terrible awareness of the body and what aging involves and the vulnerabilities it brings. I suppose I think that being a feminist in relation to all that is . . . to do with . . . watching, being aware . . . trying to think about the experiences rather than let them just all batter you [laughs]. It's hard, aging.

STUART HALL: So the relationship between us has not only *equalized* but has been *reversed*. So now, you know, I am 80, and getting old, and she's 66, with her creative life still opening up ahead of her.... We'll never be that idyllic picture of two people who have been in love all their lives, who then have a retirement together.... [Pauses] So that's a matter for regret, but I *can't* regret the fact that, as I would put it, nevertheless, I stole her life.... That is ... just the most important transforming thing that ever happened to me.[157]

7 HAPPINESS: LATE FEMINIST LIVES AND BEYOND IN THE 2000s

"One, two, three, four, we want a bloody damn sight more. Biology isn't destiny. Equal pay now. Bed or wed, are you free to choose? I'm not just a delectable screwing machine. Capitalism breeds sexploitation. Freedom!"[1] These were some of the slogans proclaimed on placards at the first National Women's Liberation march in London, celebrating International Women's Day on March 6, 1971. Among the four-thousand-plus marchers braving sleet and snow was Jill Tweedie. Aged thirty-four, a leading feminist journalist for the *Guardian*'s "women's section," she nervously attended with her friend Ivy, not sure what to expect.[2] May Hobbs and Jean Mormont, waving a placard for "The Cleaners' Action Group," marched with a few from the Night Cleaners' campaign.[3] Twenty-seven-year-old Lynne Segal was also there. Having moved from Sydney six months before, and separated from her husband, she felt "relatively friendless," though a visiting libertarian friend, George Molnar, marched companionably alongside her.[4] As a single mother, she might have been cheered by the sight of the giant model of an Old Woman's Shoe, in protest at the lack of childcare. She exchanged a word with a fellow Aussie, the celebrated Germaine Greer, whom she knew from back home. Then there was the theatrical Mary Ann "Buzz" Goodbody, bearing a tall and teetering mannequin of a woman's body, decorated to look like Joan of Arc's martyred corpse.

Did Tweedie feel different as a journalist, or did her cruel marriage awaken a bond? Hobbs was one of the best-remembered speakers at the rally, but she left for Australia by the late 1970s.[5] Jean Mormont, when interviewed in 1977 by Sheila Rowbotham and Jean McCrindle, was still ready to support the cause but was little connected to its networks, bringing up her seventh child and still cleaning to support her family.[6] Segal, to her surprise, is now an influential feminist academic, prolific and a little naughty. Her friend George attempted to sidestep a capitalist career by becoming a clerk.[7] Greer's ups and downs are better known, though her recent cause, restoring a patch of rainforest in southeast Queensland, has fuelled a brilliant turn to ecofeminism.[8] Goodbody, the Royal Shakespeare Company's talented first female director, committed suicide in 1975.

And what of the many who did not march because they did not live in London, or did not want to mark that movement moment? Clearly there was no simple pattern to a feminist life, nor a "happily ever after." But this is precisely the point: the great variety reflects activists' success in challenging expected life courses for women of all backgrounds. So, to the oft-raised question "Did the movement succeed?", we can answer first by understanding that liberation, as feminists saw it, did not mean simply being happy, but rather, being able to make choices. Moreover, feminists of the 1970s and 1980s insisted that the choices women need are about what matters in life—work, love, justice—going far beyond questions of the consumer lifestyle that dominate debates today. Facing up to these harder choices is demanding. Protest nevertheless can offer pleasure, audible in the music and song that often so joyfully interrupts an oral history recording. And such music offers clues to the deep satisfaction involved in living with feminist commitments. The end of a feminist life is remarkable for showing how enduring that satisfaction can be: S&A interviewees Mary McIntosh, Sheila Kitzinger, Audrey Jones, and Una Kroll have died since the S&A project concluded, yet they were politically purposeful to the end—Jones was taken ill returning from a United Nations women's meeting.[9] This sense of purpose is indeed a kind of faith. The story of Nadira Mirza, Muslim educator and Bradford activist, can spotlight exactly what this might mean in twenty-first-century contexts where religion has reemerged as a political frontline for women's liberation.

Choices: So Long as the Women Aren't Free, the People Aren't Free

"When I was young you were meant to meet people [laughing] in your twenties, settle down, have children and . . . live in a kind of peaceful elderly middle age, and I've found my life's never gone according to that plan from early times—I initially rebelled against that pattern, but as I've got older I've been amazed that all the things that people expect to happen never seem to fit."[10] The S&A oral history includes reflections such as this, from Sheila

Despite sleet and snow, a crowd of four thousand marked International Women's Day in March 1971 by staging the United Kingdom's first national women's liberation march in London. A group of women friends including the rising theatre director Mary Ann "Buzz" Goodbody carried a teetering tailor's mannequin, decorated to look like Joan of Arc's martyred corpse. *Photo courtesy of Mirrorpix*

Rowbotham, for whom the movement was part of a personal transformation through and in which their lives became utterly different from what they had expected. Novelist Zoë Fairbairns describes her middle-class mother in textbook "unhappy housewife heroine" terms: an unwaged domestic labourer, with a husband who did not love her, no conception of divorce, three children, no material help. Fairbairns describes the thrilling realization, around 1969, that she did not have to marry or have children; she stopped assessing herself for heterosexual attractiveness, decided to eat what she wanted, and became economically self-sufficient.[11] Rowena Arshad speaks of rejecting her Chinese Malaysian mother's conservative views of women's self-sacrifice.[12] Jan McKenley, whose mother came from Jamaica, said:

> My mother has led quite an interesting life, but she's lived it very much in private and in her own family and within . . . a very *narrow* set of four walls, and she hasn't lived it in the world and she doesn't choose to. And I think I lived in the world of London and more widely in England in a time of change. . . . I saw something *rushing* past my window and I *knew* . . . it was something I had to get involved in, and I was glad to have done that.[13]

But not all our interviewees presented conversion narratives. For many, political socialization began from the start, including Amrit Wilson, whose mother was a human rights activist in India, and Valerie Wise, who chaired the Women's Committee of the Greater London Council in the 1980s, and whose mother, Audrey Wise, was a member of Parliament (MP) who powerfully supported working-class women's rights. The Communist mothers of Beatrix Campbell and Barbara Taylor became so interested in feminism that they at times irritated their radical daughters by interfering.[14] In fact, about half of our sixty interviewees were raised in left-wing or anti-imperialist families, seven of whose mothers were or became activists.

Our interviewees came from three social generations: a handful born between 1925 and 1942; a large group of postwar early baby boomers born between 1943 and 1955; and a second tranche of late baby boomers born from 1955 to 1964. All were to a greater or lesser extent positioned in relationship to the Second World War. Some were defined by immigration to the United Kingdom and anticolonial struggle: Jewish in the 1930s escaping Nazism, and Caribbean and South Asian in the 1950s and 1960s. Powerful diasporic ethnic identities sometimes crossed with experiences of poverty and racism. As the WLM and anticolonial, black power, and Northern Irish struggles began to connect through the 1970s, it was typically the second generation of migrants from former colonies who articulated distinctive "feminisms" that were also critiques of parental patriarchies.

In this light, activists' lives appear as an exaggerated version of a multigenerational, and often multicultural, shift toward liberalism, youth culture, nontraditional, and antimaterialist lifestyles. Certainly, this pattern holds in relation to paid employment. Although many S&A interviewees came of age when the public sector in the United Kingdom was growing, like former New Left activists, they are concentrated in the "helping" professions and are more likely than their age peers to have experienced an episodic or nontraditional work history.[15] About one-third became academics; just under one-third public-sector workers, including teachers, equality consultants, or social workers; and most of the rest worked in grassroots and voluntary organizations. A handful became professional politicians, including Jane Hutt, who moved impressively from managing Welsh Women's Aid to becoming finance minister in the Welsh devolved administration. A few make a living in the arts, including the writer Michelene Wandor, artist Mary Kelly, photographer Grace Lau, and musician Alison Raynor. A few are businesswomen, and not conventionally so: Ursula Owen, one-time director of the feminist Virago Press and eco-builder Barbara Jones; Elizabeth Armstrong works for the Scotland Co-operative Group's Credit Union. Sue Lopez was also exceptional as a professional football player and coach.

Take Jalna Hanmer, Mary McIntosh, Cynthia Cockburn, Ellen Malos, Betty Cook, Una Kroll, Grace Lau, Mary Kennedy, Sheila Kitzinger: academics, a nurse, a doctor, a photographer, an adult educator, and a birth activist, respectively. Despite their very different class and ethnic backgrounds, had they followed their mothers' paths, they would all have been housewives, though some also domestic servants, small-business owners, and shopkeepers. Kroll's impoverished housekeeper mother hoped her daughter would break through and become a brilliant surgeon. Instead, Kroll gave up medical school to become a nun, though she later became a family doctor, and a lay priest in old age, after women could finally be ordained in the Church of England in 1994, and Wales in 1997. Poignantly, at that stage, despite her campaigning, she was too old, at seventy-one, to gain a full-time post.[16] Jo Robinson, born in 1942 and thus more typical of our WLM cohort, is the daughter of a Blackpool butcher and dreamed of becoming a film director. Instead, she worked first in a radical print collective, then as an art teacher, then as a midwife. She is now a gardener, a late-life job characteristic of a feminist of this generation. In her interview, she offers no regrets but is clear that she imagined none of it on leaving home in 1964. "I thought that you got engaged at eighteen, married at twenty-one, and had children at twenty-three; that's what I thought that you did. I was told and I believed that, and then when I got to that age it wasn't like that at all . . ."[17]

Such life-course effects belong to the category of unintended consequences of movement actions.[18] But although some examples suggest that activism may have involved material self-sacrifice, our archive also records upward mobility. This may be overdetermined by the fact that our oral history was focused on those who were instigators in some form, and thus likely to have come into the movement with educational capital and eventual financial resource. This trend among interviewees parallels studies suggesting that white lower/middle-class grammar-school (for pupils with higher exam grades) girls form the nucleus of UK activists, with only three of our interviewees identifying today as working class.[19] Though many of these women gave up a certain security, their activism did not typically prevent a midlife improvement in circumstance and sometimes enabled it, through teaching women's studies or other professionalized feminist activities.

Welsh dockworker's daughter Deirdre Beddoe, who at primary school was told she could be a sailor's wife but not a sailor, became a history professor in part thanks to her pioneering histories of Welsh working women.[20] We could also cite Betty Cook, Mary Kelly, Karen McMinn, Mukami McCrum, and many others who in some way found that their politics has underwritten a profession that has enabled them to live at least as comfortably as their peers and certainly more than they had expected. Cook moved dramatically from life as a miner's wife to become an educational advisor, McCrum from a farming family in Kenya to a policy worker for the Scottish government. Successive UK governments' divisive favouring of house ownership also overdetermined the fortunes of activists who could buy property in the 1960s–80s.

Feminists are less comfortable talking about these gains, a discomfort that reflects the movement's loftier ideals than mere equality of opportunity. Rosalind Delmar, whose father was a building labourer in a Teeside steelworks and whose mother was a housewife, expresses the disappointment she felt in the 1980s when "friends of mine in the women's movement who had moved on to have careers related to the movement, like in women's studies . . . , were not particularly interested in keeping up the connection when I had children. I thought that was *very* ironic as well, that . . . the focus was on . . . who was getting what *job*. . . . I was sad to see [pause] women in the women's movement behaving, when they *did* get university jobs and so on, rather like *male* professors behaved."[21] This is perhaps the more striking given that Delmar was by then a psychotherapist and well known as a movement intellectual who had previously moved into the world of university and adult education as well as literary translation.

If activists themselves have been so abashed about modest career gains, popular opinion is quick to disdain feminists as "white and middle class." This stereotyping simplifies the mobile and precarious class and race status that our oral histories often reveal, though perhaps it confirms how progressive politics can provoke suspicion, especially when women are in the lead. The stereotype has certainly haunted feminists in ironic ways. The marketization of Western economies in the 1980s propelled a new generation of professional women who did not profess feminist allegiances but seemed to demonstrate that women were now "liberated." Women were sometimes overly innocent about the general economic as well as political opportunity that underwrote their protests. But they could also be overly ashamed about having successfully carved out niches of employment in academia, local government, and the voluntary sector.

Today, most people support the principles of equal pay and even equal value—an achievement. But entrenched gendered divisions of labour, particularly at home, holds women's pay at roughly 60 percent of men's in the United Kingdom today. Equal opportunities? Discrimination in the job market is now illegal, and commitments by the Labour Party and Liberal Democrats to have women-only shortlists to promote female candidates in a number of UK elections have helped transform political representation, especially in Scotland and Wales.[22] But the prominence of women such as Theresa May notwithstanding, women are still notably absent from jobs in politics and beyond, especially in the private sector. The media loved reporting in 2016 that there were more people called John than women running *Financial Times* Stock Exchange (FTSE) 100 companies.[23]

With hindsight, we can see that some of the internal arguments over difference within the UK movements reflected a generational lag in opportunity, as only in the 1980s did most women gain the toehold that white middle-class women had begun to find in the 1960s. Stella Dadzie cites the poverty, educational exclusion, and policing that black women faced in the 1970s as the reason she was drawn to pan-African liberation movements rather than feminism at the time. Yet Dadzie's own story shows the complex interaction of class and identity, as she explains her own career as the daughter of a frail, impoverished white mother and a fêted Ghanaian diplomat father. Like many black women activists of her generation, she has become a freelance equal opportunities trainer and writer, having made her name with a groundbreaking book about resistance in 1985. She also talks honestly about her financial naiveté, at one point choosing to turn down the chance to become a well-paid manager in a radical college.[24] And, in any case, the period of relative plenty in the United Kingdom provided by sixteen consecutive years of economic growth up until 2007 has been undermined by global crashes, sharpening economic and social divisions once more, despite rhetoric from chief executive officers and celebrity feminists of "leaning in."[25]

The mobility and flux of women's life courses is just as crucially defined by love, childbearing, and sexuality as by paid work. Transforming these aspects of life is at the heart of the WLM's aspirations. Some things have changed for the better. Rape within marriage has been a crime in the United Kingdom since 1991, following a Court of Appeal ruling. Assisted childcare and rights to parental leave were significantly improved under the Labour government after 2001. The definition of domestic violence now includes coercive control. Activists' lives have changed as well. Typically in their early twenties, most came into the movement unmarried and without children. The average age of becoming a mother in the United Kingdom in the 1970s was around twenty-seven; the mean age for women to marry in 1971 in England and Wales was twenty-two.[26] Only a couple of our older interviewees had done that. The sizeable minority who were mothers when they joined the movement, typically from our older cohort, creatively represented a new kind of life course. Ann Oakley, Catherine Hall, and Jenni Murray, for example, experimented with nonsexist childrearing, had male partners sharing the housework, gave birth at home, and combined mothering, activism, and paid work. Lynne Segal, like Jo Robinson and Cynthia Cockburn, was a single mother who lived in a collective, as an alternative to the nuclear family. But since a key demand was for women to have reproductive choices, an alternative consequence was that women who did not have biological children could more easily resist a sense of failure. Many, like Beatrix Campbell, talk of the joy of parenting others' children, and lesbian women began to claim mothering as a life stage, particularly after gaining reproductive rights in 2002.[27]

Of course, participation in the WLM did not magically solve the challenges of women's reproductive years. Forty-one of our sixty interviewees became biological mothers, having one or two children. Two of them adopted children. In this way, we can say that they were more likely than their age peers not to have children: just less than one fifth (18 percent) of women born in 1969 were childless at age forty-five, which was high compared with their mothers' generation before them (though in fact broadly comparable with the picture in the United Kingdom across the twentieth century as a whole).[28]

Many of those who did raise children, typically in their thirties in the 1980s, say that this coincided with a retreat from activism, though sometimes different political preoccupations emerged at this stage in their lives. They recounted divisions between biological and nonbiological mothers and child-free women, ambivalence around contraception and abortion, children who have been unhappy with or rejected their own feminist values, the work and cost as well as the pleasures of childcare. Older interviewees more directly faced maternalistic expectations, but all three generations testify to ongoing struggles to be "good enough" mothers or caregivers.[29] At the same time, new expectations that women would compete with men professionally meant that some women delayed mothering until it was too late to conceive naturally. Those activists who found themselves in this situation, admittedly only a few, feel the irony particularly acutely, for obvious reasons. Zoë Fairbairns, witty and steadfast in her refusal of maternity as destiny, comments that the absence of biological children has an impact in later life too:

> I've chosen not to have kids, and this is a joint choice with John, my partner. He never wanted to have kids either. And I look around and I see friends, contemporaries who have ... got these amazing grown-up kids who've all got wonderful jobs and they've got *kids*. And ... the

> parents have got *grandchildren* and these people are going to be a consolation to them . . . and look out for them in old age. And suddenly I think, "Oh! *That's* what it was all about." . . . But, and then I think, "but you *can't* just have the good bits." And . . . if I run the video of my life, there's no point at which I think, "Right, *stop*, that would be a point at which I could have kids and it would have worked out." I think that my decision not to have kids was the right decision for me, albeit perhaps made for the wrong reasons.

Fairbairns proposes that what defines a feminist life course is autonomy, and that this includes being able to take responsibility for one's youthful decisions in later life.

Feminists' feelings about childbearing also entwine with those about sexuality, marriage, and monogamy. Former New Left activists are more likely than their age peers to have divorced, married later, or remained single, even in the context where lifelong heterosexual marriage has crumbled for the majority.[30] However, these were not always chosen results, even for members of a movement where patriarchal marriage and heterosexuality were the targets of protest. It is a cliché now to talk of the baby boomer activist looking back bemusedly on a youth of nonmonogamous experimentation, but this does describe many of our interviews. Not one woman said that she still lived in an open relationship, and forty-five have settled with a long-term partner, married, or entered a civil partnership.

Yet it is obvious that the prism of sexual rights has had enormous consequences in their unanimous insistence on sexual as well as economic equality in their later relationships. Many say how glad they are to have escaped the marital traps that ensnared parents before the Divorce Reform Act of 1969 came into force in England and Wales in 1971, extended to Northern Ireland in 1978. This for the first time meant neither partner had to prove "fault," even if they have found their own relationships a struggle. Those who are single enjoy their sense of independence and sometimes celibacy. Several "live apart together," and all strive to share housework fairly. Catherine and Stuart Hall's fifty-year marriage stands as a high-profile example of how a marriage preceded and survived the movement, in part because of a commitment to embrace the other's political causes. Comparing the S&A interviews with Olive Banks and Brian Harrison's biographical studies of suffrage activists shows a striking continuity in the role of supportive men.[31]

A different kind of impact is evident in queer or lesbian relationships. Perhaps 250,000 queer women aged over seventy in the United Kingdom today owe their sense of sexuality in part to the WLM.[32] Of the seventeen lesbian or bisexual women in our cohort, four defined themselves as having entered the movement as lesbian; some, like Mary McIntosh, attempted to link their gay liberation activism with feminism. However, thirteen said their sexuality evolved in the movement, and many more spoke of a period of bisexuality that was directly part of activist life. Political nurturing of women's sexual fluidity entwined with more autonomous women-centred relationships. Encouraging sexual confidence has also been important in extending sex life itself into older age. Lynne Segal's searing analysis of her male partner's departure for a younger woman later allows her, in her sixties, to enjoy a new life with a woman lover, not unlike Susie Orbach's glamorous marriage to the novelist Jeanette Winterson.[33]

One final biographical consequence of activism, physical and mental health, came up frequently. Sheila Rowbotham's record of the ignominy of being treated for candida in the mid-1960s as if it were a shameful sexual disease is an ordinary but telling glimpse of the way that women's bodies were pathologized.[34] In contrast, feminism provided language and services that celebrate women's bodily lives. Many interviewees mentioned the transformative effects of the feminist health handbook *Our Bodies, Ourselves*, reworked in the United Kingdom by Angela Phillips and Jill Rakusen, and of alternative beauty ideals.[35] This new approach to the body also helped them at turning points later in their life course: consider hormone replacement therapy (HRT) inventor Robert Wilson's description of menopause as a "crippling disease" that "desexed women" in his disgustingly titled 1966 book *Feminine Forever*.[36] Journalist Wendy Cooper defended HRT in 1973 as another key to "biological lib."[37] Although HRT's promises are as ambiguous as the Pill's, the feminist principle that women's biology must be destigmatized, that women should be allowed to choose, has helped challenge patriarchal healthcare policy and provision.

But the relationship to mental health is more ambiguous. One of the most striking findings of our oral histories is how far activists became preoccupied with their own or others' states of mind, where early political consciousness raising turned into prolonged therapeutic experiences in midlife. Of our sixty interviewees, thirty-two talk about having been depressed, with twenty-eight having sought therapy or counseling, though also, importantly, many say their mothers had been depressed in the "Valium generation" of housewifery. WLM historian Barbara Taylor, who has written a beautiful "memoir of madness," subtly links her breakdown in part to the effects of psychoanalytic treatment—though to it she also attributes her cure.[38] Feminists have typically diagnosed social injustice as the cause of women's depression.[39] Still, we must ask why so many feminists have seemed troubled, and some of the most brilliant exponents—Shulamith Firestone, Kate Millett in the United States, and Hannah Gavron in the United Kingdom, for example—spectacularly so.

Could we posit that in some sense being a feminist *made* one unhappy, even ill? This proposition is risky in the face of stereotypes of feminists as dour. However, the challenges of refusing conventional life courses and activist burnout might have contributed to mental struggles. People come to social movements because they are seeking meaning, change, or remedy. There is a correspondence between "biographical availability" for activism and its consequences.[40] Feminists' attention to private life fuelled new ambitions that brought new vulnerabilities, shaped within a postmodern culture of confession and self-fashioning and a therapeutic industry not at all feminist in origin or intent.[41] Primarily, feminists' unhappiness reflects a more general mood, an apparent epidemic of unhappiness across the developed world in the first decade of the new millennium.

This epidemic became the focus of high-profile debate and a mushrooming field of happiness economics. Scholars now address the paradox of malaise in a time of relative plenty and safety for most in the developed world, calculating, for example, that people achieve little emotional gain from increases in their earnings after reaching an annual income of $75,000.[42] Theories of contemporary unhappiness have suggested different, sometimes contradictory causes: genes, exercise, digital technology, family and community breakdown, work instabilities, layoffs, migration, increased perceived risks in daily life, and the loss of belief. For women, raised aspirations in the context of multiple and conflicting domains, social insecurities, and increased household risk are argued to have provoked new anxiety and neuroticism.[43] But for feminists, including feminist economists, the broadest reason for today's malaise is inequality and isolation. Global capitalism has been a disappointment even for the winners, especially after the 2008 economic crash.

Yet part of the problem is an ideology of happiness itself. Along with the "angry black woman," the "feminist killjoy," "unhappy queer," and "melancholic migrant" become contagiously miserable people to avoid. Particularly insidious too are the contractual aspects of happiness—especially for girls, on whose "happiness" (for example, the correct marriage) the happiness of parents depends. However, the philosophical alternative—to live a virtuous life, even if not a happy one—is also difficult from a feminist perspective. As the WLM perceived, being a good girl is just the other side of being a bad one.[44]

Instead, feminists now turn toward vitality and moments of collective joy, to seek pleasure among struggle.[45] Here the unhappy housewife's complaints in the 1960s anticipate today's critiques of material plenty without control or community. Activists of the 1970s and 1980s felt they were going farther than "equality" feminists of the midcentury in seeing the importance of choice, but also rejected the individualistic nirvana of counterculturists, the forerunners of today's new ageisms. Instead, the distinguishing feature of post-1960s feminist philosophy was its focus on autonomy as the central term of liberation. Autonomy in this sense includes being able to control one's fertility or property, rather than simply having access to opportunities and resources.[46] Though the word "autonomy" in the nineteenth-century women's movement was associated with liberalism, as opposed to socialism, in the WLM (which largely descended from the socialist end of the suffrage movement), it offers a rounder and more connected vision of independence. Understanding this idea reinforces the point that feminists are often motivated not by personal misery, but quite the opposite: idealism, education, ambition, or simply friendship. In Rowbotham's words, "It was not that every woman suddenly became unhappy, but that significant numbers of women felt entitled to a destiny which was not simply domestic."[47] Nadira Mirza, surprised to remember her brother perceiving her as "angry" as a younger activist, concludes, "My happiness and sense of worth is derived from thinking I can make a difference for others, and in effect that's a difference for me as well."[48]

But lived autonomy is challenging. Michele Ryan, who found agitprop and the International Socialists in Bradford, remembers reading Doris Lessing's *The Golden Notebook* on a bus

> and feeling, yes, this is *absolutely* where I'm at [breathing out], and I've got to, kind of, *hold* my centre a bit better. But . . . when the relationship ended, you know, it was somebody that I really wanted to be with, and, just, emotions of abandonment. *I* had made the decision to end it, but, but there didn't seem to be any other way of dealing with it, there wasn't a future. . . . I can see through a *lot* of my life, that, I suppose because I *did* have politics, I *did* have the women's movement, I *did* have the theatre at the time, I had things that belonged to *me*, and I wasn't going to let *go* of those, in order to *fit into* a man's life.[49]

It is not surprising, then, that feminist philosophy, as it evolved in the 1970s and 1980s—via kitchen table talk, therapy, creative writing, and song as much as in women's studies—focused less on free will, or even Marxist agency, than the emotional, personal, nonuniversal aspects of personhood.[50] Ethics also dominated as the branch of philosophy that explores care alongside reason: How does one balance care for others with care for oneself? Ethics is a way to better interpret the meaning of the long lives of feminists, in which self-invention is continually imagined through relationships, and desires for more emancipated forms of love and family jostle with the realities of attachment, the inequalities inherent in dependency. Vitality also includes failure. As Michelene Wandor puts it:

> Feminism and socialism . . . really . . . formed my *thinking* and the way I approach things. It has made life *extremely* difficult and I've done some very, very *stupid* things and made some very *stupid* decisions. . . . But [pause] . . . I think it gave me a kind of *wisdom* which I haven't always been able to live by . . . It's what's enabled me to make sense of the world, and make sense of what I have wanted to *do* even though I have been very, very rarely been able really to do it.[51]

Indeed, woman after woman ends her interview reflecting on the greater freedom of choice she had compared with her mother, but without claiming any kind of idealized solution. In Catherine Hall's words:

> I've just been so fortunate to live in a different time [from that of my mother]. And I think . . . that being able to combine having children with having a *really, really* satisfying working life has been—I think it's a great privilege to have that. . . . I don't mean at *all* that I've always been contented and happy, 'cause I haven't [laughing], but then I don't think it's very much part of the human condition to be contented and happy.[52]

The challenge for feminism today is that the notion of choice, facilely equated with happiness, has become associated precisely with anti- or "post"-feminism. Typically, a rejection of feminism is articulated around physical presentation and desire, in which feminists are imagined as puritans who deny other women self-determination. Finn McKay, a prominent younger radical voice, tackles this point:

> Politics of all kinds, not just feminism, is about looking into what "choices" are available to us and just how much of a choice they really

are. We also need to look at who or what benefits from those choices. That is not the same as saying that women cannot be feminists if they dress a certain way or do not dress a certain way. There is no feminist uniform; any woman can be a feminist.[53]

McKay rejects the notion that women who make choices seemingly against their own interests are suffering from false consciousness. But she affirms their essential feminist critique: "How could we begin to interrogate these kinds of choices though, or begin to try something different? Rather than no-makeup selfies, how about no-makeup weeks, how about no-makeup months? Think of the time and money that women could save. How about women supporting one another to try out not shaving their body hair for a while?"[54]

The combat zone of appearance, within which young women stake independence from mothers or elders, engages deeply with perceived femininity and sexuality: it is not superficial. Many third-wave feminist manifestos pitched themselves against the WLM generation on these grounds.[55] Yet the wider understanding of choice and liberation that the WLM generations sought are too easily lost. Gendered "choice" can now be shifted from the issue of femininity and sexuality to all the other territories in which autonomy for all genders can be reconfigured. Jan McKenley's exploration of black Caribbean parents' choosing their children's school in a deregulated educational market is in its own way a feminist issue.[56]

The S&A feminists, then, defend the principle of choice and tell narratives of good and bad picks with little regret. But they lament the betrayal, impoverishment, confusion over the contemporary dilution of what they had hoped for. The painful trend was clear by the early 1990s: women in Britain have greater autonomy, though not greater equality.[57] While interviewees stand by their ideals of autonomy, many conclude by confessing they feel like "relics," warning of the limits of an age of rich and fetishized consumer choice, including over gender and sexuality, but few choices regarding income, childcare, housing, parliamentary representation, nationality, pension, and care in old age. Furthermore, they worry that even with all the choices and comforts, it is wrong to be happy when so many still suffer. Sara Ahmed's reclaiming of anger for the feminist and black woman reflects this challenge. Indeed, one of her most powerful insights is that it is difficult to be happy once you have opened your political eyes:

> Any politics of justice will involve causing unhappiness even if that is not the point of our action. So much happiness is premised on, and

promised by, the concealment of suffering, the freedom to look away from what compromises one's happiness. To revolt can hurt not only because you are proximate to hurt but also because you cause unhappiness by revealing the causes of unhappiness. *You become the cause of the unhappiness you reveal.* . . . That is why feminist, queer, and antiracist archives are collective weaves of unhappiness, even when we struggle for something, even in the moment of aspiration, even when we dance in the gap between inheritance and reproduction. . . . To share what deviates from happiness is to open up to possibility, to be alive to possibility.[58]

This "collective weave of unhappiness," woven precisely as a pathway to "possibility," is certainly expressed in the oral historical archive of feminist feeling.

However, even as feminism is not principally about being happy, happiness matters. In Ahmed's schema, solidarity and the joys of battle must sustain us.[59] But the oral histories are perhaps less demanding. Older voices, remembering long political lives, vibrate with foolishness, incongruity, wit, the comfort of home, love, achievement—and care. Mukami McCrum poignantly remembers a turning point when her mother remarked, "Something changed about you—you sound aggressive, angry, sad." She explains "because of that I try to make sure that things—bad things that happen to me or to people I know or around me, whether it is racism or discrimination, don't—*take root* inside me . . . because I think they were slowly destroying me."[60]

Yet she continues with a smile, "Assertiveness is about influencing the outcome without necessarily destroying other people's by banging the table."[61] Ros Delmar, remembering herself as an "angry young woman" in the 1950s, felt sorry for young women students "depressed" rather than angry in the 1980s: "I thought, the world is a more difficult place for them than it was for me, actually, although I didn't recognize it in some ways."[62] But Delmar chuckles throughout her interview, at whether she was right about Engels, her love of travelling, the deliciousness of Italian literature, the hubris of activism. Gail Chester clearly enjoyed the opportunity to perform her love of women's community and an argument. And at one point, confessing she had underestimated the Greenham Common women's protest, she begins to sing:

Oh my g-o-d! Actually, this was one that I . . . sang last week. OK. So, [singing] "The river is flowing, flowing and growing. The river is flowing, down to the sea. Mother Earth, carry me, child I will always be. Mother Earth, carry me, down to the sea." [breathes in] And there's a second verse . . . [singing] "With my lovely feathers I wi-il-l fly, with my lovely feathers I wi-il-l fly. I'll circle around, I'll circle around the *something* of the Earth." [quietly] I don't think it's *perimeter*. [Laughs.][63]

You Can't Kill the Spirit: Singing, Funk, and Greenham

Chester tells me that music has been constantly present in her feminist life. She founded the Pre-Madonnas in 1981, inspired after hearing the Philadelphia Feminist Choir and meeting Cathy Roma from the US women's choral movement. She sings with radical choirs at Laurieston Hall in Scotland and Women in Tune festivals in Lampeter, Wales. The Pre-Madonnas, formerly the Feminist London Choir, sang of many feminist political issues, from lesbian pride to the destruction of the Greater London Council. Kirsten Hearn, among others, set parody lyrics to old tunes for it, such as "Breaking Up Is Hard To Do": "Don't take your grant away from me, don't you leave my group in misery, if you go then I'll be blue, 'cos breaking up is hard to do . . . remember when the GLC paid for all our facilities, think of all these things brand new, 'cos breaking up is hard to do."[64] Hearn purrs with pleasure about being in the Tokens, a disabled women's singing group, and playing the clarinet, adding, "I'm still . . . likely to get up and play the guitar badly and sing some revolutionary song about something."[65]

Chester was not alone in breaking into song in her oral history. Sandie Wyles doo-be-doos throughout, a soundtrack to her evolution from a Scots-Irish family of singers to playing in lesbian *ceilidh* band the Reel Aliens. She even gets out her fiddle and guitar. "Now that just hit them! Do the bass and the *dum-doo-doo-doo-doo*. [sings] 'We want sex but don't want to get pregnant' *doo-doo-doo-doo*."[66]

Cynthia Cockburn, in response to my invitation to add something at the end of the recording, tells me about Raised Voices, a way of "meeting each other once a week, and singing nice songs, and going out on demos [demonstrations] together and singing at meetings and conferences and things, but *also* it's been a vehicle through which I've been able to *write* songs. 'Stand where I stand, see what I see. Your truth and my truth shall keep company.' . . . Catholic and Protestant, Arab and Jew."[67]

The antisexist men from the Cardiff men's movement, recorded for the Unbecoming Men oral history, get going too:

FIVE: There was—there was some antisexist verses, wasn't there, umm . . . err . . . [singing]: "Don't walk home alone across the park . . . A woman can't feel safe out after dark . . ."

PETE: Yeah!

FIVE: [still singing]: "In this enlightened age that's just one bar of the cage... How can a woman stand such times and live...?"[68]

Ponderous comedy, but their voices swell with the pleasure that fed the life of protest. This "exultation of the 'we'" that music brings to a social movement is evident at moments of confrontation, fear, and isolation.[69] A striking example comes from Jocelyn Wolfe, who sang to keep calm after being arrested when supporting women chaining themselves to the railings outside Parliament in support of the Equal Pay Act in 1975. Because she was the only black woman there, the police singled her out on no evidence: outrageous racism, which she told them was "a bit like a *Monty Python* sketch":

> Now, my singing's not pretty [gentle huh]. But I remember I just sang. I sang, anything. I sang everything. I sang nursery rhymes, "Humpty Dumpty." I sang "We Shall Overcome." I sang hymns. I sang... Anything that came into my *head*, I sang it. I sang Elvis Presley, I'd just, I would just... And they wouldn't be whole songs, they would be just snatches because I would lose track and forget, but I'll just keep singing. And all of a sudden [wondrously] I could hear voices... singing "We Shall Overcome," from somewhere *else*. And then, a woman's voice shouting and saying, "It's OK, sister, we're here," you know, "Keep singing," and what have you. Oh! I just—oh, I can feel it now—it was just the *best* thing that can happen. [Inhales.][70]

Music made fundraising fun, conferences cathartic, and everyday life endurable. This is not unusual: protest music is a key to converting people and reinforcing group identity but also enables "distraction, contemplation, legitimation as well as contestation."[71] As Wolfe hints in remembering "We Shall Overcome," these elements have been crucial to black liberation movements.[72] In addition to gospel and its reinvention in soul, a black Atlantic culture of resistance in this period melded Caribbean reggae and ska, African American blues, African jive, and British jazz, as well as early rap.[73] However, in women's movements across race and region, singing also encouraged women to find a public voice. Women endorsed each other's noise, learned to listen, felt the physical changes in singing together in hundreds of small choirs as well as on marches or protests. Mal Finch wrote the "anthem" of Women Against Pit Closures during the miners' strike in 1984–85 with "Women of the Working Class."[74] Most iconic was the US acappella group Sweet Honey in the Rock, a huge influence in the United Kingdom. Jocelyn Wolfe remembers the "magic" of hearing their record at the first Organisation for Women of Asian and African Descent (OWAAD) conference in 1978, Stella Dadzie having brought it hot off the press. Mia Morris, coordinator for the Black Cultural Archives' Heart of the Race oral history, comments that "if there was a soundtrack to the women's movement, Sweet Honey in the Rock would have to be alongside it."[75] Donna Pieters from the Lewisham Black Women's Group even remortgaged her house to finance the group's first UK tour in 1983.[76]

Musical endeavors such as these help illustrate the cultural achievements of feminism during this period. Frankie Green and D-M Withers's Women's Liberation Music Archive features more than 150 artists and groups, and an oral history of gigs, festivals, jam sessions, dances, street shows, and living room music swaps. Withers hears in their jaunty rhythms an expression of "*values* of feminist nonviolence," embodied through instrumentation.[77] Groups like the Northern Women's Liberation Rock Band (1973–76) and the Fabulous Dirt Sisters (1981–89) opted for music that women could "bop" to, eschewing "heavier sounds (if not amplification entirely)."[78]

As with manual trades, sport, or cooking, part of the aim was to change *how* music was done, as much as getting a foot in the door. Pianist and singer Terri Quaye, with family roots extending into Afro-British jazz, said of her all-women's jazz band Moonspirit, "women who go into music want to create their own sound . . . not to *impersonate the male sound*."[79] Celtic music was equally retuned while building on long traditions of political protest for national identity, and English folk music, consciously disdaining nationalism, emerged in feminist guise from the left-wing postwar British folk revival. In Frankie Armstrong's words, it was a way for women to learn their own "sound."[80]

Michelene Wandor, as a professional clarinetist specializing in Renaissance music, similarly explains her multilayered performances as "a socialist/feminist critique of concert performance, really."[81] (She found classical music through becoming obsessed with the Bach signature tune from the BBC's *Woman's Hour* as a child.) Wandor's view of the unique "groundswell of autodidacticism" in the 1970s also describes a collective self-teaching about "instruments, equipment, sound engineering, and recording—usually a male domain, and having control over the distribution of our music," the latter by Caroline Hutton of the Birmingham-based Women's Revolutions Per Minute (WRPM) from 1979 to 1999.[82] Alison Rayner, who taught herself bass guitar as part of Jam Today, remembers: "A couple of women there who were trying to say that actually we should make our own instruments and

Terri Quaye led the pioneering women's jazz band Moonspirit and ran a feminist disco, The Cauldron, at The Sols Arms pub in London, seen here in 1978. With family roots extending into Afro-British jazz, she said at the time, "Women who go into music want to create their own sound, . . . not to impersonate the male sound."
Photo courtesy of Terri Quaye

Deirdre [laughs], . . . who was about nineteen, bursting into tears and saying [weepy voice], 'It's difficult enough to *play* the guitar, I don't want to have to *make* it as well.' [Hooting.]"[83]

"If I can't *dance*, I don't want to be part of your revolution." Early twentieth-century anarchist Emma Goldman was thus paraphrased in many feminist publications of the period.[84] However, preserving that "life and joy" presents a conundrum for activists who are disciplining themselves to confront injustices that the majority avoid. The long history of white expropriation of black music, as well as the tensions between women's movements, was a case in point. Gail Chester remembers this in relation to the many African freedom songs sung by mixed social movements: "There were big debates about, if you were all white, whether you could sing a song which said, 'We are children of Africa.' And then, so, this gave rise to *huge* issues about, you know, singing songs in solidarity, or songs that related to *your* personal struggle. [Big sigh.]"[85]

Rock Against Racism was itself problematic. Supported by Women Against Racism and Fascism, it roused thousands to attend carnivals organized by the Anti-Nazi League, a group that mobilized in 1970s Britain as the racist National Front was gaining ground.[86] But in composition and focus, Rock Against Racism, says historian Natalie Thomlinson, "ironically revealed the whiteness of the WLM."[87] Another awkward element of feminist music was that professional musicians prefer to be paid for performing, difficult enough in the commercial scene, and especially so in poor egalitarian circles.

Yet, song, instinctively springing from interviewees' throats, recalls the cheer of a feminist life, perhaps especially in moments of self-indulgent escape. As with feminist standup comedy and cartooning, singing could make men the butt of the joke (for once) but also joked about the restraints that feminist community imposed.[88] The S&A recordings capture snatches of mothers' lullabies or pop songs, amusing stories of enjoying distinctly unfeminist entertainment. Jan McKenley slipped off to a Teddy Pendergrass concert after the second OWAAD conference, "nothing more . . . sloppy, romantic, kind of slushy, you know, big ballad singing, sort of *macho* bloke." Discovering that some other women from the conference were also there, and had evidently left early to get dressed up, she remembers: "They'd got high heels on and *dresses* and we were still in our feminist *conference* gear . . . . It was the *funniest* thing. [smiling broadly] . . . the music was unreconstructed and fabulous and very culturally black and we . . . hadn't abandoned those things and we weren't particularly purist about that, and then this very right-on conference we'd all been at in the daytime."[89]

Music's transcending qualities are nowhere more widely remembered than from the most celebrated feminist protest of this period, the Greenham Common Women's Peace Camp (1981–2002). Although Greenham was a protest against the siting of US nuclear missiles in the United Kingdom rather than an obviously women's cause, it was women-led, and within a few months women-only. Begun by a Welsh group, "Women for Life on Earth," it soon attracted seventy thousand Campaign for Nuclear Disarmament supporters in a human chain linking the base to Aldermaston, and fifty thousand came a year later, despite the arrival of the missiles. Greenham probably mobilized at least half a million supporters in all, roused through an extraordinary network of telephone trees, chain letters, support groups, sister camps including

Seneca, in upstate New York (from where the missiles came), Comiso in Italy, an anti-uranium mining camp in Namibia, and Pine Gap in Australia.

Spectacular actions like the New Year's Day 1983 break-in, when women entered the base to dance on the missile silos, made it a media staple.[90] Women decorated the military fence with everything from flowers to tampons. Then there were the iconic woollen webs that activists used to confuse and resist arresting policemen. Breaking into a military base where soldiers had orders to shoot on sight often involved dressing up, for example as witches or teddy bears. Some of this style was distasteful to activist old hands, and the long history of the camp includes bitter internal divisions.[91] But, undoubtedly, Greenham's appeal was astonishingly broad, from mothers afraid for their children, leftie peaceniks, and Communist grandmothers to—increasingly—lesbians wanting to create a utopian, independent community out of doors and on the edge.

"You can't kill the spirit, she is like a mountain . . ." Chanted, untutored and sentimental, like food cooked on an open fire much better out of doors, Greenham's anthem epitomized its exhilaration. Singing was part of the dangerous, dirty, dull life around the fence, a tactic in court and in prison. And it also enhanced the experience of the campfire and mud, sending it mythically outward, as another of its theme tunes, Peggy Seeger's "Carry Greenham Home," encouraged. The latter, sung to the Scots melody "Mari's Wedding," was an example of folk's repurposing; Greenham music also reworked African American spirituals and civil rights music, as in "Were You There When They Bombed Hiroshima?" (based on "Were You There When They Crucified My Lord?"), or (white) American women's music, such as Holly Near's "We Are a Gentle, Angry People." Many remember gleeful parodies of classics such as "Lily of the Arc Lights," sung to the tune of "Lily Marlene," or "At the Peace Camp, Newbury, Berkshire" to the tune of "An English Country Garden."[92] A much photocopied camp songbook and a record with "You Can't Kill the Spirit" and "Yesterday's Children" were put together by a Manchester support group who congregated at Orange Gate, one of the camps named after colours of the rainbow at the nine entrances around the perimeter.[93]

Singing connected the causes of nonviolence, feminism, and environmentalism. Protestors were outraged that the airbase had been built on traditionally common land. They were outraged again when in January 1983 Newbury District Council revoked the common land bylaws for Greenham Common, becoming the private landlord for the site and instituting court proceedings to reclaim eviction costs; happily, these actions were ruled illegal by the Court of Appeal in 1990. Such protests tapped into a rich vein of English history,

Music and song enlivened the dangerous, dirty, dull life at Greenham Common women's peace camp and was a defiant tactic in court and prison. It also sent the protest mythically outward, as expressed by one of its theme tunes, Peggy Seeger's "Carry Greenham Home." Here Rebecca Johnson (left), with her friend Ruth from Sheffield, singing as the authorities attempted to evict the camp in 1984. *Photo courtesy of Janine Wiedel*

as recaptured in "The World Turned Upside Down," Leon Rosselson's song about the Diggers' fight for land rights after the English Civil War (1642–1651), and taken up in Billy Bragg's 1985 chart hit reprise. "You Can't Kill the Spirit" was indeed originally about Native American land rights, written by the Chicana Californian Naomi Littlebear Morena.[94] There is something ticklish about its West Coast imagery of mountains being reinvented in the English home counties. But it captured the sense of a primeval battle for earth's survival in the Cold War, inspired as well by the mystical associations of nearby Salisbury Plain and Stonehenge.

Rebecca Johnson, who lived at the camp for five years, describes standing on huge boulders that the Newbury council had dumped to try to prevent the protesters from camping:

> I'd been singing and quite defiantly. And then . . . a couple of women suddenly came to me and [laughs] and said . . . [softly] "Can you hide these?" and I—one was a bag of nails and I just dropped it down by my feet and it went . . . in between the holes . . . and the other was a

hammer and I . . . tossed that in some bushes behind me, and started singing the mountain song [sings], "I have dreamed on this mountain since first [takes breath] I was my mother's daughter and you can't just take my dreams away, not with me watching, you may drive a big machine, but I was born to be a great strong woman [crescendo] and you can't just take my dreams away without me resisting."[95]

An accomplished political balladeer, Johnson had a silvery voice that springs from early training in Hutterite acapella singing and captures the sense that these songs could be performances *to* police, soldiers, the press, or any onlookers who had come to gawk or support. Words tumbled out of her—hers was a twenty-hour interview—but her cadence is of a public speaker, for years now as a lobbyist for nuclear decommissioning. Her understanding of the power of the voice is evident when she describes the effect of hearing a woman's voice cutting through the hectoring of men at her first CND demo at Hyde Park in 1981. It's there as well in accounts of how Greenham women learned to speak to the media or their adroit use of walkie-talkies.[96] Yet at other times she is back at Greenham, in the circle, inhabiting the identity and the place. Singing and the practice of collective keening worked to bring not only unity and courage but a ritualistic transformation of everyday self. Keening, as Annie Tunicliffe explained in an article for *Spare Rib* in the camp's first year, "is something traditionally done by women, though now usually confined to mourning. It is an expression of feeling, a setting up of sound vibration, the sound coming from deep within the body and throat. The higher sounds are described as wailing."[97]

This uncanny sound bonded the thirty thousand women who sang together at the Embrace the Base action in December 1982. For many, its decentred harmony epitomized Greenham culture at its best. Johnson explains:

> One woman pitches a note and then other women come in above it or below it or on the same note, but it becomes a kind of harmonic chord, and it's actually both very powerful and very beautiful [gentle voice], and it rises or falls, and at different points in that different women take a different chord, you know, so it sometimes it'll fall away and then another woman will pick up another note, and so it sort of ebbs and flows but it's—it's . . . energizing, and particularly for somebody like me who loves music.[98]

Such ritualistic sharing of sound and song stirred the magic of Greenham's women-only community and resolution in the face of danger, not only from nuclear war but from hostile locals and military police, a danger so frighteningly expressed when Helen Thomas, a twenty-two-year-old Welsh woman, was killed by a police vehicle in 1989. But the sense that trials must be faced—indeed, that they will one day be overcome—is a general aspect of protest: a point of faith, perhaps. Political faith is a crucial aspect of WLM activism and frames the sometimes extraordinary deaths as well as the lives of activists.

Endings: Feminist Dying, Faith, and Nadira Mirza's Story

Feminists challenged expectations associated with age as well as with gender. Sometimes this meant reordering rites of passage (late-life courtship), reinventing them (collective living; cooperative working), or rejecting them (choosing friends or pets rather than children). The feminist challenging of ageism indeed explicitly anticipated the "postmodernization of the life course" that now defines mainstream urban societies, "declining to decline."[99]

But what happens as death approaches? Oddly, this is difficult to explore in oral history, even though interviews are classically undertaken late in life. One unembarrassed interviewee was Mary McIntosh. A sociologist, she was the first of the S&A interviewees to die, aged seventy-seven in 2013. When I interviewed her in 2011, she said:

> I went through a *little* patch, especially after I had a . . . partial breast removal of, you know, *wanting* to die and thinking I was *useless* and so forth, but actually *now* I feel, oh I *could* die, and therefore you kind of choose life and I live from day to day somewhat. But I don't choose to die, oddly, and I'm quite positive about the next few years, is as far ahead as I look. It's a strange sort of feeling, though I *do* feel, the more I look at my body, the more I think that, you know, that term "use-by" [laughing gently] which they put on goods . . . applies specially to your body; it becomes less and less *useful* and more and more past its use-by date and certainly past its sell-by date. So, you know, I *actually* think that—well, my mother used to say, "Don't get old, there's no future in it" [chortling], and that is certainly true![100]

Her calm, dry tones are not easy to convey in transcript, nor her musing that she is relieved not many will remember her. Although she was a luminary of the Gay Liberation Front and then the WLM, and a brilliant sociologist (anticipating Foucault's history of sexuality), McIntosh took early retirement in 1996, having consulted "somebody who specialized in mid-life changes of direction." Supported by her partner Angela Stewart-Park, a graphic designer (also a dashing sometime revolutionary feminist, originally on the "opposite side" in the feminist sex wars), McIntosh became an Age Concern volunteer, raising awareness of older LGBT lives. She put her papers in the Hall-Carpenter archives, both legacy-making and a shedding. What would she have made of the obituaries by old Gay Liberation Front comrades and the memorials in feminist communities?[101] Though I want to illuminate her individuality and achievement, I also cherish her equanimous approach to death and reputation. Her matter-of-fact, even cheerful tone itself suggests her secular, materialist attitude toward the body after death.

Listening to Sheila Kitzinger's recording also offers insight into what we might call feminist dying. Kitzinger, who died in 2015, was a pioneer for natural childbirth, influential in health and maternity rights campaigns.[102] Her five daughters became active feminists. In her 2012 interview, she says that "passing from this life" is

> a great hurdle, which we often cope with *very, very* badly, which like the transition *into* life has been challenging me for years and years and years, and now I've learnt from my daughters too that this is the *other* thing to which we need direct attention ... They actually do *say* to me, many of the phrases I use about *birth* and the way we want to face up to birth and deal with birth are *exactly* like the ones when we move towards death. And ... as I get older, I think, yeah, they're absolutely right.[103]

For Kitzinger, "facing up to birth" was about refusing unnecessary medical intervention, women learning "how to take control of their bodies ... trusting them, living through them, expressing themselves. And that affects sex of course and our feelings about our sexuality, whatever it is, as well as childbirth."[104] Now it affects dying too.

As the UK *Our Bodies, Ourselves* imagined "women growing older," this is more than "turning around decades of a certain kind of dependency on doctors."[105] It is to reclaim the stage of life in which women's bodies have been archetypally abjected, from the insulting connotations of "old woman" to the "atrophying" vagina. However different McIntosh and Kitzinger's self-styling, they converge on women's ability and right to decide for ourselves even at the end. An early inspiration came from photographer Jo Spence, who focused the camera on herself when she was diagnosed with breast cancer in 1982.[106] As iconic in the United Kingdom as Audre Lorde's 1980 *Cancer Journals* was in the United States, Spence's photos asserted identity at the end as well as middle of life.

"Dealing with Dying" in *Spare Rib* (1984) illuminates similar impulses. Here Esther Green, Sue Krzowski, and Sheila Ernst wrote about the death of Pam Smith, a colleague at the Women's Therapy Centre and psychiatric social worker.[107] Pam was furious to be moved onto light duties by her university employers as her cancer developed; the Women's Therapy Centre instead kept her going until she was ready to hand over her responsibilities. Managing death beyond the nuclear family was also important. Smith had chosen not to have children, marry, or live with her lover—seemingly with no regrets when anticipating an early death. She also found herself a therapist and arranged her own funeral. In this tradition, and informed by the accident that left a sister in a coma, Kitzinger's daughters Celia and Jenny are campaigning for greater control over situations of persistent vegetative states. Raising awareness of living wills and advance directive forms, they support an ethics of self-care and autonomy.

But as life expectancy lengthens, and chronic illnesses and dementia introduce need and dependency, so feminists nuance their ideas of autonomy, as do disability rights activists. What is a feminist relationship to new biological technology? It is already wrestling with questions of how surgery or hormonal treatment can be deployed to shape gender identity. In a similar way, can we, should we, control death and disease? Kitzinger and McIntosh's approaches reflect the stoicism of the prewar generation and the privilege of having a clear mind at death surrounded by a loving feminist family. In contrast, Lynne Segal critiques the buoyancy of the most public figures of second-wave feminism—Greer, Friedan, and Steinem—for their "celebration of the rebirth of self-sufficiency" in old age, the illusion that we can age agelessly.[108] We hear echoes of Ahmed's challenge to go beyond happiness as a goal. But unlike exhilarating anger, or the fun of wearing purple, Segal explores the vital preciousness of being needed across the life course.[109]

This is timely: more than a third of over-sixty-five people live alone, while around one in eight adults are caregivers. Many are themselves old. The number of over-eighty-fives in England responsible for the care of loved ones rose by 125 percent between the census years 2001 and 2011 to reach nearly 90,000. Interestingly, more than half in this older group are men.[110] Who is there at the end also illustrates again the inequalities between women, sharply measured in the concentration of migrants and black women in caregiving work. But feminist age activists like Segal argue that a positive and collective approach to late life can help prevent loneliness and ill health while also providing work for new generations (properly compensated). They welcome the fact that more men are learning to be caregivers, even if only in late life.

A feminist's attempt to reveal the meaning of family, care, and choice can be starkly symbolized at the funeral, where we see not only whose lives are "grievable," but whose grief counts. Death can pull those who "left home" back into family structures and ideologies with mixed and material consequences, as a recent study of feminist and LGBTQI wills suggests.[111] In the United Kingdom, the marriage of Prince William and Catherine Middleton in April 2011 focused attention on the fact that the rules of succession to the British Crown favoured boys over girls irrespective of who might be born first. In December 2011, the House of Commons stated that the rules were to be amended, and the Succession to the Crown Act 2013 made the royal family lineage gender-neutral, so that the eldest child, regardless of gender, would precede his or her siblings. The status of widows is being equalized, partly after feminist campaigns to end the discriminatory pension system, although the age at which women get the state pension in the United Kingdom has increased. However, inheritance is still governed by marriage or civil partnership, particularly in the absence of a will, which over half of the population do not have.[112] Typically feminists have chosen to formalize relationships in late life because common-law partners or friends receive nothing by default. Increasing class, race, and regional inequalities determine vastly different legacies.

The generations to which the WLM belonged inherited less comparatively than previous generations partly because they lived in a time of the greatest redistribution through welfare state tax policy. But while some have done well from progressive pensions policy in the 1970s, others cruelly lost out as occupational pension plans closed, or because they were on the "wrong" side of the volatile housing market. Notwithstanding stereotypes of greedy baby boomers squandering the family's inheritance, they are giving more to the next generation before they die, typically to help with housing costs, paying their own spiraling healthcare costs, and—why not?—enjoying active and independent late lifestyles.[113]

But the death of a feminist raises a question arguably far more important than material legacies: the purpose of life itself. Kitzinger's ceremony, as described by her daughters, hints at her own answer. Her memorial website, maintained by her daughters, offers a quote from her poetry, appropriate to Kitzinger's interest in birth and matriarchy:

> After the soaring, a peace
> like swans settling on the lake.
> After the tumult and the roaring winds,
> Silence.[114]

If this is a final expression of rest, her posthumously published autobiography suggests ongoing aspirations to influence midwifery and childbirth practices. Perhaps she did not anticipate a heavenly afterlife, but plainly she hoped for one on earth. This approach is even more striking in the closing words of Una Kroll, who died in 2017, the oldest of the S&A interviewees. Kroll was the best-known campaigner for the Movement for the Ordination of Women. When the Archbishop of Canterbury asked for silent prayer after the bishops voted against women's ordination in 1978, she famously pierced the silence with a cry from the gallery: "We asked you for bread, and you gave us a stone!" But strikingly, when I interviewed her in 2012, aged eighty-six, she admitted she did not know—or care—about the afterlife.[115]

Honouring the death of activists—and reflecting on their lives of activism—reveals the extent to which feminism can become a sustaining, if not systemic, faith. Perhaps by definition it is a belief in a cause that goes beyond self. A love of women and an interest in emancipated gender relations and identities are guided by a moral compass and conscience. It has often been observed that social movements contain or refigure structures of religious faith in this way: well over two-thirds of the S&A interviewees had some kind of religious upbringing. Religious institutions are one of "four seedbeds for future social movements," along with colleges and universities, stable residential neighbourhoods, and organizations, partly for this reason.[116] Yet most in the WLM, like the atheist McIntosh and eco-Quaker Kitzinger, had left such faith behind. They saw organized religion as patriarchal, misogynistic, homophobic, and reactionary for good reason. Though religious groups are often important to causes that feminists support—Drop the Debt, Occupy, the sanctuary movement, the living wage, Campaign for Nuclear Disarmament, Amnesty International—they are as likely to fuel social movements for conservative and antifeminist causes. Moreover, the WLM generations, like the black power and pan-Africanist movements, were deeply influenced by Marxist atheism.

Yet forms of feminist belief evolved in their own way. A few activists, notably Asphodel Long and Monica Sjoo, sought to define Goddess-based theologies. Feminist theologian Melissa Raphael describes a "female sacrality" as a high point at the Greenham peace camp, where lesbian

Una Kroll was the best-known campaigner for the ordination of women priests. When the Archbishop of Canterbury asked for silent prayer after the bishops voted against the measure in 1978, she famously pierced the silence with a cry from the gallery: "We asked you for bread, and you gave us a stone!" *Photo courtesy of the Women's Library Collection @ LSE*

feminism was infused with the green and animal rights movements, neopaganism (Gaia, Mother Earth), Catholicism (Marianism in particular), Aboriginal and Native American spiritualities (weaving, the rainbow serpent), Wicca (spiders, hagiographies, witches), Quakers (peace witness), and Romanticism.[117] Anglicans such as Una Kroll, Anglo-Catholic theologians Sara Maitland and Ianthe Pratt, lesbian rabbis Sheila Shulman and Elizabeth Tikvah Sarah, Baptist minister Kate Coleman, and others appealed to ethical codes of tolerance and love, reread religious texts to find where women are not destined to obey but rather to lead or partner and where women's sexuality is not defiling but enhancing.

Reclaiming religion in this way has been particularly important for minority ethnic and working-class groups. Christian churches remain mainstays for black civil rights struggles. Notably, of the nine S&A interviewees who describe themselves as still practicing a faith, most are of African Caribbean or African background. Mukami McCrum, who grew up Presbyterian in Kenya, was upfront about the prejudices of new fundamentalist Christianity in Africa and Scots Methodism: "It's turned out that women were more in solidarity with churches than the other way around."[118] However, she returned to the Church of Scotland and became a commissioner of the World Council of Churches for women and indigenous groups, after encouragement from African American pioneering minister Yvonne Delk. This gave her back "a whole life all centred around the church and the community."[119]

Feminists who have sought to reform organized religions from within are becoming newly significant in the postsecular 2010s, where religion is being "deprivatized."[120] Anglican church attendance continues to drop, but evangelical branches and minority religions are growing. "Multifaithism" has been a key UK government policy since 1997, promoted as a response to marginalized faith communities. This policy has been especially directed at the fast-growing number of British Muslims, although the struggles inside and outside the Middle East and the war on terror have compromised progressive intentions. Muslim women have been caught in backlashes by fundamentalist versions of Islam.

The privileges that the Anglican Church enjoys as the state religion—representation in the House of Lords and, pertinently, legal exemptions from the 1993 Sex Discrimination Act—have allowed other religions, in Yasmin Alibhai-Brown's words, to "legitimately press the ruling elite for their bit of power, their strand of hair."[121] Separatist faith schools, restrictions on abortion rights, and toleration of religious courts promising to handle family violence, divorce, or polygamy are now part of the landscape.[122] Pragna Patel, a founding member of Women Against Fundamentalism (WAF), confesses in her oral history that she is still wrestling with why state funding for "moderate" Muslims to combat radicalization so often involves a "tradeoff" of women's rights. From her perspective, seemingly progressive multifaith policies designed to support a multicultural United Kingdom have in fact crushed a more empowering coalitional "black" identity.[123]

A final story drawn from the S&A oral histories opens up the question of feminist faith and its relationship to religious belief: that of Nadira Mirza, who was director of lifelong education at the University of Bradford until she was laid off in 2016. Mirza's connection to UK women's movements, both black and white, clearly shaped her community work with Muslim women and girls in Bradford for more than forty years. Born in Glasgow in 1955 to a white English mother and a Muslim Indian father, but brought up largely in Pakistan, she was educated in Islam and today, in her words, is known by everyone as "part of the Muslim community."[124] Yet in tracing her path, what stands out is how her life of service and mediation expresses a political conscience as much as a religious one. This conscience is articulated in terms of socialism, feminism, and antiracism but also as what has given meaning, resilience, and purpose to a life in which she, now in her sixties, intends to continue in activism. In many ways, it embodies what I mean by feminism as itself a faith.

Mirza suggests that her political formation lay in observing her mother's balancing of a teaching career and family, and in her sense of guilt about having domestic servants. In her unorthodox marriage Mirza's mother had rejected a conservative British upbringing. The family moved in 1955 to Karachi, Pakistan, where Mirza's father worked for an American oil company. Mirza was brought up in a domestic compound and extended family, and was tutored in the Quran at her mother's instigation to enable her children to integrate; neither parent was practicing, but both felt religion was important to know about. Mirza considers that, like Pakistani as well as English expatriate upper-middle-class women, her mother had a "nervousness," a "lack of confidence" to act on her moral convictions; "part of a Valium . . . women's generation of the '50s."[125] As a teenager she was aware of the 1970 student protests against the inequalities of the new nation: "We were part of a Pakistan that was developing . . . and I think my brother and I, we were very aware that we were at the top rung of all that. And it didn't sit easy with us."[126]

This all ended when, after a tumultuous year of war and military defeat, Zulfikar Ali Bhutto became president and imposed emergency rule, precipitating the family's exile to the United Kingdom in 1972. Mirza was seventeen. Her British state school did not recognize her previous education and her career advisor presumed her parents would only want her to get married, reluctantly suggesting she take teacher training at Oxford Polytechnic. Mirza hated the programme, but as a student discovered antiausterity, antiapartheid, and antiracist protests, and after graduating applied for her first job as a community worker in 1979.

Mirza trained in Southall in west London, known for its large British Asian community and a hub of antiracist activism, where the black power–inspired Asian youth movement emerged, bringing Muslim and Sikh men together. Southall also was where Asian and African Caribbean women were organizing together in the newly launched Southall Black Sisters (SBS), founded in 1979. Reading Amrit Wilson's 1978 *Finding a Voice: Asian Women in Britain* was also formative for her.

Funded through a new Department of Education and Science initiative supporting black and minority ethnic workers, Mirza moved to Bradford to promote Asian girls' involvement in youth services through the National Association for Asian Youth (NAAY). She remembers it was snowing, gray, and bleak on her first day in Bradford in 1981: "You *hardly* saw . . . young people, absolutely *no* black minority ethnic, Pakistani heritage young people and barely any Muslim women *at all*. And of course now it's changed radically. . . . But it's a bit of a sad city centre now that has more pound shops [shops selling goods cheaply] than anything else. At that time . . . the Wool Exchange was a beautiful place in itself, and when the wool wasn't being exchanged there were . . . wonderful flea markets."[127]

Bradford had been a boomtown of the Industrial Revolution and the British Empire but has had to reinvent itself since the decline of its textile industries in the mid-twentieth century. Although there are areas of high social deprivation, it is nonetheless a major economic centre and has been designated by the United Nations Educational, Scientific and Cultural Organization (UNESCO) as the first city of film, in honour of its outstanding film heritage. A quarter of its population are British Asian, migrants who came for a better life and worked in the textile mills in the 1950s and 1960s, or joined families who had already settled. The city witnessed race riots in 1976 (the year of the Race Relations Act); in 1982, the "Bradford 12" were acquitted of charges of conspiracy to cause explosions and endanger lives in a landmark legal case where they argued that "self-defence is no offence."

Mirza was politically inspired, having married a local activist who took part in the 1976 uprisings, but she really settled when she found "the women's network," especially when friend Pratibha Parmar was appointed to lead a sister project in Leicester's Gujarati and Hindu community, the two women "matching" the ethnicity of their patch. Together they wrote a government report "Encounters of a Cultural Kind," which controversially asked whether it mattered if girls and young women did not want to use youth services; they also contributed to *Spare Rib*, advocating British Asian young women's interests.[128]

While Parmar went into filmmaking and writing, Mirza immersed herself in local community work. After the job with the NAAY, she advised on equalities law as a Bradford city council race relations officer, successfully lobbying for a Muslim Asian girls' centre and refuge.[129] She campaigned on behalf of Zoora Shah, a Bradford woman imprisoned for killing her abuser, supported by SBS. When public funding for equalities work contracted in the

1990s, she developed "Inner City Studies" and a weekend "Junior University" at the University of Bradford, notably in response to local unrest and riots in 1995 and 2001. Transforming street kids' alienation as "global citizens," she developed sister programmes at neglected universities in rural Mirpur, from where many of Bradford Pakistanis originate. More recently, she has been part of a research project "Born in Bradford," which explores the life chances of its citizens, and of conflict resolution initiatives, paralleling the criminalization of young Irish men during Northern Ireland's Troubles and young Muslims in Bradford.

Work of this type involved a kind of faith. But what kind? Mirza herself asks whether "you need an organized religion to have that spiritual wellbeing and … to get a moral route and pathway." "Some people need that," she says.[130] She, by implication, does not. Here, her approach is different from that of the women who, since the 1990s, have sought a feminism that takes its legitimacy from Islam. British-based Iranian anthropologist Ziba Mir-Hosseini is one such, distinguishing Shari'a as sacred justice from its "outdated, human" interpretations.[131] Although the term "Islamic feminism" is claimed by often opposing groups, Mir-Hosseini's hope lies with internal lobbies for legal reform of unjust family law, such as the Malaysia-based nongovernmental organization, Sisters in Islam.[132] The Women's Islamic Initiative in Spirituality and Equality (WISE), established in 2006 in the United States to build a cohesive, global movement of Muslim women, is another faith-based progressive group that includes training women to become *muftiyyahs*, legal scholars with the right to interpret the Quran.[133]

Atheist, often Marxist-inspired women of Muslim background have more generally been recognized in the feminist West: women such as Egyptian writer, activist, physician, and psychiatrist Nawal el Sadaawi, who has been publishing since the 1970s, or Moroccan writer and sociologist Fatima Mernissi, whose classic *Beyond the Veil* was published in 1975. Others of Muslim descent such as Haleh Ashfar, who wrote influentially in UK WLM publications, focused on the crushing of women's rights in Iran after the Islamic revolution of 1979.[134] However, since then, disillusioned women in Iran's Republic have sought to challenge the gender biases of Muslim family laws. In other words, as Islamist forces co-opted popular demands for social justice, their regressive gender policies provoked their own critique, feminism the "unwanted child" of political Islam.[135] This flowering of Islamic feminism has certainly been fuelled as well by the orientalist bias of many Western or Western-educated feminists, which has allowed progressive politics to be co-opted by neocolonial forces.[136] Meanwhile, young Muslim women, in Mirza's terms, wear the hijab as a form of "cultural dress and a personal statement and a way of being noticed," sometimes despite parental opposition.[137]

Mirza steers between these paths with apparent ease. A WISE member, she says little about religious faith directly in her interview. "There's no *one* way of being a Muslim feminist," she says.

NADIRA MIRZA: I think what we do is sort of pick and choose parts of the traditional, if you can call it a traditional, women's feminist movement and parts of Islam. But why I'd call *myself* a Muslim feminist really is because I would *challenge* aspects of community and religion which I thought were oppressive, mm? But at the same time being part of it.
RACHEL COHEN: So, reforming from within rather than sort of—
NM: Yeah, yeah. But I think a lot of us, when we first started getting involved with the women's movement, it was about leaving *everything* behind and attacking it from the outside, not being part of it. And . . . the whole sort of movement around antiracism, antifascism . . . if anyone said, "Oh, I'm fighting it from *within*," you'd really sort of laugh hysterically 'cause you'd think, "It can't be done!" But I think probably around . . . religion and feminism, that's probably the *only* way to make a change. Because I work and live and take part in a lot of *highly* traditional activity in Bradford *and* in my international work, because to actually understand what's going on, you've got to be round that table.[138]

Mirza's self-positioning seems pragmatic, perhaps influenced as well by her husband, whom she described as a "free-floating, spiritualist" with probably an agnostic/atheist approach and an interest in Buddhism and Hinduism, despite his orthodox Muslim upbringing. While shared antiracism action has been a bond in their nearly forty-year marriage, she perseveres with Pakistan, which he thinks difficult to change. This difference reflects their backgrounds—he was a working-class "Bradford-born lad" of Pakistani descent, whose parents ran the first Asian restaurant in the city, whereas she grew up in Karachi "with a silver spoon in her mouth." Her family lost status, his became wealthy through business. But most striking is her comment that her youthful self would have "laughed hysterically" at the thought of "fighting from within." What once seemed impossible is now politically, rather than theologically, necessary.

Perhaps Bradford is a test case. "People who don't understand the city and the citizens . . . feel that the district is like a tinderbox that anything could go off," as Mirza puts it.[139] In 1989 local men burned Salman Rushdie's satirical

238 • SISTERHOOD AND AFTER

novel *The Satanic Verses*, shortly before Iran's Ayatollah Khomeini issued a fatwa calling for Rushdie and his publishers to be killed. This early but high-profile outburst of Islamic fundamentalism severely tested the kind of cultural relativism that had grown up with multiculturalism, dividing leftist and feminist activists as they struggled to understand. It was the reaction to anti-Rushdie protests that in London propelled the formation of WAF after a meeting at SBS, whose slogans included "Our tradition: struggle not submission" and "Religious leaders don't speak for us." WAF cleverly campaigned by pairing speakers and causes from different religions, following the Rushdie defence with a campaign against the abortion prohibition in Ireland. But the group foundered in 2010 because of issues on what position to take on the human rights of Taliban supporters held at Guantanamo Bay.[140]

Mirza views seem similar to those in WAF: she has adamantly stuck to a "very strong secular line" against pressures, because "without secularism we wouldn't be a multifaith society." Her position in this sense reflects her feminist faith: "The purpose of organized religion *is* . . . controlling women in the long run. If you look at a lot around, you know, Christianity, Judaism and Islam, it's—all three religions, Judeo religions, are *obsessed* with women, women's behaviour and women's role."[141]

At the same time, her suspicion of niche groups is of a par with her consensual approach in general:

> So I work with imams of *all* sorts of different views and then also with . . . women's groups and young people who . . . will have nothing to do with them at all. But I think one of my skills has always been the acceptable face of everything really [smiling voice], and therefore I feel I've been able to *change* a lot more and *mediate* a lot more as well. So when I go to Pakistan I'll go and see some of the Sufis as well that are quite influential in Bradford communities and . . . sit with them and listen to them and just try and get to—it's a bit about my own knowledge—it's my *own* lifelong learning really, you know, trying to understand what is the hold that people like that have, and why do they need to have that hold, and why do people need to be held? And . . . why so many people can't operate without either being controlled or controlling?[142]

Describing a recent reunion with her Pakistani school friends, she observed how pop-loving teenagers had become religiously observant. She compares herself to Muslim colleagues and friends who track their daughters' dating behaviour, insist on ethnically appropriate marriages, or are settling for "pottering" along. She refuses all of this, amused too by the little dodges (a sneaky cigarette behind the shop in Ramadan), but "if it makes them happy [laughs], it's fine." As with the new popularity of veiling, she is sympathetic to the identity pressures and pride involved: "Those of us who have sort of gone out to America or other parts of UK and Europe seem to be more—um—entrenched in Islam than those who are in Pakistan."[143]

At a time when the wealthy of the West are beset by "affluenza" but the poor by ever more insecurity, religious fundamentalisms and racist patriarchal nationalisms all too readily fill the unhappiness gap. Mirza's approach is one of links and bridges. Yet evidently, she herself draws on values that were formed through decades of work for social justice, a faith that can survive the slow pressures to conform as well as direct attack. When I met Mirza in 2017, it emerges that she has been laid off from her beloved "lifelong learning" project because of a restructure at the university. She reflects on the experience of losing her own little "empire," now in her sixties, looking to reconnect with feminist initiatives and explore her own further education. Her daughter has married in "a lovely fusion-y type of wedding," involving civil registration and the Islamic *nikah* at the same time (only two mosques in Bradford do this), "Asian film-y" music as well as pop hits by singer-songwriter Ed Sheeran. Her father had died, and she sought "the most liberal imam" to consecrate the ground to allow him to be buried alongside her mother, appreciating the local white English gravedigger who specializes in Muslim burials. Mirza's "exploratory and inquisitive attitude to everything" also emerges in how she dealt with breast cancer:

> I just . . . looked at it as something that was an *adventure*, really, a new type of journey. . . . I had to put the illness into a . . . perspective and think that, well, it's a bit like diabetes. There are ways of dealing and controlling it, right, but firstly I've got to get on top of my own emotions and . . . understand it's not going to kill me today or tomorrow. And once I . . . got an emotional grip on it, then it was quite straightforward.[144]

This account echoes that feminist principle of control over body and self-image, evident in Mary McIntosh's and others' accounts, also in Mirza's imagined end as a "pretty humanitarian burial ground out in Skipton." Its anonymity, as she describes it, would be "quite Islamic," since you are not buried in a coffin but wrapped in a sheet: "And then you're buried like that in an

240 • SISTERHOOD AND AFTER

Nadira Mirza collects money to help fund cancer research in her Bradford hometown. Mirza's connection to UK women's movements, both black and white, has shaped her community work with Muslim women and girls in the city for more than forty years, whilst her life of service and mediation expresses a political conscience as much as a religious one. *Photo courtesy of Bradford Telegraph & Argus*

unmarked grave. So that's how it's meant to be. So in some ways you could say we're going back to our roots. Equal, you know, equal is . . . the right thing for today, isn't it."[145]

Feminism consistently poses different narratives of purpose that stress autonomy and equality entwined with care and responsibility. This is often more a question of consolation than ease. Mirza believes in an end, but it is hardly scriptural:

> There has to be something, but I really, really don't know what. Perhaps, you know, your afterlife is *here* 'cause most people's lives are hell and happiness, hell and happiness in the West anyway, I mean. Other places it could be pure hell all the time. So it feels like there should be more. I mean if there's—it's . . . interesting whether this is just part of the human *search* . . .[146]

But perhaps this is the point for women like Mirza, whose feminist faith is about making progress here on earth: "I think the day that I felt . . . I wasn't part of any change would be the day that I'd think, 'Oo-hh, my work's done.'"[147]

Just as well. For, by current measures, there is a very long way to go to eradicate exploitative gender relations. Zoë Fairbairns's recent response to being asked by a man, "How will you know when you've won?" was to show him a list of the WLM's demands, saying, "I'll know we've won when each of those demands has been met, and when they look as old-fashioned as campaigning for the right to vote."[148]

If the WLM generations will not live to see the transformations they hoped for, this is not their fault. The UK political system is difficult to change—feminism under New Labour and in the first years of Scottish and Welsh devolution and the Northern Ireland Women's Coalition's work in the 1990s peace process now look like a high point to recapture.[149] But patience is a late-life lesson—it is a question of faith. Moreover, what counts as a movement's success must include shifting public opinion and increasing cultural equality as much as legislation and policy change. The WLM's insight that women's liberation is a whole-life question remains essential for gender activists of all kinds looking to a better future.

CONCLUSION

ARCHIVING HOPE: THE FUTURE OF FEMINIST MEMORY

Oral history affirms the value of people whose lives were unwritten; it can also complement the documentary archive. But equally, oral history composes a past with which the teller can live. For the activists of the 1970s and 1980s women's movements, this process was often a challenge and a delight. Remembering when they "left home" (at whatever age), they recalled a society of self-making, collectivity, purpose. S&A interviewees testify to a politics they still believe in, even when it brings memories of struggle, abuse, or splits. This element of "composure" makes the oral history record partial and unreliable, which is perhaps especially obvious when interviewees lose composure. I have therefore contextualized these memories to show more of what was in fact involved in the politics of experience, to temper the romanticism. But oral history's unreliability is inseparable from its narrative magic, both for the speaker and, in a different and equally important sense, for the listener and wider audience. Even as memory remains contested, no one doubts its significance.[1] Memory energizes the relationship between past and present. For listeners of the same age, sharing memories can be a form of mutual witnessing. For others, it can create valuable intergenerational relationships, in which past and present become future.

Such remembering has a special role in the functioning of social movements, particularly during political "doldrums" for isolated feminists.[2] It is no accident that Sheila Rowbotham titled her 1989 history of the WLM *The Past Is Before Us*. Historians like Rowbotham by definition never see the past as dead or irrelevant. But when people of an older generation engage with the young, they must draw upon political memory to drive the lesson of possibility, and this depends on adroit narrative structures. There has been progress, yes—no more knitting needles for homemade abortions, "pin money" pay, and disregard of marital rape.[3] But there has been loss, too, in new obstacles to feminist demands in the age of austerity. WLM analyses of labour, skill, reproduction, culture, sexuality, gender, care, and faith remain pertinent. But even as we return to these powerful ideas, we must be careful not to tell our histories in ways that alienate or exclude subsequent generations of activists.[4]

In any case, very few of the S&A interviewees spoke this way. Rather, their narrative structures emerged from our invitation to tell their life course, beginning with the story of their name and then their mother's. We closed by asking whether they found the method effective in capturing their life and that of a movement. Invariably, they were uncertain about the political future but satisfied they had been able to speak about life as a whole. Personal memories of habits, bodies, and domestic cultures—the everyday unvalued femininized bedrock—are especially significant for feminists. When women put these on record, history appears much less like a linear march of progress than a spiral of mothers and daughters, a way of thinking about time that for me is profoundly more human than the ever-faster rush of contemporary life.

Admittedly, images of spirals and indeed of generations bring their own risks. Think how the divisive portrayal of rapacious elderly baby boomers pauperizing their generation Y grandchildren skews the narrative. Think how queer theorists have argued that metaphors of time as a passage of inheritance privilege heterosexual partnering and children—although LGBTQI and postpatriarchal families are taking the sting out of this argument.[5] Imagining activism as generational, and social movements as waves, has rightly been critiqued for overgeneralized constructions of the players and their successors, as well as the undue influence of the popular media in styling them.[6] This way of imagining political continuity can also fall prey to the romanticism of familial inheritance and the bitterness when it disappoints. As with metaphors of fellow activists as sisters, mothers, and grandmothers, they can reduce complex histories of resource and opportunity to psychological plots and hurt those who do not feel included in the family.

I analyze the WLM as generational, therefore, not in relation to internal arguments but as radical baby boomers and their allies. The WLM was fuelled by demographic as well as political and economic opportunity. Conversely, its internal segmentations of race, class, and nation also reflected the external contexts. The autonomous black women's movement was scarred by parents' disappointments as well as by white racism, anti-immigration forces, and anticolonial struggles. For the white Jewish men prominent in the men's movement, histories of trauma and assimilation entwined with their wish to be different from their fathers. For places where large numbers of young people are similarly growing up with education, aspiration, and blocked opportunities (North Africa, for example, as well as in parts of the United States and Europe), new social movements are emerging that inevitably also reflect age, family, and life-course dynamics as well as wider inequalities. Here feminist insights remain brilliantly illuminating.

Just as feminists can challenge the inheritance of families and classes, it is also possible to redistribute and talk back to political legacies. In struggle, it is not, therefore, always wicked to spiral and repeat.[7] However, I am not proposing the repetition of traumatic memory.[8] The real lesson from this history is not to fetishize experiences of suffering over those of organizing. Many of the interviews show the value of practical experience, leadership, networking, stamina, an ability to work within organizational structures as well as outside and on the edge of them. Sally Alexander's "secret" of an activist's endurance is a case in point: to "make a commitment for whatever it is, six months, a year . . . or two years perhaps . . . steady regular routine work so that people feel there's something there, there's something to fall back on when they need a bit of support."[9] On the other hand, there must be tolerance and patience in coalitions, including those across age. Ros Delmar puts it this way:

> I'm very interested in the . . . current women's movement [pause] because I felt quite clearly that there were . . . historical problems that are *always* there for women, and this choice between . . . maternity and work is always there . . . and every generation has to solve it in its own way. I didn't think *we'd* solved it for the next generation, by any means. . . . That's a big *difference* from when we started, because there were these older women who . . . didn't know what we were going on about! And they'd *done* it all, and, you know, "Why on earth are you making a fuss? We've achieved all that!" [mock indignant voice] and so on, the successful women in the older generation.[10]

The WLM had mixed feelings about its own forbears. Activists were mostly uninterested in the Fawcett Society, the Six Point Group, and the midcentury focus on Parliament and married women's legal rights, to these older activists' frustration.[11] They were more attracted to their grandmothers' struggles, especially the spectacular heritage of suffrage campaigning, including in early oral history projects and the 1974 BBC TV miniseries *Shoulder to Shoulder*.[12]

Yet these elderly activists did not always reciprocate. The three campaigners Margaret Drabble interviewed for the *Radio Times* on *Shoulder to Shoulder* under the strapline "force fed, imprisoned, handcuffed—three respectable women remember" characteristically proposed that "we *had* to do these things; young women now don't need to."[13]

Nor was the suffrage movement wholly embraced as a genealogy. S&A interviewees spoke of it primarily to stake positions over recurring strategic questions about militancy versus reformism, sexual versus economic rights, separatism versus inclusion. Jenni Murray paralleled the WLM's relationship to Barbara Castle, who held a number of ministerial positions in the Labour governments of the 1960s and 1970s, with the irritating suffragettes (who got all the press coverage) versus the sensible suffragists (who lobbied Parliament behind the scenes).[14] Bronagh Hinds talks of how the 1970s women's rights movement in Northern Ireland had to field nationalist and civil rights movements in the same way that Northern Irish suffragettes did.[15] Pragna Patel mentions suffrage as a human right for which she is fighting today.[16] But Sheila Rowbotham, researching *Hidden from History* (confessing she had wanted to find the key to what had failed in previous revolutionary groups), remembers

> ringing the Fawcett Library and asking them for stuff on . . . women in revolutions [giggling] and was met by a very *blank* response by a woman on the telephone because they specialized in the *suffrage* movement. And I didn't *really* connect up with the suffrage movement because I was interested in this [other] idea of revolutionary transformation. And then a few books were coming out about Cuba, and I found these things in French about women in the Algerian revolutions, and in China.[17]

Moreover, black women could feel alienated by memories of the suffrage generation, entwined as it was with the British Empire, as reflected in responses to Abi Morgan's 2015 film *Suffragette*, the first mainstream feature on the subject. For all its gritty focus on a working-class laundry worker rather than the Pankhursts, some were critical that it did not include suffragists of colour, and that the marketing of the film repeated the Pankhurst line, "I'd rather be a rebel than a slave."[18] While Morgan foregrounded the historical accuracy of her story's setting, the politics of commemoration is also about which stories one chooses to tell. Yet, as any artist knows, it is impossible to tell all stories at once.[19]

Former suffragette Jane Lunnon meets young women outside Westminster Hall in London in March 1968. Her placard reprises the suffragette slogan—"Purple, green, and white puts tyranny to flight"—while her "I'm backing Britain" carrier bag recalls a short-lived and controversial campaign aimed at boosting Britain's ailing economy. *Photo courtesy of Mirrorpix*

The WLM in turn continues to pay its political inheritance tax as it encounters the mixed reviews of younger feminists. Artist Mary Kelly, known for her 1978 "Post-Partum Document" (a six-year exploration of the mother-child relationship), admits her generation failed to "really grasp" the significance of the trans movement and its "disconcerting questions... about what is a man, what is a woman." For her, LGBTQI students are taking up the theoretical legacy of "anti-essentialist feminism."[20] But clearly some trans activists' angry attacks on older feminists who do not get it or who disagree show the difficulty of transmission. In each feminist generation's longing to pass on the torch, it is possible to understand the members' paradoxically fierce suspicions over who will receive it. For this reason, feminist archives can be fought over as mythical sites of memory. And oral history is always more than "data" as it channels generational debates over institutional versus grassroots activism and what political lessons they carry.

But that is fine. These emotional records can be listened to critically, as traces, as displaced, deferred, and repressed hopes and fears, "political primal scenes," as Kelly puts it. Her 2007 art installation "Multi-Story House," produced in collaboration with her partner, Ray Barrie, visualizes this kind of exchange and documents the WLM's own postpartum life. The installation takes the shape of an illuminated house large enough to enter, in which the visitor finds multiple "stories" about feminism that relate obliquely to each other. Memories from Kelly's WLM friends are inscribed inside, younger people's ideas about 1970s and 1980s women's movements outside. She comments that the work was

> an acknowledgment and a homage to something that had gone before us but in the form of [pause] *testimonies* really more than about their campaigns. . . . So it's about their *voices*. And this is the very crucial thing for me through *all* of the works, is that there's a certain quality of the voice and the way that it can, I suppose, witness something? You know, that you feel it too, you have a little *way* of *hearing* something that happened.[21]

Her own oral history, as part of many thousands of activist recordings, might be part of this witnessing that hopes to engender feeling and identification. But, as the writings on the outside walls illuminate, newer generations feel feminism is no longer fresh and transformative nor necessarily a meaningful heritage. Here, oral history, like the house, is a symptom and a scene. What it offers is the opportunity to link stories, to see, feel, listen plurally—ideally—enough to build.

The contradictions and conditions of an oral history are easier to appreciate now that digitization enables us, finally, to hear the power of the recorded voice. Many interviewees are horrified when receiving their oral history transcript. Lauded stylist Barbara Taylor, for example, was shocked by her "habit of repetition."[22] But anyone who *listens* to Taylor's recording will be mesmerized by her slow, thoughtful Canadian-infused drawl. The dramatically elongated vowels, parenthetical rushes, the drop at the end of the sentence—repetition is here the first rule of style. This beautiful voice brings social cues missed by traditional transcription, including in the enhanced method I have employed when quoting in this book. Accents of place (Taylor's Saskatchewan childhood, her life in London) and of class (her hothouse education, the absence of any Jewish or Welsh dialect that her parentage could have put there) are part of the movement story.

We might compare these varied voices to the clipped "received pronunciation" of the British upper middle classes that, even in the late 1960s, was still the modus operandi for public speaking. Listeners today are instantly alienated by archaic articulations of privilege, even when, as with the few WLM speakers who gained airtime in the 1960s and 1970s, voicing good causes. But oral histories capture many others who never spoke like that, or who have since rejected those terms of authority. On the other hand, they also starkly contrast with the "high rise terminals" (every sentence ends as a question?) promoted to young Anglophone women today. Older feminists' speech styles talk of pre–social media public spheres, of hard-won authority and increasing social diversity. Yet they do not speak with the guttural vocal fry of the seen-it-all Kardashians or Lena Dunham.[23] Taylor's mezzo delivery, at once confident and vulnerable, articulates inner struggle as well as outer achievement.

Listening like this is hard, slow work. But where there is nothing to see, the emotional detail is easier to hear, an aural "punctum" or piercing of the merely informational.[24] It is not just the singing that breaks into memories of protest; consider also the timbre of lovely late-life voices (quavering or rough, low or silvery), the unsettling background noises, the inadvertent interruptions. When Ellen Malos wonders if we should turn the light on while I persist with my questions, when a pile of policy papers tumbles as if pushed by an invisible finger as Rebecca Johnson recounts Greenham tales, when Mary Kelly's partner appears with "Oh—sorry!" just while we are musing on his own artistic ups and downs, we understand a little more of the scene of memory and who is invested in its power. I have attempted to feed this into the difficult reconstruction of the history of emotion itself, whether the complicated emotions generated by the fight for abortion rights, the joy of purposeful community, or the shame felt by men wanting relationships with feminist women. These vital elements in oral histories of feminism can generate as well as capture feeling.

Public historians, archivists, artists, educators, and activists know this when they take oral history out of the archive and the book. Alison Marchant projected the recorded voice of her millworker aunt within the walls of Barchant cotton mill.[25] Cathy Lane's 1999 installation *Hidden Lives* juxtaposes field recordings, archival materials, interviews, conversations, and synthesized instrumental sounds to explore the house as the repository of memories, with women as the curators.[26] While Anne Butler and Gerri Sorenson imagine women's oral history as a patchwork and celebrate their transcripts in quilt form, Suzanne Lacy choreographed women aged over sixty to share their stories while they sat in a grid that was formed in the shape of a quilt.[27] Lacy's *Silver Action* reprised this performance art in 2014 at the Tate Modern with hundreds of UK feminists—including some from S&A—telling protest stories at patterned tables, scribed by young men, projected in real time on gallery walls, tweeted by young women.[28] The Striking Women oral history of British Asian women's resistance created comic strips of the Grunwick strike for schoolchildren.[29] Lizzie Thynne experimented with S&A's own soundwork, "Voices in Movement," an impressionistic installation that interwove interview fragments to mimic the political process of consciousness raising.[30] Radio broadcasts, sound walks, podcasts, interactive maps, and plaques as well as heritage community projects bring oral history onto the street and into the home.

Indeed, we inhabit a digital golden age of oral historical reception, giving hope for the future of feminist memory, where the archives of yesteryear are not merely opened but reimagined. Here, more transforming than aesthetic play (however delightful) is the principle of interactivity, as evident in ventures like the black power oral history project Do You Remember Olive Morris? and the WLM Music Archive blogs.[31] Often maintained on free software or independent sites, their born-digital curators publish, record, edit, caption, illustrate, and, where linked through social media, circulate with a reach hardly dreamt of by older oral historians. D-M Withers runs open, free, collective metadata-making workshops for feminist archives.[32] Working with the British Library, the S&A team members were also privileged to be part of a visible process of archival democratizing. Our interviewees did not want us putting the full S&A recordings and transcripts online, but I am happy to see the S&A website bustling with clips, searchable transcriptions, videos, images, thematic narratives, and teachers' packs—and thrilled that the site is being visited, tweeted, discussed, and argued over. The feminist school workshops, intergenerational conferences, television as well as collecting initiatives of S&A's curator Polly Russell make plain that the library is no more monolithic than the university or state.

This newly public oral history feeds political education that we have seen was essential to the women's movements' own precipitation, especially its hardwon lessons of coalition and strategy. But as document-based, positivist historiography is left behind, the questions that feminist oral historians have asked about voice as conduit for a collective consciousness become more pressing. Digitization squelches lingering romantic ideals of its authenticity as the voice can be manipulated, disguised, or entirely manufactured through video streams, Skype calls, lip-synching apps, voice synthesis, searchable speech, and biometric listening software.[33] Similarly, the postfactual "news" circulating in today's digital public sphere puts the WLM's suspicion of the media in the shade. This inevitably strains and tests contracts with interviewees who find their stories going out into a much less predictable world. Death may see posthumous voices float still more readily away from original moorings. In this way, privacy, sustainability, traceability, and authority are being rediscovered as vital conditions for oral historians to respect.

In addition, I propose, paradoxically, that silence be part of the new oral history. Silence may be a deliberative element of protest, as solidarity in witness or mourning or as negotiating tactic. But the silence I encourage here is simply that of critical thought and mutual respect, a silence "at the edge of sound"; not resigned, nor repressed, but one astutely listening, ready, indeed, to return to the archive and listen again.[34] Here, the old have as much to hear as the young, as we seek ways to protect a critical dialogue with the past and enable the presence of young people who are questioning the present. It is this deep listening, as much as digital technology, that will allow us to redream history from below in the growing, connected, interactive, and global archive of feminist memory.

Nadira Mirza imagines that young feminists see her generation as "eccentric."[35] Readers must be the judge of that. But how in turn would an activist today want to be remembered in fifty years? Who will be listening, where, and how? The issue for many feminists is no longer invisibility but management and interpretation in today's world of multimediated loudness wars, compressed speech, and intimate yet unboundaried publics. Today, when "feminism" plays a prominent role in public discourse yet is so easily misused and abused, we need to tune into the frequencies of the future.

So, put this book down and listen. Listen to the speeches and the stories, the inner voices, laughter, tears, tones, and sighs, the prickling air nearby. Then act.

NOTES

INTRODUCTION

1. Sheila Rowbotham, "Women's Liberation and the New Politics," in *The Body Politic: Women's Liberation in Britain*, ed. Michelene Wandor (London: Stage 1, 1972), 6.
2. Ibid., 7.
3. Ibid., 6.
4. Significant published oral history anthologies or histories that inform this book include Lisa Power, *No Bath but Plenty of Bubbles: An Oral History of the Gay Liberation Front, 1970–1973* (London: Cassell, 1995), and Sam Carroll, ed., *Brighton Trans*formed* (Brighton: QueenSpark Books, 2014).
5. Brian Howard Harrison, *Prudent Revolutionaries: Portraits of British Feminists between the Wars* (Oxford: Clarendon Press, 1987).
6. Raymond Williams, *Marxism and Literature* (Oxford: Oxford University Press, 1977), 132–34.
7. Here I build on Ann Cvetkovich's call to contribute to the histories of sexual minorities and dissidents as "archives of feeling" in *An Archive of Feelings: Trauma, Sexuality, and Lesbian Public Cultures* (Durham, NC: Duke University Press, 2003), 241.
8. Mary Chamberlain, *Fenwomen: A Portrait of Women in an English Village* (London: Quartet Books for Virago, 1975), 1.
9. Helen (charles), "The Language of Womanism: Rethinking Difference," in *Black British Feminism: A Reader*, ed. Heidi Safia Mirza (London: Routledge, 1997).
10. Angela McRobbie, *The Aftermath of Feminism: Gender, Culture and Social Change* (Los Angeles: SAGE, 2009), 1.
11. Alison Phipps, *The Politics of the Body: Gender in a Neoliberal and Neoconservative Age* (Cambridge: Polity, 2014), 21.
12. Sara Ahmed, *The Promise of Happiness* (Durham, NC: Duke University Press, 2010), 50–87.

CHAPTER 1

1. Michelene Wandor, ed., *Once a Feminist: Stories of a Generation* (London: Virago, 1990), 13.
2. J. P. Becker, "The British Women's Health Movement: An Analysis of the Establishment, Work and Achievements of Women's Health Centres since 1970" (PhD thesis, University of Essex, 2000); Na'ama Klorman-Eraqi, "Feminism and Photography in Britain in the 1970s and Early 1980s" (PhD thesis, State University of New York at Binghamton, 2014).
3. Juliet Mitchell published a contextual account of the WLM's origins in *Woman's Estate* (Harmondsworth, UK: Penguin, 1971; repr. 1981).
4. Anna Coote and Beatrix Campbell, *Sweet Freedom: The Struggle for Women's Liberation*, 2nd ed. (Oxford: Basil Blackwell, 1987), 9–10.
5. 8SUF/B/157, Papers of Jessie Stephen, The Women's Library @ LSE; Susie Fleming and Gloden Dallas, "Jessie Stephen," *Spare Rib*, no. 32 (1975): 10–13.
6. Beatrix Campbell, *S&A*, C1420/01, transcript p. 84, track 5.
7. 7SEB, Papers of Amanda Sebestyen, The Women's Library @ LSE. The pamphlet was reprinted in Feminist Anthology Collective et al., eds., *No Turning Back: Writings from the Women's Liberation Movement, 1975–80* (London: Women's Press, 1981).
8. Sheila Jeffreys, *Anticlimax: A Feminist Perspective on the Sexual Revolution* (London: Women's Press, 1990).
9. Amrit Wilson, *Finding a Voice: Asian Women in Britain* (London: Virago, 1978); Beverley Bryan, Stella Dadzie, and Suzanne Scafe, *The Heart of the Race: Black Women's Lives in Britain* (London: Virago, 1985).
10. Bryan, Dadzie, and Scafe, *The Heart of the Race*, 148–49.
11. Andy Beckett, *When the Lights Went Out: Britain in the Seventies* (London: Faber, 2009), 221.
12. Sara Maitland, ed., *Very Heaven: Looking Back at the 1960's* (London: Virago, 1988), including Angela Carter, "Truly, It Felt Like Year One," 209–16.
13. Sheila Rowbotham, *S&A*, C1420/10, transcript p. 94, track 3.
14. Rosalind Delmar, *S&A*, C1420/3, transcript p. 100, track 4.
15. Sheila Rowbotham, *S&A*, C1420/10, transcript p. 94, track 3.
16. Jenny Diski, *The Sixties* (London: Profile, 2009), 4–5.
17. Sheila Rowbotham, "Women's Liberation and the New Politics," in *The Body Politic: Women's Liberation in Britain*, ed. Michelene Wandor (London: Stage 1, 1972), 3–30.
18. Sheila Rowbotham, *S&A*, C1420/10, transcript p. 94, track 3.
19. Sheila Rowbotham, *Promise of a Dream: Remembering the Sixties* (London: Verso, 2001), 210.
20. Ibid.
21. Rowbotham, "Women's Liberation and the New Politics," 3.
22. Sheila Rowbotham, "Appreciating Our Beginnings," in *Threads through Time: Writings on History and Autobiography* (London: Penguin, 1999), 73.

23. Sheila Rowbotham, "The Beginnings of Women's Liberation in Britain," in Wandor, *Body Politic*, 93.
24. Sheila Rowbotham, *Women, Resistance, and Revolution: A History of Women and Revolution in the Modern World* (New York: Pantheon Books, 1972); *Woman's Consciousness, Man's World* (Harmondsworth, UK: Penguin Books, 1973); *Hidden from History: Rediscovering Women in History from the 17th Century to the Present* (New York: Pantheon Books, 1975); *The Past Is before Us: Feminism in Action since the 1960s* (London: Pandora, 1989).
25. Debbie Cameron, "Telling It Like It Wasn't: How Radical Feminism Became History," *Trouble & Strife* 27 (Winter 1993): 11–15.
26. Lynne Harne, "From 1971: Reinventing the Wheel," in *'68, '78, '88: From Women's Liberation to Feminism*, ed. Amanda Sebestyen (Bridport, UK: Prism, 1988), 65.
27. Lynne Harne and Elaine Miller, *All the Rage: Reasserting Radical Lesbian Feminism* (London: Teachers College Press, 1996).
28. Martin Pugh, *Women and the Women's Movement in Britain, 1914–1999* (New York: St. Martin's Press, 2000).
29. Barbara Caine, *English Feminism 1780–1980* (Oxford: Oxford University Press, 1997), 260–62.
30. Sunit Singh, "Darkness & Emancipation: Talking to Juliet Mitchell," *Platypus Review* 38 (2011): unpaginated, http://platypus1917.org/2011/08/05/emancipation-in-the-heart-of-darkness-an-interview-with-juliet-mitchell/.
31. Lesley Abdela, *Women with X Appeal: Women Politicians in Britain Today* (London: Optima, 1989); Jill Tweedie, *Letters from a Fainthearted Feminist* (London: Robson Books, 1982); Shirley Conran, *Superwoman: Everywoman's Book of Household Management* (Harmondsworth, UK: Penguin, 1977).
32. Caine, *English Feminism*, 270–71.
33. Joni Lovenduski and Vicky Randall, *Contemporary Feminist Politics: Women and Power in Britain* (Oxford: Oxford University Press, 1993), 3.
34. Joyce Gelb, "Feminism and Political Action," in *Challenging the Political Order: New Social and Political Movements in Western Democracies*, ed. Russell J. Dalton and Manfred Kuechler (Cambridge: Polity Press, 1990), 137–55; Fiona Mackay, "The State of Women's Movement/s in Britain: Ambiguity, Complexity and Challenges from the Periphery," in *Women's Movements: Flourishing or in Abeyance*, ed. Sandra Grey and Marian Sawer (Oxford: Routledge, 2008), 17–32; Kate Nash, "A Movement Moves . . . Is There a Women's Movement in England Today?," *European Journal of Women's Studies* 9, no. 3 (2002): 311–28.
35. Kathy Davis and Mary Evans, *Transatlantic Conversations: Feminism as Travelling Theory* (Burlington, VT: Ashgate, 2011).
36. In 2016, 6.2 million UK employees were trade union members, 23.5 percent of the total workforce. The proportion of female employees who were in a trade union was around 25.9 percent, compared with 21.1 percent for male employees. These figures show the fall in union membership in the United Kingdom from

a peak of 13 million in 1979, 55 percent of the total workforce then. See "Trade Union Statistics," accessed October 15, 2017, https://www.gov.uk/government/collections/trade-union-statistics.
37. House of Commons Debate, vol. 757, January 19, 1968, columns 879–82, accessed October 28, 2017, http://hansard.millbanksystems.com/commons/1968/jan/29/hull-trawler-st-romanus.
38. Brian W. Lavery, "Bilocca, Lillian (1929–1988)," in *Oxford Dictionary of National Biography*, ed. H. C. G. Matthew, Brian Harrison, and Lawrence Goldman (Oxford: Oxford University Press, 2013).
39. "What Was the Headscarf Campaign? Interview with Mary Denness," in *Local Heroes: Hull's Trawlermen*, 2008. Transcript and edited clip at www.mylearning.org/local-heroes-hulls-trawlermen/p-/video/1794/ (accessed October 28, 2017). See also Rowbotham, *Promise of a Dream*, 234.
40. Nigel Cole, *Made in Dagenham* (London: Paramount, 2010); Rupert Goold, *Made in Dagenham, the Musical* (London: Adelphi, 2014).
41. Sheila Cohen, "Equal Pay—or What? Economics, Politics and the 1968 Ford Sewing Machinists' Strike," *Labor History* 53, no. 1 (2012): 51–68. Before its 1967 regrading exercise, Ford's four grades were "Male Skilled," "Male Semi-Skilled," "Male Unskilled," and "Female." See Sue Hastings, "The Story of the Ford Sewing Machinists," in Recording Women's Voices: A TUC Oral History Project on Equal Pay (London: Trades Union Congress, 2006), 1–4.
42. Cited in Jonathan Moss, "'We Didn't Realise How Brave We Were at the Time': The 1968 Ford Sewing Machinists' Strike in Public and Personal Memory," *Oral History* 43, no. 1 (2015): 42.
43. George Stevenson, "The Women's Movement and 'Class Struggle': Gender, Class Formation and Political Identity in Women's Strikes, 1968–78," *Women's History Review* 25, no. 5 (2016): 741–55.
44. Lovenduski and Randall, *Contemporary Feminist Politics*, 181.
45. Rose Boland, interviewed by Sabby Sagall for *Socialist Worker* 1968, reprinted in "Ford Machinists' Strike, 1968: An Inspiring Demand for Women's Rights," accessed November 5, 2017, www.socialistworker.co.uk/art.php?id=15057. See also Moss, "'We Didn't Realise How Brave We Were at the Time.'"
46. "What Was the Headscarf Campaign?"
47. Brian W. Lavery, *The Headscarf Revolutionaries: Lillian Bilocca and the Hull Triple-Trawler Disaster* (Hull, UK: Barbican Press, 2015).
48. Rowbotham, "Appreciating Our Beginnings," 80–81. For how the Hull WLM group evolved, see Jane L. Thompson, *Women, Class and Education* (London: Routledge, 2000), chap. 6.
49. Rowbotham, *Promise of a Dream*, 234.
50. Audrey Wise, "Interview," in *Once a Feminist: Stories of a Generation*, ed. Michelene Wandor (London: Virago, 1990), 201–2.

51. Maureen Jackson interviewed for Recording Women's Voices, transcript pp. 3–4, track 1.
52. Lucy Delap, *Knowing Their Place: Domestic Service in Twentieth-Century Britain* (Oxford: Oxford University Press, 2011), 131.
53. Joanna Bourke, *Working-Class Cultures in Britain, 1890–1960: Gender, Class and Ethnicity* (London: Routledge, 1994), 51–79.
54. Gail Lewis, "Black Women's Employment and the British Economy," in *Inside Babylon: The Caribbean Diaspora in Britain*, ed. Winston James and Clive Harris (London: Verso, 1993).
55. Eileen Evason, *On the Edge: A Study of Poverty and Long-Term Unemployment in Northern Ireland* (London: Child Poverty Action Group, 1985).
56. "What Was the Headscarf Campaign?"
57. Stevenson, "The Women's Movement and 'Class Struggle'"; George Stevenson, "The Forgotten Strike: Equality, Gender, and Class in the Trico Equal Pay Strike," *Labour History Review* 81, no. 2 (2016): 141–68.
58. Betty Cook, *S&A*, C1420/59, transcript pp. 137–38, track 5.
59. Alberto Melucci, John Keane, and Paul Mier, *Nomads of the Present: Social Movements and Individual Needs in Contemporary Society* (London: Hutchinson Radius, 1989); Alain Touraine, *The Voice and the Eye: An Analysis of Social Movements* (Cambridge: Cambridge University Press, 1981).
60. Sheila Rowbotham, "Jolting Memory: Nightcleaners Recalled," in *Plan Rosebud: On Images, Sites and Politics of Memory*, ed. Maria Ruido (Santiago de Compostela, Spain: CGAC, 2009), 2; Dominic Sandbrook, *Seasons in the Sun: The Battle for Britain, 1974–1979* (London: Allen Lane, 2012), 12.
61. Jeffreys, *Anticlimax*.
62. Beverley Skeggs, *Formations of Class and Gender: Becoming Respectable* (London: SAGE, 1997); Lisa B. Thompson, *Beyond the Black Lady: Sexuality and the New African American Middle Class* (Champaign: University of Illinois Press, 2009).
63. Natalie Thomlinson, *Race, Ethnicity and the Women's Movement in England, 1968–1993* (Houndsmills, UK: Palgrave, 2016), 60–62.
64. Diana Watt and Adele Jones, *Catching Hell and Doing Well: Black Women in the UK—The Abasindi Cooperative* (London: Trentham, 2015), 130–35.
65. Sheila Capstick and Rachel Van Riel, *A Woman's Right to Cues* (Castleford, UK: Yorkshire Art Circus, 1988), http://www.yorkshireeveningpost.co.uk/news/club-women-win-fight-for-equal-rights-at-last-1-2091901.
66. Mukami McCrum, *S&A*, C1420/39, transcript p. 82, track 4. Margaret Howell, interviewed by Margot Farnham, *The Women's Liberation Movement Interviews*, 1992–2003, C546, cassette number 3.
67. Erin Pizzey, *This Way to the Revolution: A Memoir* (London: Peter Owen, 2011), 32.

68. Eve Setch, "The Face of Metropolitan Feminism: The London Women's Liberation Workshop, 1969-79," *Twentieth Century British History* 13, no. 2 (2002): 171-90. Setch describes the London Women's Liberation Workshop's ongoing difficulties securing a permanent building, and implies that in 1969 it operated mainly from people's homes until securing a temporary rental in Lower Marsh, South London, in 1970.
69. Rosalind Delmar, *S&A*, C1420/03, transcript p. 103, track 4.
70. Sasha Roseneil, *Disarming Patriarchy: Feminism and Political Action at Greenham* (Buckingham, UK: Open University Press, 1995), 72; Thomlinson, *Race, Ethnicity and the Women's Movement*, 35.
71. Beatrix Campbell, *S&A*, C1420/01, transcript pp. 70-72, track 3.
72. Eileen Evason, *S&A*, C1420/32, transcript p. 37, track 1.
73. David Bouchier, *The Feminist Challenge: The Movement for Women's Liberation in Britain and the USA* (London: Macmillan, 1983), 56-57.
74. Rowbotham, "Beginnings of Women's Liberation in Britain," 97.
75. Caine, *English Feminism*, 263.
76. Barbara Taylor, "History Workshop Journal," in *Making History* (2008): unpaginated, http://www.history.ac.uk/makinghistory/resources/articles/HWJ.html.
77. Rowbotham, *Promise of a Dream*, 251.
78. Michelene Wandor, ed., *The Body Politic: Women's Liberation in Britain* (London: Stage 1, 1972; reprint, 1978), 2.
79. Crockford interviewed in Lizzie Thynne, "In the Beginning We Demanded," in Sisterhood and After: The Women's Liberation Oral History Project (University of Sussex, 2013).
80. Wandor, *Once a Feminist*, 2, 4-5.
81. Ibid.
82. Thomlinson, *Race, Ethnicity and the Women's Movement*, 34-36.
83. King Alfred's in London. Jolly, Margaretta, Polly Russell, and Rachel Cohen. "Sisterhood and After: Individualism, Ethics and an Oral History of the Women's Liberation Movement." *Social Movement Studies* 11, no. 2 (2012): 211-26, 223. Haverstock Hill School in Camden is another that emerges as a connector in the interviews, though more ambiguously. A comprehensive (public high) school, its catchment area included middle-class Hampstead intelligentsia, and former pupils include David and Ed Milliband. Of our interviewees, Cynthia Cockburn and Anna Davin both chose to send their children there on political principle.
84. Rowbotham, *Promise of a Dream*, 177; Sally Alexander, "Interview," *Once a Feminist*, 83; Jo Robinson, *S&A*, C1420/43, transcript p. 115, track 07.
85. Rowbotham, *Promise of a Dream*, 236.
86. Audrey Battersby, "Interview," in Wandor, *Once a Feminist*, 113.
87. Gail Lewis, "Feminist Subjects," keynote lecture at *Ruskin wlm@40* (Ruskin College, University of Oxford, 2010).
88. Ibid.

89. Julia Sudbury, *Other Kinds of Dreams: Black Women's Organisations and the Politics of Transformation* (London: Routledge, 1998). See also Christine Bolt, *Sisterhood Questioned?: Race, Class and Internationalism in the American and British Women's Movements, c. 1880s–1970s* (London: Routledge, 2004).
90. Thomlinson, *Race, Ethnicity and the Women's Movement*, 66.
91. Farrukh Dhondy, cited in Robin Bunce and Paul Field, *Darcus Howe: A Political Biography* (London: Bloomsbury, 2013), 139.
92. Ibid., 122–27, 139.
93. Bean asserts Pat Smith from Essex University was the only other black woman at Ruskin, though she laughingly notes "there were a few brothers but they were running the crèche [nursery]"—probably referring to Stuart Hall. Gerlin Bean, interviewed for Oral Histories of the Black Women's Movement: The Heart of the Race, 2008–2010, Black Cultural Archives, London, catalogue reference ORAL/1/BWM 32.
94. Ibid. See also Selma James, "Interview," in Wandor, *Once a Feminist*, 183–99.
95. Black Women's Action Committee, Black Unity and Freedom Party, "The Black Woman," in *The Body Politic: Women's Liberation in Britain*, ed. Michelene Wandor, 84–89 (London: Stage 1, 1978; originally published 1972), 88.
96. Thomlinson, *Race, Ethnicity and the Women's Movement*, 67–68. Women in this party also included Afruika Bantu (formerly Annette Blair), Sonia Chang, and Leila Hassan.
97. Black Women's Liberation Group, "Statement on Birth Control," 89.
98. Ibid.
99. Stella Dadzie, *S&A*, C1420/20, transcript p. 62, track 5; Anna Colin et al., *Do You Remember Olive Morris?* (London: Gasworks and Remembering Olive Morris Collective, 2010), 120.
100. Colin, *Do You Remember Olive Morris?*, 120.
101. Agnes Quashie, "Talking Personal, Talking Political: Agnes Quashie Interviews Gail Lewis, Melba Wilson and Olive Gallimore About the Brixton Black Women's Group," *Trouble & Strife* 19 (1990): 44–52. The Manchester Black Women's Co-operative was cofounded by radical black activist Kath Locke. See Watt and Jones, *Catching Hell and Doing Well*.
102. Stella Dadzie, *S&A*, C1420/20, transcript p. 68, track 05.
103. Beckett, *When the Lights Went Out*, 358–403.
104. Jan Rath, *Immigrant Businesses: The Economic, Political and Social Environment* (London: Macmillan in association with Centre for Research in Ethnic Relations, University of Warwick, 2000), 13.
105. Linda McDowell, Sundari Anitha, and Ruth Pearson, "Striking Similarities: Representing South Asian Women's Industrial Action in Britain," *Gender, Place & Culture* 19, no. 2 (2011): 133–52.
106. Amrit Wilson, *S&A*, C1420/19, transcript pp. 97–98, track 04.

107. Peter Strafford, "The Sad, Lonely Lives of Britain's Asian Women," *Times* (August 11, 1978), 18.
108. Now the Karibu Centre.
109. Judith Lockhart, interviewed for Oral Histories of the Black Women's Movement: The Heart of the Race, 2008–2010, Black Cultural Archives, London, catalogue reference ORAL/1/BWM 05.
110. Bryan, Dadzie, and Scafe, *The Heart of the Race*. See "OWAAD Draft Constitution," DADZIE /1/1/4-6, Black Cultural Archives.
111. Stella Dadzie, *S&A*, C1420/20, transcript, pp. 69–70, track 05.
112. Sudbury, *Other Kinds of Dreams*, 247.
113. Thomlinson, *Race, Ethnicity and the Women's Movement*, 70.
114. Jan McKenley, *S&A*, C1420/15, transcript p. 90, track 3.
115. Alessandro Portelli, "What Makes Oral History Different," in *The Oral History Reader*, ed. Robert Perks and Alistair Thomson (London: Routledge, 2006), 32–42.
116. Sheila Rowbotham, *S&A*, C1420/10, transcript p. 121, track 4.
117. Penny Summerfield, "Culture and Composure: Creating Narratives of the Gendered Self in Oral History Interviews," *Cultural and Social History* 1, no. 1 (2004): 65.
118. Thomlinson, *Race, Ethnicity and the Women's Movement*, 176–79.
119. Clare Hemmings, *Why Stories Matter: The Political Grammar of Feminist Theory* (Durham, NC: Duke University Press, 2011), 3.
120. Ibid., 3–4. For example, see Sue Morgan, *The Feminist History Reader* (London: Routledge, 2006), 2.
121. Hemmings, *Why Stories Matter*, 5–6.
122. Ibid., 53.
123. Beatrix Campbell, *S&A*, C1420/01, transcript pp. 57–58, track 3.

CHAPTER 2

1. Sheila Rowbotham, *Hidden from History: Rediscovering Women in History from the 17th Century to the Present* (New York: Pantheon, 1975); Joanna Bornat and Hanna Diamond, "Women's History and Oral History: Developments and Debates," *Women's History Review* 16, no. 1 (2007): 19–39.
2. Mary Chamberlain, *Fenwomen: A Portrait of Women in an English Village* (London: Quartet Books for Virago, 1975), 1.
3. Nan Alamilla Boyd and Horacio N. Roque Ramírez, eds. *Bodies of Evidence: The Practice of Queer Oral History* (New York: Oxford University Press, 2012), 2–5.
4. "Women's History Issue" (London: Oral History Society, 1977); "Women's History" (London: Oral History Society, 1982); "Women's Lives" (London: Oral History Society, 1993); "Women's Narratives of Resistance" (London: Oral History Society, 1993).

5. Joanna Bornat et al., "Introduction," *Oral History* 5, no. 2 (1977): 1–5.
6. Xiaolan Bao, "Feminism and Listening to the Voice of Women: Meaning, Methods and Thoughts," *Journal of Shanxi Teachers University* 1 (2000): unpaginated.
7. Joy Webster Barbre and the Personal Narratives Group, "Interpreting Women's Lives: Feminist Theory and Personal Narratives" (Bloomington: Indiana University Press, 1989).
8. Elizabeth Roberts, *A Woman's Place: An Oral History of Working-Class Women, 1890–1940* (Oxford: Blackwell, 1984); Hall Carpenter Archives and Lesbian Oral History Group, eds., *Inventing Ourselves: Lesbian Life Stories* (London: Routledge, 1989).
9. Carolyn Steedman, *Landscape for a Good Woman* (London: Virago, 1986); Penny Summerfield, *Reconstructing Women's Wartime Lives: Discourse and Subjectivity in Oral Histories of the Second World War* (Manchester: Manchester University Press, 1998).
10. Amrit Wilson, *Finding a Voice: Asian Women in Britain* (London: Virago, 1978); Judith Okely, *The Traveller-Gypsies* (Cambridge: Cambridge University Press, 1983).
11. *Daughters of Radical Suffragists Oral History Collection*, 1976–82, The Women's Library @ LSE, 8DRS. See also Jill Liddington, "Rediscovering Suffrage History," *History Workshop Journal* 4 (1977): 192–202; Jill Liddington and Jill Norris, *One Hand Tied Behind Us: The Rise of the Women's Suffrage Movement* (London: Rivers Oram, 2000); Amanda Sebestyen, "Gwen Coleman, Suffragist," *Trouble & Strife* 7 (1985): 45–46.
12. Then the Fawcett Library. Oral Evidence on the Suffragette and Suffragist Movements: The Brian Harrison interviews, 1974–1981, The Women's Library @ LSE, 8SUF.
13. Jean McCrindle and Sheila Rowbotham, eds., *Dutiful Daughters: Women Talk about Their Lives* (London: Allen Lane, 1977).
14. Beverley Bryan, Stella Dadzie, and Suzanne Scafe, *The Heart of the Race: Black Women's Lives in Britain* (London: Virago, 1985).
15. Michelene Wandor, ed. *Once a Feminist: Stories of a Generation* (London: Virago, 1990).
16. Transcripts available in the Papers of Betty Heathfield, The Women's Library @ LSE, 7BEH.
17. *National Life Stories: Fawcett Collection*, 990. British Library Sound & Moving Image, C468. See also Rebecca Abrams, *Woman in a Man's World: Pioneering Women of the Twentieth Century* (London: Methuen, 1993).
18. See also Miriam Bearse, "An Oral History Project at Work: A Reflection on Current Research on the WLM in Britain," paper presented at Feminisms: Past, Present and Future Conference (University of Cardiff: Women's Studies Network UK, 1996).
19. Margaretta Jolly, *In Love and Struggle: Letters in Contemporary Feminism* (New York: Columbia University Press, 2008); "Speaking Personally, Academically," *Feminist Theory* 6, no. 2 (2005): 213–20. See also Sara Maitland, ed., *Very Heaven:*

Looking Back at the 1960s (London: Virago, 1988); Amanda Sebestyen, *'68, '78, '88: From Women's Liberation to Feminism* (Bridport, UK: Prism, 1988); Joan Scanlon, ed., *Surviving the Blues: Growing Up in the Thatcher Decade* (London: Virago, 1990).

20. Malin Lidström Brock, *Writing Feminist Lives: The Biographical Battles over Betty Friedan, Germaine Greer, Gloria Steinem, and Simone De Beauvoir* (New York: Palgrave Macmillan, 2016).

21. Joan Sangster, "Telling Our Stories: Feminist Debates and the Use of Oral History," in *The Oral History Reader*, ed. Robert Perks and Alistair Thomson (London: Routledge, 1998), 87–100.

22. Ann Oakley, "Interviewing Women: A Contradiction in Terms," in *Turning Points in Qualitative Research: Tying Knots in a Handkerchief*, ed. Yvonna S. Lincoln and Norman K. Denzin (Walnut Creek, CA: AltaMira, 2003), 243–64.

23. Kathryn Anderson, Susan Armitage, Dana Jack, and Judith Wittner, "Beginning Where We Are: Feminist Methodology in Oral History," *Oral History Review* 15, no. 1 (1987): 103–27.

24. Sherna Berger Gluck and Daphne Patai, *Women's Words: The Feminist Practice of Oral History* (New York: Routledge, 1991), 2. See also Katrina Srigley, Stacey Zembrzycki, and Franca Iacovetta, eds., *Beyond Women's Words: Feminisms and the Practices of Oral History in the Twenty-First Century* (London: Routledge, 2018).

25. Liz Stanley, *The Auto/Biographical I: The Theory and Practice of Feminist Auto/Biography* (Manchester: Manchester University Press, 1992), 3–4.

26. Alistair Thomson, "Four Paradigm Transformations in Oral History," *Oral History Review* 34, no. 1 (2007): 49–70.

27. Sherna Berger Gluck, "Has Feminist Oral History Lost Its Radical/Subversive Edge?," *Oral History* 39, no. 2 (2011): 63.

28. The HLF distributes the heritage share of National Lottery funding to support a variety of projects across the United Kingdom. See https://www.hlf.org.uk/.

29. See "The Making of Oral History," *Making History*, accessed August 30, 2017, http://www.history.ac.uk/makinghistory/resources/articles/oral_history.html#resources; *Records of Bolton Women's Liberation (History) Group, 1970–2010*, The Women's Library @ LSE, 5BWG; Sam Carroll, ed. *Brighton Trans*formed* (Brighton: QueenSpark Books, 2014); "Women's Work and Working Women: A Longitudinal Study of Women Working in the British Film and Television Industries, 1933–1989" (University of Newcastle, 2013–2017); *Pathways of Women's Empowerment* (Institute of Development Studies, 2006–2015).

30. Sally Alexander, *S&A*, 1420/45, transcript pp. 78–80, track 02.

31. "Sisterhood & After," The British Library, accessed August 30, 2017, bl.uk/sisterhood.

32. See also Margaretta Jolly, Polly Russell, and Rachel Cohen, "Sisterhood and After: Individualism, Ethics and an Oral History of the Women's Liberation Movement," *Social Movement Studies* 1, no. 2 (2012): 211–26.

33. Jill Radford, "History of Women's Liberation Movements in Britain: A Reflective Personal History," in *Stirring It: Challenges for Feminism*, ed. Gabriele Griffin (London: Taylor & Francis, 1994), 40; Barbara Caine, *English Feminism, 1780–1980* (Oxford: Oxford University Press, 1997), 263.
34. These workshops were held in Cardiff, Belfast, Edinburgh, Leeds, and London. About 240 witnesses attended. Archived as Records of the Women's Liberation Movement Research Network 2008–2009, The Women's Library @ LSE, 11TWL/K/01. It should be noted that this project ran when The Women's Library was held at London Metropolitan University.
35. Mia Morris, *S&A*, C1420/08, transcript pp. 28–29, track 02.
36. Beatrix Campbell, *S&A*, C1420/01.
37. Charles Tilly, *From Mobilization to Revolution* (Reading, MA: Addison-Wesley, 1978).
38. Verta A. Taylor and Nella Van Dyke, "'Get Up, Stand Up': Tactical Repertoires of Social Movements," in *The Blackwell Companion to Social Movements*, ed. David A. Snow, Sarah Anne Soule, and Hanspeter Kriesi (Oxford: Blackwell, 2004), 262–93; Suzanne Staggenborg, "Introduction to Special Issue on Qualitative Methods in the Study of Social Movements," *Qualitative Sociology* 21, no. 4 (1998): 353–55.
39. Myra Marx Ferree and Carol McClurg Mueller, "Feminism and the Women's Movement: A Global Perspective," in *The Blackwell Companion to Social Movements*, ed. David A. Snow, Sarah Anne Soule, and Hanspeter Kriesi (Oxford: Blackwell, 2004), 594.
40. Lesley Abdela, *S&A*, C1420/13, transcript p. 203, track 07.
41. Fifteen of them had already publicly archived their papers and fourteen had already archived an oral history elsewhere, while a further six had done an unarchived oral history. We prioritized those who were frail or in ill health for obvious reasons.
42. Esther Breitenbach and Fiona Mackay, *Women and Contemporary Scottish Politics: An Anthology* (Edinburgh: Polygon at Edinburgh, 2001).
43. Juliet Mitchell, cited in Jolly, Margaretta, Polly Russell, and Rachel Cohen, "Sisterhood and After: Individualism, Ethics and an Oral History of the Women's Liberation Movement," *Social Movement Studies* 11, no. 2 (2012): 211–26, 211.
44. Juliet Mitchell, "Women: The Longest Revolution," *New Left Review* 1, no. 40 (1966): 11–37.
45. Jeff Goodwin and James M. Jasper, *The Social Movements Reader: Cases and Concepts*, 3rd ed. (Chichester, UK: Wiley-Blackwell, 2015), 102.
46. Others include Women's Aid; Greenham Common Women's Peace Camp; Women and Manual Trades; Fawcett Society; Women Against Pit Closures; The 300 Group; Movement for the Ordination of Women; Organisation of Women of Asian and African Descent; Sisters Against Disablement; Southall Black Sisters; Gingerbread; Northern Ireland Women's Rights Movement; Women's Research and Resources Centre; Working Women's Charter; National Abortion Campaign; Women's Health Centre; Gay Liberation Front.

47. Zoe Fairbairns and John Petherbridge, *S&A*, C1420/24, transcript pp. 69–77, track 03. See chap. 6.
48. "Unbecoming Men: Interviews on Masculinities and the Women's Movement, 1970–1991," British Library Sound & Moving Image, C1667.
49. Recording Women's Voices: A TUC Oral History Project on Equal Pay, Union History, in "Voices from the Workplace," Winning Equal Pay, accessed October 16, 2017, http://www.unionhistory.info/equalpay/voices.php.
50. Joanna Bornat, "Biographical Methods," in *The Sage Handbook of Social Research Methods*, ed. Pertti Alasuutari, Leonard Bickman, and Julia Brannen (Los Angeles: SAGE, 2008), 346.
51. Sherry Gorelick, "Contradictions of Feminist Methodology," in *Feminism and Social Change: Bridging Theory and Practice*, ed. Heidi Gottfried (Urbana: University of Illinois Press, 1996).
52. Michael H. Frisch, *A Shared Authority: Essays on the Craft and Meaning of Oral and Public History* (Albany: State University of New York Press, 1990).
53. Paul Thompson identifies this as the "third and final choice" that an oral historian has to make in *The Voice of the Past: Oral History*, 3rd ed. (Oxford: Oxford University Press, 2000), 269.
54. Olive Banks, *Becoming a Feminist: The Social Origins of "First Wave" Feminism* (Brighton: Wheatsheaf, 1986); Brian Howard Harrison, *Prudent Revolutionaries: Portraits of British Feminists between the Wars* (Oxford: Clarendon Press, 1987).
55. Sarah F. Green, *Urban Amazons: Lesbian Feminism and Beyond in the Gender, Sexuality, and Identity Battles of London* (New York: St. Martin's Press, 1997); Joanne Hollows, "*Spare Rib*, Second-Wave Feminism and the Politics of Consumption," *Feminist Media Studies* 13, no. 2 (2012): 268–87.
56. Marco G. Giugni, "Personal and Biographical Consequences," in *The Blackwell Companion to Social Movements*, ed. David A. Snow, Sarah Anne Soule, and Hanspeter Kriesi (Oxford: Blackwell, 2004), 489–507.
57. Gail Lewis, *S&A*, C1420/14, transcript p. 177, track 07.
58. Marie-Francoise Chanfrault-Duchet, "Narrative Structures, Social Models, and Symbolic Representation in the Life Story," in *Women's Words: The Feminist Practice of Oral History*, ed. Sherna Berger Gluck and Daphne Patai (New York: Routledge, 1991), 77–92.
59. Susan Nicholls, Su Hutton, Caroline Mumford, and Kerry Cable were the professional transcribers for S&A.
60. Lucy Delap, "Feminism, Masculinities and Emotional Politics in the Late Twentieth Century," *Cultural and Social History* 15, no. 4 (2018): 1–23; Luisa Passerini, *Autobiography of a Generation: Italy, 1968* (Middletown, CT: Wesleyan University Press, 2004).
61. Julie Stephens, "Our Remembered Selves: Oral History and Feminist Memory," *Oral History* 38, no. 1 (2010): 81–90.

62. Jean Williams, "The Lady Footballers: Struggling to Play in Victorian Britain," *International Journal of the History of Sport* 29, no. 13 (2012): 1928–30; Jayne Caudwell, "Gender, Feminism and Football Studies," *Soccer & Society* 12, no. 3 (2011): 330–44.
63. Jean Williams, personal email and phone call, February 2012; Jayne Caudwell, personal email, February 2012.
64. Andrew Ward and John Williams, *Football Nation: Sixty Years of the Beautiful Game* (London: Bloomsbury, 2009), 122.
65. Sue Lopez, *S&A,* C1420/57, transcript p. 31, track 01.
66. Sue Lopez, *Women on the Ball: A Guide to Women's Football* (London: Scarlet Press, 1997), 2, 6.
67. Sue Lopez, *S&A,* C1420/57, transcript pp. 50 and 38, track 01.
68. Ibid, p. 49, track 01.
69. Scotland was the only country to vote against the motion for member countries to take control of women's football in UEFA's 1971 motion. See Lopez, *Women on the Ball*, 59.
70. Ward and Williams, *Football Nation*, 127.
71. Lopez, *Women on the Ball*, 59.
72. Ibid., 57, 92.
73. Sue Lopez, *S&A,* C1420/57, transcript p. 71, track 02.
74. Ibid., transcript p. 92, track 02.
75. Ibid., transcript p. 85, track 02.
76. Ibid., transcript p. 105, track 02.
77. Ibid., transcript p. 56, track 01.
78. Jayne Caudwell, "Women's Football in the United Kingdom: Theorizing Gender and Unpacking the Butch Lesbian Image," *Journal of Sport & Social Issues* 23, no. 4 (1999): 390–402.
79. Sue Lopez, *S&A,* C1420/57, transcript p. 118, track 02.
80. Lopez, *Women on the Ball*, 56.
81. Under the Equality Act 2010 if one sex or age is generally at a disadvantage compared to the other, it is lawful to hold separate sporting competitions: "Equality Act 2010, Part 14, General Exceptions, Section 195, Sport," Legislation.gov, accessed September 9, 2017, http://www.legislation.gov.uk/ukpga/2010/15/section/195.
82. Lopez, *Women on the Ball*, 26. See also Martin Parkin, "Theresa Finds a Gap in the FA's Defence," *Guardian*, June 9, 1979, 28.
83. Sue Lopez, *S&A,* C1420/57, transcript pp. 124–25, track 02.
84. For Peter Harte, I changed the question and asked how his life compared to his father's.
85. Anna Kessell, "England Women's Long, Historic Journey to Meet Germany at Wembley," *The Observer*, November 22, 2014.

CHAPTER 3

1. Marsha Rowe, ed., *Spare Rib Reader* (Harmondsworth, UK: Penguin, 1982), 233.
2. Avtar Brah and Rahana Minhas, "Structural Racism or Cultural Difference: Schooling for Asian Girls," in *Just a Bunch of Girls: Feminist Approaches to Schooling*, ed. Gaby Weiner (Milton Keynes, UK: Open University Press, 1985), 14–25; Diana Watt and Adele Jones, *Catching Hell and Doing Well: Black Women in the UK—The Abasindi Cooperative* (London: Trentham, 2015), chap. 6.
3. Simon Biggs and Ariela Lowenstein, "Toward Generational Intelligence: Linking Cohorts, Families and Experience," in *Kinship and Cohort in an Aging Society: From Generation to Generation*, ed. Merril Silverstein and Roseann Giarrusso (Baltimore: Johns Hopkins University Press, 2013), 159–75.
4. The periodization of these generations is contested and variable. Popular American historians William Strauss and Neil Howe define the baby boomer generation as those born between 1943 and 1960; these dates correspond with studies in the UK context. There were sharp peaks in the number of live births in the United Kingdom at the end of both world wars. Live births peaked at near postwar levels again in 1964 (875,972 births), but since then lower numbers have been seen, with the lowest in 1977; see Office for National Statistics, 2015: http://visual.ons.gov.uk/birthsanddeaths/.
5. Sheila Blackburn, "How Useful Are Feminist Theories of the Welfare State?," *Women's History Review* 4, no. 3 (1995): 369–94; Liz Heron, ed., *Truth, Dare or Promise: Girls Growing Up in the Fifties* (London: Virago, 1985), 6.
6. Office for National Statistics (UK), Number of live births in the United Kingdom (UK) from 1931 to 1960, accessed November 14, 2018, https://www-statista-com.ezproxy.sussex.ac.uk/statistics/281965/live-births-in-the-united-kingdom-uk-1931-1960/; Heron, *Truth, Dare or Promise*, 4.
7. Siobhan Molloy, *S&A*, 1420/37, transcript p. 2, track 1.
8. Meg Stacey, "Older Women and Feminism: A Note About My Experience of the WLM," *Feminist Review* 31, no. 1 (1989): 140–42.
9. These are known in the generational literature as "War children," born between 1925 and 1936, and "Depression children," born between 1937 and 1942, or sometimes "the Silent Generation."
10. Jalna Hanmer, *S&A*, 1420/04, transcript pp. 10 and 26, track 01.
11. William Strauss and Neil Howe, *Generations: The History of America's Future, 1584 to 2069* (New York: Morrow, 1991).
12. Particular historical conditions defined these, including the Commonwealth Immigrants Acts in 1962, 1968, and 1971, which redefined black British passport holders as noncitizens and black women as dependents. Julia Sudbury, *Other Kinds of Dreams: Black Women's Organisations and the Politics of Transformation* (London: Routledge, 1998), 33.
13. Michelene Wandor, *S&A*, 1420/09, track 1; Ursula Owen, *S&A*, 1420/36, track 1.

14. Amrit Wilson, *S&A,* 1420/19, track 1; Grace Lau, *S&A,* 1420/60, track 1.
15. Anna Davin, "What Is a Child?," in *Childhood in Question: Children, Parents and the State,* ed. Anthony Fletcher and Stephen Hussey (Manchester: Manchester University Press, 1999), 15–36.
16. Siobhan Molloy, *S&A,* 1420/37, transcript p. 33, track 2.
17. Sandie Wyles, *S&A,* 1420/22, transcript p. 20, track 01.
18. "Education: Historical Statistics," House of Commons Library, published November 28, 2012, accessed October 16, 2017, http://researchbriefings.parliament.uk/ResearchBriefing/Summary/SN04252. It was not until 2000 that more women graduated than men: 133,316 to 109,930.
19. Dominic Sandbrook, *State of Emergency: The Way We Were: Britain, 1970–1974* (London: Allen Lane, 2010), 436.
20. Ibid., 430.
21. Anna Davin, *S&A,* 1420/02, transcript p. 98, track 3.
22. Rosalind Delmar, *S&A,* 1420/03, transcript pp. 17–18, track 1.
23. Heron, *Truth, Dare or Promise,* 3.
24. Jan McKenley, *S&A,* C1420/15, transcript p. 21, track 01.
25. Beatrix Campbell, *S&A,* C1420/01, transcript p. 32, track 02.
26. Ibid., p. 31, track 02.
27. Karen McMinn, *S&A,* C1420/26, transcript p. 79, track 02.
28. Lesley Abdela, *S&A,* C1420/13, transcript p. 52, track 03.
29. Rebecca Johnson, *S&A,* C1420/34, transcript pp. 73–75, track 02.
30. Gail Chester, *S&A,* C1420/27, transcript p. 54, track 01.
31. Kate Fisher, "'Lay Back, Enjoy It and Shout Happy England': Sexual Pleasure and Marital Duty in Britain, 1918–60," in *Bodies, Sex and Desire from the Renaissance to the Present,* ed. Kate Fisher and Sarah Toulalan (Houndsmills, UK: Palgrave Macmillan, 2011), 181.
32. Sandbrook, *State of Emergency,* 425–29.
33. Ibid., 425.
34. Jo Robinson, *S&A,* C1420/43, transcript p. 89, track 06; Anna Davin, *S&A,* C1420/02, transcript pp. 125–26, track 04; Gail Lewis, *S&A,* C1420/14, transcript p. 47, track 02.
35. Beatrix Campbell, *S&A,* C1420/01, transcript p. 53, track 03.
36. Jan McKenley, *S&A,* C1420/15 transcript p. 59, track 02.
37. Gail Chester, *S&A,* C1420/27, transcript p. 50, track 01.
38. Jane Traies, *Lives of Older Lesbians: Sexuality, Identity & the Life Course* (London: Palgrave Macmillan, 2016), 61.
39. Mary McIntosh, *S&A,* C1420/11, transcript pp. 25–30, track 01.
40. Kirsten Hearn, *S&A,* C1420/44, transcript pp. 33–50, track 01–02.
41. Rosalind Delmar, *S&A,* C1420/03, transcript pp. 64–65, track 03.
42. Sheila Rowbotham, *Promise of a Dream: Remembering the Sixties* (London: Verso, 2001), 24–25; Jenni Murray, *S&A,* C1420/48, transcript pp. 26–27, track 02.

43. Gail Lewis, *S&A,* C1420/14, transcript p. 74, track 03.
44. Jalna Hanmer, *S&A,* C1420/04, transcript p. 24, track 1.
45. Katie Barclay et al., "Introduction: Gender and Generations: Women and Life Cycles," *Women's History Review* 20, no. 2 (2011): 175–88.
46. Stevi Jackson, "The Desire for Freud: Feminism and Psychoanalysis," in *The Trouble & Strife Reader*, ed. Deborah Cameron and Joan Scanlon (London: Bloomsbury, 2010), 123–33.
47. Jean McCrindle and Sheila Rowbotham, eds., *Dutiful Daughters: Women Talk about Their Lives* (London: Allen Lane, 1977), 4.
48. Pragna Patel, *S&A,* C1420/18, transcript pp. 54–63, track 03. See also Pragna Patel, "Flying by the Nets of Racism, Patriarchy and Religion," in *Women against Fundamentalism: Stories of Dissent and Solidarity*, ed. Sukhwant Dhaliwal and Nira Yuval-Davis (London: Lawrence and Wishart, 2015), 52–66.
49. Jenni Murray, *Memoirs of a Not So Dutiful Daughter* (London: Black Swan, 2009).
50. Jenni Murray, *S&A,* C1420/48, transcript pp. 37–40, track 02.
51. Ibid., 44. See also Murray, *Memoirs of a Not So Dutiful Daughter*, 142.
52. Cynthia Cockburn, *S&A,* C1420/42, transcript p. 7, track 01.
53. Beatrix Campbell, *S&A,* C1420/01, transcript p. 42, track 03.
54. Ibid., p. 13, track 01.
55. Michèle Barrett and Mary McIntosh, *The Anti-Social Family*, 2nd ed. (London: Verso, 1991); "Ethnocentrism and Socialist-Feminist Theory," *Feminist Review*, no. 80 (2005): 64–86.
56. Mary McIntosh, *S&A,* C1420/11, transcript pp. 106, 108, track 05.
57. This was reprinted with new reflections in 2005, in Kum-Kum Bhavnani and Margaret Coulson, "Transforming Socialist-Feminism: The Challenge of Racism," *Feminist Review*, no. 80 (2005): 87–97.
58. Mukami McCrum, *S&A,* C1420/39, transcript pp. 51–52, track 02.
59. Natalie Thomlinson, *Race, Ethnicity and the Women's Movement in England, 1968–1993* (Houndsmills, UK: Palgrave, 2016), 54–57; Carmen et al., "Becoming Visible: Black Lesbian Discussions," *Feminist Review* 17 (1984): 53–72; Ann Phoenix, "Theories of Gender and Black Families," in *Black British Feminism: A Reader*, ed. Heidi Safia Mirza (London: Routledge, 1997), 50–63.
60. Sandbrook, *State of Emergency*, 436.
61. Joni Lovenduski and Vicky Randall, *Contemporary Feminist Politics: Women and Power in Britain* (Oxford: Oxford University Press, 1993), 268–69; Beatrix Campbell, *S&A,* C1420/01, transcript p. 137, track 06.
62. Mary McIntosh, "Introduction to an Issue: Family Secrets as Public Drama," *Feminist Review* 28 (1988): 12.
63. Mary McIntosh, *S&A,* C1420/11, transcript p. 120, track 05.
64. Ibid., 122.
65. Ibid., 124.

66. Sara Ahmed, *The Promise of Happiness* (Durham, NC: Duke University Press, 2010), 52.
67. Jenni Murray, *S&A,* C1420/48, transcript p. 41, track 02, and p. 116, track 5.
68. Marianne Hirsch, *The Mother/Daughter Plot: Narrative, Psychoanalysis, Feminism* (Bloomington: Indiana University Press, 1989).
69. Barbara Castle, "No Kitchen Cabinet," in *Very Heaven: Looking Back at the 1960's*, ed. Sara Maitland (London: Virago, 1988), 51.
70. Angela Davis, *Modern Motherhood: Women and Family in England, c. 1945–2000* (Manchester: Manchester University Press, 2012).
71. Elizabeth D. Hutchison, ed., *Dimensions of Human Behavior: Person and Environment*, 4th ed. (Los Angeles: Sage Publications, 2011), 548.
72. Amrit Wilson, *S&A*, C1420/19, transcript p. 9, track 1; Barbara Taylor, *S&A*, C1420/38, transcript pp. 195–97, track 8; Beatrix Campbell, *S&A,* C1420/60, transcript p. 13, track 1.
73. Jean McCrindle, "The Hungarian Uprising and a Young British Communist," *History Workshop Journal* 62, no. 1 (2006): 194–99.
74. Olive Banks, *Becoming a Feminist: The Social Origins of "First Wave" Feminism* (Brighton: Wheatsheaf, 1986), 8–9.
75. Sheila Rowbotham, *S&A,* C1420/10, transcript p. 30, track 1; Elaine Showalter, *Inventing Herself: Claiming a Feminist Intellectual Heritage* (London: Picador, 2001), 261.
76. Jenni Murray, *S&A,* C1420/48, transcript p. 40, track 02.
77. Amrit Wilson, *S&A,* C1420/19, transcript p. 27, track 2; Mukami McCrum, *S&A,* C1420/39, transcript pp. 15–16, 32, track 01.
78. Doug McAdam, "Recruitment to High-Risk Activism: The Case of Freedom Summer," *American Journal of Sociology* 92, no. 1 (1986): 64–90.
79. Rebecca E. Klatch, *A Generation Divided: The New Left, the New Right, and the 1960s* (Berkeley: University of California Press, 1999), 37.
80. Aldon D. Morris and Suzanne Staggenborg, "Leadership in Social Movements," in *The Blackwell Companion to Social Movements*, ed. David A. Snow, Sarah Anne Soule, and Hanspeter Kriesi (Oxford: Blackwell, 2004), 175.
81. Jenni Murray, *S&A,* C1420/48, transcript p. 90, track 04.
82. Davin, "What Is a Child?"
83. Sandie Wyles, *S&A,* 1420/22, transcript p. 79, track 04.
84. Susie Orbach, *S&A,* C1420/25, transcript p. 25, track 01.
85. Ibid., transcript p. 6, track 01.
86. Ibid., transcript p. 7, track 01.
87. Ibid., transcript p. 4, track 01.
88. Ibid., transcript p. 67, track 03.
89. Ibid., transcript p. 73, track 03.
90. Ibid., transcript p. 30, track 01.

91. Ibid., transcript p. 42, track 01.
92. Ibid., transcript pp. 51–52, track 02.
93. Edward Steichen, *The Family of Man: The Greatest Photographic Exhibition of All Time—503 Pictures from 68 Countries* (New York: Museum of Modern Art, 1955). Another S&A interviewee, Barbara Taylor, discusses this in *The Last Asylum: A Memoir of Madness in Our Times* (London: Hamish Hamilton, 2014), 16–19.
94. Susie Orbach, *S&A,* C1420/25, transcript p. 112, track 04.
95. Susie Orbach, *Fat Is a Feminist Issue: The Anti-Diet Guide: Conquering Compulsive Eating + Fat Is a Feminist Issue II* [one volume] (London: Arrow, 2006).
96. Susie Orbach, *S&A,* C1420/25, transcript p. 131, track 06.
97. Orbach, *Fat Is a Feminist Issue*, 86, 353–55.
98. Joan Dickinson, "Some Thoughts on Fat," in *Shadows on a Tightrope: Writings by Women on Fat Oppression*, ed. Lisa Schoenfielder and Barb Wieser (Iowa City, IA: Aunt Lute, 1983), 39–42.
99. Cynthia Cockburn, *S&A,* C1420/42, transcript p. 90, track 05.
100. Susie Orbach, *S&A,* C1420/25, transcript pp. 168–69, track 09.
101. Susie Orbach, "Mining Bodies: The New Colonialism," *HuffPost*, https://www.huffingtonpost.co.uk/susie-orbach/mining-bodies-the-new-colonialism_b_1326712.html.
102. Ibid., p. 229, track 12.
103. Sue Krzowski and Pat Land, *In Our Experience: Workshops at the Women's Therapy Centre* (London: Women's Press, 1988); Susan Gutwill, Andrea Gitter, and Lisa Rubin, "The Women's Therapy Centre Institute: The Personal Is Political," *Women & Therapy* 34, no. 1–2 (2010): 143–58.
104. Lynne Segal, *S&A,* C1420/28, transcript p. 70, track 02.
105. John Rowan, *The Horned God: Feminism and Men as Wounding and Healing* (London: Routledge & Kegan Paul, 1987), 21.
106. Susie Orbach, *S&A,* C1420/25, transcript p. 176, track 09.
107. Ibid., pp. 176–77, track 09.
108. Luise Eichenbaum and Susie Orbach, *Between Women: Love, Envy, and Competition in Women's Friendships* (New York: Viking, 1988).
109. Susie Orbach, *S&A,* C1420/25, transcript p. 210, track 12.
110. Ibid., pp. 153–54, track 9.
111. Ibid., p. 147, track 08.
112. Ibid., p. 254, track 14.
113. Jeanette Winterson, "The New Happily Ever After," *Guardian Saturday Review* 8 (April 2017): 2–3.
114. Susie Orbach, *S&A,* C1420/25, transcript p. 254, track 14.
115. Ibid., pp. 277–78, track 16.
116. Callum G. Brown, *Religion and the Demographic Revolution: Women and Secularisation in Canada, Ireland and USA since the 1960s* (Woodbridge, UK: Boydell, 2012).

117. Ronald Inglehart, *Culture Shift in Advanced Industrial Society* (Princeton, NJ: Princeton University Press, 1990), 497.
118. Richard A. Easterlin, *Birth and Fortune: The Impact of Numbers on Personal Welfare*, 2nd ed. (Chicago: University of Chicago Press, 1987); Klatch, *A Generation Divided*.
119. Doug McAdam, "The Biographical Impact of Activism," in *How Social Movements Matter*, ed. Marco Giugni, Doug McAdam, and Charles Tilly (Minneapolis: University of Minnesota Press, 1999), 135–36.
120. Jane Pilcher, *Women of Their Time: Generation, Gender Issues and Feminism* (Aldershot, UK: Ashgate, 1998).
121. Patricia Meyer Spacks, "Stages of Self: Notes on Autobiography and the Life Cycle," in *Autobiography: Concepts in Literary and Cultural Studies*, ed. Trev Lynn Broughton (London: Routledge, 2007), 199–212.

CHAPTER 4

1. William Hirst and David Manier, "Towards a Psychology of Collective Memory," *Memory* 16, no. 3 (2008): 12.
2. Andy Beckett, *When the Lights Went Out: Britain in the Seventies* (London: Faber, 2009); Colin Hay, "Chronicles of a Death Foretold: The Winter of Discontent and Construction of the Crisis of British Keynesianism," *Parliamentary Affairs* 63, no. 3 (2010): 446–70.
3. Zoë Fairbairns, Helen Graham, Ali Neilson, Emma Robertson, and Ann Kaloski, *The Feminist Seventies* (York: Raw Nerve Books, 2002), 93–104.
4. Lynne Segal, *Why Feminism?: Gender, Psychology, Politics* (Cambridge: Polity Press, 1999), 17; *Nightcleaners*, Berwick Street Film Collective, 1975.
5. George Stevenson, "The Women's Movement and 'Class Struggle': Gender, Class Formation and Political Identity in Women's Strikes, 1968–78," *Women's History Review* 25, no. 5 (2016): 741–55, 746.
6. Sheila Rowbotham, "The Nightcleaners' Campaign," in *Conditions of Illusion: Papers from the Women's Movement*, ed. Sandra Allen, Lee Sanders, and Jan Wallis (Leeds: Feminist Books, 1974); "Jolting Memory: Nightcleaners Recalled," in *Plan Rosebud: On Images, Sites and Politics of Memory*, ed. Maria Ruido (Santiago de Compostela, Spain: CGAC, 2009); Sally Alexander, S&A, C1420/45, transcript pp. 74–77, track 2. See also "The Night Cleaners: Transcripts," The Women's Library @ LSE 7SHR/D/02; and *Dutiful Daughters: Women Talk About Their Lives*, ed. Jean McCrindle and Sheila Rowbotham (London: Allen Lane, 1977), section on Jean Mormont, 139–56. Thomlinson discusses the racial politics of this campaign—more than half the cleaners were black—in Natalie Thomlinson, *Race, Ethnicity and the Women's Movement in England, 1968–1993* (Houndsmills, UK: Palgrave, 2016), 50–51.
7. May Hobbs, *Born to Struggle* (London: Quartet Books, 1973), 85.

8. Stevenson, "The Women's Movement," 747.
9. Hobbs, *Born to Struggle*, 82–84; *Nightcleaners*, Berwick Street Film Collective, 1975. The collective was founded by Marc Karlin, Humphry Treveleyan, Richard Modraunt, and James Scott, joined during filming by WLM artist Mary Kelly.
10. This demand was typically misunderstood as endorsing heartless collectivization. See Barbara Holland, "Inside a Soviet Nursery," *Spare Rib* 116 (1982): 18–20, and Sheila Rowbotham, *The Past Is before Us: Feminism in Action since the 1960s* (London: Pandora, 1989).
11. Mary McIntosh, *S&A*, C1420/11, transcript p. 82, track 3.
12. Mariarosa Dalla Costa and Selma James, *The Power of Women and the Subversion of the Community*, 3rd ed. (Bristol: Falling Wall Press, 1975); Ellen Malos, *The Politics of Housework* (Cheltenham: New Clarion Press, 1995).
13. Rosalind Delmar, *S&A*, C1420/03, transcript p. 127, track 5.
14. Leeds Revolutionary Feminist Group, *Love Your Enemy? The Debate between Heterosexual Feminism and Political Lesbianism* (London: Onlywomen Press, 1981).
15. Juliet Mitchell, *Woman's Estate* (Harmondsworth, UK: Penguin, 1981 [1971]), 68.
16. Zoë Fairbairns, *S&A*, C1420/24, transcript p. 8, track 1.
17. In turn, it inspired the Gay Liberation Front's invasion of the Christian Festival of Light the following year. Lisa Power, *No Bath but Plenty of Bubbles: An Oral History of the Gay Liberation Front, 1970–1973* (London: Cassell, 1995), 431.
18. Jo Robinson, *S&A*, C1420/43, transcript p. 156, track 9.
19. Sally Alexander, personal communication, October 17, 2017.
20. Lynne Segal, *S&A*, C1420/28, transcript p. 51, track 2.
21. Zoë Fairbairns, *S&A*, C1420/24, transcript pp. 54–55, track 2.
22. Dieter Rucht, "The Strategies and Action Repertoires of New Movements," in *Challenging the Political Order: New Social and Political Movements in Western Democracies*, ed. Russell J. Dalton and Manfred Kuechler (Cambridge: Polity Press, 1990); Joni Lovenduski and Vicky Randall, *Contemporary Feminist Politics: Women and Power in Britain* (Oxford: Oxford University Press, 1993), 181.
23. Sue O'Sullivan, *S&A*, C1420/40, transcript p. 129, track 6.
24. Anna Coote and Polly Pattullo, *Power and Prejudice: Women and Politics* (London: Weidenfeld and Nicolson, 1990), 90.
25. Freya Johnson Ross, "What State Are We In?: Activism, Professional Feminists and Local Government" (PhD thesis, University of Sussex, 2015).
26. The Women's Library @ LSE, 5WRR/B/02, Records of the Women's Research & Resources Centre, *WIRES* newsletter, probably from summer 1976.
27. The Women's Library @ LSE, 5WRR/B/06, Records of the Women's Research & Resources Centre, Folder: Letters to Sally Thomlinson 1971–1977. See Celia Hughes, *Young Lives on the Left: Sixties Activism and the Liberation of the Self* (Manchester: Manchester University Press, 2015), 256, on Wainwright's ability to take charge even with the International Marxist Group.

28. Eve Setch, "The Face of Metropolitan Feminism: The London Women's Liberation Workshop, 1969–79," *Twentieth Century British History* 13, no. 2 (2002): 171–90; David Bouchier, *The Feminist Challenge: The Movement for Women's Liberation in Britain and the USA* (London: Macmillan, 1983), 177, estimated ten thousand members by counting all named groups he could find in the literature and estimating an average of fifty active members in each; see also Sue Bruley, "Women's Liberation at the Grass Roots: A View from Some English Towns, c. 1968–1990," *Women's History Review* 25, no. 5 (2016): 729, which counts forty women's centres in the country in 1979.
29. Lovenduski and Randall, *Contemporary Feminist Politics*, 181; Hazel Ashatroo's research suggests a *Spare Rib* circulation figure of 35,000 in 1981, based on a Women's Committee report by Controller of Finance, 15.12.82, in GLC Collection, London Metropolitan Archives, GLC/DG/WCSU/1/53/S22. It is likely that four times as many read *Spare Rib* as bought it. I am grateful to Hazel Ashatroo for pointing me toward this figure and source.
30. Pat V. T. West, interviewed by Viv Honeybourne, Feminist Archive South Oral Histories, Personal Histories of Second Wave Feminism Oral History Project (2000–2001), University of Bristol DM2123/1/Archive Boxes 79. See also http://feministarchivesouth.org.uk/wp-content/uploads/2013/02/Personal-Histories-of-the-Second-Wave-of-Feminism.pdf.
31. D-M (formerly Deborah M.) Withers, *Sistershow Revisited: Feminism in Bristol 1973–1975* (Bristol: HammerOn Press, 2011).
32. Harriet Harman, *A Woman's Work* (Milton Keynes, UK: Allen Lane, 2017), 18, 29, 388–91.
33. Ibid., 25.
34. Sheila Rowbotham, *S&A*, C1420/10, transcript p. 106, track 3.
35. The group included Barbara Yates, Roslyn Smythe, Mary McIntosh, Elizabeth Wilson, Angie Weir, and Sarah Grimes. Elizabeth Wilson remembers "The Maoists" as "a caricature of themselves," reading *The Little Red Book* on a dais behind a red curtain in the church hall where everyone was sleeping, in Power, *No Bath but Plenty of Bubbles*, 128–29.
36. Gail Chester, *S&A*, C1420/35, transcript p. 142, track 2.
37. Rosalind Delmar, *S&A*, C1420/03, transcript p. 127, track 5.
38. Headline from the *Daily Mirror*, 1970, cited in Kaitlynn Mendes, "Framing Feminism: News Coverage of the Women's Movement in British and American Newspapers, 1968–1982," *Social Movement Studies* 10, no. 1 (2011): 55.
39. Women in Media 1972–80, The Women's Library @ LSE, 2IAW/2/B/26.
40. Barbara Burford, *The Threshing Floor: Short Stories* (London: Sheba Feminist Publishers, 1986); Siona Wilson, *Art Labor, Sex Politics: Feminist Effects in 1970s British Art and Performance* (Minneapolis, MN: University of Minnesota Press, 2009); Nicola Streeten Plowman, "A Cultural History of Feminist Cartoons and Comics in Britain from 1970 to 2010" (PhD thesis, University of Sussex, 2017).

Spare Rib is available through the British Library with a rich set of contextual essays at bl.uk/spare-rib.

41. Elizabeth Bird, "The Academic Arm of the Women's Liberation Movement: Women's Studies 1969–1999 in North America and the United Kingdom," *Women's Studies International Forum* 25, no. 1 (2002): 139–49; Sue Jackson, "Networking Women: A History of Ideas, Issues and Developments in Women's Studies in Britain," *Women's Studies International Forum* 23, no. 1 (2000): 1–11.

42. See The Women's Library @ LSE, 5WRR, Records of the Women's Research & Resources Centre (London), Box 1, Folder A/02; Lucy Delap, "Feminist Bookshops, Reading Cultures and the Women's Liberation Movement in Great Britain, c. 1974–2000," *History Workshop Journal* 81, no. 1 (2016): 171–96.

43. Jo Sutton and Jalna Hanmer, "Writing Our Own History: A Conversation about the First Years of Women's Aid between Jo Sutton and Jalna Hanmer," *Trouble & Strife*, no. 4 (1984): 55–60; Jeska Rees, "'Taking Your Politics Seriously': Lesbian History and the Women's Liberation Movement in England," in *Sapphists and Sexologists*, ed. Sonja Tiernan and Mary McAuliffe (Newcastle upon Tyne: Cambridge Scholars, 2009), 106–27. Lesley Abdela, *S&A*, C1420/13, transcript pp. 138–39, track 5. For more on Colquhoun see Matthew Parris and Kevin MacGuire, *Great Parliamentary Scandals: Four Centuries of Calumny, Smear and Innuendo* (London: Robson Books, 1997), 236–41.

44. Barbara J. Love, *Feminists Who Changed America, 1963–1975* (Urbana: University of Illinois Press, 2006), 405.

45. Michelene Wandor, "The Small Group," in *The Body Politic: Women's Liberation in Britain*, ed. Michelene Wandor (London: Stage 1, 1978), 114–15.

46. Sheila Rowbotham, "Women's Liberation and the New Politics," in *The Body Politic: Women's Liberation in Britain*, ed. Michelene Wandor (London: Stage 1, 1978), 31.

47. Sandie Wyles, *S&A*, C1420/22, transcript p. 122, track 8.

48. Rosalind Delmar, *S&A*, C1420/03, transcript pp. 123–24, track 5.

49. Jalna Hanmer, *S&A*, C1420/04, transcript p. 54, track 2.

50. Michelene Wandor, *S&A*, C1420/09, transcript p. 163, track 1.

51. Nadira Mirza, *S&A*, C1420/17, transcript p. 75, track 4.

52. Gill Philpott, "Consciousness Raising: Back to Basics," in *Spare Rib Reader*, ed. Marsha Rowe (Harmondsworth, UK: Penguin, 1982), 585–87.

53. Sidney G. Tarrow, *Power in Movement: Social Movements, Collective Action, and Politics* (Cambridge: Cambridge University Press, 1994), 50.

54. Donatella Della Porta and Mario Diani, *Social Movements: An Introduction*, 2nd ed. (Oxford: Blackwell, 2006), 188–89.

55. See Lesley Hoggart, "Feminist Principles Meet Political Reality: The Case of the National Abortion Campaign," accessed November 28, 2013, http://www.prochoiceforum.org.uk/al6.php.

56. Ibid. Corrie withdrew his bill on March 26, 1980, before the third reading, while the House of Commons was still debating amendments. It had become clear that

the bill would not succeed as it stood and Corrie was unwilling to compromise until it was too late.
57. Ibid. The bill passed by a 242–98 vote on July 13; the rally took place on July 14.
58. Elizabeth Meehan, "British Feminism from the 1960s to the 1980s," in *British Feminism in the Twentieth Century*, ed. Harold L. Smith (Aldershot: Elgar, 1990), 189–204.
59. Susan Hemmings, "October 28th," *Spare Rib*, no. 89 (December 1979): 237.
60. Dominic Sandbrook, *Seasons in the Sun: The Battle for Britain, 1974–1979* (London: Allen Lane, 2012), xviii–xix.
61. Anna Coote and Beatrix Campbell, *Sweet Freedom: The Struggle for Women's Liberation*, 2nd ed. (Oxford: Basil Blackwell, 1987), 147–48.
62. Emine Saner, "The Working Women's Charter: Forty Years on, Women Are Still Struggling," *Guardian*, November 10, 2014. The Employment Protection Act 1975 for the first time protected female employees from being dismissed from their job due to pregnancy. See also Tara Martin, "The Beginning of Labour's End? Britain's 'Winter of Discontent' and Working-Class Women's Activism," *International Labor and Working-Class History* 75, no. 1 (2009): 49–67.
63. Beatrix Campbell, *S&A*, C1420/60, transcript pp. 71–72, track 3. See also Peta Steel, "Terry Marsland, Union Leader Who Devoted Her Career to Fighting for Women's Rights," *Independent*, June 25, 2011, 42.
64. Stephen Brooke, *Sexual Politics: Sexuality, Family Planning, and the British Left from the 1880s to the Present Day* (Oxford: Oxford University Press, 2011).
65. Drew Halfmann shows how the British Medical Association initially fought the Abortion Act, for professional rather than ethical interests. Drew Halfmann, "Historical Priorities and the Responses of Doctors' Associations to Abortion Reform Proposals in Britain and the United States, 1960–1973," *Social Problems* 50, no. 4 (2003): 567–91.
66. Sandbrook, *State of Emergency*, 430–31. However, Anna Coote in *Marxism Today* quotes the much lower figure of a total of 112,055 abortions performed on residents of England and Wales in 1978. See Anna Coote, "Focus: Abortion," *Marxism Today*, November 1979, 2.
67. Sandbrook, *Seasons in the Sun*, 401–2.
68. Sandbrook, *State of Emergency*, 694.
69. Sandbrook, *Seasons in the Sun*, 431.
70. Coote and Campbell, *Sweet Freedom*, 148.
71. The Labour Abortion Reform Committee was led by Jo Richardson and Maureen Colquhoun and supported by Michael Foot, Labour leader and leader of the opposition, 1980–83. See Brooke, *Sexual Politics*, 214–15.
72. 374 Gray's Inn Road also housed Women's Aid, Rights of Women, Homeless Action, and Lesbian Line.
73. Jan McKenley, *S&A*, C1420/60, transcript p. 73, track 2.
74. Ibid., p. 52, track 2.
75. Ibid.

76. Sheila Rowbotham, "Women . . . How Far Have We Come?," in *Dreams and Dilemmas: Collected Writings* (London: Virago, 1983), 92.
77. See also Joni Lovenduski, "Parliament, Pressure Groups, Networks and the Women's Movement: The Politics of Abortion Law Reform in Britain (1967–1983)," in *The New Politics of Abortion*, ed. Joni Lovenduski and Joyce Outshoorn (London: Sage, 1986), 49–66.
78. Michael Litchfield and Susan Kentish, *Babies for Burning: The Abortion Business in Britain* (London: Serpentine Press, 1974).
79. Brooke, *Sexual Politics*, 201; Coote, "Focus: Abortion."
80. Polly Toynbee, "Behind the Lines: Ironing in the Soul," in *Women of the Revolution: Forty Years of Feminism*, ed. Kira Cochrane (London: Guardian Books, 2010), 124.
81. Leeds Revolutionary Feminist Group, *Love Your Enemy?*, 6. Jessica Wood's letter, reprinted in this publication, describes campaigning with the NAC as an example of her former oppressed, heterosexually focused life, 52.
82. This approach is also obvious in Coote's article for *Marxism Today* (Coote, "Focus: Abortion").
83. Julia Sudbury, *Other Kinds of Dreams: Black Women's Organisations and the Politics of Transformation* (London: Routledge, 1998), 135.
84. Anon, "Black Women Together: The Need for a United and Autonomous National Black Women's Organisation," *Spare Rib*, no. 47 (October 1979): 42–45. See also William E. Nelson, *Black Atlantic Politics: Dilemmas of Political Empowerment in Boston and Liverpool* (Albany: State University of New York Press, 2000), 272.
85. Gail Lewis, *S&A*, C1420/60, transcript p. 151, track 5.
86. Black Unity and Freedom Party, The Black Women's Action Committee, "The Black Woman," in *The Body Politic: Women's Liberation in Britain*, ed. Michelene Wandor (London: Stage 1, 1972), 84–89.
87. Ibid., 89.
88. Gail Lewis, *S&A*, C1420/60, transcript p. 152, track 5.
89. Ibid., pp. 46–53, track 2. See also Gail Lewis, "Birthing Racial Difference: Conversations with My Mother and Others," *Studies in the Maternal* 1, no. 1 (2009): 1–21.
90. Gail Lewis, *S&A*, C1420/60, transcript p. 48, track 2.
91. Suzanne Scafe, "The Heart of the Race," in *Hearing Her: New Feminist Oral Histories* (presentation paper, University of Sussex, April 11, 2013).
92. Kirsten Hearn, *S&A*, C1420/60, transcript p. 67, track 3.
93. Ibid., p. 107, track 4.
94. Jan McKenley, *S&A*, C1420/60, transcript p. 79, track 2; Marie-Thérèse McGivern, *S&A*, C1420/46, transcript p. 80, track 3.
95. Jan McKenley, *S&A*, C1420/60, transcript p. 102, track 4.
96. Ibid., p. 58, track 2.
97. Angela Phillips and Jill Rakusen, *The New Our Bodies, Ourselves* (London: Penguin, 1996).

98. Zoë Fairbairns, *Benefits: A Novel* (Nottingham: Five Leaves, 1998), xii.
99. Ibid., 37–39.
100. Judith Wilt, *Abortion, Choice, and Contemporary Fiction: The Armageddon of the Maternal Instinct* (Chicago: University of Chicago Press, 1990).
101. Jeska Rees, "A Look Back at Anger: The Women's Liberation Movement in 1978," *Women's History Review* 19, no. 3 (2010): 346–47.
102. Sheila Rowbotham, Lynne Segal, and Hilary Wainwright, *Beyond the Fragments: Feminism and the Making of Socialism*, 3rd ed. (Boston: Merlin Press, 2013).
103. Thomlinson, *Race, Ethnicity and the Women's Movement*, 87; Anonymous, "Black Women Together: The Need for a United and Autonomous National Black Women's Organisation," *Spare Rib* 47 (1979): 42–45.
104. Marinella Marmo and Evan Smith, "Is There a Desirable Migrant: A Reflection on Human Rights Violations at the Border: The Case of Virginity Testing," *Alternative Law Journal* 35, no. 4 (2010): 223–26.
105. Marie-Thérèse McGivern, *S&A*, C1420/46, transcript pp. 81–82, track 3.
106. For example, Sandbrook, *State of Emergency*, 368–419.
107. Randeep Ramesh, "Britons More Liberal, Cynical and Individual Than 30 Years Ago, Says Survey," *Guardian*, September 10, 2013, 13.
108. Sandbrook, *Seasons in the Sun*, 431; Sandbrook, *State of Emergency*, 427.
109. Lovenduski and Randall, *Contemporary Feminist Politics*, 220–58. Compare sexual choice to the uneven legacy of the Employment Protection Act of 1975, making it illegal to fire a woman if she is pregnant.
110. Sandbrook, *Seasons in the Sun*, 439–45.
111. Halfmann, "Historical Priorities," 585. Less typically white-centric is Dr. Sheila Abdullah, a well-known Liverpool general practitioner who worked at Prince's Park health centre and appeared on the BBC "Doctor's Dilemmas" radio programme on abortion, January 12, 1983. Audrey Leathard, *The Fight for Family Planning: The Development of Family Planning Services in Britain, 1921–74* (London: Macmillan, 1980), mentions her as a prominent campaigner when discussing the varied regional reception of physicians to the Abortion Act.
112. SPUC claimed a membership of 26,000 and LIFE 20,000 in 1980 (figures cited in Lovenduski and Randall, *Contemporary Feminist Politics*, 222).
113. Quoted in Brooke, *Sexual Politics*, 194.
114. Editor, "Changing the Abortion Law," *Daily Mail*, July 16, 1979.
115. Raymond Williams, *Marxism and Literature* (Oxford: Oxford University Press, 1977), 132–34.
116. Ann Rossiter, *Ireland's Hidden Diaspora: The "Abortion Trail" and the Making of a London-Irish Underground, 1980–2000* (London: IASC, 2009).
117. Karen McMinn, *S&A*, C1420/26, transcript pp. 107–108, track 3. It should be noted that in fact the Kingsmill Massacres resulted in ten shot dead and one wounded, rather than twelve as McMinn remembers here.
118. Just a few of the others involved were Marie Queray from the Women's Centre, Evelyn Collanz from the Equal Opportunities Commission, Ann Hope from

Northern Ireland Women's Rights Movement, and Marie Abbott from Belfast Women's Collective. Joanna McMinn was appointed as worker.

119. Eileen Evason, *Hidden Violence: Battered Women in Northern Ireland* (Belfast: Farset Co-operative Press, 1982); *Against the Grain: The Contemporary Women's Movement in Northern Ireland* (Dublin: Attic Press, 1991).

120. See Christina Loughran, "Armagh and Feminist Strategy: Campaigns around Republican Women Prisoners in Armagh Jail," *Feminist Review* 23, no. 1 (1986): 59–79, "Writing Our Own History—Organising against the Odds: 10 Years of Feminism in Northern Ireland," *Trouble & Strife*, no. 11 (1986): 48–54; Margaret Ward, "Feminism and Nationalism in Ireland: Can We Learn from History?," *Journal of Gender Studies* 1, no. 4 (1992): 492–99.

121. In 1975 Northern Ireland Women's Rights Movement formed "to spread a consciousness of Women's oppression and mobilize the greatest possible numbers of women on feminist issues" (NIWRM Manifesto 1974). They called specifically for the extension of Britain's Sexual Discrimination Act to Northern Ireland, accessed November 5, 2017, http://www.encyclopedia.com/international/encyclopedias-almanacs-transcripts-and-maps/womens-movement-northern-ireland.

122. Erin Pizzey, *This Way to the Revolution: A Memoir* (London: Peter Owen, 2011).

123. Jonathan Dean, *Rethinking Contemporary Feminist Politics* (Basingstoke, UK: Palgrave Macmillan, 2010), 118.

124. Karen McMinn, "Women's Aid: Feminism at the Grass Roots," *Fortnight*, no. 220 (1985): 13.

125. Sandra Laville, "Violent Crimes against Women in England and Wales Reach Record High," *The Guardian*, September 6, 2016, unpaginated, accessed April 12, 2019, https://www.theguardian.com/society/2016/sep/05/violent-crimes-against-women-in-england-and-wales-reach-record-high.

126. In April 1990, the 1967 Abortion Act was amended to take account of medical advances to reduce the limit for terminations from 28 to 24 weeks.

127. "British Attitudes to Abortion," NatCen, by Eleanor Attar Taylor, senior researcher, posted August 3, 2017, accessed October 16, 2017, http://www.natcen.ac.uk/blog/british-attitudes-to-abortion.

128. Hannah Betts, "On Abortion, Beware the Overshare," *Guardian*, July 18, 2012, 26.

129. Dean, *Rethinking Contemporary Feminist Politics*.

130. Ibid., 101.

131. Mukami McCrum, *S&A*, C1420/39, transcript pp. 104–105, track 5.

132. Sudbury, *Other Kinds of Dreams*, 134–35.

133. Jane Hutt, *S&A*, C1420/21, transcript pp. 53–56, track 2.

134. Johnson Ross, "What State Are We In?," 203; Sudbury, *Other Kinds of Dreams*, 173.

135. Sheila Gilmore, *S&A*, C1420/29, transcript pp. 58–59, track 3.

136. Karen McMinn, *S&A*, C1420/26, transcript p. 140, track 4.

137. Ibid., p. 141, track 4.
138. Ibid.

CHAPTER 5

1. Ann Cullis, "The Dinner Party, Judy Chicago. Victoria Hall, Edinburgh," *Spare Rib*, no. 148 (1984): 34–35. The Dinner Party also displayed at The Warehouse in London March–May 1985. Germaine Greer spoke at the opening and thousands visited the huge installation in the following months. It is now part of the permanent collection at the Brooklyn Museum.
2. Ann Oakley, *Housewife* (London: A. Lane, 1974).
3. Rita Felski, "The Invention of Everyday Life," in *Doing Time: Feminist Theory and Postmodern Culture* (New York: New York University Press, 2000).
4. Lynne Segal, *Making Trouble: Life and Politics* (London: Serpent's Tail, 2007), 97.
5. Jo Robinson, *S&A*, C1420/43, transcript pp. 60, 67, 122, 133, track 8.
6. Carmen Callil, interviewed by Sue Lawley, *Desert Island Discs*, December 6, 1992, BBC Radio 4.
7. Catherine Hall, *S&A*, C1420/54, transcript pp. 46–47, track 2; Sue Bruley, "Women's Liberation at the Grass Roots: A View from Some English Towns, c. 1968–1990," *Women's History Review* 25, no. 5 (2016): 726.
8. Donna Jackman and Carol Leeming, interviewed for Oral Histories of the Black Women's Movement: The Heart of the Race, 2008–2010, Black Cultural Archives, London, ORAL/1/BWM 18; Diana Watt and Adele Jones, *Catching Hell and Doing Well: Black Women in the UK—the Abasindi Cooperative* (London: Trentham, 2015), 61.
9. Ama Gueye, interviewed for Oral Histories of the Black Women's Movement: The Heart of the Race, 2008–2010, Black Cultural Archives, London, ORAL/1/BWM 16; Jocelyn Wolfe, *S&A*, C1420/06, transcript p. 171, track 4.
10. Bronagh Hinds, *S&A*, C1420/50, transcript p. 71, track 2.
11. Sandie Wyles, *S&A*, C1420/22, transcript pp. 32–33, track 2.
12. Ellen Malos, *S&A*, C1420/06, transcript p. 140, track 3.
13. See Watt and Jones, *Catching Hell and Doing Well*, 18–19, for how this happened in Moss Side, Manchester.
14. Pragna Patel, *S&A*, C1420/18, transcript p. 27, track 2.
15. Stella Dadzie, *S&A*, C1420/20, transcript pp. 10–11, track 1.
16. Zoë Fairbairns, *Benefits: A Novel* (Nottingham: Five Leaves, 1998), 3.
17. Dominic Sandbrook, *State of Emergency: The Way We Were: Britain, 1970–1974* (London: Allen Lane, 2010), 19.
18. Jenni Murray, *S&A*, C1420/48, transcript p. 84, track 4.
19. Ibid., 85.
20. Jean McCrindle and Sheila Rowbotham, eds., *Dutiful Daughters: Women Talk About Their Lives* (London: Allen Lane, 1977), 5.

21. Jenny Lynn, *S&A*, C1420/16, transcript p. 84, track 2.
22. Pragna Patel, *S&A*, C1420/18, transcript p. 87, track 4.
23. Sarah F. Green, *Urban Amazons: Lesbian Feminism and Beyond in the Gender, Sexuality, and Identity Battles of London* (New York: St. Martin's Press, 1997), 28; Marion Brion, *Women in the Housing Service* (London: Routledge, 1995).
24. Siobhan Molloy, *S&A*, C1420/37, transcript pp. 77–80, track 3.
25. "Big Flame," "We Won't Pay: Women's Struggle on Tower Hill," *Big Flame Journal* 1974–75, 1, unpaginated.
26. Sheila Rowbotham, *Promise of a Dream: Remembering the Sixties* (London: Verso, 2001), 117.
27. Ibid., 182–83.
28. Sheila Rowbotham, *S&A*, C1420/10, transcript p. 133, track 4.
29. Pat Thane, *Happy Families? History and Family Policy* (London: British Academy Policy Centre, 2010), 12.
30. Sheila Rowbotham, Lynne Segal, and Hilary Wainwright, *Beyond the Fragments: Feminism and the Making of Socialism*, 3rd ed. (Boston: Merlin Press, 2013), 16.
31. Ibid., p. 19.
32. According to the Anglia Building Society, the numbers of women buying property doubled over the 1980s. But poorer women suffered disproportionately. In Scotland, according to the 1981 census, 78 percent of single-parent families were living in public housing (they were also likely to be in the poorest accommodation). Cited in Joni Lovenduski and Vicky Randall, *Contemporary Feminist Politics: Women and Power in Britain* (Oxford: Oxford University Press, 1993), 54, 51.
33. Ibid., 203, and Janet Newman, *Working the Spaces of Power: Activism, Neoliberalism and Gendered Labour* (London: Bloomsbury Academic, 2012).
34. Valerie Wise, *S&A*, C1420/31, transcript p. 100, track 2.
35. Natalie Thomlinson, *Race, Ethnicity and the Women's Movement in England, 1968–1993* (Houndsmills, UK: Palgrave, 2016), 74.
36. Julia Sudbury explains that "funding has been seen as a strategy to co-opt grassroots struggle into more manageable forms of activity, by turning activists into service deliverers, black working class struggle into ethnic enclaves and creating a tier of 'race relations professionals' to control black youth energies" in *Other Kinds of Dreams: Black Women's Organisations and the Politics of Transformation* (London: Routledge, 1998), 82, see also 44, 83–84; Floya Anthias, Nira Yuval-Davis, and Harriet Cain, *Racialized Boundaries: Race, Nation, Gender, Colour and Class and the Anti-Racist Struggle* (London: Routledge, 1996); Pratibha Parmar, "The Past before Us: Twenty Years of Feminism," *Feminist Review* 31 (1989): 56.
37. Beatrix Campbell, *S&A*, C1420/06, transcript p. 96, track 5.
38. Rowbotham, Segal, and Wainwright, *Beyond the Fragments*, 20.
39. CAITS was the Centre for Alternative Industrial and Technological Systems.

40. Valerie Wise, *S&A*, C1420/31, transcript pp. 73–74, track 2.
41. Ibid., p. 81, track 2.
42. Ibid., pp. 171–72, track 4.
43. Betty Cook, *S&A*, C1420/59, transcript p. 137, track 5; for the whole poem, see "Here We Go!" (Anon.), cited in Katy Shaw, "Striking Women: (Re) Writing 1984–5," *Women's Studies* 36, no. 8 (2007): 622.
44. Betty Cook, *S&A*, C1420/59, transcript pp. 77–78, track 2.
45. Ibid., p. 2, track 1.
46. Ibid., p. 92, track 4.
47. Sheila Rowbotham and Jean McCrindle, "More Than Just a Memory: Some Political Implications of Women's Involvement in the Miners' Strike, 1984–85," *Feminist Review*, no. 23 (1986): 109–24.
48. "Greetings Card: The First Banner of the Barnsley Miners Wives Action Group," *Past Pixels*, accessed September 1, 2017, http://pastpixels.co.uk/en/product/greetings-card-first-banner-barnsley-miners-wives-action-group. For a discussion of Cook's poetry, see Carol Stephenson and Jean Spence, "Pies and Essays: Women Writing through the British 1984–1985 Coal Miners' Strike," *Gender, Place & Culture* 20, no. 2 (2013): 218–35.
49. Betty Cook, *S&A*, C1420/59, transcript p. 75, track 2.
50. Jean McCrindle interviewed by Louise Brodie, *National Life Stories Collection*, C464/83, British Library.
51. Cynthia Cockburn, *S&A*, C1420/42, transcript p. 182, track 7.
52. Una Kroll, *S&A*, C1420/49, transcript pp. 149–50, track 5.
53. Michele Roberts, *Paper Houses: A Memoir of the '70s and Beyond* (London: Virago, 2007).
54. Kirsten Hearn, *S&A*, C1420/44, transcript p. 73, track 3.
55. Ibid.
56. Valerie Wise, *S&A*, C1420/31, transcript pp. 194–95, track 4; Betty Cook, *S&A*, C1420/59, transcript p. 91, track 4.
57. Dominic Sandbrook, *Seasons in the Sun: The Battle for Britain, 1974–1979* (London: Allen Lane, 2012), 17.
58. Delia Smith and Ivan Ripley, *How to Cheat at Cooking* (London: Coronet, 1973).
59. Shirley Conran, *Superwoman: Everywoman's Book of Household Management* (Harmondsworth, UK: Penguin, 1977), 172–73, 55.
60. Ibid., 43.
61. Griselda Pollock, "Food Co-Ops," *Spare Rib*, no. 27 (1974): 28.
62. Joanne Hollows, "Second-Wave Feminism and the Politics of Consumption" (paper presented at the Centre for Research in Memory, Narrative and Histories Seminar Series, University of Brighton, December 3, 2014). See also Joanne Hollows, *Domestic Cultures* (Maidenhead: Open University Press, 2008).
63. Segal, *Making Trouble*.

64. Kum-Kum Bhavnani, "Recipe for Thought," in *Turning the Tables: Recipes and Reflections from Women*, ed. Sue O'Sullivan (London: Sheba Feminist Publishers, 1987).
65. Sue O'Sullivan, *S&A*, C1420/40, transcript p. 24, track 1.
66. Angela Carter, "Potato Soup," in *Turning the Tables: Recipes and Reflections from Women*, ed. Sue O'Sullivan (London: Sheba Feminist Publishers, 1987), 111–13.
67. Carol Adams, "Meat and Vegetables," *Trouble & Strife*, no. 18 (1990), 4–11.
68. Shaheen Haque and Pratibha Parmar, "Tamarind Mango Pickle and Bhajias," in *Turning the Tables: Recipes and Reflections from Women*, ed. Sue O'Sullivan (London: Sheba Feminist Publishers, 1987), 59–61; Linda Bellos, "Salad Niçoise," in *Turning the Tables: Recipes and Reflections from Women*, ed. Sue O'Sullivan (London: Sheba Feminist Publishers, 1987), 61.
69. Dena Attar, "A Feminist Cookbook?," in *Turning the Tables: Recipes and Reflections from Women*, ed. Sue O'Sullivan (London: Sheba Feminist Publishers, 1987), 7–19.
70. Rosamund Urwin, "The Five Rules for Feminist Cooking," *Evening Standard*, October 22, 2013.
71. Rachael Scicluna, "Thinking through Domestic Pluralities," *Home Cultures* 12, no. 2 (2015): 183.
72. Betty Cook, *S&A*, C1420/59, transcript p. 69, track 2.
73. "Greetings Card: The First Banner of the Barnsley Miners Wives Action Group."
74. See chap. 1.
75. Jocelyn Wolfe, *S&A*, C1420/06, transcript p. 132, track 3.
76. Viv Albertine, *Clothes, Clothes, Clothes, Music, Music, Music, Boys, Boys, Boys* (London: Faber & Faber, 2014), 83. Karen McMinn, *S&A*, C1420/26, transcript p. 74, track 2.
77. Beatrix Campbell, *S&A*, C1420/06, transcript p. 41, track 3.
78. Anna Davin, *S&A*, C1420/02, transcript p. 155, track 5.
79. Joanne Hollows, "*Spare Rib*, Second-Wave Feminism and the Politics of Consumption," *Feminist Media Studies* 13, no. 2 (2012): 268–87.
80. Nadira Mirza, *S&A*, C1420/17, transcript p. 54, track 1.
81. Watt and Jones, *Catching Hell and Doing Well*, 106.
82. Jan McKenley, *S&A*, C1420/15, transcript pp. 120–21, track 5.
83. Gail Chester, *S&A*, C1420/27, transcript p. 74, track 1.
84. Haleh Afshar, "Khomeini's Teachings and Their Implications for Women," *Feminist Review*, no. 12 (1982): 59–72.
85. Lisa Power, *No Bath but Plenty of Bubbles: An Oral History of the Gay Liberation Front, 1970–1973* (London: Cassell, 1995), 222.
86. Mary McIntosh, *S&A*, C1420/11, transcript p. 71, track 3.
87. Hollows, "*Spare Rib*, Second-Wave Feminism and the Politics of Consumption."
88. *Spare Rib* (March 1982), cover photograph by Brenda Prince.
89. *Spare Rib* (March 1982): 33.
90. Ibid.

91. Kirsten Hearn, *S&A*, C1420/44, transcript p. 77, track 3.
92. Elizabeth Wilson, *Adorned in Dreams: Fashion and Modernity* (London: I. B. Tauris, 2003), 228.
93. Janice Winship, "Dress Sense," in *Cracks in the Pavement: Gender/Fashion/Architecture*, ed. Lynne Walker (London: Sorella Press, 1992), 1–18.
94. Lesley Abdela, *S&A*, C1420/13, transcript pp. 119–20, track 5.
95. Ibid.
96. Merl Storr, *Latex and Lingerie: Shopping for Pleasure at Ann Summers* (Oxford: Berg, 2003).
97. *Spare Rib* (April 1984): 33.
98. "Story of Sh!: The UK's First Women's Sex Shop," *Sh!*, accessed September 1, 2017, https://www.sh-womenstore.com/our-story.
99. Grace Lau, *S&A*, C1420/60, transcript p. 87, track 3.
100. Sheba Collective, *Serious Pleasure: Lesbian Erotic Stories and Poetry* (London: Sheba Feminist Publishers, 1989); Sue O'Sullivan, *More Serious Pleasure* (London: Sheba, 1990).
101. Clare Short, *Dear Clare . . . This Is What Women Feel About Page 3* (London: Hutchinson Radius, 1991).
102. Barbara Jones, *S&A*, C1420/53, transcript p. 81, track 3. Jones started the disco for the New Year 1986–87 as a fundraiser for a woman in Broadmoor high-security psychiatric hospital.
103. Susan Ardill and Sue O'Sullivan, "Sex in the Summer of '88," *Feminist Review*, no. 31 (1989): 126–34.
104. Green, *Urban Amazons*, 2.
105. Ibid., 22.
106. Joe Moran, *Armchair Nation: An Intimate History of Britain in Front of the TV* (London: Profile Books, 2013), 267.
107. Ibid., 191.
108. Alison Rayner, *S&A*, C1420/47, transcript p. 122, track 4.
109. Pragna Patel, *S&A*, C1420/18, transcript pp. 131–32, track 6.
110. "Eco Hub at Lordship Recreation Ground, Haringey, London," *Low Energy Building Database*, accessed October 8, 2017, http://www.lowenergy-buildings.org.uk/viewproject.php?id=300#images; "Can a Straw Bale House Reach Passivhaus Standards?" *House Planning Help*, accessed October 8, 2017, http://www.houseplanninghelp.com/hph042-can-a-straw-bale-house-reach-passivhaus-standard-with-fran-bradshaw-from-anne-thorne-architects/.
111. Barbara Jones, *S&A*, C1420/53, transcript p. 88, track 3.
112. Liz Heron, "Getting on Top of the Job: Women in Manual Trades," *Spare Rib*, no. 72 (1978): 52.
113. Julia Dwyer and Anne Thorne, "Evaluating Matrix: Notes from inside the Collective," in *Altering Practices: Feminist Politics and Poetics of Space*, ed. Doina Petrescu (London: Routledge, 2007), 41–43.

114. Ibid., 42.
115. Barbara Jones, *S&A*, C1420/53, transcript p. 68, track 3.
116. Ibid., p. 71, track 3.
117. Clara Greed, "Builders: Class, Gender and Ethnicity in the Construction Industry," *Construction Management and Economics* 30, no. 11 (2012): 1013–17. In 1945, they made up 3.8 percent of the total construction workforce, but despite the acute labor shortage after the war, Minister of Labour Ernest Bevin refused to recruit any women into the skilled trades, while at the same time demanding that all men up to the age of sixty with any building experience register for reconstruction work. Linda Clarke and Christine Wall, "Omitted from History: Women in the Building Trades" (paper presented at the Proceedings of the Second International Congress on Construction History, Cambridge, 2006), 47, 49.
118. Clark and Wall, "Omitted from History," 51.
119. Katie King, *Theory in Its Feminist Travels: Conversations in U.S. Women's Movements* (Bloomington: Indiana University Press, 1994), 124.
120. Barbara Jones, *S&A*, C1420/53, transcript p. 113, track 4.
121. *Straw Works,* accessed September 1, 2017, http://www.strawworks.co.uk/design/.
122. Barbara Jones, *S&A*, C1420/53, transcript p. 116, track 4.
123. Dwyer and Thorne, "Evaluating Matrix," 42.
124. Barbara Jones, personal correspondence with the author, 2012. See also Barbara Jones, "Intimate Questions," *Trouble & Strife*, no. 16 (1989): 22–25.
125. Cited in Hollows, "Second-Wave Feminism and the Politics of Consumption."
126. Gwenda's Garage in Sheffield, founded by Ros Wall, Annette Williams, and Roz Wollen in 1985, was the first garage in the north of England to be run by women and staffed entirely by female mechanics: https://www.theguardian.com/lifeandstyle/2017/jul/31/annette-williams-obituary. See also Angela Phillips, "*Spare Rib*, the Business," The British Library, http://www.bl.uk/spare-rib/articles/spare-rib-the-business.
127. Liz Armstrong, *S&A*, C1420/33, transcript pp. 108–9, track 4.
128. Laurence Marks, "PROFILE: Sheila McKechnie/The Consumer's Choice," *The Independent*, January 1, 1995.
129. Clarke and Wall, "Omitted from History," 52.
130. "Women in Construction," Union of Construction, Allied Trades and Technicians, accessed October 9, 2017, https://www.ucatt.org.uk/women-construction
131. Marsha Rowe, "*Spare Rib* and the Underground Press," The British Library, https://www.bl.uk/spare-rib/articles/spare-rib-and-the-underground-press.
132. Barry Miles, *London Calling: A Countercultural History of London since 1945* (London: Atlantic, 2010), unpaginated.
133. Dwyer and Thorne, "Evaluating Matrix," 41–42.
134. Susie Orbach, *S&A*, C1420/25, transcript p. 35, track 1.
135. "Straw Bale Building," *Straw Works,* accessed September 1, 2017, http://www.strawworks.co.uk/design/.

136. Juliet Mitchell and Ann Oakley, *What Is Feminism* (Oxford: Basil Blackwell, 1986).
137. Judith Walkowitz, personal correspondence with the author, 2013; Doug McAdam, "The Biographical Impact of Activism," in *How Social Movements Matter*, ed. Marco Giugni, Doug McAdam, and Charles Tilly (Minneapolis: University of Minnesota Press, 1999), 119–48.
138. Green, *Urban Amazons*, 60.

CHAPTER 6

1. Zoë Fairbairns, *S&A*, C1420/24, transcript p. 79, track 03.
2. John Petherbridge, *S&A*, C1420/24, transcript p. 87, track 03.
3. Ibid., p. 84, track 03.
4. Ibid., p. 88, track 03.
5. Ibid., p. 90, track 03.
6. Ibid., p. 88, track 03.
7. Paul Morrison, *Unbecoming Men*, C1667/15, transcript p. 4, track 01.
8. For a classic example, see Sylvia Ann Hewlett, "Executive Presence," in *Talks at Google* (2014), https://www.youtube.com/watch?v=i2QOAfWLedE.
9. Hélène Cixous, Keith Cohen, and Paula Cohen, "The Laugh of the Medusa," *Signs: Journal of Women in Culture and Society* 1, no. 4 (1976): 875–93.
10. 6WIM/B/01-08 Box 4, Women In Media, The Women's Library@LSE; Jenni Murray, *S&A*, C1420/48, transcript p. 50–51, track 03.
11. Una Kroll, *S&A*, C1420/49, transcript p. 179, track 05. See also Una Kroll, *Bread Not Stones: The Autobiography of an Eventful Life* (Winchester: Christian Alternative, 2014), 31.
12. Harriet Harman, *A Woman's Work* (Milton Keynes, UK: Allen Lane, 2017), 318.
13. Lisa Power, *No Bath but Plenty of Bubbles: An Oral History of the Gay Liberation Front, 1970–1973* (London: Cassell, 1995), 104 and 118.
14. Lynne Segal, *S&A*, C1420/28, transcript p. 40, track 01.
15. Sheila Rowbotham, *Promise of a Dream: Remembering the Sixties* (London: Verso, 2001), 220.
16. Loretta Ross, "Voices of Feminism: Linda Burnham," *Meridians: Feminism, Race, Transnationalism* 13, no. 2 (2016): 192.
17. W. Chris Johnson, "Guerrilla Ganja Gun Girls: Policing Black Revolutionaries from Notting Hill to Laventille," *Gender & History* 26, no. 3 (2014): 661–87; Robin Bunce and Paul Field, *Darcus Howe: A Political Biography* (London: Bloomsbury, 2013), 139.
18. Power, *No Bath but Plenty of Bubbles*, 127–33.
19. May Hobbs, *Born to Struggle* (London: Quartet Books, 1973), 85.
20. Malcolm Bradbury, *The History Man* (London: Picador, 2000).
21. Susie Orbach, *S&A*, C1420/25, transcript p. 99, track 04.

22. Harman, *A Woman's Work*, 56.
23. Sue Hastings, "The Story of the Ford Sewing Machinists," in Recording Women's Voices: A TUC Oral History Project on Equal Pay (London: Trades Union Congress, 2006), 1–4. Bernie Passingham was interviewed for "A Woman's Worth: The Story of the Ford Sewing Machinists" as part of the Recording Women's Voices project. See http://www.unionhistory.info/equalpay/display.php?irn=619&mediaindex=2.
24. "Cooking up a Storm—Julie Hayward's Equal Value Victory," in Recording Women's Voices, 1–4. See http://www.unionhistory.info/equalpay/display.php?irn=621.
25. Linda McDowell, Sundari Anitha, and Ruth Pearson, "Striking Similarities: Representing South Asian Women's Industrial Action in Britain," *Gender, Place & Culture* 19, no. 2 (2011): 145.
26. Juliet Mitchell, "Women: The Longest Revolution," *New Left Review* 1, no. 40 (1966): 11–37.
27. Catherine Hall, *S&A*, C1420/20, transcript p. 36, track 01.
28. Examples of such men included Raphael Samuel, Gareth Stedman Jones, David Widgery, Robin Blackburn, Bob Rowthorn, Tariq Ali, Vic Seidler, David Fernbach, Alan Sinfield, Stuart Hall, Darcus Howe, Eddie Lacointe, and C. L. R. James. Aldon D. Morris and Suzanne Staggenborg, "Leadership in Social Movements," in *The Blackwell Companion to Social Movements*, ed. David A. Snow, Sarah Anne Soule, and Hanspeter Kriesi (Oxford: Blackwell, 2004), 175.
29. Ibid., 188–89.
30. Jan McKenley, *S&A*, C1420/15, transcript p. 88, track 03.
31. Lynne Segal, *Slow Motion: Changing Masculinities, Changing Men* (New Brunswick, NJ: Rutgers University Press, 1990), 284.
32. Lenny Henry's critique of conventional masculinities, including black machismo, can be seen in his comedy character soul singer Theophilus P. Wildebeeste in *The Lenny Henry Show*, 1984–88, and Comic Relief stage shows. See http//www.youtube.com/watch?v=BVPvqkMHk3o.
33. Natalie Thomlinson, *Race, Ethnicity and the Women's Movement in England, 1968–1993* (Houndsmills, UK: Palgrave, 2016), 107.
34. Amanda Goldrick-Jones, *Men Who Believe in Feminism* (Westport, CT: Praeger, 2002), 163; Daniel Cohen, *Unbecoming Men*, C1667/04, transcript p. 26, track 01.
35. Paul Morrison, "Looking Back on 40 Years in the 'Men's Movement,'" in *Insideman: Pioneering Stories about Men and Boys*, ed. Dan Bell and Glen Poole (Leicestershire: Matador, 2015), 148–52.
36. Segal, *Slow Motion*, 284.
37. Harman, *A Woman's Work*, 30–31.
38. Paul Smith, *Unbecoming Men*, C1667/12, transcript pp. 1–3, track 02.
39. Colin Thomas, *Unbecoming Men*, C1667/25, transcript p. 1, track 01
40. In 1980, 1,208 convictions for homosexual "solicitation" were obtained, an increase of 247 percent since 1977; in February 1984, two men were arrested and fined £100

for kissing in Oxford Street: Susan Kingsley Kent, *Gender and Power in Britain, 1640–1990* (London: Routledge, 1999), 351.
41. Mary McIntosh, *S&A*, C1420/11, transcript p. 70, track 03; Power, *No Bath but Plenty of Bubbles*, 233–46.
42. Angela (Weir) Mason originally joined GLF as a "delegate" from the WLM and eventually became head of Stonewall.
43. Power, *No Bath but Plenty of Bubbles*, 110. Power's oral history is at its most moving in showing how GLF released both men and women from the "meat market" of underground clubs.
44. Scott Lauria Morgensen, "The Representability and Responsibility of Cisgender Queer Men in Women's Studies," *Women's Studies* 42, no. 5 (2013): 534–58; John Stoltenberg, *Refusing to Be a Man: Essays on Sex and Justice* (London: UCL Press, 2000).
45. John Rowan, *The Horned God: Feminism and Men as Wounding and Healing* (London: Routledge & Kegan Paul, 1987), 23, as cited.
46. Five Cram and Peter Goodridge [Pete 6], *Unbecoming Men*, C1667/30, transcript p. 67, track 03.
47. Lucy Delap, "Feminism, Masculinities and Emotional Politics in the Late Twentieth Century," *Cultural and Social History* 15, no. 4 (2018): 571–93.
48. Misha Wolf, *Unbecoming Men*, C1667/28, transcript p. 9, track 03.
49. Dave Baigent, *Unbecoming Men*, C1667/02, transcript p. 2, track 01.
50. Rowan, *The Horned God*, 33–37; "*Achilles Heel* and the Anti-Sexist Men's Movement," *Psychotherapy and Politics International* 3, no. 1 (2005): 58–71. Red Therapy was initially mixed, and when it dissolved two of its members, Sheila Ernst and Lucy Goodison, joined the Women's Therapy Centre: Rowan, *The Horned God*, 21.
51. Commitments Collective, 1980, reproduced in Rowan, *The Horned God*, 49.
52. Daniel Cohen, *Unbecoming Men*, C1667/04, transcript p. 14, track 01.
53. Lucy Delap, "Uneasy Solidarity: The British Men's Movement and Feminism," in *The Women's Liberation Movement: Impacts and Outcomes*, ed. Kristina Schulz (New York: Berghahn, 2017), 214–36.
54. Rowan, *The Horned God*.
55. Daniel Cohen, *Unbecoming Men*, C1667/04, transcript p. 10, track 01.
56. Kobena Mercer, *Welcome to the Jungle: New Positions in Black Cultural Studies* (New York: Routledge, 1994), 10.
57. Segal, *Slow Motion*, 305.
58. Matt Cook, "'Archives of Feeling': The Aids Crisis in Britain 1987," *History Workshop Journal* 83, no. 1 (2017): 51–78.
59. Lynne Segal, *Is the Future Female? Troubled Thoughts on Contemporary Feminism* (London: Virago, 1987); Ann Oakley and Juliet Mitchell, *Who's Afraid of Feminism?: Seeing through the Backlash* (London: Hamish Hamilton, 1997).

60. Julia Sudbury, *Other Kinds of Dreams: Black Women's Organisations and the Politics of Transformation* (London: Routledge, 1998), 192–93.
61. Thomas Foster, Carol Siegel, and Ellen Berry, eds., *The Gay '90s: Disciplinary and Interdisciplinary Formations in Queer Studies* (New York: New York University Press, 1997).
62. Pratibha Parmar, "The Past before Us: Twenty Years of Feminism," *Feminist Review* 31 (1989): 108.
63. Gayatri Chakravorty Spivak, "Can the Subaltern Speak?," in *Marxism and the Interpretation of Culture*, ed. Cary Nelson and Lawrence Grossberg (Urbana: University of Illinois Press, 1988), 271–316.
64. Sherna Berger Gluck and Daphne Patai, *Women's Words: The Feminist Practice of Oral History* (New York: Routledge, 1991), 9.
65. Jacques Derrida, *The Post-Card: From Socrates to Freud and Beyond*, trans. Alan Bass (Chicago: University of Chicago Press, 1980), 472.
66. Laura Mulvey, "Afterthoughts on 'Visual Pleasure and Narrative Cinema' Inspired by *Duel in the Sun*," in *Feminism and Film Theory*, ed. Constance Penley (New York: Routledge, 1988), 57–68.
67. Grace Lau, *S&A*, C1420/60, transcript p. 66, track 02.
68. Mercer, *Welcome to the Jungle*.
69. Natasha Walters, *The New Feminism* (London: Virago, 1999).
70. Jim Wild, ed., *Working with Men for Change* (London: Taylor and Francis, 1999).
71. Daniel Cohen, *Unbecoming Men*, C1667/04, transcript p. 16, track 01.
72. "Crime Survey for England and Wales, 2017/18," Office for National Statistics, accessed June 6, 2019, https://www.ons.gov.uk/peoplepopulationandcommunity/crimeandjustice/articles/domesticabusefindingsfromthecrimesurveyforenglandandwales/yearendingmarch2018.
73. Finn Mackay, *Radical Feminism: Feminist Activism in Movement* (London: Palgrave, 2015), 52–53.
74. Jalna Hanmer, *S&A*, C1420/04, transcript p. 97, track 03; Jalna Hanmer and Sheila Saunders, *Well-Founded Fear: A Community Study of Violence to Women* (London: Hutchinson in association with Explorations in Feminism Collective affiliated to the Women's Research and Resources Centre, 1984).
75. Pragna Patel, *S&A*, C1420/18, transcript p. 82, track 04; Pragna Patel, "Flying by the Nets of Racism, Patriarchy and Religion," in *Women against Fundamentalism: Stories of Dissent and Solidarity*, ed. Sukhwant Dhaliwal and Nira Yuval-Davis (London: Lawrence and Wishart, 2015), 58–59.
76. Vera Baird, *S&A*, C1420/51, transcript p. 66, track 02.
77. Harman, *A Woman's Work*, 244–49.
78. Women Overcoming Violence and Abuse, "Abstracts" (International Conference on Violence, Abuse and Women's Citizenship, Brighton, November 10–15, 1996).
79. Gillian Whitlock, *Postcolonial Life Narratives: Testimonial Transactions* (Oxford: Oxford University Press, 2015), 13.

80. Commission on the Status of Women, "Report of the Fourth World Conference on Women: Beijing, September 4–15, 1995" (New York: United Nations, 1996), 208. These were also fed by the first clear international legal mandate for gender equality, the adoption by the United Nations of the Convention on the Elimination of All Forms of Discrimination Against Women (CEDAW), also in 1979.
81. Beatrix Campbell, *S&A*, C1420/01, transcript p. 81, track 04.
82. Anna Reading, *Gender and Memory in the Globital Age* (Basingstoke, UK: Palgrave Macmillan, 2016).
83. Marianne Hirsch, *Family Frames: Photography, Narrative, and Postmemory* (Cambridge, MA: Harvard University Press, 1997).
84. Jennifer Helgren, "A 'Very Innocent Time': Oral History Narratives, Nostalgia and Girls' Safety in the 1950s and 1960s," *Oral History Review* 42, no. 1 (2015): 50–69.
85. Mackay, *Radical Feminism*, 20.
86. Ratna Kapur, "In the Aftermath of Critique We Are Not in Epistemic Free Fall: Human Rights, the Subaltern Subject, and Non-Liberal Search for Freedom and Happiness," *Law and Critique* 25, no. 1 (2014): 25–45.
87. I have not given citations to these to avoid undue focus on these parts of whole life transcripts, but all are available in the *S&A* collection.
88. Jenni Murray, *S&A*, C1420/48, transcript p. 46, track 03.
89. Jan McKenley, *S&A*, C1420/15, transcript p. 40, track 01.
90. Marie-Thérèse McGivern, *S&A*, C1420/46, transcript pp. 77–78, track 03.
91. Jeff Hearn, *Unbecoming Men*, C1667/07, transcript p. 34, track 02.
92. Ibid., p. 35, track 02.
93. Ibid., p. 40, track 02.
94. Five Cram and Peter Goodridge, *Unbecoming Men*, C1667/30, transcript p. 12, track 01. Pete 6 was named thus to distinguish himself from the other men called Pete in the men's group and Five to find some identity, with a gender-neutral name, as an unconfident, shy man. Sadly, Peter Goodridge died in 2017.
95. Segal, *Slow Motion*, 186, 246.
96. Ibid., 252.
97. Lynne Segal, *S&A*, C1420/28, transcript p. 95, track 03.
98. Ibid.
99. Adrian Bingham, Lucy Delap, Louise Jackson, and Louise Settle, "Historical Child Sexual Abuse in England and Wales: The Role of Historians," *History of Education* 45, no. 4 (2016): 411–29.
100. Eileen Maitland, "Woman to Woman: An Oral History of Rape Crisis in Scotland 1976–1991" (Glasgow: Rape Crisis Scotland, 2009), accessed September 8, 2017, https://www.rapecrisisscotland.org.uk/resources/Woman-to-Woman.pdf.
101. Elizabeth Butler-Sloss, "Summary of the Cleveland Inquiry," *British Medical Journal* 297, no. 6642 (1988): 191.

102. Joni Lovenduski and Vicky Randall, *Contemporary Feminist Politics: Women and Power in Britain* (Oxford: Oxford University Press, 1993), 263.
103. Anne Seymour, "Aetiology of the Sexual Abuse of Children: An Extended Feminist Perspective," *Women's Studies International Forum* 21, no. 4 (1998): 415–427.
104. Beatrix Campbell, *Unofficial Secrets: Child Sexual Abuse: The Cleveland Case*, 2nd ed. (London: Virago, 1997).
105. Gisli H. Gudjonsson, "Accusations by Adults of Childhood Sexual Abuse: A Survey of the Members of the British False Memory Society," *Applied Cognitive Psychology* 11, no. 1 (1997): 3–18.
106. Cited in Segal, *Slow Motion*, 53.
107. Beatrix Campbell, S&A, C1420/01, transcript p. 139, track 06.
108. Ellen Bass and Laura Davis, *The Courage to Heal* (New York: Harper & Row, 1988); Elizabeth F. Loftus, "The Reality of Repressed Memories," *American Psychologist* 48, no. 5 (1993): 518–37.
109. Janice Haaken, *Pillar of Salt: Gender, Memory, and the Perils of Looking Back* (London: Free Association Books, 1998).
110. Lovenduski and Randall, *Contemporary Feminist Politics*, 299–300.
111. Ibid., 260.
112. Ibid., 268–69.
113. Jeff Hearn, "It's Time for Men to Change," in *Working with Men for Change*, ed. Jim Wild (London: Taylor and Francis, 1999), 7.
114. Mavis Best, interviewed for *Oral Histories of the Black Women's Movement: The Heart of the Race* by Ego Ahiame, 2008–10, Black Cultural Archives, London, catalogue reference ORAL/1/BWM 32, copyright BCA. However, some knew her at the time as Mavis Clarke.
115. Roger Hewitt, *White Backlash and the Politics of Multiculturalism* (Cambridge: Cambridge University Press, 2005).
116. Pat Thane, *Happy Families? History and Family Policy* (London: British Academy Policy Centre, 2010).
117. S&A interview, anonymized by agreement.
118. Power, *No Bath but Plenty of Bubbles*.
119. Delap, "Feminism, Masculinities and Emotional Politics."
120. Harriet Harman, *Twentieth-Century Man, 21st-Century Woman: How Both Sexes Can Bridge the Century Gap* (London: Vermilion, 1993); Harman, *A Woman's Work*, 291.
121. Among the S&A interviewees, this included Karen McMinn, Bronagh Hinds, Cynthia Cockburn, and Stella Dadzie.
122. Lynn Abrams, *Oral History Theory* (London: Routledge, 2010), 187.
123. See also Delap, "Feminism, Masculinities and Emotional Politics."
124. Paul Morrison, *Unbecoming Men*, C1667/15, transcript p. 9, track 01.
125. Berenice Fisher, "Guilt and Shame in the Women's Movement: The Radical Ideal of Action and Its Meaning for Feminist Intellectuals," *Feminist Studies* 10, no. 2 (1984): 185–212.

126. Rowbotham, *Promise of a Dream*, 177.
127. Zoe Strimpel, "Heterosexual Love in the British Women's Liberation Movement: Reflections from the Sisterhood and After Archive," *Women's History Review* 25, no. 6 (2016): 903–24.
128. Thomlinson, *Race, Ethnicity and the Women's Movement in England*, 40–41.
129. Amrit Wilson, *S&A*, C1420/19, transcript pp. 92–93, track 04.
130. Sarita Srivastava, "'You're Calling Me a Racist?': The Moral and Emotional Regulation of Antiracism and Feminism," *Signs* 31, no. 1 (2005): 29–62.
131. Ursula Owen, *S&A*, C1420/36, transcript p. 117, track 04.
132. Amrit Wilson, *S&A*, C1420/19, transcript pp. 103–104, track 04.
133. Thomlinson, *Race, Ethnicity and the Women's Movement in England*, 82–84.
134. Amrit Wilson, *S&A*, C1420/19, transcript pp. 99–100, track 04.
135. Thomlinson, *Race, Ethnicity and the Women's Movement in England*, 146–50.
136. Beatrix Campbell, *S&A*, C1420/01, transcript p. 96, track 05.
137. Barbara Taylor, *S&A*, C1420/38, transcript p. 193, track 07.
138. Barbara Taylor, *S&A*, C1420/38, transcript p. 149, track 06.
139. Thomlinson, *Race, Ethnicity and the Women's Movement in England*, 175 and 199.
140. Colin Thomas, *Unbecoming Men*, C1667/25, transcript p. 13, track 01.
141. Jeska Rees, "'Are You a Lesbian?' Challenges in Recording and Analysing the Women's Liberation Movement in England," *History Workshop Journal* 69, no. 1 (2010): 177–87.
142. Rachel Beth Cohen, "Researching Difference and Diversity within Women's Movements: Sisterhood and After," *Women's Studies International Forum* 35, no. 3 (2012): 138–40.
143. Rita Felski, "The Doxa of Difference," *Signs* 23, no. 1 (1997): 1–70.
144. Alison Phipps, *The Politics of the Body: Gender in a Neoliberal and Neoconservative Age* (Cambridge: Polity, 2014).
145. "National Opinion Survey," *Guardian*, October 6, 2016.
146. Sam Carroll, ed., *Brighton Trans*formed* (Brighton: QueenSpark Books, 2014), 36.
147. Ibid., 66.
148. Angela Phillips and Jill Rakusen, *Our Bodies, Ourselves: A Health Book by and for Women* (London: Penguin Allen Lane, 1978).
149. Carroll, *Brighton Trans*formed*, 17. See also Susan Stryker and Stephen Whittle, *The Transgender Studies Reader* (London: Routledge, 2006).
150. Mackay, *Radical Feminism*, 250.
151. Jacqueline Rose, "Who Do You Think You Are?," *London Review of Books* 38, no. 9 (2016): 3–13; 9.
152. Ibid.
153. Sarah Lamble, "Retelling Racialized Violence, Remaking White Innocence: The Politics of Interlocking Oppressions in Transgender Day of Remembrance," *Sexuality Research & Social Policy* 5, no. 1 (2008): 24–42.

154. Power, *No Bath but Plenty of Bubbles*, 244–45, 52–53; Roz Kaveney, *Tiny Pieces of Skull: Or, a Lesson in Manners* (London: Team Angelica Publishing, 2015); Stephen Whittle, "Where Did We Go Wrong? Feminism and Trans Theory—Two Teams on the Same Side?," in *The Transgender Studies Reader*, ed. Susan Stryker and Stephen Whittle (New York: Taylor and Francis, 2006), 194–202.

155. Excerpts from Catherine Hall, *S&A*, C1420/54 and Stuart Hall, *Pioneers of Qualitative Research*, C1416/42, both at the British Library.

156. Subsequent to the interview, Catherine discovered that her father was adopted by the parents of his supposed stepsister, who was in fact his mother. Personal communication to the author, November 14, 2017.

157. Stuart Hall was interviewed by Paul Thompson at his home in West Hampstead, London, and Thompson's home in Wivenhoe, Essex, in spring 2012. Stuart Hall died on February 10, 2014. Catherine Hall was interviewed by Rachel Cohen in the British Library in spring 2012. Her most recent project is "The Structure and Significance of British-Caribbean Slave-Ownership, 1763–1833" (2013–16), funded by the Economic and Social Research Council and the Arts and Humanities Research Council.

CHAPTER 7

1. Slogans as cited in Jill Tweedie, "Women March for Liberation in London," *Guardian*, March 8, 1971.
2. Ibid.
3. "The Nightcleaners: Transcripts," The Women's Library @ LSE, 7SHR/D/02; Sheila Rowbotham, "Jolting Memory: Nightcleaners Recalled," in *Plan Rosebud: On Images, Sites and Politics of Memory*, ed. Maria Ruido (Santiago de Compostela, Spain: CGAC, 2009), 9.
4. Lynne Segal, *Making Trouble: Life and Politics* (London: Serpent's Tail, 2007), 70–71.
5. Anna Coote, "'I'm Just a Speaker. I've Spoke to Thousands. I'm Glad I'm No Cleaner No More, It's Bleedin' 'Ard Work,'" in *Women of the Revolution: Forty Years of Feminism*, ed. Kira Cochrane (London: Guardian Books, 2010), 16–20.
6. Jean Mormont, in *Dutiful Daughters: Women Talk About Their Lives*, ed. Jean McCrindle and Sheila Rowbotham (London: Allen Lane, 1977), 139–56.
7. Susan Varga, "Twice the Man," *Sydney Morning Herald*, August 9, 2003.
8. Germaine Greer, *White Beech: The Rainforest Years* (London: Bloomsbury, 2013).
9. Audrey Jones, a founder of the Wales Assembly for Women who died in 2014, aged eighty-four, fell ill returning from preparing for a United Nations Committee on the Elimination of Discrimination against Women (CEDAW) conference. Jean Silvan Evans, "Audrey Jones," *Welsh Dictionary of National Biography*, 2017, unpaginated. I also want to acknowledge the death of John Petherbridge in 2014, whose oral history is discussed in chap. 6.

10. Sheila Rowbotham, *S&A*, C1420/10, transcript p. 137, track 5.
11. Zoë Fairbairns, *S&A*, C1420/24, transcript p. 8, track 1.
12. Rowena Arshad, *S&A*, C1420/21, transcript pp. 126–27, track 3.
13. Jan McKenley, *S&A*, C1420/60, transcript p. 164, track 6.
14. Valerie Wise, *S&A*, C1420/31; Amrit Wilson, *S&A*, C1420/19; Barbara Taylor, *S&A*, C1420/38; Beatrix Campbell, *S&A*, C1420/60.
15. Marco G. Giugni, "Personal and Biographical Consequences," in *The Blackwell Companion to Social Movements*, ed. David A. Snow, Sarah Anne Soule, and Hanspeter Kriesi (Oxford: Blackwell, 2004), 494.
16. Una Kroll, *S&A*, C1420/49, transcript p. 169, track 5.
17. Jo Robinson, *S&A*, C1420/43, transcript p. 71, track 5.
18. Giugni, "Personal and Biographical Consequences," 489.
19. Martin Pugh, *Women and the Women's Movement in Britain, 1914–1999* (New York: St. Martin's Press, 2000).
20. Deirdre Beddoe, *S&A*, C1420/23.
21. Rosalind Delmar, *S&A*, C1420/03, transcript p. 150, track 5.
22. Fiona Mackay, "The State of Women's Movement/s in Britain: Ambiguity, Complexity and Challenges from the Periphery," in *Women's Movements: Flourishing or in Abeyance*, ed. Sandra Grey and Marian Sawer (New York: Routledge, 2008); Harriet Harman, *A Woman's Work* (Milton Keynes, UK: Allen Lane, 2017), 138–46.
23. Rob Davies, "Number of Women in UK Boardrooms Still Low," *Guardian*, July 7, 2016.
24. Stella Dadzie, *S&A*, C1420/20, transcript p. 93, track 5.
25. Sheryl Sandberg and Nell Scovell, *Lean In: Women, Work, and the Will to Lead* (New York: W. H. Allen, 2013).
26. "Statistical Bulletin: Births in England and Wales, 2013," Office for National Statistics, published July 16, 2014, http://www.ons.gov.uk/ons/dcp171778_371129.pdf; Pat Thane, *Happy Families? History and Family Policy* (London: British Academy Policy Centre, 2010), 24.
27. Sue Allen and Lynne Harne, "Lesbian Mothers: The Fight for Child Custody," in *Radical Records: Thirty Years of Lesbian and Gay History, 1957–1987*, ed. Bob Cant and Susan Hemmings (London: Routledge, 2010), 181–94.
28. "Statistical Bulletin: Births in England and Wales, 2013."
29. Angela Davis, *Modern Motherhood: Women and Family in England, c. 1945–2000* (Manchester: Manchester University Press, 2012).
30. Doug McAdam, "The Biographical Impact of Activism," in *How Social Movements Matter*, ed. Marco Giugni, Doug McAdam, and Charles Tilly (Minneapolis: University of Minnesota Press, 1999).
31. Olive Banks, *Becoming a Feminist: The Social Origins of "First Wave" Feminism* (Brighton, UK: Wheatsheaf, 1986); Brian Harrison, *Prudent Revolutionaries: Portraits of British Feminists between the Wars* (Oxford: Clarendon Press, 1987).

32. Jane Traies's study of older lesbians reveals that at least half came out explicitly because they discovered feminism after its revival in the 1960s: *Lives of Older Lesbians: Sexuality, Identity & the Life Course* (London: Palgrave Macmillan, 2016).
33. Segal, *Making Trouble*, chap. 6.
34. Sheila Rowbotham, *Promise of a Dream: Remembering the Sixties* (London: Verso, 2001), 131.
35. Angela Phillips and Jill Rakusen, *The New Our Bodies, Ourselves* (London: Penguin, 1996).
36. Robert Anton Wilson, *Feminine Forever* (London: W. H. Allen, 1966).
37. Jenni Murray, *Is It Me, or Is It Hot in Here?: A Modern Woman's Guide to the Menopause* (London: Vermilion, 2001), 56.
38. Barbara Taylor, *The Last Asylum: A Memoir of Madness in Our Times* (London: Hamish Hamilton, 2014).
39. Pearlie McNeill, Maria McShea, and Pratibha Parmar, *Through the Break: Women and Personal Crisis* (London: Sheba, 1986).
40. Catherine Corrigall-Brown, *Patterns of Protest: Trajectories of Participation in Social Movements* (Stanford, CA: Stanford University Press, 2012).
41. Eva Illouz, *Cold Intimacies: The Making of Emotional Capitalism* (Cambridge: Polity, 2007), 25–30.
42. Daniel Kahneman and Angus Deaton, "High Income Improves Evaluation of Life but Not Emotional Well-Being," *Proceedings of the National Academy of Sciences USA* 107, no. 38 (2010): 16,489–493.
43. Betsey Stevenson and Justin Wolfers, "The Paradox of Declining Female Happiness," *American Economic Journal: Economic Policy* 1, no. 2 (2009): 190–225.
44. Sara Ahmed, *The Promise of Happiness* (Durham, NC: Duke University Press, 2010), 5, 45, 78–80, 219–20; Lynne Segal, *Radical Happiness: Moments of Collective Joy* (London: Verso, 2017).
45. Segal, *Radical Happiness*.
46. Cited in Joni Lovenduski and Vicky Randall, *Contemporary Feminist Politics: Women and Power in Britain* (Oxford: Oxford University Press, 1993), 24.
47. Sheila Rowbotham, *The Past Is before Us: Feminism in Action since the 1960s* (London; Boston: Pandora, 1989), 7.
48. Nadira Mirza, *S&A*, C1420/17, follow-up interview, May 13, 2017; transcript pp. 51–52, track 01.
49. Michele Ryan, *S&A*, C1420/35, transcript p. 76, track 3.
50. Lynn Jamieson, "Intimacy Transformed? A Critical Look at the 'Pure Relationship,'" *Sociology* 33, no. 3 (1999), 477–94; Morwenna Griffiths, "Feminism, Feelings and Philosophy," in *Feminist Perspectives in Philosophy*, ed. Morwenna Griffiths and Margaret Whitford (Basingstoke, UK: Macmillan, 1988), 131–51.
51. Michelene Wandor, *S&A*, C1420/09, transcript p. 132, track 5.
52. Catherine Hall, *S&A*, C1420/54, transcript p. 88, track 3.
53. Finn Mackay, *Radical Feminism: Feminist Activism in Movement* (London: Palgrave, 2015), 269.

54. Ibid.
55. Natasha Walters, *The New Feminism* (London: Virago, 1999).
56. Jan McKenley, *Seven Black Men: An Ecological Study of Education and Parenting* (Bristol: Aduma, 2006).
57. Lovenduski and Randall, *Contemporary Feminist Politics*, 364.
58. Ahmed, *The Promise of Happiness*, 196.
59. Ibid., 214.
60. Mukami McCrum, *S&A*, C1420/39, transcript pp. 23–24, track 1.
61. Ibid.
62. Rosalind Delmar, *S&A*, C1420/03, transcript p. 65, track 3.
63. The word in fact was "boundaries." Gail Chester, *S&A*, C1420/27, transcript p. 206, track 4.
64. "The Pre-Madonnas," the Women's Liberation Music Archive, accessed October 12, 2017, https://womensliberationmusicarchive.co.uk/p/.
65. Kirsten Hearn, *S&A*, C1420/44, transcript p. 95, track 3.
66. Sandie Wyles, *S&A*, C1420/22, transcript p. 88, track 5.
67. Cynthia Cockburn, *S&A*, C1420/42, transcript p. 191, track 7.
68. Five Cram and Peter Goodridge [Pete 6], *Unbecoming Men*, C1667/30, transcript p. 64, track 2.
69. Jeff Goodwin, James M. Jasper, and Francesca Polletta, "Emotional Dimensions of Social Movements," in *The Blackwell Companion to Social Movements*, ed. David A. Snow, Sarah Anne Soule, and Hanspeter Kriesi (Oxford: Blackwell, 2004), 413–32.
70. Jocelyn Wolfe, *S&A*, C1420/12, transcript p. 111, track 3.
71. Johanna Siméant and Christophe Traini, *Bodies in Protest: Hunger Strikes and Angry Music* (Amsterdam: Amsterdam University Press, 2016).
72. Eileen M. Hayes, *Songs in Black and Lavender: Race, Sexual Politics, and Women's Music* (Urbana: University of Illinois Press, 2010).
73. Paul Gilroy, *The Black Atlantic: Modernity and Double Consciousness* (London: Verso, 1993), 75.
74. Jaclyn J. Gier Viskovatoff and Abigail Porter, "Women of the British Coalfields on Strike in 1926 and 1984: Documenting Lives Using Oral History and Photography," in *Women's Oral History: The Frontiers Reader*, ed. Susan Armitage, Patricia Hart, and Karen Weathermon (Lincoln: University of Nebraska Press, 2003), 367.
75. Mia Morris, *S&A*, C1420/08, transcript p. 82, track 4.
76. Donna Pieters, interviewed for Oral Histories of the Black Women's Movement: The Heart of the Race, 2008–2010, Black Cultural Archives, London, ORAL/1/BWM 30.
77. D-M (formerly Deborah M.) Withers, *Feminism, Digital Culture and the Politics of Transmission: Theory, Practice and Cultural Heritage* (London: Rowman & Littlefield, 2015), 108.
78. Ibid.
79. Quoted in ibid., 108.

80. Marion Fudger, "Frankie Armstrong," *Spare Rib* 33 (March 1975): 44–45.
81. Michelene Wandor, *S&A*, C1420/09, transcript p. 133, track 5.
82. Withers, *Feminism, Digital Culture and the Politics of Transmission*, 38, 96.
83. Alison Raynor, *S&A*, C1420/47, transcript pp. 95–96, track 4.
84. Emma Goldman, *Living My Life: Autobiographical Reminiscences* (New York: Knopf, 1931), 56.
85. Gail Chester, *S&A*, C1420/27, transcript p. 212, track 4.
86. David Widgery, *Beating Time* (London: Chatto & Windus, 1986), 134; Natalie Thomlinson, *Race, Ethnicity and the Women's Movement in England, 1968–1993* (Houndsmills, UK: Palgrave, 2016).
87. Thomlinson, *Race, Ethnicity and the Women's Movement in England*, 132.
88. Nicola Streeten Plowman, "A Cultural History of Feminist Cartoons and Comics in Britain from 1970 to 2010" (PhD thesis, University of Sussex, 2017).
89. Jan McKenley, *S&A*, C1420/60, transcript p. 88, track 3.
90. Sasha Roseneil, *Common Women, Uncommon Practices: The Queer Feminisms of Greenham* (London: Cassell, 2000), 31.
91. Elaine Titcombe, "Women Activists: Rewriting Greenham's History," *Women's History Review* 22, no. 2 (2013): 310–29.
92. Roseneil, *Common Women, Uncommon Practices*, 86–87.
93. "Greenham Common Women's Peace Camp Songbook," Antiwar Songs, accessed October 12, 2017, https://www.antiwarsongs.org/canzone.php?lang=en&id=6934.
94. "Lyr Req: You Can't Kill the Spirit (Naomi Morena): 03 Dec 12," The Mudcat Café, accessed October 12, 2017, http://mudcat.org/thread.cfm?threadid=90948.
95. Rebecca Johnson, *S&A*, C1420/34, transcript p. 183, track 8.
96. Ibid., p. 274, track 11.
97. Annie Tunicliffe, "Greenham Common Women Camp On," *Spare Rib* 33 (March 1982): 16.
98. Rebecca Johnson, *S&A*, C1420/34, transcript p. 175, track 8.
99. Margaret Morganroth Gullette, *Aged by Culture* (Chicago: University of Chicago Press, 2004).
100. Mary McIntosh, *S&A*, C1420/11, transcript pp. 139–40, track 6.
101. Jill Roe, "Mary McIntosh (1936–2013)," *Australian Feminist Studies* 28, no. 77 (2013): 245–46; Jeffrey Weeks, "Obituary," *Sexualities* 16, no. 5–6 (2013): 743–46.
102. Belinda Phipps and Gillian Fletcher, "The Potential of Service User Groups to Support Evidence-Based Midwifery," in *Evidence-Based Midwifery: Applications in Context*, ed. Helen Spiby and Jane Munro (Oxford: Wiley-Blackwell, 2010), 154.
103. Sheila Kitzinger, *S&A*, C1420/58, transcript pp. 36–37, track 1.
104. Ibid., p. 18.
105. Phillips and Rakusen, *The New Our Bodies, Ourselves*, 466.

106. Jo Spence, *Putting Myself in the Picture: A Political, Personal and Photographic Autobiography* (London: Camden Press, 1986).
107. Esther Green, Sue Krzowski, and Sheila Ernst, "Dealing with Dying," *Spare Rib* 141 (April 1984): 6–8.
108. Lynne Segal, *Out of Time: The Pleasures and Perils of Ageing* (London: Verso, 2013), 93.
109. Ibid., 260.
110. Caroline Lodge, Eileen Carnell, and Marianne Coleman, *The New Age of Ageing: How Society Needs to Change* (Bristol: Policy Press, 2016), 154. "Life Expectancy," *Woman's Hour*, BBC Radio 4, April 8, 2015, http://www.bbc.co.uk/programmes/b05pntyq.
111. Sue Westwood, "Complicating Kinship and Inheritance: Older Lesbians' and Gay Men's Will-Writing in England," *Feminist Legal Studies* 23, no. 2 (2015): 181–97.
112. "Making a Will: Sharp Rise for Intestate Queries," May 19, 2016, *BBC News*, http://www.bbc.co.uk/news/uk-36325871.
113. Lodge, Carnell, and Coleman, *The New Age of Ageing: How Society Needs to Change*, 68, 201.
114. Celia and Jenny Kitzinger, "How to Plan for a Good Death," *Guardian*, June, 19, 2015, unpaginated. https://www.theguardian.com/lifeandstyle/2015/jun/19/how-to-plan-for-a-good-death-sheila-kitzinger. Kitzinger's death is also described by daughters Jenny and Celia on *Woman's Hour*, BBC Radio 4, May 7, 2015.
115. Una Kroll, *S&A*, C1420/49, transcript pp. 158–59, track 5.
116. Elizabeth D. Hutchison, "Spirituality, Religion, and Progressive Social Movements: Resources and Motivation for Social Change," *Journal of Religion & Spirituality in Social Work* 31, no. 1–2 (2012): 105–27.
117. Sally Munt, "Queer Spiritual Spaces," in *Queer Spiritual Spaces: Sexuality and Sacred Places*, ed. Kath Browne, Sally Munt, and Andrew K. T. Yip (Farnham, UK: Ashgate, 2010), 13.
118. Mukami McCrum, *S&A*, C1420/39, transcript p. 27, track 1.
119. Ibid., p. 30.
120. José Casanova, *Public Religions in the Modern World* (Chicago: University of Chicago, 1994).
121. Yasmin Alibhai-Brown, "Secularism: What Does It Mean to You?," *Guardian*, November 26, 2013.
122. Sukhwant Dhaliwal and Nira Yuval-Davis, "Introduction," in *Women against Fundamentalism: Stories of Dissent and Solidarity*, ed. Sukhwant Dhaliwal and Nira Yuval-Davis (London: Lawrence and Wishart, 2015), 7–51.
123. Pragna Patel, *S&A*, C1420/18, transcript p. 107, track 5.
124. Nadira Mirza, *S&A*, C1420/39, transcript p. 59, track 1, follow-up interview, May 13, 2017.

125. Ibid., p. 106, track 4.
126. Ibid., p. 21, track 1.
127. Ibid., p. 56, track 3.
128. Ibid., pp. 38–40, track 1; Pratibha Parmar and Nadira Mirza, "Growing Angry, Growing Strong," *Spare Rib*, no. 111 (1981), 18–21; Pratibha Parmar, "Gender, Race and Power: The Challenge to Youth Work Practice," in *Multi-Racist Britain: New Directions in Theory and Practice*, ed. Philip Cohen and Harwant S. Bains (Basingstoke, UK: Macmillan, 1988).
129. Bridget Lockyer, "An Irregular Period? Participation in the Bradford Women's Liberation Movement," *Women's History Review* 22, no. 4 (2013): 643–57.
130. Nadira Mirza, *S&A*, C1420/39, transcript pp. 77–78, track 4.
131. Ziba Mir-Hosseini, accessed October 12, 2017, www.zibamirhosseini.com.
132. Ziba Mir-Hosseini, "Towards Gender Equality: Muslim Family Laws and the Shari'a," in *Wanted: Equality and Justice in the Muslim Family*, ed. Zainah Anwar (Kuala Lumpur: Musawah, An Initiative of Sisters of Islam, 2009).
133. WISE is a programme of the American Society for Muslim Advancement.
134. Haleh Afshar, "Khomeini's Teachings and Their Implications for Women," *Feminist Review*, no. 12 (1982): 59–72.
135. Mir-Hosseini, "Towards Gender Equality."
136. Haideh Moghissi, *Muslim Diaspora: Gender, Culture, and Identity* (New York: Routledge, 2006).
137. Nadira Mirza, *S&A*, C1420/39, transcript p. 89, track 4.
138. Ibid., pp. 99–100, track 4.
139. Ibid., p. 74, track 1, follow-up interview, May 13, 2017.
140. Dhaliwal and Yuval-Davis, "Introduction."
141. Nadira Mirza, *S&A*, C1420/39, transcript p. 89, track 4.
142. Ibid., pp. 99–100, track 4.
143. Ibid., p. 64, track 2, follow-up interview, May 13, 2017.
144. Ibid., p. 82, track 4.
145. Ibid., p. 76, track 2, follow-up interview, May 13, 2017.
146. Ibid., p. 76, track 2.
147. Ibid., p. 107, track 4.
148. Zoë Fairbairns, "Saying What We Want: Women's Demands in the Seventies and Now," in *The Feminist Seventies*, ed. Helen Graham, Ann Kaloski, Ali Neilson, and Emma Robertson (York: Raw Nerve Books, 2002), 95.
149. Paul Bagguley, "Contemporary British Feminism: A Social Movement in Abeyance?," *Social Movement Studies* 1, no. 2 (2002): 169–85.

CONCLUSION

1. Brian Harrison, James McMillan, and Patricia Hilden, "Some Feminist Betrayals of Women's History," *Historical Journal* 26, no. 2 (1983): 375–89.

2. Leila J. Rupp and Verta A. Taylor, *Survival in the Doldrums: The American Women's Rights Movement, 1945 to the 1960s* (New York: Oxford University Press, 1987).
3. Zoë Fairbairns, "Five Decades, Five Feminisms: The Sue Innes Memorial Lecture 2016," presentation at *Feminisms: Histories, Ideas & Practice* (Glasgow: Women's History Scotland, 2016).
4. Clare Hemmings, *Why Stories Matter: The Political Grammar of Feminist Theory* (Durham, NC: Duke University Press, 2011).
5. Judith Halberstam, *In a Queer Time and Place: Transgender Bodies, Subcultural Lives* (New York: New York University Press, 2005).
6. Candis Steenbergen, "Passing on Feminism" (PhD thesis, Concordia University, 2009).
7. Sally Alexander, "Feminism: History: Repetition, Some Notes and Queries," in *Becoming a Woman: And Other Essays in 19th- and 20th-Century Feminist History* (London: Virago, 1994), 243–47.
8. Ann Cvetkovich, *An Archive of Feelings: Trauma, Sexuality, and Lesbian Public Cultures* (Durham, NC: Duke University Press, 2003), 235.
9. Sally Alexander, *S&A*, C1420/45, transcript pp. 75–76, track 02.
10. Rosalind Delmar, *S&A*, C1420/03, transcript pp. 150–51, track 05.
11. Barbara Caine, *English Feminism 1780–1980* (Oxford: Oxford University Press, 1997), 238–39.
12. Midge Mackenzie, *Shoulder to Shoulder: A Documentary* (London: Allen Lane, 1975).
13. Margaret Drabble et al., "Shoulder to Shoulder: A *Radio Times* Special," *Radio Times*, August 29, 1974.
14. Jenni Murray, *S&A*, C1420/48, transcript pp. 71–72, track 03.
15. Bronagh Hinds, *S&A*, C1420/50, transcript pp. 85–86, track 02.
16. Pragna Patel, *S&A*, C1420/18, transcript p. 138, track 06.
17. Sheila Rowbotham, *S&A*, C1420/10, transcript p. 110, track 03.
18. Andrew Pulver, "Meryl Streep Defends Feminist Credentials as Suffragette Opens London Film Festival," *Guardian*, October 7, 2015.
19. Anita Anand, *Sophia: Princess, Suffragette, Revolutionary* (London: Bloomsbury, 2015).
20. Mary Kelly, *S&A*, C1420/58, transcript p. 83, track 02.
21. Ibid., p. 74, track 02.
22. Barbara Taylor, *S&A*, C1420/38, transcript p. 205, track 08.
23. "Vocal Fry + Speech Patterns in Young Women," *Woman's Hour*, BBC Radio 4, July 31, 2015.
24. Ken Cormier, "Writing the Tape-Recorded Life," *a/b: Auto/Biography Studies* 27, no. 2 (2012): 423.
25. Alison Marchant, "Treading the Traces of Discarded History: Oral History Installations," in *Women's Oral History: The Frontiers Reader*, ed. Susan Armitage, Patricia Hart, and Karen Weathermon (Lincoln: University of Nebraska Press, 2003).

26. Cathy Lane, "Voices from the Past: Compositional Approaches to Using Recorded Speech," *Organised Sound* 11, no. 1 (2006): 3–11.
27. Suzanne Lacy, Moira Roth, and Kerstin Mey, *Leaving Art: Writings on Performance, Politics, and Publics, 1974–2007* (Durham, NC: Duke University Press, 2010), xxviii–xxx.
28. "Silver Action (2013)," *Suzanne Lacy*, accessed October 9, 2017, http://www.suzannelacy.com/silver-action-2013/
29. Sundari Anitha and Ruth Pearson, "Striking Women—Striking Out," *Feminist Review*, no. 108 (2014): 61–70. See also *Striking Women*, accessed October 9, 2017, http://www.striking-women.org/.
30. Margaretta Jolly, "Voices in Movement: Feminist Family Stories in Oral History and Sound Art," *Life Writing* 12, no. 2 (2015): 139–59.
31. *Remembering Olive Collective*, accessed October 9, 2017, https://rememberolivemorris.wordpress.com/ and *Women's Liberation Music Archive*, accessed October 9, 2017, https://womensliberationmusicarchive.co.uk/
32. D-M (formerly Deborah M.) Withers, *Feminism, Digital Culture and the Politics of Transmission: Theory, Practice and Cultural Heritage* (London: Rowman & Littlefield, 2015), 123. See also Bonnie J. Morris and D-M Withers, *The Feminist Revolution: The Struggle for Women's Liberation* (London: Virago, 2018).
33. I thank Rob Gallagher at Kings College London for this point.
34. Sheena Malhotra and Aimee Carrillo Rowe, *Silence, Feminism, Power: Reflections at the Edges of Sound* (New York: Palgrave Macmillan, 2013).
35. Nadira Mirza, *S&A*, C1420/39, transcript p. 79, track 1, follow-up interview, May 13, 2017.

SELECTED BIBLIOGRAPHY

ORAL HISTORIES

Sisterhood and After: The Women's Liberation Oral History Project

The project interviewed sixty feminists who had been active in the women's liberation movement in the United Kingdom in the 1970s, 1980s, and 1990s. The collection comprises audio interviews, verbatim transcripts, and ten documentary short films, created from March 2010 to March 2013. Partners in the project were the British Library, the University of Sussex, and the Women's Library. The project was carried out by Margaretta Jolly, Rachel Cohen, and Freya Johnson-Ross from the University of Sussex and Polly Russell at the British Library. The short films were made by filmmaker Lizzie Thynne, supported by Peter Harte. For more information, including links to the interviews and films, see www.bl.uk/sisterhood.

Some interviewees edited their interview transcripts, which are also available alongside the verbatim transcripts. The majority are copyright of the British Library Board and the University of Sussex. All the interviews are catalogued at the British Library under the prefix C1420. Each individual interview is then numbered, as below (name of interviewee, name of interviewer, date of interview):

01 Beatrix Campbell interviewed by Margaretta Jolly, 2010
02 Anna Davin interviewed by Rachel Cohen, 2010
03 Rosalind Delmar interviewed by Rachel Cohen, 2010
04 Jalna Hanmer interviewed by Margaretta Jolly, 2010
05 Mary Kennedy interviewed by Rachel Cohen, 2010
06 Ellen Malos interviewed by Margaretta Jolly, 2010
07 Juliet Mitchell interviewed by Margaretta Jolly, 2010
08 Mia Morris interviewed by Rachel Cohen, 2010
09 Michelene Wandor interviewed by Rachel Cohen, 2010
10 Sheila Rowbotham interviewed by Rachel Cohen, 2010

11 Mary McIntosh interviewed by Margaretta Jolly, 2010
12 Jocelyn Wolfe interviewed by Rachel Cohen, 2011
13 Lesley Abdela interviewed by Margaretta Jolly, 2011
14 Gail Lewis interviewed by Rachel Cohen, 2011
15 Jan McKenley interviewed by Margaretta Jolly, 2011
16 Jenny Lynn interviewed by Rachel Cohen, 2011
17 Nadira Mirza interviewed by Rachel Cohen, 2011 and by Margaretta Jolly, 2017
18 Pragna Patel interviewed by Rachel Cohen, 2011
19 Amrit Wilson interviewed by Margaretta Jolly, 2011
20 Stella Dadzie interviewed by Rachel Cohen, 2011
21 Rowena Arshad interviewed by Rachel Cohen, 2011
22 Sandie Wyles interviewed by Rachel Cohen, 2011
23 Deirdre Beddoe interviewed by Rachel Cohen, 2011
24 Zoë Fairbairns and John Petherbridge interviewed by Margaretta Jolly, 2011
25 Susie Orbach interviewed by Polly Russell, 2011
26 Karen McMinn interviewed by Rachel Cohen, 2011
27 Gail Chester interviewed by Margaretta Jolly, 2011
28 Lynne Segal interviewed by Margaretta Jolly, 2011
29 Sheila Gilmore interviewed by Freya Johnson-Ross, 2011
30 Audrey Jones interviewed by Rachel Cohen, 2011
31 Valerie Wise interviewed by Freya Johnson-Ross, 2011
32 Eileen Evason interviewed by Rachel Cohen, 2011
33 Elizabeth Armstrong interviewed by Margaretta Jolly, 2011
34 Rebecca Johnson interviewed by Margaretta Jolly, 2011
35 Michele Ryan interviewed by Rachel Cohen, 2011
36 Ursula Owen interviewed by Rachel Cohen, 2011
37 Siobhan Molloy interviewed by Rachel Cohen, 2011
38 Barbara Taylor interviewed by Margaretta Jolly, 2011
39 Mukami McCrum interviewed by Freya Johnson-Ross, 2011
40 Sue O'Sullivan interviewed by Rachel Cohen, 2012
41 Jane Hutt interviewed by Margaretta Jolly, 2012
42 Cynthia Cockburn interviewed by Margaretta Jolly, 2012
43 Jo Robinson interviewed by Polly Russell, 2011
44 Kirsten Hearn interviewed by Rachel Cohen, 2012
45 Sally Alexander interviewed by Rachel Cohen, 2012
46 Marie-Thérèse McGivern interviewed by Rachel Cohen, 2012
47 Alison Rayner interviewed by Rachel Cohen, 2012
48 Jenni Murray interviewed by Margaretta Jolly, 2012
49 Una Kroll interviewed by Margaretta Jolly, 2012
50 Bronagh Hinds interviewed by Freya Johnson-Ross, 2012
51 Vera Baird interviewed by Rachel Cohen, 2012
52 Interview by Margaretta Jolly in progress.

53 Barbara Jones interviewed by Margaretta Jolly, 2012
54 Catherine Hall interviewed by Rachel Cohen, 2012
55 Mary Kelly interviewed by Margaretta Jolly, 2012
56 Ann Oakley interviewed by Margaretta Jolly, 2012
57 Sue Lopez interviewed by Margaretta Jolly, 2012
58 Sheila Kitzinger interviewed by Louise Brodie, 2012
59 Betty Cook interviewed by Rachel Cohen, 2012
60 Grace Lau interviewed by Margaretta Jolly, 2012

For information about and links to Lizzie Thynne's Sisterhood and After films go to www.bl.uk/sisterhood/about-the-project. All the films are catalogued at the British Library under the prefix C1420. Each individual film is then numbered, as below (name of interviewee, date of filming):

11/02 Edited video interview with Mary McIntosh, 2011
13/02 Video interview with Lesley Abdela, 2012
15/02 Unedited video interview with Jan McKenley, 2011
15/03 Edited video interview with Jan McKenley, 2011
26/02 Video interview with Karen McMinn, 2012
34/02 Video interview with Rebecca Johnson, 2012
35/02 Video interview with Michele Ryan, 2012
50/02 Video interview with Bronagh Hinds, 2012
53/02 Video interview with Barbara Jones, 2012
61/02 Video interview with Sue Crockford, 2012

Other British Library Collections

The oral history collections at the British Library cover a diverse range of subject areas. For more information go to www.bl.uk/subjects/oral-history. This book has drawn on the following areas within the British Library collection:

C546, The Women's Liberation Movement interviews, 1992–2003: four interviews with activists in the women's movement in Britain and overseas.

C1416/42, Stuart Hall interviewed by Paul Thompson; in Pioneers of Qualitative Research, 2007.

C464/83, Jean McCrindle interviewed by Louise Brodie; in National Life Stories Collection, 2011–12.

C1667, Unbecoming Men: Interviews on Masculinities and the Women's Movement, 1970–91: Thirty-three audio interviews and verbatim transcripts carried out by Dr. Lucy Delap from the University of Cambridge. The project ran from 2012 to 2013 and interviewed men who had been active in antisexist initiatives in the United Kingdom in the 1970s–1990s.

302 • Selected Bibliography

Other Collections

Black Cultural Archives, London: Oral Histories of the Black Women's Movement: The Heart of the Race, 2008–2010, Black Cultural Archives, London ORAL/1/BWM 32. Thirty-six oral history interviews with women involved in the black women's movement of the 1970s–1980s.

Glamorgan Archives, Cardiff and Swansea Civic Centre: Papers of historian Ursula Masson, who, with Deirdre Beddoe, helped found Archif Menywod Cymru/Women's Archive Wales in 1998. The collection (DWAW30) includes oral history recordings.

Glasgow Women's Library: Speaking Out: Recalling Women's Aid in Scotland GB (1534 SWA): Exhibition featuring oral history recordings alongside material from the Scottish Women's Aid archive, curated to mark the fortieth anniversary of Scottish Women's Aid. For more information go to http://womenslibrary.org.uk/?s=Speaking+Out%3A+Recalling+Women%27s+Aid+.

Hull Maritime Museum: *Local Heroes: Hull's Trawlermen*, 2008: Part of a comprehensive collection that explores the history of Hull's fishing industry, and life and work within Hull's fishing community. It also focuses on the impact of the 1968 triple trawler disaster and the subsequent women's action. For more information go to http://www.mylearning.org/local-heroes-hulls-trawlermen/p-/video/1794/.

Imperial War Museum: Greenham Common Women's Peace Camp 1981–2000: The sound archive has been interviewing women since the early 1990s who were living at, or involved with, the Greenham Common Women's Peace Camp, as well as military personnel working inside the base. For more information go to http://www.iwm.org.uk/collections/search?query=Greenham+Common+Women%27s+Peace+Camp&items_per_page=10.

Lambeth Archives: IV/279/2 Do You Remember Olive Morris? Oral History Project, recorded interviews, summary and transcriptions, 2009.

Subverting Stereotypes: Asian Women's Political Activism: A Comparison of the Grunwick and Gate Gourmet Disputes: Thirty interviews with Asian women workers involved in workplace struggles during the Grunwick strike of 1976–77 and the Gate Gourmet strike of 2005, undertaken as part of an academic research project based at Leeds and Oxford universities, led by Ruth Pearson, Anitha Sundari, and Linda McDowell and funded by the Arts and Humanities Research Council (AHRC). These interviews are not open to the public at the time of publication of this book, but to see more about the project go to http://www.leeds.ac.uk/strikingwomen/about.

Trades Union Congress (TUC): Voices from the Workplace: A TUC Oral History Project on Equal Pay, 2006: A series of short films about the fight for equal pay produced by Jo Morris, directed by Sarah Boston and Jenny Morgan, with commentaries by Sue Hastings, Mary Davis, Adina Batnitzky, and the Public and Commercial Services Union (PCS) and jointly funded by the TUC, the

Wainwright Trust, and the European Social Fund. To see the films go to http://www.unionhistory.info/equalpay/voices.php.

The films consist of oral history interviews with women and union representatives involved in major equal pay cases, beginning with the 1968 strike by Ford sewing machine operators, accompanied by notes and transcripts. The films were made as part of the learning resource Winning Equal Pay: The Value of Women's Work, a collaboration between London Metropolitan University and the TUC to record the long campaign to achieve equal pay for women.

An additional archive on the national struggle to achieve pay, and holding all the TUC archive currently available for public examination, is located at the Modern Records Centre at the University of Warwick, developed in conjunction with the TUC. The Modern Records Centre is the largest repository of trade union and industrial relations records in the United Kingdom. For more information go to http://mrc-catalogue.warwick.ac.uk/.

University of Bristol Library Special Collections, Bristol: Feminist Archive audio tapes and mini disks DM2123/1/Archive Boxes 79: Personal Histories of Second Wave Feminism Oral History Project (2000–2001) DM2123: Feminist Archive South conducted a series of oral histories with women involved in feminist activism in Bristol in the 1970s and 1980s, with summaries by Viv Honeybourne and Ilona Singer; *Women's Liberation Music Archive 1970s–1990s*, DM2598: The archive was collected by Frankie Green and D-M Withers as the Women's Liberation Music Archive project, 2011. Material relates to bands formed in the 1970s–1980s and is available in various formats: documents and posters, cuttings, printed books, photographs, audio recordings, audiovisual recordings, digitized images/audio/audiovisual held on iPad. For more information go to https://womensliberationmusicarchive.co.uk/.

University of Leeds Special Collections: Oral History Project on the Women's Liberation Movement in Bradford and Leeds 1969–79: Transcripts of two interviews undertaken by Elizabeth Arlege Ross and Miriam Bearse for Feminist Archive North (FAN) 1995–96 for Women in the Women's Liberation Movement in Leeds and Bradford 1969–79. Audio recordings are housed in Box 08. For more information go to https://library.leeds.ac.uk/special-collections-explore?.

The Women's Library @ LSE: Oral Evidence on the Suffragette and Suffragist Movements: the Brian Harrison interviews 1974–1981 (8SUF): The collection consists of 205 interviews available in digital audio file format and one folder of contextual material relating to the interviews, including essays and reports by Brian Harrison. The digital files are copies of the original oral history interview recordings that are held on reel-to-reel cassette; records of the Women's Liberation Movement Research Network 2008–2009 (11TWL/K/01): typescripts of workshops; DVDs of witness workshops on the history of the women's liberation movement in the United Kingdom; one MP3 file of three workshops; and a folder of contextual material relating to the project. For more information go to http://www.lse.ac.uk/Library/Collections/Collection-highlights/The-Womens-Library.

PUBLISHED ORAL HISTORIES

Carroll, Sam, ed. *Brighton Trans*formed*. Brighton: QueenSpark Books, 2014.

Hall Carpenter Archives, and Lesbian Oral History Group, eds. *Inventing Ourselves: Lesbian Life Stories*. London: Routledge, 1989.

Maitland, Eileen. "Woman to Woman: An Oral History of Rape Crisis in Scotland 1976–1991." Glasgow: Rape Crisis Scotland, 2009; available at https://www.rapecrisisscotland.org.uk/resources/Woman-to-Woman.pdf (accessed April 12, 2019).

McCrindle, Jean, and Sheila Rowbotham, eds. *Dutiful Daughters: Women Talk About Their Lives*. London: Allen Lane, 1977.

Power, Lisa. *No Bath but Plenty of Bubbles: An Oral History of the Gay Liberation Front, 1970–1973*. London: Cassell, 1995. (Power contextualizes these in a fantastically thorough narrative.)

Wandor, Michelene, ed. *Once a Feminist: Stories of a Generation*. London: Virago, 1990.

PAPERS

The Women's Library @ LSE, London

Papers of Jessie Stephen (8SUF/B/157).
Records of Women in Media 1971–99 (6WIM).
Records of the Women's Research & Resources Centre 1965–1981 (5WRR).
Records of Sheba Feminist Press 1981–94 (6SFP).

The Black Cultural Archives, London

Papers of Stella Dadzie (DADZIE/).
Papers of Jan McKenley (McKENLEY/).

London Metropolitan University Archives, Trades Union Congress Library Collections

Rights for Women, National Council of Civil Liberties newsletter, 1982–86 (HD 6050).
Women and Manual Trades newsletter, 1980–93 (HD 6050).
Women's charter, Working Women's Charter Campaign, 1975 (HD 6050).

PERIODICALS

FOWAAD (newsletter of the Organisation of Women of Asian and African Descent [OWAAD], 1978–83).
Red Rag (c. 1973–80).
Shrew (1969–78).
Spare Rib (1972–93). See bl.uk/spare-rib.

Trouble & Strife (1983–2001).
WIRES (Women's Information and Referral Service, 1975–84)
Women's Liberation Workshop Newsletter (1970–75).

PUBLISHED TEXTS

Ahmed, Sara. *The Promise of Happiness*. Durham, NC: Duke University Press, 2010.
Alexander, Sally. "Feminism: History: Repetition, Some Notes and Queries." In *Becoming a Woman: And Other Essays in 19th- and 20th-Century Feminist History*, 243–47. London: Virago, 1994.
Banks, Olive. *Becoming a Feminist: The Social Origins of "First Wave" Feminism*. Brighton: Wheatsheaf, 1986.
Barrett, Michèle, and Mary McIntosh. *The Anti-Social Family*. 2nd ed. London: Verso, 1991.
Barrett, Michèle, and Mary McIntosh. "Ethnocentrism and Socialist-Feminist Theory." *Feminist Review*, no. 80 (2005): 64–86.
Bhavnani, Kum-Kum, and Margaret Coulson. "Transforming Socialist-Feminism: The Challenge of Racism." *Feminist Review*, no. 80 (2005): 87–97.
Bornat, Joanna, and Hanna Diamond. "Women's History and Oral History: Developments and Debates." *Women's History Review* 16, no. 1 (2007): 19–39.
Bouchier, David. *The Feminist Challenge: The Movement for Women's Liberation in Britain and the USA*. London: Macmillan, 1983.
Breitenbach, Esther, and Fiona Mackay. *Women and Contemporary Scottish Politics: An Anthology*. Edinburgh: Polygon at Edinburgh, 2001.
Browne, Sarah. *The Women's Liberation Movement in Scotland*. Manchester: Manchester University Press, 2014.
Bruley, Sue. "Women's Liberation at the Grass Roots: A View from Some English Towns, c. 1968–1990." *Women's History Review* 25, no. 5 (2016): 723–40.
Bryan, Beverley, Stella Dadzie, and Suzanne Scafe. *The Heart of the Race: Black Women's Lives in Britain*. London: Virago, 1985, republished by Verso, 2018.
Caine, Barbara. *English Feminism, 1780–1980*. Oxford: Oxford University Press, 1997.
Cameron, Deborah, and Joan Scanlon, eds. *The Trouble & Strife Reader*. London: Bloomsbury, 2010.
Carmen, Gail, Shaila, and Pratibha. "Becoming Visible: Black Lesbian Discussions." *Feminist Review*, no. 17 (1984): 53–72.
Cochrane, Kira. *Women of the Revolution: Forty Years of Feminism*. London: Guardian Books, 2010.
Cohen, Rachel Beth. "Researching Difference and Diversity within Women's Movements: Sisterhood and After." *Women's Studies International Forum* 35, no. 3 (2012): 138–40.
Coote, Anna, and Beatrix Campbell. *Sweet Freedom: The Struggle for Women's Liberation*. 2nd ed. Oxford: Basil Blackwell, 1987.

Cvetkovich, Ann. *An Archive of Feelings: Trauma, Sexuality, and Lesbian Public Cultures*. Durham, NC: Duke University Press, 2003.

Dean, Jonathan. *Rethinking Contemporary Feminist Politics*. Basingstoke: Palgrave Macmillan, 2010.

Delap, Lucy. "Uneasy Solidarity: The British Men's Movement and Feminism." In *The Women's Liberation Movement: Impacts and Outcomes*, edited by Kristina Schulz, 214–36. New York: Berghahn, 2017.

Della Porta, Donatella, and Mario Diani. *Social Movements: An Introduction*. 2nd ed. Oxford: Blackwell, 2006.

Dhaliwal, Sukhwant, and Nira Yuval-Davis, eds. *Women against Fundamentalism: Stories of Dissent and Solidarity*. London: Lawrence and Wishart, 2015.

Evason, Eileen. *Against the Grain: The Contemporary Women's Movement in Northern Ireland*. Dublin: Attic Press, 1991.

Fairbairns, Zoë. *Benefits: A Novel*. Nottingham: Five Leaves, 1998.

Fairbairns, Zoë. "Saying What We Want: Women's Demands in the Seventies and Now." In *The Feminist Seventies*, edited by Helen Graham, Ali Neilson, Emma Robertson, and Ann Kaloski, 93–104. York: Raw Nerve Books, 2002.

Feminist Anthology Collective, Michèle Barrett, Sue Bruley, Gail Chester, Maggie Millman, Sue O'Sullivan, Amanda Sebestyen, and Lynne Segal, eds. *No Turning Back: Writings from the Women's Liberation Movement 1975–80*. London: Women's Press, 1981.

Gelb, Joyce. "Feminism and Political Action." In *Challenging the Political Order: New Social and Political Movements in Western Democracies*, edited by Russell J. Dalton and Manfred Kuechler, 137–55. Cambridge: Polity Press, 1990.

Giugni, Marco G. "Personal and Biographical Consequences." In *The Blackwell Companion to Social Movements*, edited by David A. Snow, Sarah Anne Soule, and Hanspeter Kriesi, 489–507. Oxford: Blackwell, 2004.

Gluck, Sherna Berger, and Daphne Patai. *Women's Words: The Feminist Practice of Oral History*. New York: Routledge, 1991.

Graham, Helen, Ali Neilson, Emma Robertson, and Ann Kaloski, eds. *Saying What We Want: Women's Demands in the Seventies and Now*. York: Raw Nerve Books, 2002.

Green, Sarah F. *Urban Amazons: Lesbian Feminism and beyond in the Gender, Sexuality, and Identity Battles of London*. New York: St. Martin's Press, 1997.

Harman, Harriet. *A Woman's Work*. Milton Keynes: Allen Lane, 2017.

Harrison, Brian Howard. *Prudent Revolutionaries: Portraits of British Feminists between the Wars*. Oxford: Clarendon Press, 1987.

Hearn, Jeff. "It's Time for Men to Change." In *Working with Men for Change*, edited by Jim Wild, 5–15. London: Taylor and Francis, 1999.

Hemmings, Clare. *Why Stories Matter: The Political Grammar of Feminist Theory*. Durham, NC: Duke University Press, 2011.

Hollows, Joanne. "*Spare Rib*, Second-Wave Feminism and the Politics of Consumption." *Feminist Media Studies* 13, no. 2 (2013): 268–87.

Jasper, James M. "Emotional Dimensions in Social Movements." In *The Blackwell Companion to Social Movements*, edited by David A. Snow, Sarah Anne Soule, and Hanspeter Kriesi, 413–32. Oxford: Blackwell, 2004.

Johnson Ross, Freya. "What State Are We In?: Activism, Professional Feminists and Local Government." PhD thesis, University of Sussex, 2015.

Jolly, Margaretta. *In Love and Struggle: Letters in Contemporary Feminism*. New York: Columbia University Press, 2008.

Jolly, Margaretta. "Recognising Place, Space and Nation in Researching Women's Movements: Sisterhood and After." *Women's Studies International Forum* 35, no. 3 (2012): 144–46.

Jolly, Margaretta. "Voices in Movement: Feminist Family Stories in Oral History and Sound Art." *Life Writing* 12, no. 2 (2015): 1–21.

Jolly, Margaretta, Polly Russell, and Rachel Cohen. "Sisterhood and After: Individualism, Ethics and an Oral History of the Women's Liberation Movement." *Social Movement Studies* 11, no. 2 (2012): 1–16.

Kanter, Hannah, Sarah Lefanu, Shaila Shah, and Carole Spedding, eds. *Sweeping Statements: Writings from the Women's Liberation Movement 1981–83*. London: The Women's Press, 1984.

Lewis, Gail. "Black Women's Employment and the British Economy." In *Inside Babylon: The Caribbean Diaspora in Britain*, edited by Winston James and Clive Harris, 73–96. London: Verso, 1993.

Lovenduski, Joni, and Vicky Randall. *Contemporary Feminist Politics: Women and Power in Britain*. Oxford: Oxford University Press, 1993.

Mackay, Finn. *Radical Feminism: Feminist Activism in Movement*. London: Palgrave, 2015.

Mackay, Fiona. "The State of Women's Movement/s in Britain: Ambiguity, Complexity and Challenges from the Periphery." In *Women's Movements: Flourishing or in Abeyance*, edited by Sandra Grey and Marian Sawer, 17–32. Oxford: Routledge, 2008.

Maitland, Sara, ed. *Very Heaven: Looking Back at the 1960's*. London: Virago, 1988.

Malos, Ellen. *The Politics of Housework*. Cheltenham: New Clarion Press, 1995.

McAdam, Doug. "The Biographical Impact of Activism." In *How Social Movements Matter*, edited by Marco Giugni, Doug McAdam, and Charles Tilly, 119–48. Minneapolis: University of Minnesota Press, 1999.

McDowell, Linda, Sundari Anitha, and Ruth Pearson. "Striking Similarities: Representing South Asian Women's Industrial Action in Britain." *Gender, Place & Culture* 19, no. 2 (2011): 133–52.

McRobbie, Angela. *The Aftermath of Feminism: Gender, Culture and Social Change*. Los Angeles: SAGE, 2009.

Meehan, Elizabeth. "British Feminism from the 1960s to the 1980s." In *British Feminism in the Twentieth Century*, edited by Harold L. Smith, 189–204. Aldershot: Elgar, 1990.

Mirza, Heidi Safia. "'Harvesting Our Collective Intelligence': Black British Feminism in Post-Race Times." *Women's Studies International Forum* 51 (2015): 1–9.

Mitchell, Juliet. "Women: The Longest Revolution." *New Left Review* 1, no. 40 (1966): 11–37.
Mitchell, Juliet, and Ann Oakley. *What Is Feminism*. Oxford: Basil Blackwell, 1986.
Morgan, Sue. *The Feminist History Reader*. London: Routledge, 2006.
Morrison, Paul. "Looking Back on 40 Years in the 'Men's Movement.'" In *Insideman: Pioneering Stories about Men and Boys*, edited by Dan Bell and Glen Poole, 148–52. Leicestershire: Matador, 2015.
Nash, Kate. "A Movement Moves... Is There a Women's Movement in England Today?" *European Journal of Women's Studies* 9, no. 3 (2002): 311–28.
Oakley, Ann. "Interviewing Women: A Contradiction in Terms." In *Turning Points in Qualitative Research: Tying Knots in a Handkerchief*, edited by Yvonna S. Lincoln and Norman K. Denzin, 243–64. Oxford: AltaMira Press, 2003.
Oakley, Ann, and Juliet Mitchell. *Who's Afraid of Feminism?: Seeing through the Backlash*. London: Hamish Hamilton, 1997.
Orbach, Susie. *Fat Is a Feminist Issue: The Anti-Diet Guide: Conquering Compulsive Eating + Fat Is a Feminist Issue II*. London: Arrow, 2006.
O'Sullivan, Sue, ed. *Turning the Tables: Recipes and Reflections from Women*. London: Sheba Feminist Publishers, 1987.
Parmar, Pratibha. "The Past before Us: Twenty Years of Feminism." *Feminist Review* 31 (1989): 55–65.
Phillips, Angela, and Jill Rakusen. *Our Bodies, Ourselves: A Health Book by and for Women*. London: Penguin Allen Lane, 1978.
Phoenix, Ann. "Theories of Gender and Black Families." In *Black British Feminism: A Reader*, edited by Heidi Safia Mirza, 50–63. London: Routledge, 1997.
Pugh, Martin. *Women and the Women's Movement in Britain, 1914–1999*. New York: St. Martin's Press, 2000.
Rowbotham, Sheila. "Appreciating Our Beginnings." In *Threads through Time: Writings on History and Autobiography*, 73–83. London: Penguin, 1999.
Rowbotham, Sheila. *Promise of a Dream: Remembering the Sixties*. London: Verso, 2001.
Rowbotham, Sheila. "Women's Liberation and the New Politics." In *The Body Politic: Women's Liberation in Britain*, edited by Michelene Wandor, 3–30. London: Stage 1, 1972.
Rowbotham, Sheila, Lynne Segal, and Hilary Wainwright. *Beyond the Fragments: Feminism and the Making of Socialism*. 3rd ed. Boston: Merlin Press, 2013.
Rowe, Marsha, ed. *Spare Rib Reader*. Harmondsworth, UK: Penguin, 1982.
Sebestyen, Amanda. *'68, '78, '88: From Women's Liberation to Feminism*. Bridport, UK: Prism, 1988.
Segal, Lynne. *Making Trouble: Life and Politics*. London: Serpent's Tail, 2007.
Segal, Lynne. *Out of Time: The Pleasures and Perils of Ageing*. London: Verso, 2013.
Stevenson, George. "The Women's Movement and 'Class Struggle': Gender, Class Formation and Political Identity in Women's Strikes, 1968–78." *Women's History Review* 25, no. 5 (2016): 741–55.

Sudbury, Julia. *Other Kinds of Dreams: Black Women's Organisations and the Politics of Transformation*. London: Routledge, 1998.

Summerfield, Penny. "Culture and Composure: Creating Narratives of the Gendered Self in Oral History Interviews." *Cultural and Social History* 1, no. 1 (2004): 65–93.

Thane, Pat. *Happy Families? History and Family Policy*. London: British Academy Policy Centre, 2010.

Thomlinson, Natalie. *Race, Ethnicity and the Women's Movement in England, 1968–1993*. Houndsmills, UK: Palgrave, 2016.

Traies, Jane. *Lives of Older Lesbians: Sexuality, Identity & the Life Course*. London: Palgrave Macmillan, 2016.

Walters, Natasha. *The New Feminism*. London: Virago, 1999.

Wandor, Michelene, ed. *The Body Politic: Women's Liberation in Britain*. London: Stage 1, 1972.

Ward, Margaret. "Feminism and Nationalism in Ireland: Can We Learn from History?" *Journal of Gender Studies* 1, no. 4 (1992): 492–99.

Watt, Diana, and Adele Jones. *Catching Hell and Doing Well: Black Women in the UK—The Abasindi Cooperative*. London: Trentham, 2015.

Wilson, Amrit. *Dreams, Questions, Struggles: South Asian Women in Britain*. London: Pluto, 2006.

Wilson, Amrit. *Finding a Voice: Asian Women in Britain*. London: Virago, 1978.

Withers, Deborah [D-M]. *Feminism, Digital Culture and the Politics of Transmission: Theory, Practice and Cultural Heritage*. London: Rowman & Littlefield, 2015.

INDEX

For the benefit of digital users, indexed terms that span two pages (e.g., 52–53) may, on occasion, appear on only one of those pages.

Note: Figures are indicated by *f* following the page number

Abdela, Lesley, 15, 46, 68, 144–45
Aberson, Arielle, 26
abortion
    Abortion Act of 1967, 12–13, 110–11, 117–18, 163
    abortion as a litmus test for gender relations, 117–18
    abortion rights as cutting across class and race, 108
    after perceived fetal viability, 117–18
    anti-abortion activism, 105–11
    illegal, 12, 242–43
    in Northern Ireland, 112–13, 117–18, 237–38
    legal and free abortion as WLM demand, 26, 90
    men's support of abortion rights, 164–65, 167
    National Abortion Campaign (NAC), 4, 46, 47, 63–64, 89, 95, 101–12, 104*f*
    personal experiences of, 68, 80–81, 104–6, 108–9
    restrictions on abortion rights, 233
    semi-legalization of in 1967, 64, 68
    TUC march for abortion rights, 21
    WLM's campaign to protect abortion rights, 112
Achilles Heel (magazine), 165, 167–68
Adorned in Dreams (Wilson), 144–45
Aftermath of Feminism, The (McRobbie), 6–7
age
    age activism, 227, 229–30, 248–49
    ageism, 215, 217
    age of marriage and motherhood, 210–12
    baby boomer generation as "winners," 11–12, 63, 243–44
    coming of age in the '70s, 89
    concerns over teenage sexuality, 103
    contradictions of old age, 101
    of core activists, 77–78
    domestic abuse and, 170–71
    education system and, 65–66
    Equality Act of 2010, 263n81

312 • Index

age (cont.)
 isolation in old age, 76
 puberty and sex education, 67–68
 selection as interviewee and, 45, 50, 62–64, 207–8
 sexuality, marriage, and monogamy, 212–13
 signs of sexual difference in adolescence, 69
 unequal age of consent, 166
 young people identifying as LGB, 185
 youth as the cultural age for everyone, 87–88
Ahluwalia, Kiranjit, 172–73
Ahmed, Sara, 6–7, 76, 217–18
Albertine, Viv, 141–42
Alexander, Sally, 26, 28, 44, 60, 91–92, 93–94
Ali, Tariq, 13
Allen, Sheila, 174–75
Anderson, Kathryn, 42–43
Andrassy, David, 134f
Anticlimax (Jeffreys), 10
anti-colonialism, 8, 10
anti-Semitism, 15–16, 80
Anti-Social Family, The (McIntosh and Barrett), 74–75
archive, ix, 2–3, 4, 5, 14, 32, 34–35, 40, 41, 42, 43–45, 47, 49, 50, 53–54, 61, 101–2, 123–24, 173, 208, 217–18, 220–21, 227–28, 242, 246, 248–49, 250, 251n7, 261n41
Armitage, Susan, 5
Armstrong, Elizabeth "Liz," 123–24, 156, 207–8
Armstrong, Frankie, 221
Arshad, Rowena, 205–6
Ashfar, Haleh, 236–37
Ashley, April, 188
Attar, Dena, 140–41
Atwood, Margaret, 3
Aurat Obaa, 34
Auto/Biographical I, The (Stanley), 43

Babies for Burning (Litchfield and Kentish), 105
Backlash (Faludi), 168–69
Baigent, Dave, 167
Baird, Vera, 172–73
Banks, Olive, 50, 212
Barber, Abi, 60
Barnsley Miners' Wives Action Group, 131–33, 134f
Barrett, Michèle, 74, 75
Barrie, Ray, 246–47
Bates, Ted, 54
Bean, Gerlin, 29–30
Bearse, Miriam, 42
Beddoe, Deirdre, 41–42, 46, 208, 221–22
Bellos, Linda, 140
Benefits (Fairbairns), 3, 109–10
Bennett, Theresa, 58–59
Best, Mavis (Clarke), 179–80
Beyond the Veil (Mernissi), 236–37
Bhavnani, Kum-Kum, 74, 139–41
Bilocca, Lillian, 14, 16–25, 18f
Bilton, Flo, 55–56
Bindel, Julie, 172–73
Bittersweet: Facing Up to Feelings of Love, Envy, and Competition in Women's Friendships (Orbach and Eichenbaum), 85–86
Black, Cilla, 77
Black Cultural Archives (BCA), 2–3, 34, 43–44, 45
Black Dwarf (radical newspaper), 13–14
Boateng, Paul, 179–80
body politics, x–xi, 92–93
Body Politic: Writings from the Women's Liberation Movement in Britain, 1969–1972, The (Wandor), 29, 99
Boland, Rose, 16–25
Booth, Cherie, 169–70
Bornat, Joanna, 49
Bornstein, Kate, 187–88
Bradbury, Malcolm, 162–63

Index • 313

Bradshaw, Fran, 154
Brah, Harpal, 162–63
Brighton Trans*formed oral history, 2–3, 44, 48–49, 185–86
Brixton Black Women's Group (BBWG), 29–30, 34, 106
Bryan, Beverley, 10–11, 11*f*, 42, 107
Burford, Barbara, 98
Butler, Anne, 248–49
Butler-Sloss, Elizabeth, 177–78

Caine, Barbara, 25–26
Callil, Carmen, 122–23
Campaign for Nuclear Disarmament (CND), 9–10, 13, 14–15, 159, 192, 226
Campbell, Beatrix
　on funding for black women's movement, 128–29
　incest survivors' and child rights campaigns, 4, 177–78
　joy of parenting others' children, 210–11
　memories of post-war rationing, 140
　memories of wedding dress, 141–42
　memories of writing *Sweet Freedom*, 37–39
　political socialization of, 207
　on racism, 183
　relationship with mother and father, 73–75, 77–78
　scorn of the Ruskin conference, 21
　selection as interviewee, 45–46
　on sexual life, 69
　Sweet Freedom: The Struggle for Women's Liberation, 9–10, 38*f*
　transformation of political understanding, 25
　views of unions, 103
　on working-class culture and education, 67
Campbell, Bobby, 69, 141–42
Cancer Journals (Lorde), 228–29

Capstick, Sheila, 23–24
Carmichael, Stokely, 28–29, 162–63
"Carry Greenham Home" (Seeger), 225*f*
Carter, Angela, 12, 140
Case, Dave, 54–55
Castle, Barbara, 4, 17–18, 19*f*, 77, 245
Caudwell, Jayne, 52
Chamberlin, Mary, 5, 41
Chersterman, John, 166
Chester, Gail
　account of sex education, 5, 68
　African freedom songs, 222–23
　distribution of WLM flyer, 99
　grassroots activism of, 3–4
　on hairstyles, 142–43
　home of, 123–24
　love of women's community, 218–19
　memories of rites of passage, 69–70
　music and feminism, 219
　on WLM demands, 97
Chicago, Judy, 121
Child Benefit Act of 1975, 122–23
Children's Act of 1989, 178–79
class
　abolishing class exploitations, 9–10
　abortion rights as cutting across, 108
　aligning gender and class interests, 110
　biases in UK educational system, 62, 65
　black and minority women's versus white working-class WLM movements, 29, 30, 105–6
　black women's versus white middle-class WLM movements, 6, 10–11
　Campbell on, 67, 73
　class inequality and women's sports, 58
　class struggle of oral against print classes, 40–41
　complexities around cross-class alliances, 8–9
　cross-class and working-class—led feminism, 138

class (*cont.*)
   cross-class experimentation through clothes swapping, 144–45
   Dadzie on interaction of class and identity, 210
   effect on interviewees' oral histories, 4, 35
   gender-class analysis, 175
   gender equality and, 185
   gender versus class-framed dystopia, 109–10
   Hall's early work on, 4
   men's violence as a unifying force, 172
   middle-class versus working-class women's employment, 158
   physical size as a new class issue, 84–85
   role in WLM's seven demands, 90–92
   Rowbotham on, 14
   UK's endemic class consciousness, 181
   WAMT and TOPs programs, 149–50, 157
   Wandor on, 27
   and women's liberation in feminist histories, 16–25
   working-class activism and socialist ideologies, 50
   working-class activism versus white middle-class feminism, 28, 45, 47–48, 57–58, 124, 131–32, 209
   working-class trade union activism, 3–4, 23, 70
Cockburn, Cynthia
   on ideologies of marriage and home, 74
   life-long struggle with overeating, 84
   memories of post-war rationing, 140
   on Raised Voices, 219
   response to questions about mother, 73
   self-chosen career of, 135, 208
   as single mother living in a collective family, 210–11
   support of feminism in her home, 136–37
Cohen, Daniel, 167–68, 169–70
Cohen, Rachel, 60, 143, 184, 237
Colquhoun, Maureen, 98
Committee in Defence of the 1967 Act (Co-Ord), 101–2
Conran, Shirley, 15, 138
consciousness raising (CR), 99–101, 106
Cook, Betty
   effect of WLM on, 3–4
   everyday life of, 137
   identification with working-class struggle, 131–33
   life course of, 208
   memories of first picket, 137–38
   as older member of WLM, 63
   profession based on experiences in WLM, 208–9
   work with Barnsley Miners' Wives Action Group, 134*f*
Cooper, Wendy, 213
Coote, Anna, 8–10, 11–12, 37, 38*f*, 103
Corbett, Arthur, 188
Corrie, John, 101–3, 105
Costa, Maria Della, 138
Coulson, Margaret, 74
Courage to Heal, The (Loftus), 178
Creasy, Stella, 117–18
Crockford, Sue, 27
Crozier, George, 105

Dadzie, Stella
   complex interaction of class and identity, 210
   first OWAAD conference, 32, 220–21
   Heart of the Race (1985), 42, 107
   memories of homelessness, 124
   photo of, 11*f*
   refutes genealogy from white-majority WLM, 10–11
   success as movement organizer, 29–30

Dagenham, Ford factory strike, 8–9, 16–25, 19f, 163
Davidoff, Leonore, 41–42
Davin, Anna, 26, 66, 68, 79, 141–42
de Beauvoir, Simone, 71–72, 76, 78
Declaration on the Elimination of Violence Against Women, 115, 172–73
Delap, Lucy, 48–49, 51–52, 164, 167, 184
Delk, Yvonne, 232–33
Delmar, Rosalind
   account of move to Little Newport Street, 24–25
   on CND executive committee, 28
   commitment to consciousness raising, 99–100
   disappointment in fellow activists, 209
   educational experiences of, 66
   feelings for young women students in the 1980s, 218
   memories of Pat Thorne's equal rights bill, 97–98
   memories of rites of passage, 69–70
   movement of WLM to politics of representation, 12
   on self-defined sexuality, 92–93
   on tolerance and patience in coalitions, 244
demands (of the WLM), 15, 26, 90–92, 91f, 97, 102, 104–5, 170–71, 241
Denness, Mary, 18–19, 21
Desai, Jayaben, 31f
Dhondy, Farrukh, 162–63
"Dinner Party" (artwork), 121
disability, 45, 137, 169–70, 229
Diski, Jenny, 12–13
Divorce Reform Act of 1969, 66, 212
Domestic Violence Matrimonial Proceedings Act of 1976, 171
Douglas, Sheila, 17
Do You Remember Olive Morris? (oral history project), 249
Drabble, Margaret, 244–45

Dunn, Pat, 55–56
Dutiful Daughters (Rowbotham and McCrindle), 42, 71, 73
Dworkin, Andrea, 92–93, 166

Education Act of 1944, 65–67
"Effeminist Manifesto" (Pitchford), 166
Egbuna, Obi, 28–29
Eichenbaum, Luise, 85–86
emotion
   contradictions and embarrassments told by, 51–52
   dark emotion flowing around women's movement, 183–84
   feminist "mood work" in relation to reproductive choices, 109–10
   joy at women's political successes and unity, 92, 115, 138, 205, 215
   public sharing of, 105–6, 117–18
   reconstruction of history of, 248
England, 3–4, 45–46, 53f, 53–54, 55, 57, 61, 74–75, 112–13, 115, 117–18, 119, 124–25, 127–28, 129, 135–36, 170–71, 191–92, 193, 199, 202, 206, 210–11, 212, 229–30, 273n66, 282n126
"Equal Opportunities for Men and Women" (consultative document), 96
Equal Pay Act of 1970, 4, 17–18, 19f, 55–56, 66, 220
Ernst, Sheila, 85, 229
Evason, Eileen, 25, 114
Exposures for Women, 169

Fabulous Dirt Sisters, 221
Fairbairns, Zoë
   Benefits (1979), 3, 109–10
   on life course, 205–6, 211–12
   reaction to Greer's pronouncement, 93
   view of mortgage debt, 126–27
   on WLM demands, 241
   work as editor for CND, 159

faith/belief
  dying and faith, 227–41
  feminism as a sustaining, 231–32
  loss of as theory of contemporary unhappiness, 214
  political faith and WLM activism, 226–27
  relationship to feminism, 233–34
  sense of purpose as, 205
Faludi, Susan, 168–69
fathers and fathering
  abusive situations and, 73
  Fathers Direct think tank, 185
  fathers' rights, 177–80
  feminists moving away from "father quest," 76
  incest, 170–71
  as inspiration for feminists, 163
  interviewees question concerning, 263n84
  Jewish experience, 243–44
  need for signature on mortgages, 125
  post-war generation, x
  respectfulness of girls' ambition, 71
  as role-model for women in trades, 149–50
Fat Is a Feminist Issue: The Anti-Diet Guide to Permanent Weight Loss (FIFI) (Orbach), 4, 83–84, 99
Fawcett Society, 16, 25–26, 42, 96, 177–78, 185, 244–45
Feather, Stuart, 142–43
Female Eunuch, The (Greer), 5, 22–23, 92–93
Feminine Forever (Wilson), 213
Feminist Archives (North and South), 2–3, 42
feminist histories
  class and women's liberation in, 16–25
  composing feminist memories, 35–39
  oral history and feminist method, 40–61
  race and nation in, 25–34
  sound of feminist memory, 1–7
  telling through oral histories, 8–16
Feminist Practice: Notes from the Tenth Year (Sebestyen), 10
Feminist Psychoanalysis Group, 92–93
Fenwomen: A Portrait of Women in an English Village (Chamberlain), 5–6, 41
Field, Yvonne, 34
Finch, Mal, 220–21
Finch, Sue, 93–94, 122–23
Finding a Voice: Asian Women in Britain (Wilson), 10, 30–31, 41–42
Firestone, Shulamith, 213–14
Fleming, Jacky, 98
Ford factory strike, 8–9, 16–25, 19f, 163
Forrester-Paton, Keith, 167
Fortune, Jenny, 93–94
French, Dawn, 164
Frontiers: A Journal of Women's Studies, 41

Garthwaite, Al, 122–23
Gavron, Hannah, 213–14
Gay Liberation Front (GLF), 2–3, 6, 92, 97, 142–43, 162, 166, 180, 188, 227–28
gender. *See also* Brighton Trans*formed oral history; transgendered liberation
  abortion as a litmus test for gender relations, 117–18
  aligning gender and class interests, 109–10
  autonomy for all genders, 217
  binary view of, 172
  challenges to gender ideologies, 21
  complex patterns of gender struggle, 6–7
  concept of gender choice, 166–67, 229
  cross-gender identification, 169
  effect on interviewees' oral histories, 4

eradicating exploitative gender
    relations, 241
gender-based violence, 173–74
gender-class analysis, 23, 175
gendered divisions of labor, 209–10
gender-equality movements, 16
gender identities shaped in childhood,
    62–63, 71
gender liberation, 47, 169–70, 231
gender-neutral rules of succession to
    the crown, 230
gender politics of WLM demands, 159
importance of considering in
    everyone's life, 43
inequalities perpetuated by UK
    education system, 65
links between class and gender
    struggles, 92
pressures on gender-atypical girls, 69
rethinking of gender itself, 159–60
revolution of gender relations, 1–2
WLM analysis of, 242–43
*Gender in a Neoliberal and
Neoconservative Age*
    (Phipps), 6–7
Gender Recognition Act of 2004, 188
generation
    activists' lives as
        multigenerational, 207–8
    baby boomer generation as "winners,"
        11–12, 63, 230, 243–44
    baby boomer generation in Northern
        Ireland, 63
    construction of generational
        chains, 76
    debates over institutional versus
        grassroots activism, 246
    distinct definitions of, 64
    feminists of Chaberlain's generation, 6
    intergenerational transmittance of
        femininity in patriarchy, 84
    memories of post-war rationing, 140
    mid-century feminism, 71

post-war generation, x, 62–63, 65, 80
    as predictor of activism, 87
    preserving the WLMs activism, 44
    public remembering across, 173
    rejection of parent's values by
        younger, 12–13
    selection of interviewees and, 207
    shift from focus on material goods to
        self-realization, 87–88
    stoicism of prewar generation, 229
    suffrage generation, 245
    teaching as an intervention in the life
        course of future, 78–79
    unifying through oral
        histories, 242–44
    "Valium generation," 213–14, 234
    view of feminism by newer
        generations, 247
    women's liberation born anew with
        each, xi
Gilmore, Sheila, 3–4, 119
girls and girlhood
    disillusioned by reality of women's
        oppression, 12
    Girls' Centre of Excellence, 57, 60
    horror of body obsession, 84–85
    of interviewees mothers, 76
    match girls strike, 20
    Mirza's work with Muslim and Asian
        girls in Bradford, 233–36
    opportunities in sports, 52,
        58–59, 79
    Orbach's work as girls' rights
        campaigner, 86–87
    Scottish National Organisation of
        Girls' Work, 79
    sexual rights for, 185
    socializing girls in the century of
        childhood, 62–70
    standards of education, 62, 142
Gittins, Diana, 41
Gluck, Sherna, 5, 42, 43–44, 169
Godard, Jean-Luc, 162–63

Golden Notebook, The (Lessing), 165–66, 215
Goldman, Emma, 222–23
Goodbody, Mary Ann "Buzz," 204–5, 206*f*
Goodison, Lucy, 85
Goodwin, Clive, 28
Graessle, Lois, 24–25
Gravill, Diana, 157
Greater London Council (GLC), 128–29, 130*f*, 130–31, 179–80, 219
Green, Esther, 229
Green, Frankie, 221
Green, Sarah F., 50–51
Greenham Common Women's protest, 2, 47, 133, 134*f*, 135–36, 168, 218, 223–27, 225*f*, 231–32
Greer, Germaine, 10–11, 22–23, 63, 76, 92–93, 147, 204–5
Grimstad, Susan, 155
Grosvenor Avenue collective, 122–23
Grunwick photo-processing laboratory strike, 8–9, 30, 31*f*, 163
Gueye, Ama, 122–23
Gunn, Rosie, 169

Haaken, Janice, 178
Halberstam, Judith, 176
Halford, Alison, 77
Hall, Catherine
    on autonomy, 216
    on becoming a feminist, 163
    as example of marriage supportive of feminism, 212
    final National Women's Liberation conference, 188–89
    Hall marriage as example of successful and supportive, 160, 202*f*
    influence on husband, 4
    on marriage and feminism, 189–203
    meaning of women's liberation, 3–4
    memories of Ruskin conference, 27
    nonsexist childrearing, 210–11
    politics of identities, 188–89
    special issues on women in *Oral History*, 41
Hall, Stuart
    as editor of *New Left Review*, 28, 163
    as example of marriage supportive of feminism, 212
    influence of wife on, 4
    on marriage and feminism, 189–203
    marriage as example of successful conversation across differences, 160, 188–203, 202*f*
    politics of identities, 188–89
    support of feminism at Ruskin conference, 27, 164*f*, 164
Hall Carpenter Archives, 41
Hanmer, Jalna, 3–4, 63, 70–71, 99–100, 171, 172–73, 174–75, 208
Haque, Shaheen, 140
Harman, Harriet, 15, 97, 162, 163, 180
Harne, Lynne, 14–15
Harris, Hermione, 135
Harrison, Brian, 42, 49, 212
Hart, Val, 122–23
Harte, Peter, 60
Harvey, Barbara, 115
Hayward, Julie, 17–18, 163
Hearn, Jeff, 175, 179
Hearn, Kirsten, 5, 63–64, 69–70, 107–8, 137, 143–45, 219
Heart of Race, The (oral history collection), 34
Heart of the Race, The (Bryan, Dadzie, and Scafe), 2–3, 10–11, 11*f*, 42, 107, 210
Heathfield, Betty, 42
Heaume, Chris, 180
Heinemann, Margot, 81
Hemmings, Clare, 36
Henry, Lenny, 164
Heritage Lottery Fund (HLF), 43–44

Hidden from History (Rowbotham), 245
Hidden Lives (Lane), 248–49
Higgs, Marietta, 177
Hinds, Bronagh, 122–23, 245
History Man, The, 162–63
Hobbs, Arthur, 55
Hobbs, May, 91–92, 204–5
Hodgkin, Luke, 68
Hollows, Joanne, 50–51, 141
Housing Act of 1977, 125–26
Housing Act of 1980, 127–28
Howell, Margaret, 23–24
How to Cheat At Cooking (Smith), 138
Hoyle, Kathryn, 146
Huebsch, Edward, 82
Hull fishermen's wives and girlfriends' campaign for trawler safety, 8–9, 16–25, 18*f*
Humphrey, Emma, 172–73
Hunter-Henderson, Roberta, 26
Hutt, Jane, 3–4, 118–19, 207–8
Hutton, Caroline, 221–22

image and imagery
  body image, 46, 83–84, 185, 239–40
  consciousness raising and, 99
  disillusionment caused by, 12
  of feminism in popular media, 35–36, 169–70
  of "grimy" Little Newport Street, 24–25
  guided imagery used to access repressed memories, 178
  made available through oral histories, 51
  male violence and, 116–17
  of Mapplethorpe's photographs, 169
  self-image and the beauty and fast-food industries, 79–80, 84–85
  self-image as women, 27, 174
  sexualized images of militant women, 13

imperialism, 235
Innes, Sue, 95
international, x–xi, 55–56, 87, 136–37, 157, 237, 257n89, 286n78, 287n80
internationalism, 27–28
International Labour Organisation, 19–20
International Marxist Group, 91–92, 270n27
International Socialists, 9–10, 205
International Women's Day (1971), 204–5, 206*f*
Inventing Ourselves: Lesbian Life Stories, 41
Ireland. *See also* Northern Ireland
  abortion prohibition in, 237–38
  Women in Ireland group, 197–98
  women's liberation groups in, 96
Islamic feminism, 236–37

Jackman, Donna, 122–23
Jackson, Maureen, 20
James, Selma, 29, 63
Jeffreys, Sheila, 10, 22–23, 92–93, 105–6
Jewish feminism, 44–45, 48, 79–81, 164–65, 168, 182, 238, 243–44
Jimenez, Margarita, 93–94
Johnson, Rebecca, 5, 68, 225*f,* 225–26, 248
Johnson-Ross, Freya, 129–30
Jolly, Margaretta, 38, 61
Jones, Audrey, 205
Jones, Barbara, 3–4, 122, 126–27, 146–47, 148–58, 207–8

Kaveney, Ros, 188
keening, 226
Kelly, Liz, 177
Kelly, Mary, 93–94, 98, 207–9, 246–47, 248
Kennedy, Mary, 208

Kentish, Susan, 105
Kitzinger, Sheila, 5, 63, 79, 205, 208, 228–29, 230–31
Koedt, Anne, 22–23, 69
Kraft, Veronica, 83
Kroll, Una, 3, 5, 62–63, 135–36, 140, 162, 205, 208, 231, 232*f*
Krzowski, Sue, 229

Lacy, Suzanne, 248–49
La Fontaine, Jean, 177
Lamborn, Harry, 163
Lane, Cathy, 248–49
Lau, Grace, 64, 69, 146, 169, 207–8
"Lavender menace," 98
Lawrence, Doreen, 179–80
Lawrence, Stephen, 179–80
Lawson, Nigella, 140–41
leadership
  black women in positions of, 32
  debates over in UK women's movements, 16
  foundations for, 78
  lack of in women's soccer, 60
  move to professionalism, 118–19
  WLM refusal of, 8, 46–47, 60
Lecointe, Althea, 28–29
Leeming, Carol, 122–23
Lefcourt, Carol, 83
Leicester Black Sisters, 122–23
lesbian
  antiviolence campaigning, 110
  bitter debates over in WLM, 15–16, 182
  black women's movement and, 23
  discrimination against accommodation for lesbians, 125–26, 152–53
  dispersal of OWAAD and, 34
  ending discrimination against lesbians, 90–91
  issue of dress codes, 147
  lack of options for in early 1970s, 66

"Lavender menace," 98
Leeds Revolutionary Feminists, 105–6
legalization of male homosexuality and, 64
lesbian-centered, ecofeminist philosophy, 154
lesbian erotica, 146
lesbian fashion, 143
link to Greenham Common Women's Peace Camp, 2, 224, 231–32
mothering as a life stage, 210–11
political lesbianism, 92–93
potential for isolation in old age, 76
pressure felt by lesbian girls, 69
public projection of, 6
radical lesbian separatist politics, 149
as regressively shite and racist, 36–37
risks of ostracism and ridicule, 57–58
socialism's view of, 162–63
taboo of lesbian desire, 12
view of all penetration as rape, 174
YBA (Why Be A) Wife campaign, 3, 92
lesbian and gay
  effect of WLM on, 213
  Gay Liberation Front (GLF), 2–3, 6, 92, 97, 142–43, 162, 166, 180, 188, 227–28
  legalization of adoption and in-vitro fertilization rights, xi
  split between lesbians and gay men, 166
  WLM effect on queer and lesbian relationships, 213
lesbian rights, x–xi
Lessing, Doris, 165–66, 215
"Letters from a Fainthearted Feminist" (Tweedie), 15
Lewis, Gail
  criticism of *The Anti-Social Family*, 74–75
  disappointment in white women's liberation movement, x, 28

Index • 321

discovery of feminism through a man, 163
experience of abortion, 68
meaning of women's liberation, 3–4
memories of rites of passage, 69–70
role of oral histories, 51
success as movement organizer, 29–30
views on sharing of feelings about feelings, 106–7
liberal feminism, 185, 207–8, 215
Liddington, Jill, 41, 42
life course
    autonomy as defining aspect of feminist, 212
    escape from expected, 57, 87, 214
    feminist insights into, 244
    gender-equality movements and, 185
    mobility and flux of women's, 210–11
    new trajectories that influenced society, 126
    questions of expected through consciousness raising, 101
    reflections of Delmar on, 209
    reflections of Fairbairns on, 205–6
    reflections of McKenley on, 205–6
    reflections of Robinson on, 208
    reflections of Rowbotham on, 205–6
    sexuality as defining aspect of, 210–11
    of social movements, 101
    teaching as an intervention of future generations, 78–79
    turning points in later years, 213, 227
    unintended consequences of movement actions, 208
    vital preciousness of being needed across, 229
Likoya, Abina, 122–23
Litchfield, Michael, 105
literature and feminism, 3, 5–6, 22–23, 27–28, 41, 87–88, 92–93, 98, 109–10, 164–65, 174–75
Livingstone, Ken, 129, 130*f*
Lockhart, Judith, 32

Loftus, Elizabeth, 178
London Women's Liberation Workshop, 24–25
Long, Asphodel, 231–32
Lopez, Sue, 3, 52–60, 53*f*, 61, 207–8
Lorde, Audre, 228–29
Lunnon, Jane, 246*f*
Lynn, Jenny, 125–26

Machal, Samora, 10–11
MacKay, Finn, 173, 187, 216–17
Made in Dagenham, 17, 19*f*
Maitland, Sara, 12
Malos, Ellen, 3–4, 96–97, 123–24, 208, 248
Mangrove Nine trial (1970), 28–29
Mapplethorpe, Robert, 169
Marchant, Alison, 248–49
marriage
    abusive marriages, 3–4, 68, 204–5
    arguments against romanticizing, 74
    arranged marriages, 84–85, 182–83
    average age of marriage and motherhood, 66, 210–12
    black feminism and, 74–75
    Declaration on the Elimination of Violence Against Women, 115, 172–73
    as defining aspect of women's life courses, 63, 76, 90, 101, 214–15
    Domestic Violence Matrimonial Proceedings Act of 1976, 171
    feminists feelings about, 212
    gender-based violence, 173–74
    Hall marriage as example of successful and supportive, 160, 188–203, 202*f*, 212
    inheritance laws and, 230
    mixed-race marriages, 124
    rape in marriage, 115, 170–71, 210–11
    sexuality, monogamy, age and, 212–13
    of transsexuals, 188
    views on pre-marital sex, 68, 103, 111

marriage (*cont.*)
  women's oppression through, 12, 21, 66, 71, 131–33
  YBA (Why Be A) Wife campaign, 3, 92
Marsland, Terry, 102
Mason, Angela, 144–45
Matrimonial Proceedings and Property Act of 1969, 66
May, Theresa, 209–10
McCrindle, Jean, 42, 71, 73, 77–78, 132, 133–35, 204–5
McCrum, Mukami
  avoidance of becoming sad and angry, x, 218
  on dress code at women's groups, 23–24
  educational experiences of, 78
  memories of childhood, 5
  on move to professionalism, 118–19
  profession based on experiences in WLM, 208–9
  religious life of, 232–33
  sense of responsibility to family, 74
McDonnell, John, 130*f*
McGivern, Marie-Thérèse, 110, 174
McIntosh, Mary
  on death and dying, 227–29
  death of, 205
  feminist approach to child abuse, 74–76
  gay liberation activism of, 213
  memories of rites of passage, 69–70
  occupation of, 208
  on organized religion, 231
  on shopping and consumerism, 142–43
  sparks debate over role of family, 74
  support of SBS, 172
  "YBA Wife" campaign, 3, 92
McKechnie, Sheila, 156
McKenley, Jan
  approach to the politics of hair, 142
  connection between sexual and women's liberation, 69
  crossing of racial divides, 4
  early messages about rape, 174
  experiences and work for National Abortion Campaign, 104–6, 108–9
  exploration of educational choices available to black Caribbean parents in the UK, 217
  generational influences on, 63–64
  memories of education, 67
  on men active in feminist movement, 163–64
  music as escape, 223
  observations on OWAAD, 34
  reflections on life course, 205–6
  success as movement organizer, 29–30, 46
  work as NAC national coordinator, 103, 104*f*
McKinnon, Catherine, 171
McMinn, Karen, 3, 67–68, 90, 112–20, 116*f*, 141–42, 208–9
McNamara, Kevin, 17
McNeil, Sheila, 96
McRobbie, Angela, 6–7
Mead, Margaret, 78
media and the WLM
  fascination of the media with the Hull women, 17
  goal of S&A project, 44
  Greenham Common Women's Peace Camp and, 223–24, 226
  hostility of WLM toward mainstream media, 4, 95, 98
  media's reliance on Orbach for source material, 79–80
  popular media images of feminism, 35–36, 40
  rejection of media sensationalizing, 9–10
  social media, 247–50
  survivors' campaigns and, 177

undue influence of media, 243
Wise as face of GLC, 131
WLM antiviolence campaigning, 171
Women in Media group, 96, 98
Memoirs of a Dutiful Daughter (de Beauvoir), 71
Memoirs of a Not So Dutiful Daughter (Murray), 71–72
memory/remembering
　by abuse survivors, 177
　collective remembering, 173
　composing feminist memories, 35–39
　future of feminist memory, 242–50
　listening as essential to transmission of memory, 1–2
　memories of the 1940s, 1950s, and 1960s
　　aspiration and inspiration for activism, 77–88
　　effect of family dynamics, 70–76
　　potential for activism, 62
　　society's impact on, 62–70
　memories of the 1970s
　　coming of age in the '70s, 89–101
　　National Abortion Campaign, 101–12
　　Women's Aid Northern Ireland, 112–20
　memories of the 1980s
　　everyday life, 121–22
　　housing and homes, 122–37
　　shopping and consumerism, 137–48
　　work and capitalism, 148–58
　memories of the 1990s
　　Catherine and Stuart Hall, 189–203
　　men, masculinity, and the question of difference, 160–70
　　men and feminism, 159–60
　　men's violence and movement identities, 170–84
　　transgendered liberation, 185–89
　memories of the 2000s
　　dying and faith, 227–41
　　life choices, 205–19
　music and feminism, 219–27
　questions of WLM success, 204–5
　oral history as an investigation of, 41
　politics of memory, 160
　Remembering Our Dead ceremony, 187–88
　Right to Memory and Right to communicate initiatives, 173
　role in functioning of social movements, 242–43
　sound of feminist memory, 1–7
Mercer, Kobena, 169
Mernissi, Fatima, 236–37
Millett, Kate, 164–65, 213–14
miners' strike of 1984-85, 121–22, 132–33, 139–41, 220–21
Mir-Hosseini, Ziba, 236
Mirza, Nadira
　on consciousness raising, 100–1
　demonstrates sense of purpose as a kind of faith, 205
　on perception of self as angry, 215
　photo of, 240*f*
　on self-help approach, 142
　work in WLM, 233–40
　young feminists view of her generation, 250
Miss America pageant, 9–10, 93
Miss World beauty pageant protest, 2, 44, 89, 93, 94*f*, 98, 122–23, 147
Mitchell, Juliet
　on becoming a feminist, 78
　on capitalism, 158
　challenge of deficit model, 168–69
　criticism of *The Female Eunuch,* 92–93
　funding for feminist causes, 157
　groundbreaking theory of women's oppression, 163
　inspirations of, 15
　as interviewee for S&A, 63
　meaning of women's liberation, 3–4
　as Ruskin conference organizer, 26–27, 47

Molloy, Siobhan, 63, 65, 67, 126
Molnar, George, 204–5
More Serious Pleasure (O'Sullivan), 146
Morgan, Abi, 245
Morgan, Robin, 166
Mormont, Jean, 91–92, 204–5
Morris, Mia, 45, 220–21
Morris, Olive, 29–30
Morrison, Paul, 161–62, 165, 167–68
motherhood and mothering. *See also* abortion
　Barrett's experience of, 75
　campaign for single mothers, 122–23
　Campbell's experiences of and views on, 21, 73, 74–75, 141–42
　Catherine Hall's experiences of, x–xi, 189–90, 216
　Chester's experiences of, 69
　choice to become mothers among WLM activists, 211–14
　Cockburn's experiences of, 73
　conventional scripts of, 89
　Cook's experiences of, 132–33
　Dadzie's experiences of, 124
　dark emotion flowing around women's movement, 183–84
　Davin's experiences with, 68, 141–42
　demands for family allowance payments, 122–23
　effect on future activists, 205–11
　Focus E15 Mums' protest of 2013, 126
　Harne's views on, 14–15
　Hearn's experiences with, 108
　interviewees reaction to questions concerning, 5, 61, 243
　Lewis's experiences of, 74–75
　Lewis's experiences with, 107
　linked to Greenham Common women's Peace Camp, 2, 224
　Lopez's experiences of, 56–57
　McCrum's experiences of, 74, 218
　McKenley's experiences with, 109, 174, 205–6
　McMinn's experiences with, 119–20
　midcentury feminism and, 71
　Mirza's experiences with, 234
　mothers' right to work, x–xi, 180
　Murray's experiences of, 71–73
　Oakley's work on, 42–43
　Orbach's experiences with, 80–81, 86–87
　O'Sullivan's experiences of, 139–40
　portpatriarchal family form, 76
　"Post-Partum Document" (Kelly), 246
　post-war experiences of, x, 62–63, 65
　Rowbotham's writings on, 14
　Scafe's experiences with, 107
　sex education and, 68
　teenage mothers, 103
　transmission of femininity in patriarchy through, 84, 85–86
　Wise's experiences of, 130–31
　WLMs view of, 77, 89
　Wyles's experiences of, 66
Motherson, Keith, 167
Movement for the Ordination of Women, 135–36, 231
"Multi-Story House" (Kelly), 246–47
Mulvey, Laura, 93–94, 169
municipal feminism, 128, 130f, 133
Murray, Jenni
　childbirth experience of, 79
　experience obtaining a mortgage, 124–25
　experience of rape, 173–74
　as important mainstreamer for WLM ideas, 3
　memories of family and growing up, 69–70, 71–73, 72f, 76, 78
　nonsexist childrearing, 210–11
　position as BBC newsreader, 162, 245
Murray, Len, 103
Muslim feminism, 236–37
"Myth of the Vaginal Orgasm, The" (Koedt), 22–23, 69

nation, 2–3, 22f, 25–35, 45, 46, 61, 71, 92, 102–3, 110, 112, 114, 127–28, 182, 234. *See also* international; transnational
final national WLM conference, 15–16, 90, 91f, 110, 188–89
first national WLM conference, 8, 14, 47
first national WLM march, 14–15, 204, 206f
nation and race, 71
national independence and liberation movements, ix, 6, 46, 115, 182, 221
nationalism, 2–3, 221, 223, 239
nationality, 217
national liberation and feminism, tensions between, 4, 6, 114, 115
national politics, x–xi
as selection criteria for oral history, 47–48
National Abortion Campaign (NAC), 4, 46, 47, 63–64, 89, 95, 101–12, 104f
National Association for Asian Youth (NAAY), 235
National Coordinating Committee, 96
National Council of Civil Liberties (NCCL), 15
National Joint Action Campaign Committee for Women's Equal Rights (NJACCWER), 19–20, 21, 22f
National Organization for Women (NOW), 98
Nelson, Sarah, 115
New Feminism, The (Walters), 169–70
New Left Review, 183–84
Newsome, Olive, 55
New Woman's Survival Catalogue (Rennie and Grimstad), 155
Night Cleaners' Action, 91–92
Norris, Jill, 42

Northern Ireland. *See also* Ireland
1970s women's rights movement in, 245
abortion debate in, 110–11
baby boomer generation in, 63
bitter debates over in WLM, 15–16
campaigns for rights of Gypsy/Roma/Traveler communities, 126
censorship of reports by Colin Thomas, 165–66
conflict resolution attempts, 180–81
criminalization of young Irish men, 235–36
Divorce Reform Act of 1969, 212
education system in, 67
Northern Ireland Women's Coalition, 241
Northern Ireland Women's rights Movement, 122–23
protests demanding "troops out of Northern Ireland," 63–64
"rape debate" in, 174
rejection of parental and peer expectations in, 12–13
selection of interviewees from, 47–48
the "Troubles" as generationally defining, 64, 89
women in national independence groups, 6
Women's Aid Northern Ireland, 3, 90, 112–20, 116f, 161
women working with political parties in, 46, 127–28

Oakley, Ann, 42–43, 121–22, 168–69, 210–11
Okely, Judith, 41–42
Once a Feminist (Wandor), 8, 13, 27, 42
On Tools (film), 150
oral history
effect of digitization on, 52, 249–50
and feminist method

oral history (cont.)
    affiliation of oral history with
        feminism, 40–44
    challenge of ethical analysis,
        50–52, 60–61
    making of S&A oral history, 44–49
    Sue Lopez's story, 52–60
    range of histories available, 2–3
    remembering activism through, 44
    telling feminist histories through
        changeable meaning of the
            past, 8–16
        class and women's liberation, 16–25
        composing feminist
            memories, 35–39
        race and nation, 25–34
Oral History (British journal), 41
Orbach, Susie
    on consciousness raising, 99
    discovery of feminism through
        men, 163
    early messages about sexuality, 69
    marriage to Jeanette Winterson, 213
    photo of, 82*f*
    position on money, 157
    role in Women's Therapy Centre, 46
    work with Dove Beauty's "real
        women" campaign, 4
    work with WLM, 79–87
Organisation for Women of African and
        Asian Descent (OWAAD)
    Dadzie's initiation of, 32
    disbanding of, 34
    inaugural meeting, 8–9,
        32–34, 33–34*f*
    McKenley's work in, 46
    men's support of feminism, 163–64
    role of music in, 220–21
O'Sullivan, Sue, 95, 139–41, 146
Other Cinema, The, 24–25
*Other Kinds of Dreams: Black
    Women's Organisations and
    the Politics of Transformation*
    (Sudbury), 168–69
*Our Bodies, Ourselves: A Health Book
    by and for Women* (Phillips
    and Rakusen), 22–23, 109, 187,
    213, 228–29
Owen, Ursula, 44, 64, 207–8

Paper Houses (Roberts), 136
parliament and parliamentary politics
    Alison Halford's work, 77
    ascent of free-market capitalism under
        Thatcherism, 15–16
    Audrey Wise's work, 20, 77–78, 128,
        130–31, 207
    campaign against sex
        discrimination, 96
    challenges of Thatcherism, 110,
        118–19, 122–58
    Corrie Bill, 105
    David Steel's work, 163
    Harriet Harman's work, x–xi, 163
    Harry Lamborn's work, 163
    Jocelyn Wolfe's support of Equal Pay
        Act, 220
    Jo Richardson's work, 111–12
    Kevin McNamara's work, 17
    lack of female MPs in 1970s and
        198s, 90, 98
    Lesley Abdela's work, 15, 68
    Lilian Bilocca's delegation to, 17
    "mainstreaming" tactics under
        Thatcher's government, 90
    Maurice Orbach's work, 79–80
    midcentury focus on, 244–45
    Pat Thorne's equal rights bill, 97–98
    report on domestic violence, 160–61
    suffrage movement's focus on, 78–79
    underestimation of the potential
        demand for abortion, 102–3
Parmar, Pratibha, 140, 168–69,
    182–83, 235–36

Passerini, Luisa, 5, 51–52
Passingham, Bernie, 163
Passing Through (Petherbridge), 161
Past Is Before Us, The (Rowbotham), 14, 242–43
Patai, Daphne, 43, 169
Patel, Pragna, 3, 62–63, 71, 124, 125–26, 147–48, 172, 233, 245
Perks, Rob, 44
Petherbridge, John, 159–62
Phillips, Angela, 109
Phipps, Alison, 6–7
Piercy, Marge, 3
Pieters, Donna, 220–21
Pitchford, Kenneth, 166
Pizzey, Erin, 24–25, 48–49, 116–17
Plath, Sylvia, 76
"Political Lesbianism: The Case Against Heterosexuality" (paper), 105–6
Pollack, Rachel, 188
Pollock, Griselda, 138
Portelli, Alessandro, 5, 35
postcolonial, x
"Post-Partum Document" (Kelly), 98, 246
Power, Lisa, 2–3, 188
Pre-Madonnas (musical group), 219
Prescott, John, 17
professional radicalism, 118–20

Quaye, Terri, 221, 222*f*
queer
　development of sophisticated queer theory, 36–37, 168–69, 176, 243
　exploring progressive genders and sexualities, 160
　impact of WLM on queer relationships, 213–15
　and models of alternative womanhood, 185–87
　queer undertone of men's groups, 166–67
　Remembering Our Dead ceremony, 187–88
　unhappiness revealed in queer archives, 217–18

race
　abolishing race exploitations, 9–10
　abortion rights as cutting across, 108
　cross-race alliances, 8–9
　effect on interviewees' oral histories, 4, 184, 209
　greater connections between women's movements across, 133
　interviewee selection criteria, 45, 47, 49
　memory politics and, 160
　men's violence as a unifying force, 172
　and nation in feminist histories, 25–34
　race debates in WLM, 182–83, 244
　race relations explored by Thomlinson, 35–36
　role of singing in women's movements, 220–21
　transgendered liberation and, 187–88
Race Relations Act of 1976, 235
Race Today, 29–30
radical feminism, 3–4, 38, 108, 117, 120, 185
Rantzen, Esther, 74–75
Raphael, Melissa, 231–32
Rayner, Alison, 147–48, 207–8, 221–22
Rees, Jeska, 184
religion
　acceptance of all women by Women's Aid, 115
　Christianity and feminism, 232–33, 238
　experience of sexual status and expectation and, 22–23
　as frontline for women's liberations, 205
　gender equality structure, 16
　Hall's experiences with, 190

religion (*cont.*)
  Islam and feminism, 233, 234, 236–37, 238
  Judaism and feminism, 238
  as method of controlling women, 238
  Orbach's experiences with, 80
  as patriarchal, misogynistic, homophobic, and reactionary, 231
  Rushdie defense, 237–38
  selection of interviewees and, 45
Rennie, Kristen, 155
Riley, Percy, 133
Roberts, Elizabeth, 41
Roberts, Michele, 136–37
Robinson, Jo, 3–4, 28, 68, 93–94, 94*f*, 122–23, 208, 210–11
Rock Against Racism, 223
Rose, Hilary, 174–75
Rose, Jacqueline, 187–88
Ross, Elizabeth Arlege, 42
Rowan, John, 167–68
Rowbotham, Sheila
  on becoming a feminist, 78
  betrayals by men, 162–63
  Dalston Women's Liberation Workshop, 97
  discovery of feminism through men, 163
  Dutiful Daughters, 42, 71, 73
  on entitlement of women, 215
  at first Ruskin conference, 26*f,* 27, 28
  idea for WLM demands, 104–5
  influence on WPAC, 133–34
  interview of Mormont, 204–5
  love of clothing and fashion, 141
  memories of early WLM work, 35
  memories of NJACCWER rally, 19–20
  memories of rites of passage, 69–70
  met with guffaws when suggesting a women's history meeting, 26
  on the pathologization of women's bodies, 213
  recollections of early homes, 126–27
  reflections on life course, 205–6
  reinvention of the Planning Unit, 128–29
  subheads, 242–43, 245
  support of oral history projects, 41–42
  on transmission of memory, 1–2, 40–41
  views of unions, 21–22
  work with WLM, 13–15
Ruskin College, WLM meeting at, 8–9, 25–34, 26*f*
Russell, Polly, 44, 60
Ryan, Michele, 215

el Saadawi, Nawal, 236–37
Samuel, Raphael, 26, 28, 133–34
Sarachild, Kathie, 99
Scafe, Suzanne, 10–11, 11*f,* 29–30, 42, 107
Scargill, Anne, 132, 134*f*
Scargill, Arthur, 132
Schwarz, Joe, 86
Scicluna, Rachael, 140–41
Scotland
  feminists working with political parites, 46
  folk revival in, 67
  National Abortion Campaign in, 104
  nationalist parties in, 127–28
  poll tax in, 119
  promotion of female candidates for election, 209–10
  radical choirs at Laurieston Hall, 219
  resistance to including women in football, 55–56
  Scotland Co-operative Group's Credit Union, 207–8
  Scotland Rape Crisis's Oral History (2009), 177

Scottish National Organisation of
  Girls' Work, 79
selection of interviewees from,
  47–48
Valerie Wise's work in, 128
Scotland Rape Crisis's Oral History, 177
Scott, Ann, 14
Scott, EJ, 185–86
Sebestyen, Amanda, 10, 42
Second Sex, The (de Beauvoir), 78
Seeger, Peggy, 225*f*
Segal, Lynne
  on ageing, 229–30
  celebrating International Women's
    Day (1971), 204–5
  challenge of deficit model, 168–69
  collective living experiments, 138–39
  gay liberation activism of, 213
  home of, 122–23, 139*f*
  ideas and opposition of radical
    feminism, 175–76
  life choices, 210–11
  love of a soft-spoken man, 162
  meaning of women's liberation, 3–4
  men's groups in Britain, 165
  reaction to "Why Miss World"
    pamphlet, 93–95
Seidler, Vic, 167–68
Serious Pleasure (O'Sullivan), 146
Sex Discrimination Act of 1975, 58–59,
  90, 97, 98, 124–25, 149
Sex Discrimination Act of 1993, 233
sexuality
  1950s as time of innocence and
    safety, 173
  age-related concerns over, 217
  autonomy for all genders, 217
  debates arising over sexual
    difference, 15–16
  as defining aspect of women's life
    courses, 210–11
  double standards, 12
  effect on professional opportunities, 21
  as enhancing rather than
    defiling, 231–32
  false promises of sexual
    liberation, 22–23
  feminists' feelings about childbearing
    and, 212
  gender-equality movements, 16
  Kitzinger's views on, 228
  Lau's photography projects dealing
    with, 169
  McKenley's views on, 174
  McKinnon's views on, 171
  new expressions of through women's
    liberation, 3–4, 169–70
  pathologization of women's bodies,
    79, 213
  patronizing and confusing messages
    about, 13–14
  as power, 177
  radical sexual rights activists, 169
  recurring strategic questions
    about, 245
  in religious texts, 231–32
  right to self-defined sexuality, 170–71
  sexual rights and equality, 212
  transgender and liberation, 185–88
  vibrator and feminist product
    advertisements, 145–46
  WLM analysis of, 242–43
  WLM effect on queer and lesbian
    relationships, 213
Sexual Offences Act of 1976, 171
Sexual Politics (Millett), 164–65
Shah, Zoora, 209
Sharma, Krishna, 172
Shaw, Robin, 169
Sheba Publishers, 140
Short, Clare, 146
Shoulder to Shoulder (BBC TV
  miniseries), 244–45
Shrew (newsletter), 96

Silver Action (Lacy), 248–49
singing/song
 African freedom songs and feminism, 222–23
 cheer of feminist life, 223
 Chester's connection to, 219
 as clue to satisfaction in living with feminist commitments, 205
 Cockburn's enjoyment of, 219
 evolving feminist philosophy and, 216
 at Greenham Common women's peace camp, 224–26, 225*f*
 Hearn's pleasure over, 219
 ritualistic sharing of, 226–27
 Wyles's demonstration of, 219
Sjoo, Monica, 167, 231–32
Slow Motion: Changing Masculinities, Changing Men (Segal), 175–76
Smith, Delia, 77, 138
Smith, Pam, 229
Smith, Pat, 29
Smith, Paul, 165
Snow, Nick, 180
socialism
 autonomy and, 215
 feminist socialism, 216
 Jones's experiences with, 154–55
 labor protests and, 21–22
 Mirza's experiences with, 233–34
 as origin for WLM, 9–10, 14, 15, 16–17
 state socialism in Eastern Europe and China, 156
 views of lesbians, 162–63
socialist feminism, ix–x, 3, 45–46, 154
Sorenson, Gerri, 248–49
Southall Black Sisters (SBS), 3, 31–32, 89, 172–73, 234
Spare Rib (WLM magazine)
 advertisements for sexual goods, 145–46
 Bellos's work for, 140
 competing priorities set out in, 105–6
 feminist fashion in, 143, 144*f*
 funding of, 128, 157
 Hearn on the cover of, 143
 launch of, 98
 Mirza and Parmar's work for, 235
 popularity of, 96
 reports on the UK school system in, 62
 TUC march coverage in, 101–2
 Wilson's work for, 30–31, 182
Spence, Jo, 228–29
Spencer, Diana, 84–85
Spivak, Gayatri, 169
Stanley, Liz, 43
Steel, David, 163
Stephen, Jessie, 9–10
Stephens, Julie, 51–52
Stewart-Park, Angela, 227–28
Stoltenberg, John, 166
strawbale building, 153
Straw Works, 153–54
Striking Women oral history, 248–49
Sudbury, Julia, 168–69
suffrage
 Anglo-American suffrage activism, 6
 biographical studies of activists, 212
 Edwardian suffrage activism, 50
 focus on Parliament, 78–79
 Jane Lunnon, 246*f*
 militant suffrage movement, 55
 oral histories of, 42, 49, 244–45
 as precursor to WLM, 245
 protest for by Jessie Stephen, 9–10
 Rowbotham's views on, 15
 socialist origins of, 215
Suffragette (film), 245
Summerfield, Penny, 35–36
Summers, Ann, 145–46
Summerskill, Baroness, 19–20
Superwoman: Everywoman's Book of Household Management (Conran), 138
Sutcliffe, Peter, 171*f*, 171

Sutherland, Eileen, 153
Sweet Freedom: The Struggle for Women's Liberation (Campbell and Coote), 9–10, 37–39, 38f

Taylor, Barbara, 41–42, 44, 163, 183–84, 207, 213–14, 247–48
Tench, Joan, 54–55
Thatcher, Margaret, 77, 89–90, 101–2, 105, 127–28, 130–31
This Way to the Revolution (Pizzey), 24
Thomas, Colin, 165–66, 184
Thomas, George, 110
Thomas, Helen, 226–27
Thomlinson, Natalie, 23, 27–28, 35–36, 182, 223
Thompson, E. P., 163
Thompson, Paul, 43–44, 133–34
Thomson, Alistair, 43
Thorne, Anne, 154
Thornton, Sara, 172–73
Threshing Floor, The (Burford), 98
Thrupp, Jackie, 96–97
Thynne, Lizzie, 60, 150, 248–49
Toynbee, Polly, 105
Trades Union Congress (TUC)
  Boland oral history, 17–18
  campaign for equal pay ad opportunity, 19–20
  Jackson oral history, 20
  march for abortion rights, 21
  support of reproductive rights, 101–2, 103
Trades Union Congress Equal Pay Story, 2–3
trade unions. *See also* Ford factory strike; Grunwick photo-processing laboratory strike; Night Cleaners' Action; Trades Union Congress (TUC)
  miners' wives' action and, 133
  National Union of Mineworkers (NUM), 132
  National Union of Seamen, 17
  National Union of Vehicle Builders, 17
  support of sexual harassment training and pensions, 168
  Tobacco Workers' Union, 102
  Trades Union Congress Equal Pay Story, 2–3
  Transport and General Workers' Union, 17, 91–92
  Union of Construction and Allied Technical Trades, 156
  working-class activism versus white middle-class WLM movements, 21–22
  working-class trade union activism, 3–4, 23, 28, 50
  Working Women's Charter, 20
Trafalgar Square, 1969 equal pay demonstration, 22f
Training Opportunities Programme (TOPS), 149–51
transgendered liberation, 1–2, 4, 185–89
transnational, 14, 50, 283n16
Tufnell Park women's liberation group, 27
Tunnicliffe, Annie, 226
Turning the Tables: Recipes and Reflections from Women (O'Sullivan), 139–41
Tweedie, Jill, 15, 204–5

Unbecoming Men oral history, 219
Union of European Football Association's (UEFA), 55–56
United Nations, x–xi
United Nations Fourth World Conference on Women: Action for Equality, Development and Peace (Beijing, 1995), x–xi
United Nations World Conference on Human Rights (Vienna, 1993), 115

Van Twest, Pat, 96–97
Vietnam War protests, 9–10, 16–17
Virago (feminist press), 5–6, 47, 64, 109–10, 122–23, 155–56, 207–8
voice
   attention to individual voices, 4
   challenges for women in public speaking, 5, 162, 226, 247–48
   as conduit for collective consciousness, 249–50
   deconstruction and politicization of, 5
   inner voice of men's movement accounts, 184
   need to tune into past voices, 1–2
   older voices, 218, 248
   oral history and, 51
   politics of voice, 160, 182–83
   power of, 226, 247
   public voices found through singing, 220–21
   recovering voices of suppressed groups, 169
"Voices in Movement: Feminist Family Stories in Oral History and Sound Art" (Thynne), 248–49
Volcano, Della Grace, 169

Wages for Housework, 128, 178–79
Wainwright, Hilary, 96, 110
Wales
   age of marriage and motherhood in, 210–11
   Archif Menywod Cymru/Women's Archive of Wales's oral history, 42
   Divorce Reform Act of 1969, 212
   feminists working with political parites, 46
   National Abortion Campaign in, 104
   nationalist parties of, 127–28
   ordination of women in, 208

   poll tax in, 119
   promotion of femal political candidates in, 209–10
   selection of interviewees from, 47–48
   violent incidents in, 170–71
   violent offenses against women, 117
   Women in Tune festival in Lampeter, 219
   Women's Aid from England and Wales, 115
   work of Jane Hutt in, 118–19
Walters, Natasha, 169–70
Wandor, Michelene
   The Body Politic: Writings from the Women's Liberation Movement in Britain, 1969–1972, 29, 99
   on consciousness raising, 99–100
   on feminism and socialism, 216
   memories of childhood, 64
   memories of Ruskin conference, 27–28
   occupation of, 207–8
   Once a Feminist, 8, 13, 42
   view of groundswell of autodidacticism, 221–22
Weeks, Jeffrey, 166
Whittle, Stephen, 188
"Why Miss World?" (pamphlet), 94–95
Williams, Jean, 52
Wilson, Amrit
   duty toward family, nation, and culture, 71
   Finding a Voice: Asian Women in Britain (1978), 3, 10, 41–42
   life influences, 64, 77–78, 207
   work at *Spare Rib,* 182–83
   work with WLM, 30–32
Wilson, Elizabeth, 144–45
Wilson, Harold, 12–13, 17, 18f
Wilson, Robert, 213
Wilson, Sarah, 93–94, 122–23
Winchester, Noreen, 115, 116f
Winship, Janice, 144–45

Winter of Discontent of 1979, 89, 101–12
Winterson, Jeanette, 86–87, 213
WIRES (newsletter), 96
Wise, Audrey, 14, 20, 77–78, 128, 207
Wise, Valerie, 3–4, 63–64, 77–78, 128–31, 130*f*, 137–38, 142, 149, 207
Wistrich, Harriet, 173
Withers, D-M, 249
Wolf, Misha, 167
Wolfe, Jocelyn, 29–30, 122–23, 141, 142, 220–21
Wollstonecraft, Mary, 15
Woman's Place: An Oral History of Working-Class Women, 1890–1940, A (Roberts), 41
"Woman's Right to Cues, A" (Capstick), 23–24
Women Against Fundamentalism (WAF), 233
Women Against Pit Closures (WAPC), 3–4, 42, 131–33, 168, 220–21
Women Against Racism and Fascism, 223
Women and Manual Trades (WAMT), 122, 149–51
"Women and the New Politics" (Rowbotham), 13
"Women of the Working Class" (Finch), 220–21
Women on the Ball (Lopez), 54–55, 58–59
Women's Aid, 23–24
Women's Aid Northern Ireland, 3, 90, 112–20, 116*f*, 161
Women's Cooperative Guild, 42
Women's Football Association (WFA), 55
Women's Liberation Movement (WLM). *See also* consciousness raising (CR); Miss World beauty pageant protest; National Abortion Campaign (NAC); *Spare Rib* (WLM magazine)
antiviolence campaigning, 171–81
as centered in white majority culture and perspectives, 6, 223
champions of, 55
cultural activism of, 98
effect of capitalist economies on, 156
exploring through oral history, 2
factionalism in, 4, 15–16, 110
feminist memories of, 35–39
first book-length history of, 9–10
first conference at Ruskin College, 8–9, 25–34, 26*f*
focus on reforming the family, 71, 75, 76
gains realized by, 89, 111–12
under Margaret Thatcher, 121–37
men's role in, 160–70
mobility and fluidity of core experience of, 47–48, 96–97, 104
organized lobbying by, 96–97
origins in socialism versus liberalism, 9–10, 14–15, 155
politics of voice and, 160
principles of equality and autonomy in, 8, 46
prominent historians of, 41–43
publications supported and launched by, 98
racial identities and, 182–84
reason for launch of, 12–14, 62, 87, 95, 243–44
Rowbotham's 1989 history of, 242–43
scorn of consumerism, 137–39
seven demands of, 15, 26, 90–92, 91*f*, 97, 102, 104–5, 170–71, 241
UK vs. other countries, 2–3
union alliances, 103
women's liberation as a whole-life question, 241

Women's Liberation Movement (WLM) (*cont.*)
   working-class versus white middle-class movements, 16–25
Women's Liberation Music Archive, 2–3
Women's Liberation Oral History Project (S&A)
   ages of interviewees, 62–63
   challenge of ethical analysis, 50–52, 60–61
   methodology, 44–49, 51–52
   occupations of interviewees, 207–8
   scope of, 2–3
   social generations and immigration status of interviewees, 207

Women's Place, A (Crockford), 27
Women's Revolutions Per Minute (WRPM), 221–22
Women's Words: The Feminist Practice of Oral History (Gluck and Patai), 43, 169
Women: The Longest Revolution (Mitchell), 47
Working Women's Charter, 20
Wyatt, Geoffrey, 177
Wyles, Sandie, 65–66, 79, 99, 219

YBA (Why Be A) Wife campaign, 3, 92
"Year of the Militant Woman" issue, 13–14

THE OXFORD ORAL HISTORY SERIES

J. Todd Moye (University of North Texas)
Kathryn Nasstrom (University of San Francisco)
Robert Perks (The British Library)
Series Editors

Donald A. Ritchie
Senior Advisor

Approaching an Auschwitz Survivor: Holocaust Testimony and Its Transformations *Edited by Jürgen Matthäus*

Singing Out: An Oral History of America's Folk Music Revivals *David K. Dunaway and Molly Beer*

Freedom Flyers: The Tuskegee Airmen of World War II *J. Todd Moye*

Launching the War on Poverty: An Oral History, Second Edition *Michael L. Gillette*

The Firm: The Inside Story of the Stasi *Gary Bruce*

The Wonder of Their Voices: The 1946 Holocaust Interviews of David Boder *Alan Rosen*

They Say in Harlan County: An Oral History *Alessandro Portelli*

The Oxford Handbook of Oral History *Edited by Donald A. Ritchie*

Habits of Change: An Oral History of American Nuns *Carole Garibaldi Rogers*

Soviet Baby Boomers: An Oral History of Russia's Cold War Generation *Donald J. Raleigh*

Bodies of Evidence: The Practice of Queer Oral History *Edited by Nan Alamilla Boyd and Horacio N. Roque Ramírez*

Lady Bird Johnson: An Oral History *Michael L. Gillette*

Dedicated to God: An Oral History of Cloistered Nuns *Abbie Reese*

Listening on the Edge: Oral History in the Aftermath of Crisis *Edited by Mark Cave and Stephen M. Sloan*

Chinese Comfort Women: Testimonies from Imperial Japan's Sex Slaves *Peipei Qiu, with Su Zhiliang and Chen Lifei*

Doing Oral History, Third Edition *Donald A. Ritchie*

A Guide to Oral History and the Law, Second Edition *John A. Neuenschwander*

Pioneers and Partisans: An Oral History of Nazi Genocide in Belorussia *Anika Walke*

Velvet Revolutions: An Oral History of Czech Society *Miroslav Vaněk and Pavel Mücke*

Escape to Miami: An Oral History of the Cuban Rafter Crisis *Elizabeth Campisi*

Inside the Clinton White House: An Oral History *Russell L. Riley*

Edward M. Kennedy: An Oral History *Barbara A. Perry*

Fly Until You Die: An Oral History of Hmong Pilots in the Vietnam War *Chia Youyee Vang*

Voices of Guinness: An Oral History of the Park Royal Brewery *Tim Strangleman*